Media Systems
in Society

Media Systems in Society

Understanding Industries, Strategies, and Power

Second Edition

Joseph Turow

The Annenberg School for Communication
University of Pennsylvania

 LONGMAN

An imprint of Addison Wesley Longman, Inc.

New York • Reading, Massachusetts • Menlo Park, California • Harlow, England
Don Mills, Ontario • Sydney • Mexico City • Madrid • Amsterdam

Media Systems in Society, Second Edition

Copyright © 1997, 1992 by Longman Publishers USA,
A Division of Addison Wesley Longman, Inc.
All rights reserved.
No part of this publication may be reproduced,
stored in a retrieval system, or transmitted
in any form or by any means, electronic, mechanical,
photocopying, recording, or otherwise,
without the prior permission of the publisher.

Longman, 10 Bank Street, White Plains, N.Y. 10606

Executive editor: Pamela A. Gordon
Associate editor: Hillary B. Henderson
Production editor: Linda Moser/Professional Book Center
Production supervisor: Edith Pullman
Cover design: Susan Moore
Compositor: Digitype

Library of Congress Cataloging-in-Publication Data

Turow, Joseph.
    Media systems in society : understanding industries, strategies,
and power / Joseph Turow. — 2nd ed.
        p.   cm.
    Includes bibliographical references and index.
    ISBN 0-8013-1704-5
    1. Mass media.   I. Title.
P90.T87 1997
302.23 — dc20   96-8986
                                                      CIP

2 3 4 5 6 7 8 9 10-MA-009998

For My Parents

Contents

CHAPTER 3   **A BIT OF HISTORY: GOVERNMENT, BUSINESS, AND MASS MEDIA**   **60**

67-88

CHAPTER 4   **MEDIA SUPPORT: PAYING THE PIPER, CALLING THE TUNE**   **89**

CHAPTER 5   **TARGETING THE AUDIENCE**   **115**

List of Figures, Tables, Boxes, and Talking Points

Preface

Ours is a world in which traditional mass media categories sometimes get in the way of understanding. Consider the term *movie industry*. Not too many years ago, a movie studio executive's job might have been described as one that helps to create audiovisual products for movie theaters. At present, if a high-level Warner Brothers studio executive believed that definition, he or she would probably not hold the job for long.

Today, movie executives must calculate global production and distribution strategies with a wide variety of locations and technologies in mind. In addition to theater screens, they must think of Pay Per View cable, ordinary pay cable, basic cable, home video, broadcast network TV, and independent broadcasting stations. By the same token, pay-cable firms such as Home Box Office (HBO) regularly release their productions to theaters, broadcast TV networks, and home-video stores around the world. For people who work at Warner Brothers and HBO (both owned, incidentally, by Time Warner) the term *movie industry* begins to blur. Where does the movie industry end and the cable industry begin?

That is only one example of the category-shattering changes taking place. We live in a boundary-blurring world where executives of some of the largest corporations are involved daily in planning ways to create and distribute stories — news and entertainment stories — across a mind-spinning galaxy of locations, many of which they themselves own. Books are made into films, films into books. Newspaper comic characters appear on greeting cards and show up on TV shows and in books. Newswork becomes the basis not only for articles in papers and magazines, but also for information in lucrative data banks owned by the news firms. Entire cross-media industries are created around stars such as Shaquile O'Neil, Howard Stern, Madonna, and Martha Stewart.

- How can we understand what goes on in the firms that carry out these activities?
- How can we think about the organizational, institutional, legal, political, economic, historical, and cultural considerations that shape the menus of choice that confront millions of people when they watch TV, read books, buy greeting cards, stare at billboards?
- What does the future hold for different mass media, why, and with what possible social consequences?

These questions raise fascinating, exciting, and important issues. *Media Systems in Society* addresses these issues and many others through a wide-ranging framework for understanding mass communication as a social and industrial process. The response to the first edition has been most gratifying, and this second edition updates that volume, keeping the basic framework but taking into account the many changes that have taken place in the media system since 1992. It also keeps the tone current by bringing fresh examples, tables, and charts.

The ideas contained in this text are a product of more than two decades of learning about, and teaching, mass communication while conducting research in many different sorts of media organizations. As an undergraduate at the University of Pennsylvania, majoring in English and dabbling in American Studies, I first started asking the questions listed here. I carried on the work during my graduate studies in communication at Penn, then at Purdue University for ten years, then back at Penn's Annenberg School for Communication, where I now teach.

I am grateful to my teachers, students, colleagues, and, not least, "subjects" of my research for leading me toward the ideas incorporated throughout this text. I am particularly grateful to the late Tren Andersen, an editor at Longman and a friend, who originally asked me to write it. Rob Blanchard and Linda Moser provided helpful comments and suggestions on the manuscript. University of Pennsylvania students Ben Wyche, Lori Silbersweig, Nadine Cantor, Kelli D'Apice, Lynn Edwards, Maggie Williams, William Hoffman, Karen Fraser, George Nimeh, and Melissa Jumper Herrmann reviewed the manuscript as it evolved, offering help and frank critiques. The following reviewers also helped in the development of this edition:

Lawrence Budner, Rhode Island College

Carl R. Bybee, University of Oregon

William F. Griswold Jr., University of Georgia

Ray Novak, University of Wisconsin, Parkside

Dan Schiller, University of California, San Diego

Katherine A. Steele, Syracuse University
Susan M. Strohm, Pennsylvania State University

Judith Turow, my wife, has followed this book and many other projects from beginning to end. Her suggestions, patience, and understanding have been invaluable. My children, Jonathan, Marissa, and Rebecca, have provided me with welcome distraction from this project long enough to have other sorts of fun.

CHAPTER 1

Mass Media Industries
What Are They?
Why Study Them?

This chapter

- sketches some of the profound changes that are taking place in the media.
- introduces the terms *media industry* and *media system* as ways to organize an approach to these changes.
- underscores the importance of understanding the media system by explaining how its activities connect to issues of culture and power in the society at large.

The purpose of this book is to give you the tools to understand U.S. media industries. These industries, running the gamut from books to movies to video games, are crucial to American society as producers of culture and as businesses. As producers of culture, mass media industries shape a large part of what Americans read, see, hear, touch, and even smell. Network TV comedies, news magazine feature stories, rock albums, comic books, scratch-and-sniff perfume ads, direct mail catalogs — these represent only a small number of the products Americans pay attention to every day. As businesses, mass media industries employ millions of people, from TV producers to popcorn vendors in theaters. They also comprise a major class of U.S. exports to the rest of the world.

Understanding U.S. media industries in the late 1990s is a challenge because they are undergoing major changes. Consider some of the alterations that are taking place:

- The three traditional television networks (ABC, CBS, and NBC) are nowhere near the powerhouse audience-grabbers they were a decade and a half ago. Whereas in the late 1970s the networks could reliably reach nearly 90% of all Americans watching television in the evening, the mid-1990s saw that figure dwindle to around 55%. Network executives are worried that advertisers who have used network TV to reach huge segments of the population will desert them.

- Cable television, hardly a competitor to over-the-air TV in the early 1980s, has been an important factor in the broadcast networks' decreasing audience. Although most cable channels still garner relatively small audiences according to industry surveys, services such as the ESPN sports network have been known to attract the numbers and kinds of viewers that bring in many advertising dollars and make them highly profitable.

- The Hollywood production industry (typically known as "the movie business") has been undergoing wrenching alterations. In the 1980s and 1990s, Rupert Murdoch's Australian firm, News Corp, gained control over 20th Century Fox; the French bank Credit Lyonnais took over an ailing MGM and United Artists; Japanese electronics manufacturer Sony bought Columbia Pictures; Time Inc. merged with Warner Communications; the new Time Warner swallowed Turner Broadcasting; ABC and Disney merged; Westinghouse took over CBS; and a new major studio — Dreamworks SKG — was created.

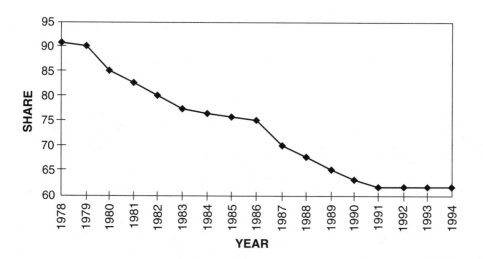

FIGURE 1.1 Combined prime time share of ABC, CBS, and NBC, 1978–1994 (SOURCE: *Channels Magazine 1986 Field Guide*, p. 82; Nielsen Media Research; and *TV Dimensions*, '94–'95.)

Since the 1970s the Big Three networks' share of the TV viewing audience has dropped about 30%.

- Beyond broadcast and cable television, a whole new world of audiovisual entertainment, news, and information is emerging. The vehicles are videotapes, video games, CD-ROM for personal computers, satellite delivery companies such as Direct TV, and on-line computer services such as the Internet and America Online. The popularity of videotapes and video games is already great in the mid-1990s; the popularity of the other products and services is growing fast. Together, they are changing the way people deal with media in and out of their homes.
- The newspaper industry has been trying to come to terms with the new electronic media environment. Major city newspapers, particularly, are seeing newspaper reading decline among younger segments of the population. New newspaper formats and new systems of news delivery are topics of major concern in an industry increasingly preoccupied with the need to attract a TV-oriented populace.
- The advertising and public relations industries have been drastically affected by the maelstrom of changes in the media they work with. The multiplication of cable channels, the decline of network TV audiences, the growth of specialty magazines, the growth of advertiser-supported media around the world, the explosive increase in the direct-selling business (what used to be called mail order) — these and other changes have forced advertising and PR executives to rethink the strategies they have used for decades. Their desire to use the new media to reach customers in innovative ways is sending huge tremors through media firms throughout the world.

This book will help you analyze these developments, ask a variety of questions about them, and figure out ways to answer them. Different kinds of questions encourage exploration of the workings of mass media industries in different ways. Looking at the industries from several viewpoints helps us better grasp the strategies behind their activities and the implications of those strategies for society.

TWO PRINCIPLES

Our approach is guided by two basic principles. First, the **mass media industries are increasingly interrelated.** It will be useful to consider ways to understand individual mass media industries — the theatrical film and cable TV businesses, for example. For people who work with movies, however, it is often impossible to know where the movie industry ends and the cable and broadcast television industries begin. Movies that show up in theaters one month may appear on pay-per-view cable the next and on homevideo cassettes a few months after that. To comprehend how media develop and what they do in society, we must step back from a focus on only one media industry. Instead, we must pay attention to the way media industries relate to one another. These interrelationships form what can be called the **media system** of a society.

Second, **in order to understand the mass media's present and future, we must gain a broad understanding of the organizations, strategies, and power considerations that guide the creation of mass media materials.** Individual people may write the particular news reports we read or direct the movies we attend. It is very important, though, that those people work with other people in their organizations to get their work completed and released to the public. Of equal importance, those organizations must interact with other organizations if the work is to be released successfully to its intended audience. All these activities involve issues of strategy and power that go beyond the individual. These issues need to be understood if the process of creating and distributing materials across media industries is to make sense.

To grasp the usefulness of this approach, we need only look at predictions from decades ago about what new media technologies would be. In many cases these prognostications ignored the interrelationship of mass media and, especially, the organizations, strategies, and power considerations that guided the creation of media technologies and the content they released. The result was a naive approach to media policy, planning, and criticism.

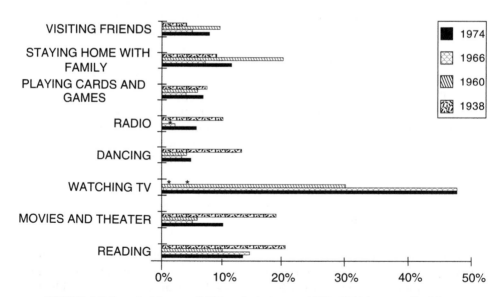

FIGURE 1.2 Favorite leisure activities, selected years, 1938–1974 (SOURCE: *Social Indicators, 1976* (Washington, D.C.: U.S. Government Printing Office, 1977, p. 492.)

*means radio received less than 1% of the responses
**indicates that television was not mentioned

The use of various mass media has clearly been an important component of people's activities for decades. Watching television has a high place unto itself as the favorite pastime.

PREDICTIONS, PAST AND PRESENT

In the mid-nineteenth century, there was no shortage of discussion on how the telegraph and the railway, both startling new vehicles of communication, would improve society. One commentator, enraptured by the possibilities of transmitting religious messages far and wide, proclaimed that the nation was "on the border of a spiritual harvest because thought now travels by steam and magnetic wires."[1] Another writer stated lyrically that in the future, "a perfect network of electric filaments" would "consolidate and harmonize the social union of mankind" by connecting people to one another.[2]

Historians Charles and Mary Beard were among those who held this **deterministic** attitude about media technology in the early twentieth century. They saw radio as one of the offspring of electricity that would emancipate humankind, bringing education and cosmopolitanism to all.[3] They also seemed to feel that the materials carried on these channels would merely add to the glorious possibilities of the technology. They did not think to ask, for example, whether violent radio dramas and speeches by bigoted radio ministers could cancel out the impulses toward international interconnections and cooperation they believed were dictated by the radio technology itself.

Current Scenarios

It is easy to point out now, decades after the introduction of radio, that ignorance, war, and parochialism still exist. Yet, while we might chuckle condescendingly about the naiveté of decades past, we often do not realize that the same type of reasoning about media exists today. Many writings on the direction of new technologies practically glow with speculation about the great advances that can be realized when consumers begin to interconnect the new gadgets with traditional mass media and, especially, the computer. Consider just a few new wonders that are possible, or nearly possible, today:

- **High-definition television (HDTV)** (also called **advanced television technology [ATV]**) can create a sharper and wider picture that makes today's TV sets seem like antiques.
- **Liquid display tubes** are being developed that can provide wall-size images that far exceed the abilities of today's projection screen devices.
- New generations of **tape and laser disc player-recorders** allow viewers to record and play noise-free music and video.
- Increasingly sophisticated satellite technology allows international transmission of mass media materials to very small dishes on the roofs of houses.
- The spread of **fiber-optic cable** and new **signal compression technology** can expand the number of audio and visual channels that stream into the home and office. The two-way capability of the cable

will allow the consumer to call up entertainment and information "servers" that access specific programs on demand.

Imagine a college student — say, a French major — preparing for a summer trip to Europe. A not-so-futuristic scenario might have her linking her TV monitor via computer and cables to the public library's tape archive to view a high-definition video about France, creating theaterlike effects at home. Or, the student might turn to the international satellite transmissions coming into her house to view the evening news on one of France's TV networks. Alternatively, she might rent a video disc of a recent French film (in stereo on a high-definition wall monitor) to bone up on the language while being entertained.

To many observers such soon-to-be-commonplace experiences will be only the most obvious manifestation of deeper alterations in the way we think and relate to our environment. They foretell that the new media will bring with them sweeping economic, political, social, and cultural changes. One author predicts that the media will cause "the most total revolution that the human race has witnessed since the industrial revolution."[4]

Such writers argue that the consumer at the computer will become the ultimate programmer, creating a personal menu of choices from a huge array of entertainment and information possibilities.[5] It has already begun, they say. The large number of channels aimed at individuals and special interest groups available through on-line services, cable television, video discs, and satellite broadcasting — a strategy called **narrowcasting** — are replacing the broadcasting of lowest-common-denominator entertainment. The future will see even more dramatic changes, these writers contend. The newspaper of tomorrow will consist of information selected by viewers to fit their needs and interests, delivered to their home via high-capacity cables.

According to this view, social historian Daniel Pope points out, even advertising will change drastically. The new interactive media systems will encourage the use of video catalogs, allowing consumers to examine, order, and pay for products at home, thus bypassing established channels of distribution. This interactivity will place a priority on individual needs, to which marketers would have to respond as never before. Producers will allow more opportunities for communication by consumers as equals. Sellers and buyers will share the same information about needs and products and therefore share power. Advertising via the media will then be a genuinely democratic dialogue.[6]

But not all writers who spin tales about where the media will lead society are optimists. A strong contingent of pessimists has insistently voiced concerns that the hundreds of possibilities available through the onslaught of homevideo equipment, satellite dishes, cable channels, and their interaction through home computers must diminish the chances for organized democratic consciousness and action. They worry that, as the number of television stations and videotapes increases, the chances of getting many people in society to learn about problems from the media, and to mobilize responses to the problems, will decrease.

The result, according to this view, is that the specialization emphasized by the new technologies will push people into their own small worlds, where they will have little appreciation for the interests and concerns of others. Consequently, Stephen Ephros, a former attorney for the Federal Communications Commission, predicts: "If my personal computer focuses on one area, and your personal computer focuses on something else, we will see what we want to see. We will not know about anything else."[7]

Another View

At first glance, it may seem difficult to decide which media observer to believe. You might even be tempted to pick one view or the other depending on whether you think you are an optimist or a pessimist. But there is a third, better way: Choose neither version of the future.

This way is better because, like the futurists of decades ago, neither camp takes into account the two principles about mass media set forth earlier. Although they may revel in the interconnection of media technologies, they do not seriously consider the interrelationship of media *industries*. As a result, they ignore forces in the industries and in society at large that control the development of these media technologies and the materials they create — the actual movies on laser discs, the actual data bases available through the computer, and so on. The resulting impression is that media technologies virtually spring up out of thin air and create materials in a vacuum. Not considered are the organizational, legal, and political forces that help define the actual role those media play in society from their point of conception onward. The following are just a few of the forces buffeting the new technologies mentioned earlier:

- Although it is possible to transmit HDTV videos on the kind of computer setup the college student of the example was using, the costs at present would make it infeasible. For international broadcasts of HDTV, both high cost and technology standards are factors. There are fierce international arguments about the standards for high-definition television. Moreover, it is not clear that U.S. media companies support HDTV. They have been pressuring the Federal Communications Commission to allocate to them the bandwidth necessary for HDTV signals. However, these companies have decided they could make more advertising money by using it to transmit not high-definition pictures but instead a number of standard-definition channels that would take up the space of one HDTV channel.
- As with advanced television, the future of some of the most advanced methods for recording and playing music and motion pictures has been guided more by the politics and economics of the marketplace than by quality of sound. Consider digital audiotape (DAT), mini discs, and the digital compact cassette (DCC), three technologies that were new in the late 1980s and early 1990s. The first brought noise-free sound to

home tape machines, though in a format incompatible with standard analog cassettes. The second, also incompatible with existing products, allowed consumers to record as well as to play seventy-four minutes of audio on 2 ½-inch discs. The third, DCC, allowed sound reproduction of a quality between that of analog and that of DAT. DCC had an important advantage over DAT, though: Its machine could also accommodate the existing analog tapes that most consumers owned.

- Each technology represented an advance in consumer electronics, but that did not guarantee success in a consumer marketplace where analog tapes and standard compact discs (CDs) have been favorites for several years. Many habits and vested interests were at stake. Recording executives found that consumers did not want to spend the hundreds of dollars required to buy the new formats. The recording companies themselves balked at having to spend the extra money required to release albums in five, rather than two or three, formats. Similarly, retailers objected to stocking the same recordings in a wide variety of formats, which took up a lot of store space and cost a lot of money.[8]

- As it turned out, all three technologies failed in the general marketplace. It was this experience, and the failure that Sony suffered with the Betamax video recorder during the 1970s, that led Sony and Philips to scrap two different types of digital video disc players (DVD) they were about to introduce in the mid-1990s. Each believed that its system was superior, but also feared that the release of competing systems would confuse retailers and consumers. The two firms agreed to compromise, to pool their technologies and release only one DVD technology, in order to maximize their chance of marketplace success.

- The future of narrowcasting must be evaluated in terms of the expense of providing media materials to very small audiences. When it comes to "network-quality" movies or other entertainment materials, the cost of creating programs (over $1 million an hour) might make narrowcasting prohibitive for very small audiences. However, producers of news, entertainment, and information (such as talk shows and travelogues) have found several ways to recoup their costs and spread their risks; these methods will be described in the course of this book. The answers that producers are formulating, depending on the materials they are creating, will guide the future of narrowcasting as much as will the availability of multiple channels.

Do not interpret these comments to mean that futuristic media will make no imprint. The new technologies may well cast large-scale impressions on society, even along lines that futurists have mentioned. Whether signs point to that happening, however, and what the social consequences might be if it does happen, are matters for intense examination and discussion. We should jump to neither optimistic nor pessimistic conclusions about the new media's implications based on a view that the social impact of a mass medium is built into the technology. If we want an evenhanded picture of the role that mass media technology will play in society, we should learn to look systematically at the forces shaping the development of technology, its use, and the content created for it. This means asking a number of questions:

- How are changes in media technology, in national and global politics, and in society at large affecting existing ways of working in mass media industries?
- How will the menu of songs, stories, and reports available to different audiences change in the face of new media?
- How will the nature of the materials themselves change?

Answering these and other questions about the present and future requires a language to talk systematically about mass media systems and industries. Such a language can help raise questions about how mass media industries operate today, how they relate to one another, and how they relate to society at large.

MEDIA STUDIES AND THIS BOOK'S APPROACH

To construct a language, this book draws on two streams of thought that began in the nineteenth century and developed in different ways through the twentieth century. One stream has been called "marxist," the other "industrial." Both have asked questions about the power of media in society, but from different perspectives.

The marxist stream is named for social philosopher Karl Marx. Its driving assumption is Marx's notion that the structure and content of a society's media of communication reflect the interests of the dominant economic class in the society. "Fundamentalist" marxist writers have tended to find direct associations between ownership patterns of media organizations and the content those media distribute. They have written that even media materials we would not consider political — cartoons, romance stories — are filled with images that reinforce the values of the capitalist system.

Most contemporary marxist scholars are not as likely as those of decades past to argue that these direct patterns of influence always exist. They often acknowledge that certain media (typically small, independent moviemakers, magazine publishers, or book companies) may go against the values of society's owners of production. For example, a movie might celebrate the labor movement in its fight against the owners of the companies — the banks, insurance companies, and the very wealthy stratum of the population. Marxist writers today are centrally concerned with the extent to and manner in which people who work in media organizations will shape media materials in ways that reinforce or resist the power of the dominant class in society.

According to their view, media workers do not always know they are reinforcing the right of the dominant class when they create their images. Often, they are simply following work rules and habits. As a result many media organizations end up being "amplifiers" that reflect the basic economic arrangements of society and the values that support it.

The industrial stream of thought is based on very different assumptions. It argues that while the ownership of society's "capital" is sometimes important for understanding how media industries and organizations work, it is not always the most important consideration. People who adopt this perspective see industrial and institutional factors, rather than ownership, as helping to explain much of what media organizations create and distribute.

Industrial factors are those influences that have to do with the way organizations work. Competition, the need to get the materials necessary to complete tasks, the mandate to get tasks done on time — these are but a few of the concerns that all organizations, including media organizations, confront.

They also confront **institutional** issues. Institutions include the military, education, medicine, business, and law, among others. As these examples suggest, an institution is a looseknit set of organizations that exercise authority over key aspects of life. Medicine, for example, covers health care concerns, and the law sees the formal rules in society as its domain. Many who espouse the industrial perspective believe that mass media organizations collectively make up an institution as well. The mass media institution has as its territory the depiction of all of society's institutions.

Marxist thinkers would not necessarily dispute this, but most would insist that at base all institutions reflect the aims of the social class that owns most of the wealth of society. The industrial perspective argues, by contrast, that the mass media institution is not always in sync with other institutions. It has stakes of its own that sometimes lead its activities to run counter to the interests of other institutions.

Television news programs, for example, frequently "expose" problems in business, military, and political institutions. According to this perspective, part of the advantage of doing so is having viewers believe the news organization is on their side. But what is good for those journalists is not necessarily good for the organization, or entire institution, they are investigating.

The assumption underlying this book, then, is that the best way to understand the emerging media system is through an industrial and institutional perspective that is open to an enormous number of influences. This approach does not dismiss the marxist idea that economic and class powers in society hold a fundamental influence over media activities. Rather than seeing it as the only influence, it finds ownership and class working along with other considerations — industrial strategies, organizational habits, institutional rivalries — that may at times be even more important in explaining media activities.

With this perspective in mind, we start our journey into the world of media organizations, strategies, and power at the very beginning: with an examination of the words we use, the process we study, and the way they are linked to crucial processes in the society at large.

DEFINING MASS MEDIA
AND MASS COMMUNICATION

The reason for using a term like *mass media* instead of simply naming specific items, such as magazines or books, is that it indicates similarities between these items. One advantage of having such an umbrella term, or **concept,** has to do with confronting the future. Once we understand what characteristics in these items lead us to group them together, we will have a way of deciding whether newly invented items should also be called by that term and analyzed according to similar patterns.[9]

Definitions help us make that decision, for they are aids to exploring the world. As concepts, they offer ideas, or points of view, that guide us to look at certain parts of the world and not others. Definitions lead us to include particular things, and to exclude other things, in our thinking. Thoughtful inclusion and exclusion often lead to innovative questions that can help us make sense of the changes going on around us.

Definitional issues arise all the time. In 1950, people had never heard of a video cassette recorder. Twenty-five years later, when VCRs were making their way into homes, writers began to casually tag them as "mass media" along with the more traditional forms. Were the writers correct? Are VCRs *always* mass media? If VCRs are excluded or included as mass media, what are the implications for understanding the strategies of mass media industries?

Answering these questions requires a definition of mass media. The one to be proposed here is fairly straightforward: **Mass media are the technological vehicles through which mass communication takes place.**

This definition may seem as if it merely passes the buck to another term, *mass communication.* In an important sense it does. Already, though, we have begun to offer an answer to the questions about VCRs. Video cassette recorders are examples of technology, and from that standpoint they fit the definition. But the definition indicates that VCRs are mass media only when they are vehicles for mass communication. The key issue is to decide what this means.

Mass communication is a concept that lies at the heart of this book. There are many definitions of mass communication. All see it as a process that involves the creation of **messages,** which are arrays of symbols that appear to be purposefully organized. In addition, conceptions of mass communication emphasize the use of technologies in the process as well as the involvement of large numbers of people.

The definition to be presented here does not necessarily cancel out or contradict other approaches. It has two purposes: One is to focus on those aspects of the process that we believe make mass communication different from other activities. The other is to highlight aspects of the process that we believe are the most relevant for learning about the **creation of messages,** the **use of technologies,** the **involvement of large numbers of people,** and the **implications** of it all.

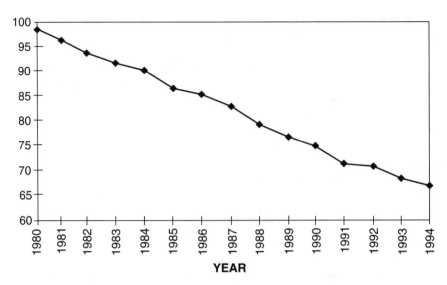

FIGURE 1.3 Declining Big Three network revenue shares (SOURCE: *TV Dimensions '95* (New York: Media Dynamics Inc), p. 40.)

This figure dramatically shows how the ABC, CBS, and NBC television networks have faced increasing competition through the 1980s and 1990s. It charts the percentage of national TV advertising revenue that the Big Three have received since 1980. In the early 1980s, ABC, CBS, and NBC were virtually the only game in town for advertisers wishing to advertise on a national basis. Over the years, though, ad-supported cable networks, the rise of national syndicated programming (see pp. 84–85), and founding of the Fox broadcast network have diminished the networks' power over advertising.

Mass communication is the industrialized production, reproduction, and multiple distribution of messages through technological devices. This definition is in sync with this book's focus on media industries, for we are arguing that mass communication's industrial nature is its most important feature.

An Industry Focus

Although the term has already been used, it will be helpful here to clarify what we mean by *industry*. An **industry** is a conglomeration of organizations that work together in a regulated fashion to create and distribute products or services. For example, we have a newspaper industry, a magazine industry, a billboard industry, and a book industry. These industries are composed of organizations that are involved in different phases of producing and distributing multiple copies of the messages.

In the case of newspapers, the same firms may control both the production and the distribution of papers. Still, many other organizations are also heavily involved in the newspaper industry: firms that sell newsprint, wire services that sell copy, advertisers that purchase space, newsstand companies that sell papers to the public, and truck dealers who rent or sell distribution vehicles.

Each production and distribution phase in a media industry is carried out through the use of technological devices. Radio broadcasters use audiotape recorders, compact discs, and transmitters; newspaper companies count word processors and delivery trucks as essential technology; and cable networks look to television cameras, videotape, and satellites for help in producing and distributing their product.

At this point, the question of whether video cassette recorders are mass media can be answered straightforwardly. Our definition emphasizes that production and distribution must be carried out by an industry in order for an apparatus to be called a **mass medium.** Therefore, a VCR that plays a movie created and distributed by a major film studio is a vehicle of mass communication. But a VCR that plays a program created by an individual or small group for distribution by hand to neighborhood friends and co-workers would not be considered a mass medium, nor would a TV set used for closed-circuit television presentations created by a company for its employees. In the last two cases, the VCR and the TV are part of an activity that uses technology for group communication or organizational communication, not for mass communication.

Some people may find reason to argue with this distinction; controversies occur over every definition of mass communication. At the same time, the definition expands the scope of our inquiry by directing us to consider as mass media a wide range of products that have not been tagged this way. The World Wide Web of the Internet, greeting cards, toys — even computer word processors — can, under certain conditions of production and distribution, be considered mass media. This does not deny that these products can be grouped under other concepts. Toys can also be termed part of the recreation industry, for example. What we are doing here is applying a **mass communication perspective** to these activities, which highlights the aspects of the phenomena involved in the industrialized production, reproduction, and distribution of messages through technological devices.

A Mass Communication Perspective

The mass communication perspective can help us see the world in a new light and ask new questions. Consider, for example, the point stressed earlier about mass media industries being increasingly interrelated. Looking at various phenomena from this point of view leads us to pay attention to the variety of industries that messages might cross, not all of which would be thought of as mass media. A character created for a cartoon — say, Donald Duck — might also find distribution on a TV program, on a video cassette, as a toy, in a magazine, and on an ice cream bar.

Notice the emphasis on "production and distribution" in the previous paragraphs. Unfortunately, distribution is often ignored in discussions of mass communication. To neglect distribution, however, is to pass over a critically important aspect of the mass communication process: Expertise in the industrialized distribution of messages through technological devices often, determines the power of various players in a mass media industry.

To illustrate this aspect, consider what would happen if you tried to be a publisher of a trade book — a work aimed at general readers that is typically sold in bookstores. If you have a laser printer and a computer with a desktop publishing program, it will not be difficult to make the pages look like a typical trade book. All you have to do is take the handsome camera-ready manuscript (or just the computer disk) to a photocopy shop. The photocopy shop can use fine paper and will probably be able to bind the copied pages in a respectable manner. A bindery, though more expensive, can give you a product that is almost indistinguishable from a volume you might find in a store. If you are willing to spend more money, you might have an artist design a jacket that the bindery will attach to each copy.

Thus, the major difference between your publishing activity and that of major publishers such as Random House and Simon & Schuster does not lie in production. One person with the cash to pay a photocopy store and perhaps a bindery can create a product that can compete favorably in appearance, and possibly in content, with something that professional publishers might turn out. It is in distribution that the fundamental distinction between a sophisticated publishing organization and a first-time operation shows itself.

As a distributor, you might want to plant your home-grown books in the B. Dalton national bookstore chain. Chances are, however, that B. Dalton's buying agents will have nothing to do with you; neither will most bookstores in the United States. Shelf space is too valuable for them to take a chance on an unknown writer with an unknown publisher. You could try to hawk your book on street corners, and perhaps you would sell a few copies. However, Random House would likely have a much easier time placing your book because it has a reputation with bookstores for choosing books that sell. Bookstores also assume that Random House will promote its books to help them move off the shelves.

Distribution clout within the media system is often an important byproduct of distribution clout within a mass media industry. As a first-time publisher, you would have a slim chance of getting your work adopted by a book club or, better still, by a movie company or a TV production firm. Random House, by contrast, has a strong reputation as a releaser of books suitable for book clubs, movies, and TV. Excerpts in magazines and newspapers are also standard fare for such a large publisher.

CONNECTING MASS COMMUNICATION
TO SOCIETY

The example just presented illustrates a crucial point about the mass communication process: It has the *potential* to distribute the same message to millions, even billions, of people. A media industry may produce and distribute materials that will reach relatively few individuals. This may be purposeful, as when a newspaper is directed to only a couple of thousand people. Or it may be unplanned, as when a trade book that its publisher had high hopes for fails to move off the shelves. It is important to stress, though, that although mass media may not always reach the largest possible audience, reaching huge populations within a relatively short period is impossible without the coordination of technologies by a variety of specialized organizations. Pursuing this point a bit deeper will lead us to yet another set of important questions to explore: the connection of mass media to the larger society.

Live Aid

A striking case in which specialized technologies and large organizations were used to reach large populations is the Live Aid concert mounted in 1985 to benefit victims of an African famine. This concert was the idea of one person: British rock musician Bob Geldof. His goal was as intimidating as the need was grave: to mobilize tens of millions of people around the world to contribute money for relief efforts.

Geldof enlisted the talents of music impresario Bill Graham and producer Michael Mitchell. They realized quickly that they needed a lot of help to achieve Geldof's goal. First, they had to create an organization that could command the support of other organizations from media industries around the world. Locations for the benefit had to be scouted and arranged; talent agencies had to be approached to coordinate the appearance of their clients; broadcasting firms throughout the world had to be contacted in the hope they would carry the concert live; satellite facilities and other telecommunications equipment had to be rented or borrowed; facilities and logistics for collecting and using donations had to be planned—all this and more needed to take place before, during, and after the concert of stellar performers was beamed live from Wembley Stadium, in London and JFK Stadium, in Philadelphia.

It was, it turned out, a monumental technological and organizational achievement. Donations of time, facilities, and energy came from corporations, celebrities, and even sailors of the Philadelphia Navy Yard. All helped Geldof and friends pull off what proved to be the most complicated live broadcast ever mounted. Fourteen satellites were used to link JFK with Wembley and the world. When it was over (with remarkably few glitches), journalists reported that Live Aid stood to make as much as $50 million and that, more astonishingly, an estimated 1.5 billion people were able to watch the show.[10]

Although the sheer size of the potential viewing audience was mind-boggling, its diversity was at least as amazing. People from 150 countries as far-flung as Iceland and Ghana tuned in to world-class rock groups. They also listened to internationally known political figures—from Bishop Desmond Tutu of South Africa to Indian Prime Minister Rajiv Gandhi—deliver prerecorded messages on world hunger. "We're using television to catalyze the world," said Michael Mitchell before the concert. Although that was an exaggeration, Live Aid was still the closest that one broadcast had ever come to doing just that.[11]

The Sharing of Messages

Ten years before Live Aid, technological drawbacks would have made such instantaneous international sharing of messages unthinkable. Even more than ten years later, this kind of event is rare, for monetary and political reasons we will explore in Chapter 9. In technologically developed countries such as the United States, however, linking large numbers of people to share the same materials virtually instantaneously has become routine for the broadcast television, radio, and cable TV industries. Just as significant is the sharing that takes place more slowly when newspapers, magazines, books, movies, billboards, and other mass media diffuse their messages across society.

Because of mass communication, millions of people in the United States who are anonymous to and separated physically from one another have the opportunity to receive the same messages within a fairly short period of time. This holds profound implications for the way we think about the world around us. For one thing, it means that huge, geographically dispersed populations can focus on the same issues at approximately the same time. For example, people throughout the country can watch and read the same news reports about a presidential campaign while the campaign is taking place.

This amazing feature of mass communication has drawn the attention of many scholars. John Dewey, John Cooley, and Robert Park, sociologists at the University of Chicago in the early twentieth century, were especially influential in their thinking about mass communication as a social "glue." They wrote extensively about the power of mass media organizations to transcend space and time and create a sense of a nation out of people who lived far from one another, in very different circumstances, with virtually no chance of meeting face-to-face. Robert Park, especially, stressed that it was important to study the process of production in order to understand why and how ideas circulate through society.

As Park understood, and as later scholars such as George Gerbner have emphasized, this sharing of messages does not mean that people share the same understanding of the messages; nor does it mean they agree with the messages. Notions of preferred ways to behave come from many areas of society, including the family, the church, and the school. What is shared, then, are depictions of the world, and these depictions are presented more broadly and more quickly through mass media than through any other vehicle of communication.

The upshot of this sharing is that **mass media create the subjects that are grist for our everyday conversation mill.** Through mass communication, individuals have a common opportunity to develop opinions about the same messages. The ideas people find in print, on the radio, on recordings, and on TV become a springboard for discussions and arguments with others. The talk may be ignited by anything — news, other types of nonfiction, advertising, or fictional materials such as movies and TV sitcoms. We should not assume, in fact, that news is necessarily the most common media-generated conversation piece. Even soap operas and prime time TV shows generate everyday talk among friends, relatives, and co-workers.

It is important to stress that the sharing of messages that takes place as a result of mass communication need not always involve huge audiences. Sometimes, the organizations that create magazines, books, records, videos, radio programs, or other media products intend to reach people with only certain characteristics — people of a certain age, for example, or a certain income. While, historically, commercial television channels have reached out to the largest number of viewers, even this has been changing. As Table 1.1 indicates, about 40% of all U.S. cable subscribers in 1994 received 54 or more TV channels. That number of channels, and the number of people receiving them is expected to grow significantly in the years to come. This means that much of the industrial process we call mass communication will be focused on "targeting" relatively small audiences profitably.

Some topics are covered so intensely by so many media that they take on a special importance as conversation pieces, if only to enable people to argue about whether so much attention should be devoted to the subjects. Mass media researchers call this process **agenda setting.** Fictional materials are sometimes raised to such significance. Special TV presentations such as the *Roots* miniseries and movies about the O. J. Simpson trial are just two examples. On a daily basis, though, nonfiction is most obviously involved in what scholars call agenda setting.

Igniting Anger and Action

Agenda setting happens, for example, when the three national TV networks and the major U.S. newspapers publicize drug addiction problems, wars in the former Yugoslavia, the issue of abortion, the O. J. Simpson trial, and the World Series. Viewers and readers might talk with others, even act toward others, as if these were the most nationally and internationally critical of subjects.

A corollary to the importance of mass media in setting discussion agendas is that they sometimes incite people to anger and action. When individuals use the mass media, they are often aware that many others are confronting the same material. Moreover, many people believe, correctly or incorrectly, that the mass media materials they dislike have the ability to affect readers or viewers in harmful ways. People have accused those who create news and nonnews materials of encouraging or reinforcing a multitude of social ills: violence, rape, illiteracy, rampant consumerism, insulting and depersonalizing advertising, political noninvolvement, cultural imperialism, and more. These claims have led to vigorous social debates, many of which have themselves been aired through one or another mass medium. Imagine a conservative religious minister who is horrified to read in the local newspaper and see on statewide TV news programs that a gubernatorial candidate's unwavering pro-choice position on abortion is increasing contributions to the candidate's primary campaign substantially. The minister is also angered by what he feels is the press's characterization of pro-lifers as fanatics. At the same time, the director of Planned Parenthood in the same town might be elated with the widespread news that the liberal candidate's popularity in the state has been helped by her stance on abortion. Both the minister and the Planned Parenthood director may feel that the appearance of the story on the front page of the newspaper signals an important development in the primary, since it focuses the attention of many people on the issue. That evaluation may lead them to gain media attention for their own particular points of view. It may also lead them to raise funds for their causes while the issue is garnering especially high visibility.

Clearly, the reactions by the minister and the Planned Parenthood director are peculiar to their interests and their backgrounds. Notice, though, that both are responding to depictions by the newspaper of parts of the world they cannot know firsthand. Notice, too, that they are drawing conclusions about the social action they should take as a result of a news report about large numbers of people they do not know, do not necessarily agree with, but with whom they feel politically and economically linked.

Shaping Notions of Society

We typically use the word society to refer to large numbers of individuals, groups, and organizations that see themselves linked politically and economically. One larger point of the minister and Planned Parenthood tale, then, is that **mass media continually help shape people's understanding of the elements that make up their society.** They do so by suggesting what individuals, groups, and organizations should care about politically and economically, and why. Mass media also tell people what others think of them and what people like themselves think of others. Finally, mass media shape people's conceptions of their society by directing their attention toward certain concerns and away from others, leading people to consider what, if anything, they ought to do about these concerns.

Mass media systems thus take on the powerful role of an **institution** in society. They portray the life of society *to* society. Many people accept media

**TABLE 1.1 CHANNEL CAPACITY OF EXISTING CABLE SYSTEMS
AS OF OCTOBER 1, 1994**

Channel Capacity	Subscribers	% of Total
54 & over	23,022,509	40.840
30–53	30,754,758	54.556
20–29	1,366,780	2.425
13–19	108,663	0.193
6–12	242,684	0.431
5 only	1,876	0.003
Under 5	517	0.001
Not Available	874,761	1.552
Total	**56,372,548**	**100**

SOURCE: Television and Cable Factbook, 1995 *(Washington, D.C.: Warren Publishing, 1995), p. 1–77.
Reprinted by permission.*

By late 1994, nearly 96% of all cable subscribers received thirty or more channels. Because of new technologies, observers predict that in the late 1990s the number of channels people get in their homes will multiply severalfold. What will be the consequences of this increase for the way society talks to itself and looks at itself?

presentations as "common sense" or "the way it is"—for others, if not for them. But for some, media images underscore what is at stake in the battle over society's self-definition. Media images lead them to want to place their version of society alongside that of others in the media, to call attention to themselves, and to gain legitimacy for their cause.

Far from being transmitters of passively accepted images, the mass media are platforms for arguments about the patterns of beliefs and activities in society, what can be called its **culture.** A key reason for studying mass media systems, then, is to understand this process of **cultural argumentation** and its relationship to conflicts over beliefs and activities elsewhere in the society.

A galaxy of fascinating and important questions flow out of this realization, such as the following:

- What considerations shape the materials that different mass media create?
- What factors cause certain parts of the media system to link up with one another more than with others?
- How do other institutions in American society relate to different mass media? For example, do physicians concerned about their public image encourage major organizations within the medical institution to influence medicine's images via various mass media? If so, how is this attempt at influence carried out, and to what extent is it successful?
- How, in general, do mass media relate to centers of power in society?
- How might we understand the influence of the many "pressure groups" outside the media on media personnel?

- What is the role of the audience in all this, and what part does it play in encouraging change or continuity in various forms of mass media materials? How, too, do the interests of international audiences and governments affect the creation and distribution of material?

THE PLAN OF THIS BOOK

The following pages are designed to help you explore answers to these and many other questions about mass media systems in society. Later chapters will explore the systems' processes as they relate to key activities that occur within and across media boundaries. Finance and support; the distribution and exhibition of media materials; government regulation; public advocacy groups; the nature of the audience and its importance; the day-to-day work of writers, directors, actors, book editors, journalists, and other production personnel; the various subcultures and hiring patterns; the risks media executives take in encouraging both continuity and change — these and other topics will be discussed and interconnected through many examples from the media world.

The emphasis will be on American mass media, but the framework developed here is applicable to all sorts of media systems. If your goal is to be a media manager, you will find challenging perspectives for understanding how media operate and interrelate, perspectives that will help you address mass media that do not yet even exist. If your interests lie primarily in becoming a more aware consumer of media materials, this book will lead you to see your environment in fresh ways. The subject is important and exciting. Read on.

CONSIDER THIS

1. How do you think societies defined themselves in the days before mass media?
2. It might be interesting to study how often during a certain period (an hour, a day) people bring media topics into their conversations.
3. An interesting way to become acquainted with media industries is to read a magazine directed to people in that industry. Examples of such trade publications are *Advertising Age, Broadcasting and Cable, Multichannel News, Editor and Publisher,* and *Variety.*

NOTES

1. Gardner Spring, quoted in James Carey and James Quirk, "The History of the Future," in G. Gerbner, L. Gross, and W. Melody (eds.), *Communications Technology and Social Policy* (New York: Wiley, 1973), p. 488.
2. Carey and Quirk, p. 492.
3. Carey and Quirk, p. 489.

4. Teresita Hermano, quoted in Michael Traber (ed.), *The Myth of the Information Revolution* (London: Sage Publications, 1986), p. 1.

5. See, for example, Nicholas Negroponte, *Being Digital* (New York: Knopf, 1995).

6. Daniel Pope, *The Making of Modern Advertising* (New York: Basic Books, 1983), pp. 295–296.

7. Stephen Ephros, quoted in Martin Koughan, "The State of the Revolution, 1982," Channels 1 (December 1981–January 1982), p. 70.

8. See Jeff Clark-Meads and Susan Nunziata, "Philips Reveals Details of DCC Launch," *Billboard*, February 16, 1991, p. 1; and Susan Nunziata, "Sony Launching New Disc Format," *Billboard*, May 25, 1991, p. 1.

9. For more on this subject, see Joseph Turow, "A Mass Communication Perspective on Entertainment Industries," in J. Curran and M. Gurevitch (eds.), *Culture, Society, and the Media,* 2nd ed. (London: Methuen, 1992); Joseph Turow, "Media Industries, Media Consequences: Rethinking Mass Communication," in J. Anderson (ed.), *Communication Yearbook* (Newberry Park, CA: Sage Publications, 1990); Joseph Turow, "The Critical Importance of Mass Communication as a Concept," in B. Ruben and L. Lievrow (eds.), *Information and Behavior* (New Brunswick, NJ: Transaction Books, 1990), pp. 9–20; Joseph Turow, "The Challenge of Inference in Interinstitutional Research on Mass Communication," *Communication Research*, 18 (April 1991), pp. 222–239; and Joseph Turow, "Cultural Argumentation and the Mass Media: A Perspective for Research," *Communication*, 8 (Autumn 1985), pp. 139–164.

10. "Rock Around the World: Live Aid Was the Biggest Charity Extravaganza Ever," *Newsweek*, July 22, 1985, pp. 56–58.

11. "Banding Together for Africa," *Newsweek*, July 15, 1985, p. 52.

CHAPTER 2

Power Roles
A Framework for Strategic Thinking

This chapter

- presents an approach to examining how various parts of a media industry work with one another.
- builds that approach around the ideas of power and resources.
- shows how this scheme applies to all sorts of media, from movies to book publishing.

Mass communication is, above all, a process that involves organizations and industries. Understanding the particulars of mass communication today and in years to come, therefore, requires an understanding of what organizations and industries are, how they operate, and how they relate to society at large. This chapter introduces the concepts required to gain such understanding. Building on these concepts, it presents a "power role framework" as a way to explore considerations that shape the creation and distribution of mass media materials.

A CRUCIAL IDEA

A crucial idea lies at the core of the framework: The creation, distribution, and exhibition of mass media materials is essentially the struggle of organizations over a broad range of society's resources.

To grasp what is meant by this struggle, it is useful to think about what an **organization** is and what it needs. An organization can be described as **an activity system that is goal-directed and boundary-maintaining.**[1]

The term **activity system** means that as members of an organization, individuals carry out certain patterns of behaviors in relation to one another. All the work that goes on at The Chicago Tribune Company to create, distribute, and plan its broad array of media operations (from a daily Chicago newspaper to national TV syndication) comprises the activity system of that organization.

Goal-directed refers to the idea that members of an organization typically act as if it had one or more goals. People who work for a newspaper company, for example, direct their work toward the creation of one or more daily newspapers. An observer would probably notice that getting the paper out on time is an important goal.

There may well be other goals, and they may conflict with one another. Generating an unimpeachably accurate product may conflict with the paper's timely appearance, for example. Even with these conflicts, the outside observer could infer that the members of the organization are not merely aimless.

Use of the word *members* brings up another feature of organizations: the idea that they are **boundary-maintaining.** This term indicates that some people are allowed to participate in the organization whereas others are excluded. Chicagoans cannot walk off the street to work on the next day's *Chicago Tribune*. Guards in the Tribune building would likely prevent people without permission from gaining access to the editorial floors. Anyone who insisted on entering could get arrested.

At base, then, an organization needs the wherewithal to keep itself intact and carry out the activity system that helps it accomplish certain goals. This is where **resources** come in. Resources are the people, supplies, information, services, and money that an organization must use to carry out its tasks. No mass media organization can possibly create all the resources it needs from scratch. Instead, the organization must try to get those resources from outside its boundaries, that is, from its **environment.**[2]

The environment provides people for recruitment into the organization; supplies used in the performance of organizational activities; required information, permission, and services to help gain the acceptability or permissibility of its activities in that environment; and money to pay for it all. At the same time, it is to the environment that the organization directs products of its activity system, often to exchange those products for resources or to gain money to purchase other resources elsewhere.

Resources are not randomly distributed throughout the environment. Rather, they are concentrated in various areas of the environment and often under the control of other organizations. Consider, as an example, just a few of the resources The Chicago Tribune Company must acquire to operate only its newspaper business. First, money must be found. Reporters, editors, business managers, delivery drivers, press workers, receptionists, and other personnel must be hired. Paper, photographic film, ink, and other exhaustible materials must be bought. Delivery trucks need to be maintained and fueled. Telephone and news wire services must be purchased.

Other requirements may not be as transparent, but they are necessary to the survival and growth of the company. For example, the newspaper organization needs law firms to protect and defend its ongoing activities. It needs lobbyists to protect its interests in government circles. It needs advertising and public relations companies to encourage target audiences to buy its product and enhance its reputation. It needs consulting firms to help its executives make decisions about the direction of the company—whether to buy other newspapers, whether to continue branching out into nonnews operations, what to do with other media properties, and how to arrange those deals.

In other words, the Tribune organization must rely on entities in its environment for resources. Moreover, those entities might demand substantial recompense for their help. This is especially true if other organizations are trying to compete for the same resources, or even if they are simply trying to block that firm from obtaining resources. The Chicago Tribune Company must consequently cope with such demands by exchanging its own resources or dealing with its needs in other ways, such as reducing them.

UNDERSTANDING POWER

Here we arrive at the concept of **power** in interorganizational relations. Power is the use of resources by one organization in order to gain compliance by another organization. An example of the exercise of power is a truckers' union that refuses to allow its members to deliver a news company's daily papers unless the firm agrees to pay them a higher salary. The union in this case is relying on the importance of a resource it controls—distribution personnel—to gain the firm's compliance.

Not all exercises of power are so obvious. In many situations, the most effective influence is that which the people being influenced do not even realize. This happens when personnel in the more powerful organization or group of organizations are able to shape the structure of relationships so that the affected parties see the situation as "common sense" or simply "the way things are." A typical way for a company to exercise such **structural power** is for its personnel to ensure that laws governing their industry benefit their firm. The rules of day-to-day industry interactions would therefore carry the imprint of that firm's power, though many who deal with the company would not remember this.

This example, along with that of the union, gives only a hint of the broadranging interorganizational struggle over resources that guides the production and distribution of mass media material. In developing a way to examine this struggle in more detail, we can locate the exercise of power in resource-controlling relationships that certain organizations hold vis-à-vis other organizations. For example, certain firms in the recording industry have developed power over the creation of product, while others hold resources that allow them to excel at distribution. Still other companies may be involved in both the production and distribution processes.

Such resource-controlling relationships can be termed **power roles.** The first step in understanding a media industry, then, is to generate a vocabulary that allows for systematic discussion about a wide range of power roles in media industries. Then, it should be possible to identify actual organizations in those roles that are struggling over resources with organizations that have taken on the same or different power roles. Finally, questions can be asked about the way those interorganizational activities affect the messages that are created and distributed to target audiences.

A POWER ROLE FRAMEWORK

A framework for accomplishing the first step is presented in Table 2.1, which is based on a scheme developed by communication researcher George Gerbner.[3] Note that each power role an organization might take on is characterized by a label for the role and the typical activities that describe it. Also listed in the table is each power role's leverage in the industry. An organization's leverage is the resources it can use to gain compliance from other organizations. An organization taking on the authority power role, for example, may be able to marshal resources of the legislative system and the police to enforce its will on producers.

The descriptions in Table 2.1 make it clear that the framework revolves around the **producer** power role. Of chief concern is the way organizations taking on different roles within a media industry influence the amount or nature of mass media materials created for release to the public. Organizations acting as **distributors, exhibitors, clients, unions,** and so on sometimes involve themselves in actions that have no impact on mass media producers. They all pay bills to the electric company, for example. Here, however, the concern is only with their activities that may affect the output of an organization taking on the producer power role.

The power role framework charts activities and lines of leverage between organizations. That is, it is essentially an **interorganizational** scheme. Nevertheless, two power roles in Table 2.1 — **creators** and **publics** — are included because of their importance, even though they cannot by their very concepts be filled by organizations. As the descriptions in the table indicate, creators and publics are by definition unorganized. Creators are people who make individual decisions about lending their talents to production firms. Publics do not even join organizations. They are consumers who, individually or (at most) in scattered small groups, make decisions about whether to buy a book, subscribe to a magazine, or watch a particular TV program.

Decisions by individual consumers have important implications for a producer's ability to survive. Directly or indirectly, publics provide a crucial resource: money. Still, it is worth noting that when individuals go beyond

TABLE 2.1 THE POWER ROLES OF A MASS MEDIA INDUSTRY

Power Role*	Typical Activities	Leverage
1. Producer	Create material for release to the public via mass media. Set and supervise content and selection guidelines.	Control over people and ideas that might get exposure to the public via mass media.
2. Authority	Provide government (or governmentally sanctioned) regulation and arbitration among other power roles.	Political and military power.
3. Investor	Contribute money in anticipation of production and purchase of material by clients. Set general conditions for the supply of capital and operating funds.	Control over monetary resources.
4. Client	Make organizational purchases in support of specific products. Contribute to producers' most direct cash flow in exchange for media material created.	Control over monetary resources.
5. Auxiliary	Provide material supplies to producers.	Control over access to supplies.
6. Creator	Provide producer with talent to conceive and arrange mass media material.	An individual creator's decision to join a production organization.
7. Union	Regulate the provision of personnel to producers. Set work standards; provide worker protection.	Solidarity and threats of work stoppage.
8. Distributor	Select and coordinate dispersal of material to the point of exhibition.	Control over channels by which material can reach exhibition.
9. Exhibitor	Offer material for public viewing or purchase.	Control over outlets through which the public chooses materials.
10. Linking pin	Move completed mass media material or people representing that material from production firms in one industry to production firms in another industry.	Control over access to new markets, new possibilities.
11. Facilitator	Help production firms carry out or evaluate mass media material.	Control over intermediary services.
12. Public advocacy	Demand favorable attention, portrayal, policy support.	Pressue through boycott, appeal to authorities.
13. Public	Purchase and/or attend to distributed messages in an unorganized fashion.	An individual decision to choose or not choose particular content. An individual decision to complain through legal or other channels.

*All but the *creator* and *public* power roles are typically carried out by organizations. See text for further details.

making these kinds of yes/no decisions or registering individual complaints, they are no longer acting as publics, according to this scheme. Rather, when consumers band together to affect production, distribution, or exhibition choices, they are acting as organizations that hold the public advocacy power role. Similarly, creators who band together take on the union power role.

Taking on Power Roles

The language about organizations' power roles is purposeful. Organizations are not in themselves power roles; rather, they carry out role-related activities. This means that organizations can take on more than one role within a mass media industry. Firms acting as producers, for example, can also be distributors and exhibitors. This ability can increase an organization's power in a mass media industry.

The power role scheme sees mass media industries as systems — that is, as forces that continually influence one another. In media systems, organizational forces interact continually to accumulate and exert influence over production. Exploring the elements of the industry systems in greater detail reveals how the industries relate to one another to create the larger mass media system in society. The following sections of this chapter begin this exploration, with a focus on specific influences that organizations in various power roles exert over mass media content.

To keep the scope manageable, the following sections draw examples from mass media industries in the United States alone. The aim is not to present exhaustive descriptions of activities and leverages associated with these roles. In fact, several especially powerful roles are introduced rather briefly, because later chapters treat them at length. Roles that take up less attention later in the book, or roles that must be described in some detail now in order to develop key points later, receive disproportionate attention in this chapter. The tack, then, is to set up avenues for further analysis and generalization.

THE PRODUCER ROLE

The producer is the central power role in the interorganizational scheme. Producers in a mass media industry must compete with one another for resources. How fierce the competition is between particular production firms depends to a large extent on the similarity of their goals and activities. The more alike two companies are in what they make and how they make it, the more fierce their competition is likely to be, because the producers would be competing for very similar, and by nature scarce, resources. The more difficult (or "expensive") it is to procure resources, the greater the competition.

An Example from Book Publishing

Consider two publishing firms. Executives of both decide to produce an expensive title—a large "coffee table" book on candle making. Moreover, they both decide that the best way to market the title is through bookstores. Here are grounds for competition; grounds for even fiercer competition might be imagined.

Suppose that to make a good profit the firms must persuade the top five national book outlets to carry their products. Suppose, further, that each chain will carry only one such candle-making title. In other words, a key resource — exhibition service — would be highly concentrated. Or suppose that the number of people interested in buying expensive books on candle making in bookstores is smaller than the number of books the two publishers must sell to make a profit. That is, the environmental capacity is lean from the standpoint of another key resource: the public's money. Both of these situations would increase competition between the two publishing firms.

Competition would be reduced if the companies did not have similar goals and activities — for example, if they chose different kinds of books to create and sell. Similarly, competition would lessen if the environment's distribution resources were less concentrated and if a larger public willing to buy the book could be found. This could happen if one of the publishers decided to use book club rather than bookstore channels to reach potential customers. The book club strategy would allow the firm to use outlets different from those of its competition. This would provide a group of potential customers who might be quite different from bookstore browsers.

Let us assume that both publishers decide to produce only coffee-table hobby books on candle making, car repair, and flower arranging. One publisher aims at the bookstore market whereas the other aims at the book club arena. Under such circumstances, one could say that each publisher had its own rather specialized niche in the book industry. The concept of "niche" refers to a distinct combination of resources that can support organizations with similar goals, boundaries, and activities.[4] Generally, when one production firm perceives a niche, attempts to exploit it, and thrives, other firms enter to compete in the niche.

Competition over Niches

In the newspaper business, an example of a much-contested niche is the suburban audience. In many areas of the United States, the growth of upper-middle-class suburbs in the 1950s and 1960s provided fertile ground for small daily and weekly papers to grow and prosper. The growth of this niche often meant the loss of resources for urban papers, as advertisers pursued their prime audiences into the suburbs. When the big city papers counterattacked, it was by expanding into the suburban niches themselves. Sometimes they did so by increasing coverage of the suburbs in the main paper, sometimes by creating special zoned editions. In some regions the strategy worked better than in others.

The growth of the suburbs is a case in which the resources of a niche were created through geographic movement. A case in which resources were created through the changing nature of the population can be seen in the development of periodicals for Americans 55 years and older. This group was a growing, increasingly affluent segment of the U.S. population in the 1980s. A magazine market that offered *Modern Maturity* to them early in the decade included by the mid-1990s *Modern Maturity, New Choices, New Choices for the Best Years, Longevity, Senior World, Senior Magazine,* and *Creative Retirement,* among others.

Executives in magazine publishing firms perceived that with increased longevity and burgeoning pension funds, a new resource became available to them: upscale people over 55 who were attractive to magazine advertisers and who might subscribe to magazines that discussed their interests and problems. As a result, these magazines came into being.

TALKING POINT 2.1   A Newspaper Tries a New Niche

Mass media production firms are continually searching for ways to increase their revenues, and that sometimes means trying to identify and exploit new niches. An example is The New York Times Company, which tried to expand the market for its news in a novel way. Executives of the firm were aware that their use of satellites to print editions of *The New York Times* around the United States on the same day was making their product increasingly a truly national newspaper of record. That kind of timeliness was not available in other countries, especially in the Far East, where even with shipment by air the *Times* was arriving long after its release in the United States.

Times executives reasoned that they had a new niche, that influential executives and politicians in the Far East would pay to receive the paper when their counterparts in New York, Chicago, and Los Angeles did. The most cost-efficient way to begin, they concluded, was through a facsimile service — sending synopses of the *Times* by phone lines to fax machines in the Far East. The service, begun in 1990, was called TimesFax and consisted of six to eight letter-sized pages of material gleaned nightly from the next morning's issue of the *Times* and transmitted from New York about 10:00 P.M. That schedule would make it available in midmorning to Tokyo subscribers.

When the new service was announced, executives said the publication would include a summary of articles that appear on the front page of the *Times* and articles on international news, U.S. news, and business news. It was also to include some editorial commentaries and columns by business writers. It is possible that TimesFax represented a relatively low-cost attempt to test the Far East waters. Perhaps *Times* executives wanted to determine if the new niche justified building a printing plant in the region that, with the aid of a satellite, could reproduce the entire paper instantly from New York.

SOURCE: *New York Times,* November 11, 1989.

Organizations stop competing in a niche (or go broke) when they no longer find it profitable. To survive in a crowded environment, producers might try to broaden or narrow the conceptions of their niche to take advantage of resources others are not pursuing. Titles such as *Grandparents, Memories,* and *Longevity* show that their publishers were trying to carve out special niches within the broad arena that advertisers call the "mature market." This positioning was designed to attract mature readers with specific interests as well as advertisers interested in paying to reach them. The fact that several of these magazines were not in business by the late 1990s indicates that in the case of the mature market, the positioning was not convincing to advertisers and audiences.

As this example suggests, "niche" is a slippery concept. It is not at all obvious where one niche ends and another begins. For example, did *Longevity* and *Lifewise* really share the same niche with *Modern Maturity?* Or did they more properly seek the same resources as magazines such as *American Health* and cable channels such as Lifetime?

The answer is that the description of a niche is negotiated territory. How a magazine company sets itself off from competition, argues the value of its existence, and seeks the resources it needs depends to a large extent on how organizations and publics that provide it with resources are willing to see it. This point directs our attention to organizations and groups that hold other power roles by virtue of their ability to supply resources to, and withhold resources from, the producers.

THE AUTHORITY ROLE

One of those power roles is that of **authority,** which involves regulating the other roles in a mass media industry. Simply put, authorities are governments. The most important resource they provide is permission — permission to publish, permission to broadcast, permission to film and record. Authorities can provide other resources as well:

> **Information** on the society or the world that production firms might find impossible or too expensive to bring together by themselves
>
> **Tax benefits** that might improve the cash flows of production firms
>
> **Training programs** to supply personnel

Of course, authorities can also withhold these resources. Such broad abilities, plus the political and military leverage to enforce decisions, make organizations taking on the authority role important for mass media organizations to have on their side. Authorities set the ground rules for the activities that go on in mass media industries.

The term *authority* covers a wide and complicated territory. It refers to various levels of government: federal, state, county, and city. It also refers to several types of organizations: courts, legislatures, executive agencies, and police. The different types of government arms are involved in setting policies, drawing up regulations, interpreting them, and enforcing them. These arms are found at all levels of government, and the different levels may have different jurisdictions over mass media industries. For example, licenses to broadcast commercial television signals in all communities across the nation are issued and regulated at the federal level by the Federal Communications Commission (FCC). By contrast, franchises for cable systems are granted at the state and/or local (city-county) level, with the understanding that these authorities adhere to minimum FCC guidelines. Similarly, expectations about the kind of material that can be carried on a local television station are found in FCC documents; local complaints about programming are evaluated on a case-by-case basis at the federal level. Expectations about the kind of material that can or should be carried on a channel originating from a cable system are generally a nonfederal affair, however, though federal laws may prevent state or local authorities from prohibiting certain programming.

Three Levels of Regulation

Authorities regulate mass media industries on three levels: structural, technical, and content. The **structural** level involves rulings that dictate actual organizational processes and relationships in a mass media industry. One example is Congress's decision in 1919 that broadcasting should be a commercial enterprise rather than a government monopoly.[5] An example narrower in scope was a 1945 decision by the U.S. Supreme Court that encouraged competition between newspapers. The decision struck down an Associated Press bylaw that permitted the wire service to grant exclusive service to a particular newspaper for a particular area.[6]

At the **technical** level, rulings relate to standards of a mechanical, electronic, or otherwise scientific nature that organizations of a mass media industry must uphold. A relevant case is Congress's decision in the early 1960s to require that all TV-set manufacturers involved in interstate commerce equip the sets with receivers capable of receiving both UHF (Ultra High Frequency — Channels 14-83) and the more popular VHF (Very High Frequency — Channels 2-13).[7] More generally, postal edicts relating to weight, size, and construction are technical regulations that affect the operations of book, newspaper, and magazine publishers, as well as direct marketers.[8]

The third level of regulation, **content,** involves specific messages and message policies. An example from broadcasting is the Federal Communication Act's requirement that broadcast licensees program "in the public interest, convenience, and necessity." More specific is the act's demand that stations that provide time to one candidate during an election allow opponents the same amount of time.[9] Relevant to all mass media are content rulings concerning free speech and its limitations on subjects such as libel, copyright, obscenity, pornography, and deceptive advertising.[10]

Content regulations obviously affect the kinds of materials mass media production organizations create. Less obvious, but equally important, is the impact that structural and technical regulations have on content. For example, the 1919 decision by Congress to allow a commercial structure in broadcasting had profound long-term consequences for the materials sent over the air. It ignited a long and complicated series of events over several decades, leading to the radio and TV networks, the advertiser-supported system, and the commercial approach to programming that guided the broadcast media through the 1980s. Exactly how that happened is explored in more detail throughout this book.

Postal rules illustrate how technical regulation can shape mass media material. Lower postal rates for books, magazines, and newspapers than for other commercial matter have historically helped encourage the growth of those media. For example, postal laws have traditionally held that magazines sent to paying subscribers ("paid-circulation magazines") may pay lower rates than magazines circulated free to a designated group of people ("controlled-circulation magazines"). This is one reason many magazines prefer paid to controlled circulation. At the same time, magazine publishers wishing to be eligible for the lower (second-class) rate must make sure that the shape and orientation of their products conform to the technical standards the post office uses to define a paid-circulation magazine:

1. It must be regularly issued at stated intervals, as frequently as four times a year. It must bear a date of issue and be numbered consecutively.
2. It must be formed of printed paper sheets, without board, cloth, leather, or other substantial bindings. Moreover, it may not be produced through the stencil, mimeograph, or hectograph process or in imitation of typewriting.
3. It must be originated and published for public dissemination, or devoted to literature, the sciences, or some special industry. It must have a legitimate list of subscribers. Also, it should not be designed primarily for advertising purposes, or for free circulation or for circulation at nominal rates.[11]

These technical criteria were created with a view of what proper magazines should look like and what they should contain. How regulatory approaches develop and how they differ among media industries are topics addressed in Chapter 3.

THE INVESTOR AND CLIENT ROLES

The leverage that investors and clients hold is straightforward: They control the money producers need to make material for release to the public.

Investment organizations include banks, stock brokerage firms, insurance companies, government and private foundations, and investment syndicates. Generally they provide money only when the expectation is that the production firm's overall activities will yield an attractive return on their initial outlays. As a result their power to veto or approve of a production company's long-range plans is enormous. The importance of the investment community is so critical, in fact, that top executives of media firms of all sizes make a point to brief their major investment communities regularly on their firms' progress and plans. It is not unusual to see the presidents of CBS and Paramount Communications giving talks to top Wall Street brokers and bankers on their firms' future. Nor is it unusual to see the heads of smaller companies trying to catch the interest of international lenders at one of the many movie and television conventions that take place throughout the year in Europe and the United States.

Sometimes, even one investment organization's loss of confidence in a company can spell disaster for that firm. This happened in 1989 to Vestron, Inc., a medium-size film producer and video distributor. In the summer of that year, Los Angeles–based Security Pacific National Bank promised the firm a six-year, $100 million line of credit. A few months later, Security Pacific withdrew its offer, arguing that Vestron's financial situation had worsened to such an extent that the bank had grounds to abort the agreement out of fear it would not be repaid. Vestron executives were stunned. Not only did they lose the promised loan, but Security Pacific's action made all other investors wary of offering Vestron long-term financing. With its survival at stake, Vestron decided to sue the bank for breach of contract and fraud.

"We relied on [Security Pacific's] contractual commitment," said Vestron's chief executive officer in a statement issued by the firm. "It was central to the company's business plan, and when the bank reneged, Vestron's long-term financing collapsed. This has forced us to abandon significant elements of our business plan and has triggered massive financial losses."[12]

The power of organizations taking on the client role is different from that of organizations acting as investors. Whereas investors lend cash in support of general long-term growth, clients provide money in support of particular products before the producer releases them for public consumption. By far the dominant client group in American mass media is the advertising industry. In many sectors of the newspaper, magazine, and broadcast television industries, banks and insurance companies invest in particular production firms on the conviction that enough advertisers will pay to be identified with the mass media material to make the investment profitable. But advertisers are not the only media clients. The "trade" sector of book publishing is a case in point. Investors provide capital to publishers with the expectation that a number of profitable stores will purchase the books and place them on sale to the public. For these publishers, their exhibition outlets (the stores) are also their clients.

In essence, then, clients are customers of producers. Dominant media clients decide by their purchases whether particular mass media materials will be released to the public. It follows that the clients' importance relates to their being most directly responsible for the production organizations' solvency. This pivotal position holds profound implications for both the process and the product of mass media producers. Chapter 4 examines these implications in detail.

THE AUXILIARY ROLE

At this point, we shift our attention from power roles that regulate or sponsor mass media production to roles that contribute to a production firm's technical ability to do its job: auxiliaries, creators, and unions. As in earlier sections, our interest is in the way these relationships may affect the amount and nature of mass media material released to the public.

There is much to consider about the ability of auxiliaries to influence mass media content. Simply, mass media material could not be created if auxiliaries did not provide producers with supplies. Consider, for example, the many supplies required to put together a movie. Of course plumbing, air conditioning, telephones, and office equipment are needed to run the facilities from which the movie is coordinated. Typical preproduction as well as in-production demands include camera, sound, lighting, setting, wardrobe, makeup, hairdressing, and transportation equipment. Other production operations require equipment for editing, special sound and visual effects, and dubbing.

Moreover, if the film is shot on location, many **ancillary services** will be needed—services that support, but do not contribute directly to, actual production procedures. Transportation must be provided for cast and crew; hotel and meal accommodations must be established; preparations must be made to use the location setting; and facilities for screening daily "rushes" by the producer and director must be set up. Even if the entire movie is made in a studio, ancillary services as diverse as security, accounting, maintenance, and film developing will be required.

The ability of a production organization to afford auxiliaries' resources typically determines whether it will get them. That, in turn, may determine whether the film is produced in the manner it was originally conceived. During the mid-1970s, for example, sharply rising costs of silver forced auxiliaries to charge more for photographic film, which led to the cancellation of a number of tightly budgeted movie projects. Of course, the possibility also exists that auxiliaries will develop new supplies or services that will revolutionize the way mass media material is produced.[13]

The Case of Printing

Other examples of auxiliary resources can be found in the newspaper and magazine industries. On a very basic level lies the price of paper, which is extremely important to firms in this business. In the mid-1990s, analysts cited as reasons for the closing of the *Houston Post,* a strong escalation of the price of newsprint, consolidations at the Times-Mirror Company (owner of the *Los An-*

geles Times and *Newsday*), and the merger of *the Milwaukee Journal* and *The Sentinel.* The situation was sufficiently grave that the Justice Department announced in 1995 that it had begun an investigation into possible collusion on high prices among the three dozen companies that produce most of the newsprint consumed in the United States.[14]

A far different example of auxiliary power is the impact of computer firms on newspapers and magazines. The ability of auxiliaries such as IBM, Merganthaler, Compugraphic, and Atex to wed data-gathering, storing, retrieving, and printing capabilities of computers to the publication of newspapers and magazines has led to significant changes in the content produced.[15] A computer-run system has encouraged editors to experiment with changes in the graphic design of periodicals much more than before. Computer facilities allow them to translate new ideas into print without using time-consuming procedures involving composition and press workers.

Computers are also beginning to give magazine publishers the ability to offer "selective binding" services to their advertising clients. Ads personalized with names of subscribers and phrases of special interest to them can be inserted automatically into a periodical. As this technology develops, it is possible that issues of major magazines will be customized as a matter of course. Computers will adjust the ads of marketers trying to reach specific individuals or types of individuals. Even changes in the articles will be made by the computer to conform to the publisher's or advertiser's knowledge of particular readers' interests.

Over the past two decades, computer-run production systems have been oriented toward a different goal: allowing editors and writers in large firms to work closer to printing and distribution deadlines than ever before.

Consider the case of *U.S. News & World Report.* Before the introduction of computer production into the weekly magazine's operation, the editorial deadline (the "closing") began at noon on Thursday and ended at 9:00 P.M. that day. Printing took place over the weekend. When new equipment arrived in the mid-1970s, final page composition and printing took much less time. As a consequence, editors and writers did not need to begin closing until late Friday.

This gain of more than a day was quite significant for a weekly news magazine. It allowed editors much greater leeway to update changing circumstances and integrate "late-breaking" stories into the body of the periodical. Such flexibility is increasingly important as other forms of advanced technologies — laptop computers, satellite communications, mobile phones, fax machines — allow reporters to transmit stories to their news organizations from around the world at the speed of light.[16]

THE CREATOR AND UNION ROLES

The key consideration that has moved newspapers and magazines toward computers in composing and printing is their ability to substantially lower labor costs. Of course, there are still areas of content selection and production in which the substitution of machines for people is prohibitively expensive, if not downright impossible. At the very least, people must participate in coming up with the ideas and deciding how they should look in the final products. Such individuals hold the creator power role — for example, magazine writers, TV actors, news reporters, set designers, television producers, movie directors, movie stuntpeople, news photographers, book editors, and record producers.

Some mass media creators become more highly recognized than others for their individual achievements. As a result they take on power that makes them independent forces in their industries in the creation of mass media material. Actor Gene Hackman, movie producer Steven Spielberg, movie director Spike Lee, and broadcast journalists Dan Rather and Diane Sawyer have the clout to personally initiate, shape, and finalize mass media works. This clout often exceeds the leverage carried by entire organizations that deal with production firms. Therefore we must include the creator power role in this essentially interorganizational scheme.

It is important to note that the kind of leverage that Hackman, Spielberg, Lee, Rather, and Sawyer hold is possessed by a very small percentage of personnel in any media industry. Most creators must work within the confines of the rules of the organizations that hire them. In fact, the relative lack of leverage that most creators find in their jobs has led them to form unions or guilds in an attempt to wield collective power with respect to production firms.[17]

Union Clout

Whether they represent creators or other personnel, organizations taking on the union power role can have substantial leverage. In 1989 an article in the *New York Times* about union problems at the *Daily News* commented that "it has been conventional wisdom in New York that no newspaper can publish without the truck drivers, a particularly tough union." Fear by *Daily News* executives that they would not be able to reach an easy agreement with its ten labor unions resulted in a campaign of "tough talk and sophisticated public relations" more than two months before the strike. The aim was to intimidate union leaders into making concessions.[18]

The ability of mass media production organizations to make use of an auxiliary organization's resources sometimes depends on the terms that organizations holding union roles negotiate with producers concerning the use of those resources. This point was dramatically demonstrated in the newspaper industry. The craft unions' anger over executives' desire to replace Linotype machine operators with computers led to bitter disputes. In a flurry of incidents in the late 1960s and 1970s, the International Typographical Union and the National Newspaper Guild tried to use the leverage of solidarity they had with union workers throughout their firms to set standards for retaining printers in the face of new technologies.

Arguments with management over the proper introduction of automation generally led to compromises acceptable to both sides. In a minority of cases, however, the disagreements erupted in bitter strikes. For a combination of reasons, the strikes resulted in the suspension or merger of newspapers, particularly in large metropolitan areas. By the 1980s it had become clear to all involved that traditional newspaper craft unions had been forced to give way to automation. Some writers suggested that the best way for the weakened unions to retain significant leverage in the current technological era was to merge.[19]

Most union demands revolve around defining and ensuring satisfactory wages for their members under nonexploitative working conditions. One way to do this is to develop industry standards for creative or technical quality that a small percentage of the potential worker population can meet. Sometimes,

---

BOX 2.1   Network TV's Major Unions

ABC, CBS, and NBC negotiate labor agreements with locals of more than a dozen unions. Below is a list of the nine largest national unions they face at bargaining tables.

Communication Workers of America (CWA): umbrella organization including the National Association of Broadcast Employees and Technicians (NABET): technicians and clerical workers at NBC and ABC.

International Alliance of Theatrical Stage Employees and Moving Picture Machine Operators (IATSE): camera, sound, and lighting technicians and stagehands at the networks, their affiliates, and the production firms.

International Brotherhood of Electrical Workers (IBEW): represents technicians at CBS.

American Federation of Television and Radio Artist (AFTRA): actors in soap operas, game shows, and programs shot in video; network and affiliate news correspondents.

Screen Actors Guild: actors in movies, commercials, and TV shows shot in film.

Directors Guild of America (DGA): directors, stage managers, and production assistants.

Writers Guild of America (WGA): script, promotional, and news writers; graphic artists; it has separate divisions on the East and West coats.

American Federation of Musicians (AFM): network studio musicians.

United Scenic Artists (USA): art and scenic directors and costume designers.

SOURCE: *Channels Magazine,* November 1986, p. 44; and an executive at the American Federation of television and Radio Artists (AFTRA), 1995.

union admission requirements and apprenticeship tracks protect these standards and regulate worker entry. These activities make the needed resources (employable workers) scarce and drive up their minimum price. In turn, the finished product reflects a "professional" approach.

The ability of unions to fix minimum wages and other terms for their members varies within and across media industries. In book publishing, for example, the Authors League has created a "model contract" for royalty terms and other aspects of writer-publisher agreements. However, the contract has no binding value, and many publishers successfully negotiate terms less generous to authors.[20] By contrast, the Writers Guild, which operates in the movie and television industries, has successfully established minimum rates that producers must pay for a "treatment" (a brief description of a proposed screenplay), for an actual screenplay, and for revisions. In addition, the guild has helped create rules about the on-screen credit that writers are given and about the kinds of rights to an original screenplay that a writer may retain when a producer buys that writer's material for a movie.[21]

At the same time, the Writers Guild has tried and failed to get production firms to agree that the writer of a movie screenplay retains creative control over that screenplay even after the material is delivered to the production firm. Production firm executives have insisted that the writer is simply an employee, not an executive. They have maintained the right to alter a screenplay any way they wish once they have paid for it.[22]

In the nature of things, compromises must be made. A union's bargaining position on a compromise is only as strong as the collective importance, and solidarity, of its members as production resources. Often, the way arguments are resolved influences the content created. The most drastic consequence of negotiations or work stoppages over wages could be producers' decisions not to work on certain products at all because of high labor costs. Producers might, however, respond to higher costs in one or more of the following ways: They might scale down the material to versions more in line with current prices; they might keep the material unchanged but raise its price to the public to meet extra costs; they might keep the material unchanged but raise the price of advertising inserts to help defray expenses; or they might keep the material unchanged but create it in ways that reduce reliance on the unions.

Getting around the Unions

One way to get around the union involves turning to auxiliaries for substitutional automated resources. Another way is to create the material in places where union regulations are absent or not as stringent. We have already seen that the use of new technologies can lead to important changes in mass media material. Choosing a production location because of a favorable union environment also may affect what the public sees, hears, or reads.

The shifting of television series programming between Los Angeles and New York during the past three decades is, to a significant extent, due to shifting union costs. From the late 1950s to the late 1970s, producers generally considered the major New York union, the International Alliance of Theatrical Stage Employees (IATSE), to be more troublesome and a lot more expensive than its counterparts on the West Coast. This, plus a parallel decline in available studio facilities, encouraged producers to forsake the Big Apple, the birthplace of TV production, for Hollywood.

In the early 1980s, however, as part of a bid by the mayor's office to attract motion picture and television work to the city, the management of the IATSE became more flexible in meeting filmmakers' demands. Moreover, a second union became more prominent, and competition between the two created an even more flexible attitude toward production. An umbrella organization, the Conference of Motion Picture and Television Unions, was formed to provide a forum for production executives and members from both unions to discuss problems of mutual concern. These activities, along with an increase in studio space, helped establish near parity in production costs between New York and Los Angeles. As a result the number of series, specials, and movies with a New York City backdrop increased.[23]

The increase may not have been permanent, though: A strike by technicians in 1991 brought moviemaking in New York to a standstill for many months. It threatened to jeopardize previous gains, as producers learned to use less expensive alternatives to Hollywood and the Big Apple.[24]

The lure of relatively low labor costs has made Toronto and Vancouver in Canada, and the state of Florida major motion picture and TV production sites. Toronto and Vancouver won popularity during the 1980s and 1990s because of favorable U.S.-Canadian money exchange rates. Florida was popular because of its laws allowing nonunion workers. Most films that were shot in these areas were represented as taking place elsewhere. In the case of the Canadian cities, some people in the movie business snickered that Toronto was too clean a city to stand in for a U.S. counterpart, which was often New York.

THE DISTRIBUTOR AND EXHIBITOR ROLES

Distribution and exhibition, like the costs of auxiliary and union resources, are critically important to producers of mass media material. If garnering specific resources to create a product is a necessary early step toward achieving influence and making a profit, placing that product in front of the people who will choose it is the equally necessary later step. Therefore, to remain viable, production firms in every industry must exert influence over the distributor and exhibitor power roles. Here we are concerned with the way such controls, combined with leverage on *producers* by distributors and exhibitors, influences the amount and kind of mass media materials producers make.

The subject, put concisely, is spectrum of choice. For executives in a production firm, the question is, How can we ensure that the spectrum of materials the public gets to choose from will include our company's products? One answer is for them to oversee an entire chain of activities leading to the marketplace, from production to distribution to exhibition. This approach, called **vertical integration,** is common in many industries. A logical next step for a vertically integrated production firm is to inhibit other firms from competing with it at the production, distribution, or exhibition level. When only one company remains, it is called a vertically integrated **monopoly.** When a few firms compete and keep others out, they are vertically integrated **oligopolies.** To a greater or lesser degree, both scenarios maximize the chances that the public will choose the production firm's products.

The Movie Majors

The Los Angeles–based (Hollywood) movie industry is an area where vertically integrated oligopolies reigned supreme for decades. Beginning in the early 1920s, a small number of production companies (Paramount, Warner, 20th Century Fox, RKO, and MGM) managed to greatly reduce their risks by owning (or being owned by) both dominant distribution firms and major nationwide theater chains (exhibition outlets). Critics of their approach claimed they were restraining trade because their lock on the marketplace was not allowing other production firms a realistic route to screens across the country. In 1948 the U.S. government, agreeing with these claims of anticompetitive behavior, forced the film industry "majors" to divest themselves of their exhibition interests.[25]

Since then, many changes in the structure and activities of the movie industry have taken place. RKO has dropped out of the "major" studio-distributor category; Buena Vista (Disney's distributor, also representing Disney's Touchstone and Hollywood Picture labels), Sony Pictures (representing Columbia and TriStar), and New Line have entered. These majors have tried to maintain dominance as theatrical film producers by controlling a substantial, sometimes oligopolistic, share of the distribution business. Movies financed and distributed outside this powerful circle can be found in theaters. In general, however, independent filmmakers with an ambition to reach huge audiences try to attach themselves to a powerful distribution arm. They agree to give the major a substantial share of the profits in return for circulating the picture. Independent filmmakers who cannot or do not want to interest the majors must often content themselves with limited distribution, usually through small theaters in only the largest cities or (for art and foreign films) in university towns.

Three major barriers to entry protect the majors' theatrical turf. One is the huge yearly amount (tens of millions of dollars) each company spends to maintain a distribution and sales force worldwide. Possible competitors would find duplicating such a setup on a comparably large scale extremely difficult. A second barrier, also related to cost, is the large amount of cash studios can get (from their distribution pipelines and revolving bank loans) to support the kind of movie slate necessary to a large distribution operation. A third barrier is the strong links the majors developed with the huge exhibition chains after 1948. Although the relationships between the two parties have sometimes been stormy, the theater owners have come to rely on the studios for providing a predictable stream of movies that bring in the high numbers needed to keep their seats filled. They are wary of dealing regularly with new firms that sport no audience-luring record.

Contested Cable Terrain

Although the major movie studios have worked hard to keep control over their traditional exhibition arena, much of the terrain of battle over distribution and exhibition has shifted away from the theaters. In 1948, movie theaters provided the primary audiovisual media experience for Americans. Broadcast television and cable TV hardly existed; the invention of video cassette recorders was years away. Today, these media are major entertainment vehicles for people in the United States and abroad, and as such have become key exhibition outlets for movies.

Yet the Hollywood majors were late in understanding the power of TV and cable to threaten their positions as the dominant moviemakers. The key distribution power in television belongs to the major networks: ABC, CBS, NBC, and, to a lesser extent, Fox. They often purchase movies and series from the major studios; in fact, Fox and ABC are part of companies that own studios (20th Century Fox and Disney, respectively). Nevertheless, the broadcast networks do not hesitate to purchase programs from companies other than the majors. The majors were also late in recognizing the importance of controlling the distribution of their movies to cable TV systems.

During the 1970s and 1980s, primary distribution of recent films in the cable TV industry belonged to Home Box Office (HBO), a division of Time Inc. Time, a magazine-publishing giant, also owned American Television and Communications (ATC), one of the largest operators of cable systems in the United States. Time executives realized the usefulness of the link between its HBO channel and cable exhibitors. Since subscribers were asked to pay extra for HBO, the channel increased the profits of ATC and other cable systems nationwide. From Hollywood's standpoint, however, HBO's grip on cable TV meant that film producers were often at Time Inc.'s mercy when it came to the selection and pricing of their pictures for cable.

By the early 1980s, strategists for the Hollywood majors were aware that it was in their firms' interests to control the movement of their product into the markets created by increasingly popular technologies, such as cable TV and homevideo. As a result all the majors, individually or with other firms, cre-

TABLE 2.2 TOP SEVEN CABLE TELEVISION MULTIPLE SYSTEM OPERATORS

Rank	Multiple System Operator	Number of Subscribers
1.	Tele-Communications Inc.	15.2 million
2.	Time Warner	7.2 million
3.	Continental Cablevision	3 million
4.	Comcast	2.9 million
5.	Cablevision Systems Corp.	2.3 million
6.	Cox Cable	1.8 million
7.	Jones Intercable	1.3 million

SOURCE: *Advertising Age, April 11, 1994, p. S10.*

Multiple system operators (MSOs) are firms that own more than one cable television system. The very biggest MSOs are especially powerful cable exhibitors, because their agreement to carry channels can make the difference between success and failure for distributors of programming. Taking advantage of its power, TCI, the top MSO, often demands a part of the profits as payment for carrying a new channel. Time Warner's ownership of the number-two system means that new cable programming ideas by HBO or other Time Warner units might have an easier chance to get tryouts than would othewise be the case.

Table 2.2 lists the seven largest MSOs according to the number of subscribers to at least their basic service in certain months of 1994. A basic service is the set of channels that consumers receive when they pay a cable company the lowest monthly subscription fee. Higher fees are charged for nonbasic services, such as more ad-supported channels (on levels called tiers), pay-TV channels (HBO, Showtime), and pay-per-view activities.

---

ated home video divisions that developed clout which mirrored their power in the theatrical marketplace. This kind of opportunity was not as easily duplicated in the cable business, which had already developed its own distribution and exhibition structure. However, a number of majors tried to make distribution inroads. Disney's creation of The Disney Channel, a cable distribution channel, was a notable example.

An even more important development was the transaction that brought Home Box Office, the leading pay-TV channel, under the control of a major movie distributor. It happened in 1989, when Time merged with Warner Communications. Through its ownership of Warner Brothers, HBO, and ATC, the new firm instantly became a vertically integrated power in the cable industry. The implications of Time Warner's status frightened a number of cable system owners, who worried that HBO would use its Hollywood production link to force cable systems not owned by Time Warner to pay higher rates for HBO, which would diminish cable systems' profits. In fact, the possibility frightened the nation's largest cable television operator, Tele-Communications, Inc. (TCI), so much that it moved to purchase half of Showtime/The Movie Channel, HBO's only serious competitor. By infusing the ailing Showtime with cash to buy films from Hollywood majors, TCI hoped to make it a viable alternative to HBO and keep the latter from raising its rates.

"The Time Warner merger has shaken up the cable world," TCI's chief executive said. "Time controls about 25% of all broadcast programming, between [subsidiaries] Lorimar, Warner, and Telepictures. . . . You tend to look for counterbalances. You are seeing new alignments take place. We need some parallel relationships."[26]

The Battle over TV Distribution

The power of HBO in Hollywood and TCI's move to shore up Showtime/The Movie Channel underscore the importance of controlling distribution in a mass media industry. By extension, the Time Warner merger illustrates the desire by companies to control production and exhibition as well as distribution in cable and in the theatrical business.

A similar desire led to increasing frustration on the part of the three major distribution powers in the television industry: ABC, CBS, and NBC. For more than thirty years, from 1948 through the early 1980s, these commercial TV networks dominated the channels that connected the great majority of TV exhibition outlets in the United States (the broadcasting stations) with TV producers. The public television network (PBS) was not a strong competitor for audiences. Moreover, there were few other broadcast channels to draw viewers away from those affiliated with one of the networks. Of 988 television stations broadcasting in 1979, only about 100 were independent of the networks.[27]

Consequently, on a typical evening in the mid-1970s, 90% or more of people watching television in the United States were viewing ABC, CBS, or NBC. In addition, the networks were the major game in the industry as far as big-money production was concerned. The power of the networks over TV distribution was so strong, in fact, that in the late 1960s the Federal Communications Commission set forth rules to limit their dominance over the availability and distribution of TV programming.

These rules stipulated that a network could not syndicate or have a financial interest in programs it had not solely produced, and could syndicate only in foreign countries any programs that it had solely produced. The Justice Department, however, was not satisfied that these "fin/syn" rules would dampen network dominance. Fearing that ABC, CBS, and NBC were using their right to produce programs themselves to inhibit competition in Hollywood, the Justice Department initiated antitrust proceedings against them. In 1978 the suit was dropped when the networks agreed to refrain until late 1990 from owning most of the entertainment programming they aired.[28]

Their control over production was nevertheless great. Production companies that wanted to create for commercial television — those that included the major film studios — were at the mercy of the networks for decisions about the number and kinds of shows that would be acceptable and the price that would be paid for them. Producers choosing to sell programs elsewhere in commercial TV had to take the **syndication** route exclusively. That is, they had to distribute their programs to individual stations or station groups market by market in the hope of obtaining enough reach and advertiser support to make the project viable.

The problem for producers through the early 1980s was that the number of independent stations, along with the percentage of national population they reached, was not enough to support syndication of expensive programs that might compete with network fare. Success in this case would be possible only if some network affiliates preempted network programs. Affiliates had an incentive to do so occasionally, because syndicated pickups do not require the station to share advertising time and revenues with the network. For the same reason, however, the networks discouraged replacement of their shows with syndicated material. Their powerful leverage lay in not renewing the station's affiliation contract. Loss of affiliation would stop the station's continuous supply of expensively mounted programs that reached large audiences and attracted local as well as national advertisers. An added element of network power was that affiliates in the very largest markets were owned by the networks themselves. This distribution clout meant that all affiliates generally "cleared" every network prime time program, and syndicating a prime time show was very difficult.

The possibilities of prime time syndication are still quite limited, for many of the reasons mentioned. However, the broadcast TV environment has changed drastically since the early 1980s, and the networks are finding their supremacy seriously challenged. We have already noted some of the challenges to network TV's audience-grabbing power: the spread of cable television to over 60% of American homes and video cassette recorders to about 80% of American homes by the mid-1990s.[29] An added challenge was the proliferation of independent television stations, usually on the UHF band. From only about 100 in 1979, the number soared to 904 just six years later.[30]

This proliferation allowed a major Hollywood studio, 20th Century Fox, to buy a number of UHF broadcast outlets in major cities, set up affiliations with others, and launch a new commercial TV network. Scheduled initially for prime time on only Saturday and Sunday, the Fox network successfully challenged its full-scale counterparts for audiences and advertisers. Over the next few years it expanded to seven days in prime time, developed a reputation for programming aimed at young adults, and built strong afternoon and Saturday morning lineups of children's shows. In the mid-1990s, Fox even managed to pry loose long-standing VHF affiliates of the Big Three networks, particularly those linked to CBS. CBS, already in trouble with advertisers because of its low ratings and its viewers, whom ad people considered too old, now had to make do with weak UHF affiliates in major markets such as Atlanta, Detroit, Cleveland, and Milwaukee. The changeover further depressed its ratings and boosted the fortunes of Fox.[31]

The Fox network's success with owning a broadcast distribution and exhibition business encouraged two other Hollywood studios, Warner Brothers and Paramount, to try the same thing. Together they created yet another force — along with cable, video, and independent TV stations generally — that steadily diminished the percentage of Americans who watched the ABC, CBS, and NBC networks even in prime time. By the mid-1990s, the three major networks together reached between 55% and 60% of TV viewers on a typical evening. The numbers represented a drop of more than twenty-five points in viewing audience share from a decade and a half earlier.

From the standpoint of ABC, CBS, and NBC executives, the erosion of their audience share meant that their power over television distribution and exhibition was dropping. Unlike the Hollywood majors, however, the three networks were prevented by government rulings from creating or owning most of the materials they distributed. They realized that power over distribution in the evolving media system is increasingly tied to a company's ability to link it to production clout — that is, to generate and control the creative product it distributes. Network executives, therefore, saw themselves hampered from competing with other large media organizations (such as Fox and Time Warner) for part of the changing media pie. As a result, they urged the FCC not to renew the regulations prohibiting them from owning a financial interest in, or syndication rights to, TV materials they air.

For their part, the network's Hollywood suppliers lobbied the FCC not to change things. They argued that giving the networks the right to own and syndicate all their programming would lead them to insist on financial equity in everything they put on the air. In turn, this would lead, they argued, to the disappearance of independent production firms, as well as to needless growth in the already substantial power that ABC, CBS, and NBC have over American culture.

In the face of lobbying by powerful constituencies on both sides, the FCC moved slowly. By the mid-1990s, however, regulators had eliminated all the rules that barred the Big Three networks from owning or distributing the programs they aired. Moreover, the Telecommunications Act of 1996 allowed companies, including the Big Three, to own stations covering 35% of the national population, up from the previous 25% limit.

Now that it was possible for ABC, CBS, and NBC to vertically integrate again, the networks began to look good to production firms that wanted to get hold of those still-key distribution channels to the home before their competitors did. For example, Disney, with its powerful movie and television production engine, merged with ABC, which brought attractive cable distribution services (ESPN, ESPN2, Lifetime) as well as a broadcast network under the Disney umbrella. Westinghouse, owner of TV stations and a powerful syndication firm, bought CBS because its stations and broadcast network would give it still more distribution and exhibition clout. And rumors were flying wildly that General Electric would either buy a studio for its NBC subsidiary or sell NBC to one.

This realignment of distribution and exhibition channels in the broadcast TV business also encouraged a major shakeup in cable. A number of weeks after the ABC and CBS merger announcements, Time Warner executives disclosed that they had completed an agreement to purchase Turner Broadcasting System (TBS). Time Warner was already a major player throughout the

TABLE 2.3 LARGEST "ENTERTAINMENT AND MEDIA" COMPANIES IN TERMS OF REVENUE

Company	Headquarters	1994 Revenue (Millions of Dollars)
Time Warner Inc.	NY, USA	15,905
Bertelsmann AG	Guetersloh, Germany	NA
Walt Disney Co.	Burbank, Calif., USA	10,055
News Corp	Adelaide, Australia, NY, LA USA	8,862
Fujisanki	Tokyo, Japan	8,175
Sony Entertainment (div)	Tokyo, Japan; NY, LA, USA	8,175
Havas	Paris, France	7,875
Fininvest	Milan, Italy	7,432
Viacom	NY, USA	7,363
Thorn EMI	London, UK	7,211
Capital Cities/ABC	NY, USA	6,379
Polygram NV	Netherlands, London, UK	4,936
Tele-Communications	Engelwood, Colo., USA	4,936
MCA, Inc. (div.)	LA, USA	4,800*
Kirch Group	Ismaning, Germany	4,286*
Gannett Co	Arlington, Virginia, USA	3,825
CBS	NY, USA	3,712
Rank Organization	London, UK	3,523
NBC (div.)	NY, USA	3,361

*estimate. (*SOURCE: "The Global 50,"* Variety, *August 28, 1995, p. 27. Reprinted with permission of Variety, Inc.*)

This is a list of what *Variety,* the weekly show-business trade magazine calls "the world's largest entertainment and media companies." Such a list is bound to be controversial, because it involves defining what kinds of companies to include and what to exclude. *Variety* chose to identify the companies that specifically dominate the film, television, and music businesses worldwide—what some call "the audiovisual sector." As a result, companies without major holdings in film, TV, or music (such as The New York Times Co. and Reuters) did not qualify. *Variety* also excluded government-supported or public broadcasters such as the British Broadcasting Corporation. The letters "div." indicate that the firm is a division of a larger firm.

Published in mid-1995, the list does not take into consideration the mergers of Time Warner with Turner Broadcasting, Disney with ABC, and Westinghouse with CBS. Nevertheless, with firms such as Polygram, Kirch, and Rank on the list, it does suggest the international dimension of media power.

media system; in fact, it was the largest media firm in the world. Yet, throughout, the conglomerate already had powerful movie, magazine, and music production and distribution businesses, the firm's leaders believed that TBS could give them unsurpassed distribution clout to home TV sets in the United States and around the world.

According to those involved in the deal, the new combination was aimed at giving the Time Warner movie production group and news/sports magazine group access to Turner's extremely powerful distribution channels. So, the idea went, Turner's WTBS and TNT cable services could work well with Warner Brothers films; Turner's Cartoon Channel could mesh with Warner's Loony Tunes cartoon library; and the staffs of *Time, People, Fortune, Entertainment Weekly, Martha Stewart,* and *Sports Illustrated* magazines could provide content for Turner's major global cable distribution engine: the Cable News Network.

Distribution in Print and Radio

As the preceding examples show, the broadcast television, cable television, and theatrical movie industries reveal intensely public bids for control over distribution. Control over distribution with the aim of maintaining a producer's access to distribution outlets is not as dramatically evident in the print media. This does not mean that control over the distribution process is not important. It does mean that many more producers have an opportunity to exert control. Four differences between print media industries, on the one hand, and the cable, broadcast, and theatrical film industries, on the other, seem to explain this difference in access to distribution:

> The relatively low cost of production and promotion that is possible in print
>
> The relatively greater number of units of material that print outlets will accept
>
> The relatively larger number of outlets that exist to exhibit print materials
>
> The relatively larger variety of outlets that exist to exhibit print materials

Comparing the theatrical movie industry with book publishing illustrates these points. Books are substantially less expensive to create than movies; bookstores, libraries, and schools carry more new titles a year than do movie exhibitors; there are more outlets for new books in the United States than there are theatrical movie outlets; and the variety of book outlets (bookstores, libraries, schools, a wide spectrum of commercial locations, book clubs, and direct-to-home sales) is much greater than the variety of first-run theatrical film outlets (essentially "hard top" movie houses and drive-ins).

In magazine publishing, the ability to distribute material to consumers directly through the mail, as well as through racks in stores, also makes it more difficult for a small number of companies to own all distribution routes. Similarly, the situation in radio, though once comparable to the contemporary TV and movie industries, is closer today to that of book publishing in its range of outlet diversity and production costs.

The change came about as a result of two parallel developments that began in the mid-1950s. One was the new advertising role for radio that emerged during the rise of television — reaching narrower publics than TV for short periods of time. The other was the increased government allocation of AM and (particularly) FM licenses. By 1989 more than 10,500 radio stations existed in

TABLE 2.4 BEST-SELLERS BY PUBLISHING CORPORATION, 1994

Company	Hardcover			Paperback		
	# of Bks.	# of Wks.	% Share*	# of Bks.	# of Wks.	% Share*
Random Inc.	37	331.5	21.7	36	276	18
Simon & Schuster	32	269.5	17.6	31	306	20
Bantam Doubleday Dell	27	190	12.4	35	239	15.6
Harper Collins	14	135	8.8	18	157	10.3
Time Warner	11	172	11.2	14	94	6.1
Putnam Berkley	19	136	8.9	21	123	8
Penguin USA	5	37	2.4	13	79	5.2
Hearst	2	14	.9	7	28	1.8
Andrews & McMeel	3	67	4.4	6	31	2
Workman	—	—	—	4	63	4.1
Norton	1	6	.4	1	27	1.8
St. Martin's	3	20	1.3	3	11	.7
Houghton Mifflin	4	22	1.4	2	6	.4
Hyperion	3	19	1.2	—	—	—

*"Share" represents the publisher's share of the 1,530 hardcover or 1,530 paperback bestseller positions on *Publishers Weekly* charts during 1994. (SOURCE: Publishers Weekly, *January 2, 1995, p. 52.*)

the United States.[32] Although traditional radio networks (ABC, Westwood One, CBS) certainly exist, a tremendous number of other production and distribution services with a wide variety of long and short programming forms also compete for stations' interests.

Note, however, that a general atmosphere of easy entry for producers at both the distribution and exhibition levels of a mass media industry does not mean that all segments of the industry are so competitive. To the contrary, it is quite likely that even in these industries, distribution channels to certain types of outlets are controlled by a small number of production firms. Hardcover "trade" books and mass market paperbacks — sectors of book publishing in which different types of retail stores are the major outlets — serve as good examples. According to *Publishers Weekly,* in 1994 eight publishing conglomerates accounted for 83.9% of all hardcover bestsellers, and 85% of all paperback bestsellers. The next six publishers brought the share to 92.6% for hardcovers and 94% for paperbacks. As *Publishers* Weekly noted, "that doesn't leave much room for the rest of the hundreds — or thousands, counting smaller independent houses — of publishing players.[33] Parallel examples of such power by producer-distributors over their markets could be drawn from the CD and tape sectors of the music industry.

When distribution channels are not controlled nationally by a small number of firms, a wide range of producers can be encouraged to try to reach the public. For example, a small firm wanting to market a magazine for first and second graders may be able to convince distributors in different cities to carry the magazine. Some might carry it, some might not. Failing that, the firm might be able to succeed by advertising and selling the magazine through the mail. Or perhaps the firm will decide that the best approach is through toy stores, where another kind of distributor will carry the material.

There are, in fact, a number of child-oriented periodicals that are sold more in toy stores and through the mail than on newsstands. *Sesame Street Magazine, Barbie Magazine*, and *Toys R Us Magazine* are the ones found in the Toys R Us toy chain, for obvious reasons. Another, more unusual, example of a periodical sold through nontraditional retail outlets was *It's Me!*, a bi-monthly aimed at large women. While it was marketed in 1981 on a test basis through magazine stands in Chicago, *It's Me!* was released in Los Angeles, New York, and Chicago through stores of its charter advertiser, the Lane Bryant clothing chain for larger women.[34] Neither the in-store nor the news-stand tests were considered successful, though, and the magazine disappeared after its first year.

Producers' Power over Exhibition

The control production firms exercise over exhibitors varies. Producers have much power over exhibitors in areas of media industries where they face little competition in the production and distribution of their products. The distribution of films provides an example. The major movie companies have managed to exert a great deal of influence over the policies of theater chains, from the amounts they charge for tickets to their right to show commercials in the theaters. This is be-cause theater chains, as large as they are, are dependent on a handful of firms for the bulk of their money-making product and do not want to alienate them.

The broadcast television networks, as producers and distributors of a flow of programming, also exercise a lot of influence over their affiliate stations. These exhibitors rely on network fare for the bulk of their programming and a large percentage of their revenues. Although the money-making capabilities of a TV network are not what they used to be, losing a link to a network could be a major financial blow in many markets.

Still, such power does not mean that the broadcast networks or major movie companies totally ignore the outlets that carry their programming. Some-times the exhibitor/distributor relationship can strongly influence the material released to the public. For example, for years the objection by affiliates that an hour-long newscast would not enhance their profits has stopped ABC, CBS, and NBC from implementing what their news divisions have sorely wanted.

Coping Strategies

Generally, exhibitors have more influence over what they carry (and thus more leverage with producers) in industries where production and distribu-tion are not dominated by a few companies. In situations where exhibitors have such power, producers must develop ways to reduce their uncertainty about whether outlets will carry their products.

Sociologist Paul Hirsch suggests four coping strategies that production firms employ to deal with this kind of uncertainty:

- Deploying contact personnel to organizational boundaries
- Overproducing and differentially promoting new items
- Co-opting mass media gatekeepers
- Bypassing outlets altogether through direct marketing[35]

It might be useful to start with the last strategy, because it totally ignores distributors and exhibitors. **Bypassing outlets through direct marketing** means using the mail or other advertising vehicles (including mass media) to inform members of the public that the item can be purchased directly from the producer.

This can be a useful strategy for media production firms with products or audiences that need special handling. It may be that a firm's product is aimed at publics that do not frequent predictable outlets in numbers high enough to make the material profitable, for example, albums of big band music aimed at retirees who do not visit record stores. It may be that the target audience is well known to, and easily reached by, the producer, for example, an audience of mass communication professors whose addresses are made available to a publisher of a scholarly book relevant to them. Or it may be that the product typically requires more explanation than can be obtained by looking at it in an outlet, such as an encyclopedia. In any of these cases, a direct-marketing approach will be the strategy of choice for the producer.

If, however, getting the product to the public via distributors and exhibitors is the goal, the other coping strategies may come into play. The first strategy, **deploying contact personnel to organizational boundaries,** involves the production firm's sales representatives.

Part of a sales representative's role may be to build trust with buyers in distribution and exhibition organizations so that the buyers will want the producer's products. Doing so might mean circulating information that tries to justify high optimism for the products' sales. The sales representative might give assurances that impressive advertising campaigns will bring the public to exhibitors in search of the product. The rep might offer outlets or distributors special discounts for carrying the product. On the dark side, gaining favor might involve bribing people with money or drugs.

The second coping strategy, **overproducing and differentially promoting new items,** means producing a large number of items (many book titles or CD titles) and promoting only those that seem to be catching on. The hope is that at least some of the products will be accepted by distributors, outlets, and, ultimately, members of the public.

Sociologist Serge Denisoff offered a good illustration of how this approach has worked in the recording industry; his example applies to many areas of book publishing as well. In the mid-1970s he pointed out that despite control by five record conglomerates of over 50% of the business, these firms found it imperative to follow what he called "the buckshot theory of record releasing."

> CBS Records, with its plant and catalog, must produce an enormous amount of product to keep its various bureaus, agencies, and departments busy. Of every 10 records released, only 2 or 3 will sell. Consequently, large companies must produce massive amounts of product to sustain their large corporate bodies. Huge investments are made and must be maintained. A concentration upon proven talent, coupled with the 7 to 3 ratio, motivates the larger companies to treat newcomers indiscriminately, at the same time competing with each other for surefire sellers. . . . Capitol [Records] operates on what [an executive] calls Formula 10, which is nearly identical to Columbia's 7 to 3 ratio. Capitol's advertising department head believes that in 10 releases at least one should be gold with several others bringing in a sizable return.[36]

As Denisoff's description suggests, use of the overproduction strategy can have both positive and negative implications for new artists breaking into the media business. The need for a large slate of releases may encourage firms to look for new faces. However, the firms' tendency to let certain releases sink or swim in the marketplace may mean that the artists do not get the kind of publicity and marketing support they need to gain the notice of distributors, exhibitors, and segments of the public.

The third strategy Hirsch mentions, **co-opting mass media gatekeepers,** is likely to be employed in combination with other strategies. **Gatekeepers** are people who make decisions about whether or not to select certain materials for production. Co-opting mass media gatekeepers involves convincing them to promote mass media items that are available for sale, rent, or viewing elsewhere.

Examples are easily found: a CD promoter who persuades a radio station program director to play a particular recording; a public relations agent who persuades a talk show coordinator to schedule the author of a new book on the show; and a movie studio publicist who persuades television network programmers to produce a special about how a new movie was made.

THE LINKING PIN ROLE

The previous examples of co-opting mass media gatekeepers point to factors that are often underestimated in considering influences on mass media production organizations. The term that will be used here to describe these factors is **linking pin** activities. They involve the movement of completed material, or people representing that material, from production firms in one industry to production firms in another industry.

Linking pin activities are key aspects of a mass media cross-fertilization process that serves to tie together publics that might have little in common. Consider how often you have seen people or subjects appear on television, in magazines, on book covers, and in the movies during a particular period. This phenomenon occurs in what journalists call "hard news" (the government, economic, and crime reports of the day), "soft news" (tales of ordinary people and discussions of the arts), and even fiction. For example, Jane Fonda might appear in a new movie, on a magazine cover, and on a TV talk show in the course of a week. Similarly, Tom Wolfe might discuss his new book on TV's *Good Morning America*, on CNN's *Larry King Show*, and with *Time* magazine on the same day.

As these examples suggest, much linking pin activity is promotional from the standpoint of the organization that initiates the interconnections. Production firms that want to ensure large audiences for their creations often turn to other mass media to spread the word. Typically they devolve this linking pin power role upon public relations companies or promotional agencies specialized in this task. At other times, the production organizations act as linking pins. Special units of the organizations arrange to tout the firms' creations in other media. In the case of the largest media conglomerates, transactions might even take place among various arms of the company—for example, when Home Box Office, a cable TV subsidiary of Time Warner, carried a program about the history of *Life*, one of Time Warner's magazines.

This sort of internal cross-promotion has become a key activity for on-line divisions of media firms. The French media conglomerate Hachette, for example, created Hachette Filipacchi New Media (HFM) in the mid-1990s to produce on-line versions of its U.S. magazines (*Car and Driver, Elle, George, Premiere,* and others) on the World Wide Web. The expectation was that the HFM "home pages" would draw money from advertisers who would want to reach young, well-off audiences who cruise cyberspace. Just as important, though, was the hope that the on-line versions would lead people browsing home pages to like what the titles stand for so much that they would purchase print subscriptions.

Apart from promotion, a major impetus for linking pin activity is the mass media's need for information. Production organizations often need the output of other media. They might do so because they want assuredly popular materials. Too, they might find that borrowing from other media is the easiest way to fill time or space in their own medium. Producers of TV's *Ricki Lake Show*, for example, who need to come up with controversial guests for five hour-long programs each week, may rely on a variety of magazines and books as sources for suggestions. And a company might buy the rights to make a film based on a popular new novel in the hope that its popularity will carry over to the movie.

Firms that are the objects of such linking pin pursuits do not discourage this situation; it means free publicity and sometimes lots of money for them. Richard Snyder, former president of the Simon & Schuster book pub-

---

TALKING POINT 2.2   Simon & Schuster's Linking Pin Role

Simon & Schuster is a book publishing division of Paramount Communications. When it released Kitty Kelly's explosive biography of Nancy Reagan in 1991, the intensive coverage was marked by an unusual contract to control how reporters got advance copies of the book.

The document said that in order for them to get an advance copy of the book, reporters could not talk or write about it until April 8, when the book was to be released. As the Associated Press commented a number of days later, the contract represented the latest example of covenants aimed at controlling news coverage.

To limit access and leaks of the book's contents, Simon & Schuster imposed stringent security on the editing and printing process. Only five manuscripts were prepared. They were numbered and a log was kept of each copy's whereabouts.

To ensure that stories about the book would appear in unison, the publisher asked the Associated Press, *The Washington Post, USA Today, The Los Angeles Times, The New York Times, The New York Daily News, Newsweek Magazine, Women's Wear Daily,* and *Entertainment Tonight* to sign the agreement. All agreed except the two New York dailies. They published stories about the book on April 7th.

Nevertheless, Simon & Schuster had orchestrated a publicity coup.

SOURCE: *Editor and Publisher,* April 27, 1991, p. 11.

---

lishing house, recognized the importance of interindustry connections when he said, "In a certain sense, we are the software of the television and movie media."[37]

Probably the most important linking pin organizations in the world are the major international news wire services: the Associated Press, Reuters, United Press International, Agence France Presse, and Interfax. These firms are producers in what can be called the **raw materials news industry,** which generates thousands of nonfiction stories that are sold across mass media boundaries as building blocks for newspapers, magazines, and even books.

Examples of a few other linking pins in the raw materials news industry are:

The **investigative journalism** collectives (the Community Information Project, the Center for Investigative Reporting, and the Better Government Association), which sell their reports to newspapers, magazines, and television networks.

The **major international picture agencies** (Sygma, Magnum, Gamma-Liaison, Sipa, Black Star, and Contact), which for a fee help photographers sell their work to newspapers, magazines, and book publishers throughout the world.

Picture libraries, such as the Bettmann Archive, which rent historical pictures on a variety of subjects to production firms in various mass media industries.

THE FACILITATOR ROLE

The role of linking pin organizations is to move mass media material, or people representing that material, from one mass media industry to another. By contrast, organizations that take on **facilitator** roles work within mass media industries. They help initiate, carry out, or evaluate mass media material in the first place — sometimes even before it is produced or distributed. Organizations taking on a facilitator role include:

Talent agencies that suggest artists to production firms and negotiate their contracts.

Law firms that help production firms deal with investors, authorities, and distributors.

Consulting firms that help producers create mass media material.

Market research firms that survey the environment for mass media material, evaluate how previous material has fared, project how current material might do, and suggest why.

The consequences of these facilitation activities for mass media material can sometimes be profound. Consider the position of a large talent agency (say, William Morris or Creative Artists) in the process. On a basic level, a talent agency's purpose is to serve as a negotiating intermediary between a particular creator — for example, an actor, director, composer, or writer — and the production organization. The agency's mandate is to get the client work and then extract the best possible deal from the firm that wants the client's services. Over the years, though, large talent agencies have developed the ability to go beyond suggesting and negotiating for individual clients. Now they often parlay their influential client lists into **packages of talent,** which they market to production firms.

A **package** is a combination of two or more creators who come together to work on a mass media project. Through clients who are writers, a talent agent knows what manuscripts are available. At the same time, through clients who are producers, directors, and actors, an agent can keep close tabs on developments in his or her creative community. By putting these people together, the agent might yield a plan for a movie or TV series that a production firm will find attractive. The production firm, for its part, might appreciate the agency's packaging activities, since it saves producers the time, effort, and money involved in trying to do the same thing.

Talent firms often act as linking pins as well as facilitators, because they frequently parlay particular groups of talent into packages that cross media boundaries. Thomas Whiteside has described this activity well:

> A script is an "element," so is a writer, so are a book, a producer, an actor or group of actors, a director. In contrast to simpler times, in which it was taken for granted that a published book originated with the author . . . [the package] does not have to take place in the mind of a writer; it can occur around a conference table in the office of a producer or an agent, who may then add to it "elements" including the writer, who is "acquired" sooner or later in the packaging process.[38]

Not all packaging deals are completed, of course. Such negotiations are very delicate for the agents involved, because they require placing value on every person in the package in relation to the others in the package. In addition, production firm executives may not want certain individuals in the package, preferring to substitute their own choices in those creative slots. Nevertheless, the use of talent agencies to facilitate the production of material has become a pervasive fact of life in mass media industries.

THE PUBLIC ADVOCACY
AND PUBLIC POWER ROLES

The last two power roles in Table 2.1 — public advocacy and the public — have already been introduced in this chapter. Little more is said about them here because the task of drawing out their actual implications for mass media material is so great that it demands a separate discussion (see Chapters 5 and 6). At this point, it is useful to note only that **publics** come into existence when scattered groups or individuals share certain mass media materials. By contrast, **public advocacy organizations** are created when those individuals or groups band together systematically. Typically, their aim is to demand that producer, distributor, or exhibitor organizations change certain approaches to mass media content.

As a member of a public, a person's leverage regarding the media is expressed in individual ways. If you like a TV show, you may view it; if you don't, you may not. If something about a program makes you especially angry, you might write a letter to the people in charge. Public advocacy organizations might have the same aims with respect to the TV show, and they might use the same tactics. In addition, they may try to force change through boycotts of the firm that creates the program, the network that distributes it, the stations that air it, and even the advertisers that support it.

It should be noted that the word *audience* is not the same as *public,* as it is used in the power role framework. The term *public* refers to the individual viewers, readers, and listeners of the mass media material, *as they see them-*

selves. By contrast, the word *audience* refers to the viewers, readers, and listeners *as they are understood and targeted* by media executives. Chapter 5 takes up the meaning of audience in much more detail, explains how it differs from the public, and shows the surprising importance it has in helping us make sense of mass media activities.

SOME IMPLICATIONS OF THE FRAMEWORK

In this chapter I have shown the usefulness of the power role approach for examining how interorganizational activities within and across mass media industries influence the creation of media materials. The power role framework developed here serves as a backdrop to our journey through media systems in the chapters that follow. Before ending Chapter 2, it is helpful to step back and examine the power role framework as a whole after having become familiar with its parts. This allows us to see issues regarding the media and the larger society that might have been missed when analyzing particular power roles.

A point made earlier bears repeating: Power roles represent interdependent activities of organizations. They are not in themselves organizations or groups. A corollary of this point is that organizations may take on more than one role in a mass media industry. Examples throughout this chapter show that producers are sometimes also distributors, exhibitors, and linking pins; that linking pins are sometimes also facilitators; and that exhibitors are sometimes also patrons. The overlapping of other roles may be harder to imagine. For example, it is rather unusual to find a case in the United States where a producer also acts as a client and auxiliary. However, in today's world of multi-level, vertically integrated conglomerates, such combinations are not at all out of the question. In some foreign countries, organizations take on the authority, producer, client, and auxiliary power roles across a variety of media industries. Only the public, public advocacy, and creator roles are, by their very nature, unable to be carried out by organizations that also act as producers.

Coalitions and Power Centers

The accumulation of roles by an organization means an accumulation of the organization's ability to obtain resources. This, in turn, means an accumulation of the organization's ability to exert leverage within (and possibly across) mass media industries. Organizations can also increase their influence by forming coalitions with other organizations holding the same or different roles. For example, a union might increase its leverage with a production firm by marshaling the support of another union. The other union might agree to help out of genuine concern for the cause, or out of an assurance that the help will be repaid.

This view of mass communication as an interorganizational struggle over resources leads us to look for power centers and alliances. Awareness of this ever-shifting struggle should put to rest any notions that mass media material results from the process of "giving the public what it wants," as some media firms would have us believe. As the power role framework shows, the public is only one factor in an industry's scheme of things. Other power roles may at times be more evident, and carry more leverage, than do scattered, individual consumers.

In every established mass media industry there is a pattern of roles that the organizations maintain with one another. This role pattern is what we mean when we refer to an industry's **structure.** The broadcast television's structure, for example, is found in the rather predictable relationships that networks, Hollywood production firms, communication law firms, market research firms, pressure groups, and other entities have with one another. An important step toward understanding the structure of an industry and its function in society lies in assessing the events that have caused various relationships to evolve. Relationships not developed, leverage possibilities not pursued, resources not exploited — these and other omissions may have their roots in incidents, power struggles, and national philosophies that shaped an industry at its birth or at later critical points. Insight into the historical processes shaping mass communication is, therefore, necessary for developing a firm understanding of the processes and strategies of media systems. To learn more about this subject, turn to Chapter 3.

CONSIDER THIS

1. Why could it be said that the distributor power role is at least as important as the producer power role?

2. Some members of the U.S. movie industry have argued that large talent agencies such as CAA, ICM, and William Morris have become the most powerful entities in Hollywood. How might their large linking pin role contribute to their enormous power?

3. Most people do not pay much attention to the publishers of books they buy. Publishing houses, though, have personalities and audience targets that they convey to bookstores through their various labels, or "imprints." Find out how many imprints a large publisher like Random House or Simon & Schuster has. Ask a bookstore manager in your area what personalities or target audiences the imprints suggest.

NOTES

1. Howard Aldrich, *Organizations and Environments* (Englewood Cliffs, NJ: Prentice Hall, 1979), p. 4.

2. See Ephraim Yuctman and Stanley Seashore, "A System Resource Approach to Organizational Effectiveness," *American Sociological Review* 32 (December 1967), p. 900.

3. George Gerbner, "Institutional Pressures upon Mass Communicators," *Sociological Review Monograph* 13 (1969), pp. 205–248.
4. Michael Hannan and John Freeman, "The Population Ecology of Organizations," *American Journal of Sociology* 82 (March 1988), pp. 929–962; and Aldrich, passim.
5. Erik Barnouw, *A Tower in Babel* (New York: Oxford University Press, 1968).
6. Richard Allen Schwartzlose, *The American Wire Services* (New York: Arno Press, 1979), p. 239.
7. Kenneth Cox, "The Federal Communications Commission," *Boston College Industrial and Commercial Law Review* 11 (May 1970), pp. 605–666.
8. Ernest C. Hynds, *American Newspapers in the '80s* (New York: Hastings House, 1975), p. 157.
9. Cox, p. 631. See also Erik Barnouw, *The Golden Web* (New York: Oxford University Press, 1970), pp. 311–347.
10. Don R. Pember, *Mass Media Law* (Dubuque, IA: William C. Brown, 1977).
11. J. W. Click and Russel N. Baird, *Magazine Editing and Production,* 2nd ed. (Dubuque, IA: William C. Brown, 1979), p. 281.
12. "Vestron, Saying Nixed Loan Triggered Woes, Sues Bank," *Variety,* June 17 1989, p. 66.
13. Lewis Jacobs, *The Rise of the American Film* (New York: Teacher's College Press, 1968), pp. 302–305; and Arthur Knight, *The Liveliest Art* (New York: Signet, 1957), pp. 142–187 and 274–312.
14. Stephen Labaton, "US Inquiry Begins on Price for Newsprint," *New York Times,* October 27, 1995, p. D1.
15. Hynds, p. 273.
16. On *U.S. News,* see Click and Baird, p. 215. Also see Jim Rosenberg, "System Changeover Under Way at AP," *Editor and Publisher,* July 8, 1989, p. 20.
17. See Charlton Heston, "Actors as Union Men," in A. William Bleum and Jason Squires (eds.), *The Movie Business* (New York: Hastings House, 1972), pp. 85–91.
18. Alex S. Jones, "New York's Daily News Prepares for a War with Its Unions," *New York Times,* September 25, 1989, p. D-9.
19. Hynds, p. 164.
20. John Dessauer, *Book Publishing* (New York: Bowker, 1974), p. 345.
21. M. William Krasilovsky, "Motivation and Control in Creative Writing," in Bleum and Squires, p. 33.
22. J. Kenneth Rotcap, "The Story Editor," in Bleum and Squires, p. 22.
23. Amy Kaufman, "It's Easier Now Than It Used to Be," *Emmy Magazine* 3 (Fall 1981), pp. 38–41.
24. Michael Fleming, "Pact Prods Pix Back to Gotham," *Variety,* May 20, 1991, p. 1.
25. Thomas Guback, "Theatrical Film," in Benjamin Compaine (ed.), *Who Owns the Media?* (White Plains, NY: Knowledge Industry Publications, 1979), p. 183.
26. Geraldine Fabrikant, "Cable Hungry for Programs," *New York Times,* November 16, 1989, p. D-1.
26. *Broadcasting Yearbook, 1979,* pp. A-1 and D-49.
28. Christopher H. Sterling, "Television and Radio Broadcasting," in Compaine, p. 201.
29. Ed Papazian (ed.), *TV Dimensions '95* (New York: Media Dynamics), p. 104.
30. Christopher H. Sterling and John M. Kittross, *Stay Tuned: A Concise History of Broadcasting* (Belmont, CA: Wadsworth, 1990), p. 637.
31. Bill Carter, "Westinghouse Visits TV Land," *New York Times,* October 30, 1995, p. D1.

32. Sterling and Kittross, p. 633.
33. Danby Maryles, "Embraced by the List: Bestsellers '94," *Publisher's Weekly,* January 2, 1992, p. 53.
34. "New Women's Magazine Aiming Big," *Advertising Age,* March 2, 1981, p. 40.
35. Paul Hirsch, "Processing Fads and Fashions," *American Journal of Sociology* 77 (January 1972), pp. 639–659.
36. R. Serge Denisoff, *Solid Gold: The Popular Record Industry* (New Brunswick, NJ: Transaction Books, 1972), pp. 97–98.
37. Thomas Whiteside, *The Blockbuster Complex* (Middletown, CT: Wesleyan University Press, 1981), p. 70.
38. Ibid.

CHAPTER 3

A Bit of History
Government, Business, and Mass Media

This chapter

- shows how the past development of media has an effect on the present.
- describes how the government's relationship with the media system evolved.
- sketches the way advertisers become the major support for many media industries.

Some people think of history as a collection of disconnected facts about eras that no longer exist. They are wrong. History is the study of the past, but seen through the eyes of the present. Historians view this study not merely as a sequence of facts, but also as a tapestry of stories built on those facts. The stories illuminate the way people used to think and live. But they do more: They serve as tools for making sense of how and why we think and live today.

A study of the past can help us understand how the media industries that exist today developed. Recall from Chapter 2 that when we talk of the structure of a media industry, we mean the roles that organizations play with one another in the course of producing, distributing, and exhibiting mass media materials. In every society, these roles have a history behind them. They develop over time in response to political and economic conditions.

In the United States, present-day power role relationships did not begin with the organizations that currently exist within mass media industries. Rather, the bases of those relationships were set decades, even centuries, ago. How is it that the federal government can regulate the content of broadcast television content but not home video? What precedents make it likely that a government law banning obscenity on the Internet will be overturned? Why are advertisers, and not state, local, and federal governments, important in financing many media?

It is virtually impossible to accurately answer these basic questions about the U.S. media system without understanding its history. In fact, if you want to become a savvy media executive or a knowledgeable consumer of media materials, you must develop an ability to reflect critically on the past in order to understand the present and realistically consider the future. This chapter aims to help you do that.

Deciding where to begin is difficult. Strictly speaking, the industrial activity called mass communication began in the nineteenth century. Yet to understand mass communication it often helps to look even further into the past. One can trace influences on American mass media all the way back to the invention of writing about 6,000 years ago. Another starting point is the invention of the printing press by Johannes Gutenberg in the mid-fifteenth century in the region of Europe that is now Germany.

Here the scope must be more modest. Our purpose is to sketch how the fundamental relationships of American media industries — those that relate to governments and advertisers — came to be. Accordingly, this chapter traces the beginnings of government–media relations and media–business relations in the United States. It is impossible to understand the government's role without understanding the role of business in the activities of U.S. mass media, because the business of media is sanctioned and regulated in a variety of ways by the authorities. Knowing why that is and how it came to be is crucial for being able to think creatively about contemporary relationships among government, business, and media.[1]

AN ADVERSARIAL RELATIONSHIP

In considering the development of government–media relations in the United States, it is instructive to think back to the American colonies of the eighteenth century and their most influential ruler, England. This was a period when ground rules were set concerning the relationship between the government and newspaper printers. The newspaper was a relatively recent phenomenon in England at the time.

They were not much like the ones we see today. The print was small and dense, and there were few illustrations. Often, articles were simply reprints or translations of pieces from other newspapers, and they were not in the style we associate with contemporary reportage. Merchants were a primary audience, because the papers informed them about events in other countries that could influence their ability to travel and sell goods.

Political dissenters were also drawn to newspapers. One reason was that papers could bring information about the activities of enemies and allies, within or outside their territory. Another was that through newspapers, they could circulate ideas that could keep supporters and would-be supporters charged up about their cause.

Commerce and Dissent

This dual function of newspapers—information provider for merchants and rallying point for political dissenters—helps explain the slow development of the medium in England and British colonial America. It might appear odd that although William Caxton set up the first press in England in 1476, nearly two centuries elapsed before the country had a newspaper printed regularly within its borders. The explanation lies in the inability of would-be publishers to fill one or the other aspect of the dual role. First, England was not yet a mercantile power. What interest there was among the British in merchant news was supplied from abroad, in English, by the enterprising Dutch. Second, and maybe even more important, the British Crown feared dissent and wanted to fully control all printing.

In 1509, for example, King Henry VIII issued a list of prohibited books and established a licensing system. Licensing meant that only people with written authority of the Crown could use a printing press. Queen Mary Tudor, who came after him, established the Stationers Company, whose members were the elite of printers. They were chosen for their loyalty to the monarchy and acted as police for the Crown's benefit. In the late 1500s, the Stationers adopted an order for a weekly search of London printing houses to report on work in progress, the number of orders on hand, the number of employees and their wages—even the identity of customers. The power of the monarchy, combined with a merchant class that was not yet preoccupied with affairs in Europe, inhibited the creation of long-lasting, openly available newspapers.

By the 1600s, though, England was beginning its ascent to greatness as a trading nation. The atmosphere was ripe for more channels of communication that would inform the growing merchant class about conditions affecting their work outside England. Also on the rise were public arguments in print by various factions of British society because the climate of governance was changing. In the early 1600s, the Crown passed from the Protestant Tudors to the Stuarts, who were Catholic. Political and religious disputes ensued and the power of the monarchy deteriorated. Paralleling the Crown's decline, the power of other elites rose as Parliament gained a voice in British society that was more substantial than in the past.

Truth in the Field

Throughout this tumultuous century, British elites argued bitterly about the extent to which the press should be allowed to publicly reflect disputes. Embattled groups that supported the right of their side to be heard developed the argument that the free expression of ideas would necessarily help leaders of society and the people to see which side contained the truth. This was the theme of John Milton in the following passage of his famous 1644 pamphlet, *Areopagitica:*

> And though the winds of doctrine were let loose to play upon the earth, so truth be in the field, we do injuriously by licensing and prohibiting to misdoubt her strength. Let her and falsehood grapple: who ever knew truth put to the worse in a free and open encounter.[2]

The idea that truth would always win out in a printed debate became the rallying cry behind those in England and America who wanted press freedoms. Among the British, it contributed directly to the establishment of the first English Bill of Rights in the 1680s, which endorsed free expression for members of Parliament. In the American colonies, it lay behind the glorification of a press system that was not only free from government control but also free to attack the government.

This ideal was established slowly in the colonies during the eighteenth century. At the century's start, newspapers such as the *Boston Newsletter* carried the phrase "by authority of the Crown," even after such announcement of fealty was not required in England. Goodwill toward the political establishment was further ensured by the fact that the publishers of many colonial papers were either postmasters appointed by the royal governor or printers who had succeeded in winning government printing contracts. In neither case was the person likely to circulate ideas that were politically suspect.

Nevertheless, printers did appear who dared to challenge the authorities, and they set important examples. One was James Franklin, printer/publisher of the *New England Courant* in the 1720s. Franklin, brother of the more famous Ben, released articles that criticized Puritan leadership in Boston during a smallpox epidemic. Franklin was imprisoned, then exiled from the city, but not before he printed a ringing defense of his actions that echoed Milton's.

> Even errors made publick, and afterwards publickly expos'd, less endanger the constitution of church or state, than they are (without opposition) industriously propagated in private conversation. Hence, to anathemize a printer for publishing the different opinions of men, is as injudicious as it is wicked.[3]

Public support for this position seems to have accelerated as a result of the 1735 trial of New York printer John Peter Zenger. He was charged with "seditious libel" for presenting information in his newspaper that criticized the generally disliked royal governor. The jury should have found Zenger guilty, because by British common law the truth of a published remark was not a relevant defense. Yet Zenger's renowned Philadelphia lawyer, Andrew Hamilton, convinced the jury that his client was not guilty by reason of the value of exposing truth. Hamilton argued that Zenger should be set free because "Nature and Laws of our Country have given us a Right — the Liberty — both of exposing and opposing arbitrary Power (in these Parts of the World, at least) by speaking and writing Truth."[4]

Hamilton's comments and the jury's verdict point to an idea that was gaining strength throughout the 1700s in the American colonies: that the newspaper could and should be used as a weapon of truth against unfair aspects of British colonial rule. Many American intellectuals were influenced by European Enlightenment philosophers of the day. They agreed with the endorsement by Bacon, Descartes, and others of the empirical methods of scientific, rational inquiry. They agreed, too, with the affirmation of Locke, Montesquieu, and other thinkers that truth, as shown by reason, would inevitably triumph when challenged by error — and that it would be recognized by the majority. As they saw it, reason would triumph in human affairs through the action of the majority in political decisions. This was, in fact, the extension of Milton's *Areopagitica* argument, and the British parliamentary Bill of Rights, to the people at large in relation to the government.

Toward the First Amendment

The contention that the press could and should play an adversarial role toward the government became particularly strong when England forced the American colonists to share costs of an expensive war with France during the 1760s and 1770s. In trying to raise money, the British made the grave mistake of imposing taxes on paper. This angered lawyers and printers, because it greatly affected their business. But lawyers and printers were a bad group to attack. They banded together and published strong condemnations of British colonial policy, which did not allow Americans voting representatives in Parliament who could speak for or against such taxes.

Such anti-British sentiments led some journalists to call for a total break with the "mother" country. This, in turn, led supporters of England to threaten, and even carry out, violence against them. It was a time that stayed clearly in the minds of the leaders of the new republic after their war with Britain ended. They were determined to ensure their ability to air arguments in the public arena.

For them the issue was not merely philosophical. As members of the various political factions that vied for primacy in the new nation, they did not wish to be prevented by more powerful parties from using the press and the orator's box. American newspapers of the late eighteenth century tended to voice the opinions of particular political parties. Their owners, and the parties they stood for, wanted to continue to do so.

As a result, the framers of the U.S. Constitution of 1787 found it necessary to agree to a Bill of Rights that would include the following words: "Congress shall make no law . . . abridging the freedom of speech, or of the press." This First Amendment to the Constitution, largely the work of James Madison, points very clearly to concern by the Founding Fathers over government manipulation of the press. The amendment does not insist that speech and the press ought to be free in some broad, abstract sense. Rather it specifically refers to freedom from congressional control, just as many of the state constitutions specify freedoms of speech and of the press from government control within their borders. The issue of private control over the avenues of knowledge — by advertisers, media conglomerates, or other means — is not a concern of the First Amendment. To the people who wrote the First Amendment, this was simply not an issue of concern.

The point of the First Amendment, in other words, was to ensure that the adversarial relationship between the press and the authorities, which had evolved during colonial times and continued into the early days of the republic, would endure. Congress did allow prohibitions that restrained the press but did not impede this adversarial relationship. Lawmakers elaborated and interpreted laws regulating slander, libel, and indecent language throughout the nineteenth and twentieth centuries. They disallowed **plagiarism** — copying someone's work without permission — as it had been under English common law. By extension, they set forth the terms whereby a person could control a work — a notion called **copyright.** Pornography was also considered actionable, though with the exception of child nudity, the courts had a difficult time specifying exactly what it was. All these were not felt to be an abridgment of press freedoms.

Even when it came to the cherished adversary relationship, government actions were not always in harmony with the celebrated ideal. For one thing, when the Constitution was written, it seems clear that the framers saw the Bill of Rights as reserved for cultured, literate white males only, who they believed were the only ones who ought to have access to a press. Moreover, within seven years of the adoption of the First Amendment, the threat of war with France led President John Adams to secure congressional approval of the **Sedition Act,** which threatened journalists with imprisonment for writing material that cast aspersions on the political leadership of the United States.

Consider, too, that even national leaders who stressed the importance of press freedoms could sometimes voice exasperation and impatience with the potpourri of scurrilous accusations served up by the nation's highly politicized newspapers. President Thomas Jefferson, for example, was distressed in 1803 by the vitriol of the Federalist press. He toyed with the thought that "a few prosecutions of the most prominent offenders" would bring the rest of the newspaper community in line. That he, and George Washington before him, did not follow this tack is testimonial to a deep belief that contending political viewpoints would help the nation arrive at truth. But the tension that Washington, Jefferson, and many succeeding government leaders felt over this adversarial relationship with the press continues today.

TOWARD A NEW SUPPORT SYSTEM

One reason the press's adversarial relationship with the government could continue was that newspapers and other public media developed forms of monetary support that were not connected directly to the government. The

First Amendment ensures only that the government will not enact laws directly controlling the content of the press. The amendment says nothing about other methods politicians can use to control what is printed. A key avenue of such control is cash. If major leaders of the government are the only ones who can support newspapers (or magazines or TV stations), the views expressed through those communication channels will effectively be controlled by those leaders.

From the start of the republic, however, it was clear that newspapers could find funds from a variety of sources to keep the adversarial relationship going. Newspapers of the early United States reveled in the kinds of political attacks that today we associate with entertainment/gossip tabloids such as *The National Enquirer*. For example, a *New York Evening Post* article reported that President Thomas Jefferson, a Republican, had paid a Richmond, Virginia, newspaper editor to spread the word that George Washington, a Federalist, had been a robber, traitor, and perjurer.[5] The combativeness within the highly politicized American press could actually be dangerous. When Benjamin Franklin Bache wrote in the *Philadelphia General Advertiser* of 1796 that "the American nation has been debauched by Washington," Federalists wrecked his office and beat him in retaliation.[6] Similarly, Vice President Aaron Burr challenged Treasury Secretary Alexander Hamilton to the duel that took Hamilton's life after an Albany newspaper published an alleged remark by Hamilton that Burr found personally insulting.[7]

Early American newspapers were typically small operations run by publishers who were also printers and editors. They drew their support primarily from the aristocracy or the upper-middle-class merchants. Many of the papers were allied with political parties. This explains why, apart from commercial notices, much of the "news" that appeared was phrased in the form of fierce political arguments against the opposition.

Some newspapers were even supported by party officials, who helped arrange lucrative government printing contracts for the editors. Readers who picked up the *Gazette of the United States* in the 1790s knew they were reading the organ of the Federalist party sponsored by Alexander Hamilton. Similarly, readers knew that the *National Gazette* was a Jeffersonian Republican mouthpiece.

The great majority of Americans did not read any of the newspapers that were printed in the closing years of the eighteenth century and the first few decades of the nineteenth. Much of the reason was illiteracy, though the number of working-class citizens learning to read was growing quickly. Even among those who could read, however, the cost of getting a newspaper was out of reach, because newspapers were still created in an expensive, labor-intensive manner. They used hand-driven presses that by the 1790s were still not much different from Gutenberg's.

Publishers charged from $6 to $10 a year in advance for a newspaper subscription. This was more than most skilled workers earned in a week and, in any case, a person of limited means could not pay that amount up front. One result was that circulations were not impressive by current standards. A circulation of 1,500 was considered adequate in all but the biggest commercial centers. Another consequence was that most of the papers tended to reflect the editorial slant of the conservative political party (the Federalist party), because the prosperous class seemed to gravitate toward that viewpoint.[8]

A Sea Change

By the 1830s, however, a number of factors were coming together to encourage a sea change in American journalism. The 1820s and 1830s marked the rise of an emphasis on the power of the "common man." Andrew Jackson's presidential victory in 1829 signaled the utility of appealing to more than just the wealthy in a nation where white male suffrage was the rule. Literacy among the working class continued to climb. In fact, the interest of workers in newspapers was evident in a number of early union-supported newspapers that had appeared briefly during the previous decade.

Added to this fascinating soup of change was the steam-powered press. Invented in Saxony (today a part of Germany) and improved in England and the United States, a steam-powered press in 1830 was able to produce 4,000 double impressions an hour. The labor-saving speed of the technology drastically lowered the per-page cost of printing. It made possible a newspaper that huge numbers of people could afford.

During the late 1820s and early 1830s, in fact, a number of entrepreneurs tried to create a paper that sold for a penny, but with little success. Then in 1833, Benjamin Day, a struggling printer, founded the *New York Sun*. Hugely successful — within six months its circulation reached 8,000 — and quickly imitated, it pointed the way toward drastic changes in the look and content of the American newspaper. It also led to a revolution in the way many mass media in the United States were financed.

The slogan on the *Sun*'s masthead was "It Shines for All," which reflected the newspaper's desire to entice great numbers of people, rather than only the merchant class. The Sun was shockingly different from the typical newspaper of the early nineteenth century. Following the example of an emerging British popular press, Day's product and its imitators emphasized not partisan politics but sensationalism, human interest, and humor. In the earliest years, hoaxes and exaggerated stories were fairly common. Over the next few decades, however, the *Sun* and other papers in this new generation (such as the *New York Herald* and *New York Tribune*) developed an approach to the organization of American journalism and the presentation of news that still exists today.

A consensus emerged about the importance of such characteristics as speed in identifying and processing news; the proper use of headlines, datelines, and bylines; distinctions between "hard news" and "features"; the optimal adversarial stance between government and journalist in a nonpartisan press; and the procedure for writing an "objective" story. These approaches became the backbone of a prosperous new newspaper industry. By the end of the century, the values and writing standards of American journalism were shared so widely (if not always implemented) that they were used to justify the professionalization of news work as taught in special journalism schools.

The nature and implications of these values and standards are discussed in chapter 7. Here it is important to point out that **the new nonpartisan approach to journalism encouraged an industrialized way of organizing and supporting production that could truly be called mass communication.**

From the start, Benjamin Day's slogan "It Shines for All" reflected his philosophy of financing the paper as well as creating its content. He and his partners believed that a penny publication would thrive by making its money back one issue at a time. His paper was sold on the streets for a penny by ambitious hawkers who made about 37 cents for every 100 copies they sold. As new presses offered faster, larger, and cheaper printruns, increased circulation meant increased profits for the publisher. Day and his competitors tried to entice more and more readers to buy their product by adding new sections to match a variety of possible interests, including those of the wealthier classes. The *New York Herald* was particularly innovative in appealing to different segments of the population in different portions of the same issue. By the late 1840s, it had a sports section, a critical review column, society news, and a strong financial section, among others.

One consequence of these developments was that newspapers became complex organizations. The single printer-publisher-editor-reporter role of the early 1800s gave way to a hierarchy of specialized positions needed to create,

---

TALKING POINT 3.1 A Whistler

The penny papers were as different from today's major dailies as they were from the traditional political-commercial papers of their day. Editors had no qualms about running unattributed stories about unnamed people doing things at unnamed times who seemed to be news simply because they were interesting. The following story ran on the front page of the *New York Sun*'s first issue, September 3, 1833:

A Whistler — A boy in Vermont, accustomed to working alone, was so prone to whistling, that as soon as he was by himself, he unconsciously commenced. When asleep, the muscles of his mouth, chest, and lungs were so completely concatenated in the association, he whistled with astonishing shrillness. A pale countenance, loss of appetite, and almost total prostration of strength, convinced his mother it would end in death if not speedily overcome, which was accomplished by placing him in the society of another boy, who had orders to give him a blow as soon as he began to whistle.

print, and market the newspaper. A related change was that through the mid-
and late nineteenth century and the early twentieth century, the newspaper
world became industrialized. Newspaper organizations entered into regular interactions with a variety of organizations and industries that provided the symbolic and material supplies necessary to do their work. From the standpoint of
actual editorial product, the chief new organizational contributors were the
telegraph company (Western Union), the news wire services (such as Reuters
and the Associated Press), and syndication firms (such as King Features). Just
as significant, the money to pay for these services came increasingly not from
readers but rather from a new set of organizations that wanted to reach them:
the advertising industry.

The Rise of Advertising

Advertising actually began well before the nineteenth century. Merchants had
advertised in newspapers from their inception, and by the time Benjamin Day
arrived on the scene, ads were taken for granted as a fact of journalistic life. In
those days, advertising was one source of extra money for a newspaper firm;
the greatest source for financing the operation was the readership. In the
decades after the rise of the penny press, however, the emphasis of financial
support shifted, and advertising became the monetary lifeblood of the journalistic enterprise.

Many considerations led to the changed relationship between advertisers
and newspaper organizations. One was that advertisers were impressed by the
substantial numbers of readers the new penny press and its descendants
reached. The papers allowed them to reach more people through one vehicle
than was previously possible. The news merchants, for their part, saw advertising revenue as a way to get the large amounts of cash required to purchase
the faster printing presses and other technologies necessary to stay ahead in
what had become a highly competitive business.

The competition typically revolved around speed. Publishers, editors, and
reporters increasingly saw news in terms of getting stories to the public faster
than their competitors. Boasting about having "the latest" news seemed to increase circulation. So did emphasizing that papers contained "the facts" uncol-
ored by political partiality. By arguing that their coverage was free of bias,
newspapers could attract people of all political persuasions.

Increasing circulation was the way to increase advertising revenues. Increased ad revenues, in turn, allowed for more speed-oriented technologies
that could bring the latest news along with a kaleidoscope of cartoons, human
interest columns, and pictures. This, publishers felt, would lift circulation to
still greater heights. It was a continuing cycle.

Advertising as an industry evolved hand in hand with the new U.S. world
of journalism. Central to that industry was the advertising agency. The first
one was conceived in 1849 as a middleman between papers and businesses
looking to purchase space for ads. In the decades that followed the American

Civil War, ad agencies developed into marketing arms for companies trying to sell goods.

Innovative and persuasive strategies for newspaper ads were most often used to hawk patent medicine products — drinks and other commodities that were supposed to cure bodily ailments. Ineffective and illegal patent medicines were outlawed in 1905 by the nation's first Pure Food and Drug Act. However, the legacy of patent medicine advertising remained: in advertisers' strong financial influence over the newspaper business, in the persuasive strategies that showed up in ads for a variety of products, and, not least, in the taint of unscrupulousness it lent to the advertising business in society at large.

By the demise of patent medicine advertising, many other goods had arrived on the advertising scene. The late nineteenth century saw rapid expansion of the U.S. economy. The Industrial Revolution was moving at full speed, and a flood of new consumer products was being released to the marketplace that needed public awareness in order to sell. Advertising agencies became vehicles for creating this awareness. The space bought by ad agencies encouraged huge circulation growth and rapid competition among big city newspapers of the late nineteenth century. Advertisers also sponsored weekly and monthly magazines (the *Saturday Evening Post, Collier's, Ladies' Home Journal*) that reached millions of people. Keeping this boom going were a rapidly

---

TALKING POINT 3.2   The Ladies' Morning Star

The phenomenal success of the first penny papers in New York City — the *Sun,* the *Transcript,* and the *Herald* — soon resulted in a number of others in New York, all of which were short-lived. The most novel of those failed undertakings was a penny paper for women, the *Ladies' Morning Star,* established by William Newell in April 1836. Two years earlier, a similar attempt, edited by an "Ann Oddbody," had failed. Newell was trying again.

Newell's idea was that the general penny press did not address what he (and others of the day) saw as the more refined sensibilities that women had over men. The police reports of the typical penny papers were, he stated in an editorial, written in a way that degraded those sensibilities. Echoing Benjamin Day's motto "It Shines for All," Newell wrote that his paper was aimed at all types of women, those married as well as "that class of young women who live by their daily labor."

The paper was praised at the time by the editor of the *Philadelphia Public Ledger.* Unfortunately for Newell, he could attract neither advertisers nor readers. Merchants apparently objected to advertising in a paper intended exclusively for women. Newell, after six months, changed the name to *The Morning Star.* That still did not help pay the bills, though, and the paper died by the end of the year.

SOURCE: William Grosvenor Bleyer, *Main Currents in the History of American Journalism* (Boston: Houghton Mifflin, 1927), pp. 168-171.

growing population of readers, favorable postal rates, further developments in high-speed printing, and the ability to reproduce photographs on high-speed presses.

The result was that newspapers and magazines entered the twentieth century with the largest audiences in their history. What is more, the audience was paying a minor portion of the actual costs of producing what it was reading. Advertisers, searching for huge numbers of likely consumers, were footing most of the bill. In about a century, American mass media had developed a support system that separated media control from political parties. A new source of financial control — advertisers and the advertising industry — had risen to take its place. One broad consequence was obvious: Rather than politics guiding the creation and content of newspapers, commerce now set the ground rules. Newspapers and magazines had become vehicles in a people-catching activity.

BUSINESS, GOVERNMENT, AND NEW MASS MEDIA

Not all U.S. mass media used advertising as their primary support at the turn of the century. The book industry still followed its centuries-old tradition of printing only announcements of related entities by the same publisher. Similarly, the new music recording industry carried no ads on its discs, although the records' paper jackets often advertised the companies' other offerings. One reason for the absence of ads on the recordings themselves may have been the short playing time of a disc. Early records had only one side, and a song plus a commercial would not fit on the same side.

This constraint did not exist in the film industry. In fact, film entrepreneurs experimented with using moving images to sell consumer products as early as the 1890s.[9] Also, local advertising projected on simple slides has appeared in movie theaters throughout the country for decades. Still, even though the promotion of "coming attractions" became standard in U.S. theaters, the practice of presenting national commercials for nonfilm products did not catch on until the 1980s. One can speculate about the reasons, but no one seems to have investigated them systematically.

Government, Business, and Radio

By not encouraging advertising, the recording and movie industries are different from almost all other mass media that have developed in the twentieth century. Radio, which emerged in the 1920s as a major mass medium, was the new technology that set the pattern in favor of ad industry sponsorship. Today, Americans may think of commercials as a natural part of radio and its offshoot, television. Advertising was never an essential part of that invention, however. In England, radio was operated through a government-run organization (the British Broadcasting Corporation) and supported by a tax on receivers. It did not develop a commercial side until the 1950s.

In the United States, neither private ownership nor commercial sponsorship was taken for granted. The federal government gave the U.S. Navy control of radio broadcasting for reasons of national security during World War I. After the war, admirals lobbied Congress vigorously to retain that monopoly. When Congress denied the Navy's request and decided that broadcasting to the public should be developed privately, many observers in and outside the radio business stated their hope that radio waves would never be used to sell products. They felt that radio stations could be financed by stores and equipment manufacturers that needed to give consumers something to listen to after they purchased sets.

Looking back on the congressional debate about the future of radio in 1919, one can see clearly how a view of the past, combined with concerns of the present, shaped the nation's approach to a new mass medium. The United States was becoming an increasingly wealthy, business-oriented society. Radio was relatively undeveloped, with its unwieldy technology, listeners who saw it as a curiosity, and no regularly scheduled programs. It was obvious, though, that the medium was on the threshold of great changes.

Leaders of commerce and government believed that the best way to develop radio's great potential was to move it from the public to the private sector. In addition, members of Congress were aware of the American tradition that kept mass media away from direct government control. A broadcast station could spread words further than an individual newspaper or a magazine. Moreover, it could reach the illiterate as well as the literate. Allowing the Navy to dictate decisions about use of the airwaves would mean involving a government agency in the potentially controversial area of controlling ideas in large segments of the population.

As a result of this debate, Congress decreed in 1919 that broadcasting was to be a privately sponsored enterprise, available to any citizen who paid for a license. Radio's split from government was not straightforward, however. Navy officials feared that opening broadcasting to all comers would mean that power over this potentially important medium could fall to parties with ill will toward the nation. To ensure that dominant control of radio would remain in friendly hands, the Navy encouraged a number of American firms that owned the major broadcast patents (notably, American Telephone and Telegraph, General Electric, and the Westinghouse Company) to form a patent trust — that is, a company that would rule U.S. radio through patents.

They called the trust the Radio Corporation of America (RCA). Its purpose was to force anyone interested in setting up a broadcasting operation to pay RCA for the infringement of RCA's radio patents. RCA, in turn, would impose certain agreed-upon conditions on use of the airwaves. In addition, RCA would be the most powerful force developing the airwaves, thereby ensuring that an entity close to the Navy would remain in the driver's seat.

The use of a patent trust to control a media industry was not new. Thomas Edison, for one, had tried it in both the record and movie industries. Moreover, like the movie and record trusts before it, the radio monopoly was broken up by the courts within a decade of its inception. The creation of RCA was different from the building of the other trusts because it was orchestrated by an arm of the federal government. Still, both the construction and destruction of these early media monopolies were indicative of a new federal approach to media in the late nineteenth century. It involved attempts by one or another branch of the government to sidestep the prohibitions of the First Amendment through **structural regulation**—that is, through laws or rulings that would guide the creative output of the industry *indirectly* by dictating broadly how its companies related to one another and to the government.

BOX 3.1   Major Dates in U.S. Media Industries (1640–1996)

1640	America's first book, *The Bay Psalm Book,* is published.
1690	America's first newspaper, *Public Occurrences,* is published in Boston by Benjamin Harris.
1704	The nation's first newspaper advertisement appears in the first issue of the *Boston News-Letter.*
1731	Benjamin Franklin establishes America's first circulation library.
1735	The Zenger trial establishes landmark precedent for freedom of the press in America—the concept that truth is the best defense for libel.
1741	The first American magazines, Andrew Bradford's *American Magazine* and Benjamin Franklin's *General Magazine,* are published.
1765	The Stamp Act Congress meets in New York and adopts "No taxation without representation" slogan.
1783	The *Pennsylvania Evening Post,* America's first daily newspaper, is published.
1793	Semaphore telegraph system invented in France by the Chappe brothers.
1798	Alien and Sedition Laws are passed by Congress.
1832	Samuel Morse invents telegraph alphabet.
1833	Benjamin Day publishes the *New York Sun* and establishes the Penny Press.
1837	First patent for commercial telegraph system given to Cooke and Wheatstone in the United Kingdom.
1844	First telegraph line extends from Washington to Baltimore.
1858	First transatlantic telegraph cable laid between United States and Great Britain.
1865	First conference of the International Telegraph Union held.
1876	Telephone patented by Alexander Graham Bell.
1877	Thomas Edison demonstrates his phonograph for the first time.
1878	First local telephone exchange opens in the United States.

(continued)

BOX 3.1   Major Dates in U.S. Media Industries (1640–1996) *(continued)*

1879	Postal Act encourages the growth of magazines ensuring quick, reasonably priced distribution for magazines.
1884	Paul Nipkow patents the scanning disk, a precursor to television.
1887	Heinrich Hertz demonstrates the existence of radio waves.
	Emile Berliner develops the gramophone.
1889	Thomas Edison films the first motion picture.
1891	The International Copyright Law is passed, expanding royalty protection to American writers.
1895	Guglielmo Marconi sends wireless messages on family estate.
1896	Marconi applies for patent in London for the invention of radio.
	Original Bell patents expire; beginning of competition in U.S. telephone industry.
1898	Sir Oliver Lodge develops a workable method for tuning radio electronics.
1899	Pupin invents loading coil, leading to the development of long-distance telephony.
1900	A Frenchman named Perskyi comes up with the word *television*.
	Ladies Home Journal is the first magazine to surpass 1 million subscribers.
1901	Marconi sends letter S across Atlantic in Morse Code, establishing radio telegraphy.
1905	Albert Einstein publishes his theory of photoelectric effect.
1906	Lee De Forest develops three-element Audion tube, which allows radio transmissions of voice and music.
1907	Russian physicist Boris Rosing patents television system.
	Peak of competition between independent telephone companies and the Bell system in the United States; Theodore Vail becomes president of AT&T.
1908	Eugene Lauste invents the first talking motion pictures.
1912	Radio Act of 1912, first U.S. law to control land radio stations, makes the Secretary of Commerce and Labor responsible for licensing.
1913	AT&T begins to purchase De Forest patents. Kingsbury Commitment with Justice Department settles antitrust suit against AT&T and allows absorption of remaining independent telephone companies.
1915	AT&T long-distance service, using vacuum-tube amplifiers, reaches San Francisco.
1919	GE forms Radio Corporation of America (RCA).
1920	AT&T becomes RCA partner.
1922	First broadcast advertisement over AT&T's radio station WEAF in New York.
	ASCAP demands royalties from radio stations.
1923	Zworykin applies for a patent for the "Iconoscope," a partly electronic television system, which replaces earlier mechanical methods of producing television images.
1925	Charles Francis Jenkins oversees the first transmission of moving pictures using motion-picture film.

1926	GE, Westinghouse, and RCA form the National Broadcasting Company.
	Book-of-the-Month Club is founded.
1927	Columbia Broadcasting System (CBS) goes on the air with a sixteen-station network.
	Two NBC networks, "red" and "blue," are in operation.
	Philo T. Farnsworth applies for patent on electronic television system.
	Radio Act of 1927 passed; Federal Radio Commission formed.
	The first feature-length motion picture, *The Jazz Singer,* opens at Warner's Theater in New York.
	Literary Guild founded.
1928	William Paley founds CBS.
	RKO formed by GE-Westinghouse-RCA and film interests.
	The first American home gets a TV set in Schenectady, New York.
1929	Paramount buys 49% of CBS.
	Bell Labs gives the first public demonstration of a working color TV system.
	RCA stock rises on Wall Street, then crashes with rest of market.
1930	David Sarnoff becomes RCA president.
	W2XBS, NBC's first TV station, goes into operation.
1931	W2XAB, CBS's first TV station, starts transmitting in New York; CBS announces the first seven-day-a-week TV broadcast schedule in America.
1932	NBC becomes wholly owned RCA subsidiary.
1933	Edwin Armstrong patents FM radio system.
	FDR's "fireside chats" play an important role in calming the banking crisis.
1934	Communications Act is passed; extends federal agency oversight to telephony and enshrines AT&T as de facto monopoly.
1935	Audimeter is used as a research tool for radio.
1938	Orson Welles broadcast of *War of the Worlds* on *Mercury Theater on the Air.*
	RCA television demonstration at the New York World's Fair.
1939	Robert de Graff introduces America's first series of paperback best-sellers, called Pocket Books.
1941	The FCC approves industry standards for black-and-white TV broadcast and reception.
	NBC's WNBT becomes the first licensed commercial television to go on the air.
	FDR's speech after the bombing of Pearl Harbor is heard in 79% of American homes.
1943	RCA sells its Blue Network to Edward Noble; it becomes ABC in 1945.
1946	First television sets go on sale.
	Color television demonstrations by CBS and NBC.
1947	The House of Representative Committee on Un-American Activities summons the Hollywood Ten to testify.

(continued)

BOX 3.1   Major Dates in U.S. Media Industries (1640–1996) *(continued)*

1948	33 $\frac{1}{3}$ and 45 rpm records appear.
	CBS inaugurates the first network nightly news broadcast, *CBS-TV News.*
1949	RCA announces the development of a color TV system compatible with current black-and-white TV sets.
1950	*Hear It Now* radio series launched by Murrow.
1951	CBS launches *See It Now.*
1952	FCC lifts freeze on license applications.
	Nixon "Checkers" speech.
1953	*TV Guide* premiere issue is published.
1955	Robert Sarnoff takes over as president of NBC.
1956	First translatlantic telephone cable laid between Great Britain and the United States.
	Consent Decree between AT&T and Justice Department opens first crack in Bell patent monopoly, but restricts AT&T from computer industry.
	Packet-switching technology, precursor to the Internet, developed in the U.S. Department of Defense Advanced Research Projects Agency (DARPA).
1960	Richard Nixon and John F. Kennedy meet in *The Great Debates* on TV and radio.
	Paperback book sales surpass trade hardcover sales for the first time.
1961	FCC authorizes FM stereo.
	FCC chairman Newton Minow finds a "vaste wasteland" on television in the United States.
1962	Telstar I inaugurates satellite relays of television programs.
1963	Networks expand evening newscasts from fifteen-minute to half-hour programs.
1964	Politically controversial "Daisy" ad aired during the Johnson-Goldwater campaign.
1966	FCC assumes jurisdiction over cable television.
	British scientists Hockham and Kao invent fiber-optic cable.
1967	Corporation for Public Broadcasting formed.
1968	"Carterfone" decision in FCC rule making allows attachment of foreign equipment to public telephone network.
1969	U.S. Department of Defense Advanced Research Projects Agency (ARPA) creates the ARPANET, a packet-switched network of networks forming an "internetwork" and linking researchers and scientists on defense projects in the United States.
1972	Home Box Office founded.
1973?	Transmission Control Protocol/Internet Protocol (TCP/IP), the Internet computer networking protocol, is developed by Robert Kahn and Vint Cerf at DARPA.
1976	WTCG-TV (later WTBS), Atlanta, begins satellite transmissions of its regular scheduling to four cable systems, thus becoming the first superstation.
	HBO begins satellite transmission via SATCOM 1.

1980	Ted Turner's Cable News Network (CNN), television's first twenty-four-hour news network, goes on the air.
1984	AT&T settles antitrust suit with Justice Department; divestiture creates Regional Bell Operating Companies (RBOCs) and AT&T (including long-distance services, Western Electric, Bell Labs, and Bellcore).
1985	First National Science Foundation Network, a backbone network linking supercomputer centers in the United States, is created. A year later, the second NSFNET forms the basis for the worldwide Internet.
	Rupert Murdoch buys Metromedia TV stations following his purchase of 20th Century Fox, setting the stage for the Fox Television Network.
1987	FCC eliminates the Fairness Doctrine.
1992	First commercial Internet service providers form in the United States.
1995	NSFNET decommissioned; worldwide Internet usage estimated at 20 million people.
	CBS/Westinghouse merger.
	Time Warner buys Turner Broadcasting.
1996	Disney buys Capitol Cities/ABC.

TENSIONS OVER CONTROL

The trend toward structural regulation reflected a complex social tension that developed around new media in the early 1900s. This tension was rooted in the same uneasiness about alleged political excesses of the press that had agitated American leaders in the early years of the republic. Added to it, however, were new concerns that moved government officials and others to search for ways to influence the mass media beyond copyright, libel, and obscenity statutes.

One feature of motion pictures and radio that concerned many observers was that these media did not use the printed word. Critics worried that movies and broadcasts could reach huge numbers of children and illiterate adults with dangerous ideas that they would not be able to handle intelligently. In another controversial development, large companies were increasingly dominating the news and entertainment businesses, and observers were troubled that powerful private corporations would gain too much power over wide-reaching communication technologies.

Activists of many political stripes called for structural regulations, such as breaking monopolistic practices of some movie companies in the hope that new companies entering the business would make more acceptable films. Many also demanded direct content regulation to protect the nation from problems they alleged were brought by the new technologies.

> **TALKING POINT 3.3   Defending Patent Medicine Advertising**
>
> Like many newspapers of the nineteenth century, the *Boston Daily Times* printed much advertising from patent medicine firms. Also like many of the papers, the *Times* received angry letters for doing so. In an 1837 editorial, it defended its practice in this way:
>
> > Some of our readers complain of the great number of patent medicines advertised in this paper. To this complaint we can only reply that it is for our interest to insert such advertisements as are not indecent or improper in their language, without any inquiry whether the articles advertised are what they purport to be. That is an inquiry for the reader who feels interested in the matter, and not for us, to make. It is sufficient for our purpose that the advertisements are paid for, and that, while we reserve the right of excluding such as are improper to be read, to the advertising public we are impartial, and show no respect to persons or to the various kinds of business that fill up this little world of ours. One man has as good a right as another to have his wares, his goods, his panaceas, his profession, published to the world in a newspaper, provided he pays for it.
>
> SOURCE: William Grosvenor Bleyer, *Main Currents in the History of American Journalism* (Boston: Houghton Mifflin, 1927), pp. 174–175.

Conservatives saw both approaches as ways to maintain the government's influence over entertainment businesses they worried would lead many people morally astray. Liberals tended to prefer structural regulation, especially when it was used to break up monopolistic activities. They argued that federal trust-busting encouraged competition and, therefore, freedom of the press, even though it meant getting the government involved in setting a media industry's rules. By fostering competition, they reasoned, the government would encourage diversity in the production, distribution, and exhibition of cultural materials. Despite their reliance on First Amendment rights, however, some liberals also believed that structural edicts would not be enough to erase problems such as racism and violence in movies or on the radio. They insisted that certain abuses demanded direct regulation of content by the government.

Inviting Government Interference in Radio

These arguments had much to do with shaping the structure and content of the American movie and radio industries in the 1920s. In the case of radio, private interests actually invited government interference. As the medium moved into the private realm, the Department of Commerce, which administered radio, felt it had no right to turn down anyone for a license. This led to an overabundance of parties willing to pay for a broadcast license and air programming. The result in many localities was that radio stations were broadcasting on top of one another.

The interference caused cacophony over the airwaves, which in turn hindered the development of stations and networks whose owners were trying to make radio broadcasting into a stable business supported by advertisers interested in reaching large numbers of people. The situation was so annoying to these powerful stations that they pressured Congress to pass a law that would allow the federal government to allocate radio frequencies selectively, with the aim of bringing order to the airwaves.

By the mid-1920s it had become clear that RCA would not be the government's answer to influence and order over radio. Wanting to aid the evolving radio industry while not losing power over it, congressional leaders adopted the argument that federal jurisdiction over the medium's structure and content was justified by the nature of the technology. Radio waves, they argued, make up a scarce public resource and, as such, their use should be guided by the government.

The ensuing deliberations led to the Federal Radio Act of 1927, which established a Federal Radio Commission as the presidentially appointed, congressionally confirmed body that would decide who should get frequencies and who should not. It was clear that Congress intended most licenses to be in private hands. Relatively few spots on the dial went to universities and nonprofit foundations.

At the same time, lawmakers composed the act to allow continuing government influence on the materials businesses were sending out. One paragraph required that broadcasters give "equal time" to political candidates. The other rulings relating to content were more general. A radio license was granted to the broadcaster for five-year terms, and it could be revoked if the licensee did not broadcast "in the public interest, convenience, and necessity."

Exactly what this phrase meant was not clear; its meaning has never been spelled out. Yet the ambiguous language was carried over into a revised Federal Communications Act of 1934, when the name of the regulatory body was changed to the Federal Communications Commission. It seems that the ambiguity was retained because it served as an important safety valve in relation to the tension between government and private control over mass media content.

The phrase allowed the executive branch and Congress to have it both ways. That is, they could express concern and power over broadcast materials while they technically retained the hands-off stance that had existed historically between government and press in the United States. The hope was that government influence over content would be exerted through **raised eyebrow** or **jawbone** methods. Companies afraid of losing the right to broadcast would adjust their programming in response to implied (raised eyebrow) or directly expressed (jawbone) complaints by regulators.

The Movies and Government Control

An obvious question confronting broadcasters was how to avoid more direct government controls in the future. The same sort of question had been faced by the movie industry a few years earlier. By 1920, Hollywood movie studios had been besieged by angry groups throughout the nation who were upset

---

TALKING POINT 3.4   Sex and the Motion Picture Code

The Production Code of the Motion Picture Producers and Directors of America went through several revisions. In each the depiction of "sex" (as the code called it) received substantial attention. The revisions helped shape the way romance, love, marriage, sexual violence, and sexually transmittable diseases were depicted. Below are the rules laid out by the code that was in effect between 1930 and 1934. Note that the Oscar-winning film *Philadelphia,* about discrimination against a homosexual with AIDS, would have been impossible under the code, as would Spike Lee's movie *Jungle Fever,* about a white-black romance.

The sanctity of the institution of marriage and the home shall be upheld. Pictures shall not infer that low forms of sex relationship are the accepted or common thing.

1. Adultery and illicit sex, sometimes necessary plot material, must not be explicitly treated or justified, or presented attractively.
2. Scenes of passion
   a. These should not be introduced except where they are definitely essential to the plot.
   b. Excessive and lustful kissing, lustful embraces, suggestive postures and gestures are not to be shown.
   c. In general, passion should be treated in such manner as not to stimulate the lower and baser emotions.
3. Seduction or rape
   a. These should never be more than suggested, and then only when essential for the plot. They must never be shown by explicit method.
   b. They are never the proper subject for comedy.
4. Sex perversion or any inference to it is forbidden.
5. White slavery shall not be treated.
6. Miscegenation (sex relationship between the white and black races) is forbidden.
7. Sex hygiene and venereal diseases are not proper subjects for theatrical motion pictures.
8. Scenes of actual childbirth, in fact or in silhouette, are never to be presented.
9. Children's sex organs are never to be exposed.

SOURCE: Garth Jowett, *Film: The Democratic Art* (New York: Little, Brown, 1976), p. 469.

over what they considered unwarranted violence and sexual displays in motion pictures. Murder and sex scandals among a few popular actors led to further demands by these advocacy groups that studios be restrained by city, state, or federal government agencies from distributing what the critics insisted were films injurious to the nation's health. Between 1909 and 1922, eight states passed some form of film censorship legislation.[10]

Legal justification for this sort of content regulation was necessarily different from that regarding broadcasting. Movies did not involve scarce radio waves. They mostly involved "entertainment," though, and in 1915 the U.S. Supreme Court ruled that motion picture fiction was "a spectacle, a show," not part of the "press," and, therefore, not protected by the First Amendment. As a result, the Court continued, films could legally be censored and regulated by authorities at the federal, state, or local level.

Fearing that a patchwork of state rules would make the separate editing of films for release to different regions of the country unmanageably expensive, the heads of major Hollywood film studios turned to self-regulation for protection. Their vehicle, created in 1922, was the Motion Picture Producers and Distributors of America (MPPDA). To underscore the MPPDA's allegiance to government authority, they followed (probably unconsciously) a course similar to the one British colonial governors had used in the early eighteenth century: They chose a postmaster with other strong ties to the establishment. Will Hays, the former U.S. postmaster general, Republican party chairman, and Presbyterian church elder, became so identified with the MPPDA that it was called the Hays Office during his twenty years there.

Hays set forth elaborate criteria that the major motion picture studios agreed to accept as indicating the boundaries of good taste in their films. A member studio could be fined for releasing a film that had not passed MPPDA inspection. The Hays Office criteria were formalized into a code in 1930. Although the code and the MPPDA's other activities did not eliminate public anger and calls for censorship of movies that groups felt were harmful, the Hays Office nevertheless was successful in staving off direct government control over film content. It is not surprising, then, that radio broadcasters followed the film industry's precedent of **self-regulation.** In fact, the National Association of Broadcasters announced a "code of ethics and standards of commercial practice" a year before the Hays Office released the public version of its code. Through these actions, the rhetoric of self-regulation became an integral part of the complex tug-of-war over government and private influence on the mass media.

REGULATORY SHIFTS

In 1952, the government's ability to influence films was reduced substantially when the Supreme Court ruled that a New York law outlawing "sacrilegious" movies was too vague and that it unconstitutionally abridged freedom of speech and the press. The High Court did not say that all censorship by government agencies was unconstitutional. However, the ruling and others that flowed from it effectively ended government authority to interfere directly with nonbroadcast media content, except in cases relating to copyright, slander, obscenity, and certain types of commercial speech. Structural regulation was still a viable option, though. The setting of postal rates, the questioning of firms' tax status, and the implementation of antitrust suits are some of the approaches government agencies have used to encourage certain types of media activities while discouraging others. Threats of such tactics, and the desire for the general public's goodwill, have kept self-regulation alive among moviemakers, pop recording companies, and other media firms.

Broadcast Regulation

As noted, broadcasting has continued to be the exception for which direct government rulings on content are allowed even though they violate the First Amendment rights of the firms' owners and managers. When television technology was being developed in the 1920s and 1930s, government officials and industry leaders considered it an extension of radio and thus agreed that the regulatory apparatus should be the same. In both media, the Federal Communications Act requires that broadcasters give equal time to political candidates; newspapers have no such obligation. Separate from the law, the FCC requires broadcasters to offer reply time to people criticized during a discussion of controversial issues; this is its "personal attack" rule. The commission also has a "political editorial" rule, which mandates that stations offer politicians reply time if a station editorializes for or against a candidate.

These rules have had both supporters and detractors, as do rules relating to children's television programming. Child advocates claim that the FCC has been too timid in trying to force television stations to become genuine educational resources for children. They argue that influential coalitions of broadcasters and advertisers have been able to derail the commission from tough programming quotas, such as a certain number of hours per week for educational shows.

Discussion has also focused on ways to ensure that children are not exposed to "adult" material through the home TV. In 1996, the rising concern of various groups about violent and sexual TV content led Congress to mandate that manufacturers install "V-chip" technology into new television sets. The chips would allow parents to prevent TVs used by their kids from receiving programs designed for adult sensibilities. Broadcast programs would be encoded with data that would turn the chip on or off. To encourage such encoding, Congress suggested that broadcasters come up with a program ratings system. If broadcasters could not agree on a system, Congress said, the FCC would have to create it.

These sorts of government requirements regarding content would be clearly unconstitutional if applied to the magazine, newspaper, or movie industry. Many people concerned about the content of fast-growing electronic media such as cable TV, home video, and on-line services would like the government to force these media to create content they feel will benefit, or at least not harm, the social and political process. Yet to claim jurisdiction over content in new electronic media, government regulators must show that those media are more like broadcasting than theatrical film or print. This means developing a justification similar to the "natural scarcity" reasoning used for broadcasting, which has proved increasingly difficult.

Home Video, On-line Services, and Cable

In considering the viability of the "natural scarcity" reasoning, home video, on-line services, and cable television are good technologies to compare. Home video, which emerged as a popular medium in the mid-1970s, has positioned itself as a counterpart to movies, magazines, and sound recordings. Because the print model of freedom of the press applies to these media, legislators and courts have agreed that it also applies to video cassettes.

This issue has been more contentious regarding on-line services. On-line services are companies that provide news, information, and entertainment to computers via phone lines while encouraging individuals and groups to send messages to each other electronically. Examples are America Online, Compuserve, and the Internet. The Internet warrants special mention because it is a public resource. It is a network of computers connected by telephone lines that was established by the Department of Defense in the 1960s as a way of encouraging government and university scientists throughout the world to send messages to one another by computer. Beginning in the late 1980s, the use of the Internet by professors and students grew dramatically. Because it is so decentralized, nobody actually owns the Internet. In the 1990s, private companies such as America Online, Compuserve, and others began to offer Internet connections to anyone willing to pay for them.

The popularity of the system exploded with the creation of the World Wide Web, a part of the Internet that displays pictures and other graphics and is easier to navigate than the older form. Inevitably, as "going on-line" became more and more popular, controversies arose regarding the political, violent, or sexual nature of discussions and images on the on-line services. Many users argued that on-line services enjoyed First Amendment rights in the same sense (and with the same limitations regarding libel, pornography, and copyright violation) as magazines and movies. Others argued that not only "pornography," but also "indecency," —lewd pictures and words— should be controlled, because many children were joining the on-line world.

The controversies came to a head in 1996, when Congress passed a broad new telecommunications bill. One provision set penalties—heavy fines and prison terms—for people convicted of distributing "indecent" sexual materials over computer networks. The implication was that the government had an authority over the on-line world that was similar to its jurisdiction over broadcasting. A broad range of groups led by the American Civil Liberties Union vigorously disagreed. They persuaded a federal court in Philadelphia to declare that part of the law unconstitutional. The government said it would appeal the decision to the U.S. Supreme Court.

Contrast this cause célèbre over on-line services with the long, tortuous path to define the government's regulatory position concerning cable TV. The federal government's approach to cable has changed drastically over the past fifty years. This technology was introduced in the late 1940s as a way to use a special wire (a coaxial cable) to bring over-the-air TV signals to populations too far from TV transmitters to receive them normally.

Until the late 1950s, the Federal Communications Commission refused to address regulatory issues regarding cable, implying that it had no jurisdiction because cable was simply an antenna service. (At the time, in fact, the business was called CATV, community antenna television.) Then, prodded by broadcasters who saw the medium as a potential competitor, the FCC announced the following logic: Because CATV was basically delivering broadcast signals to people, it was a service ancillary to broadcasting and, therefore, it could be regulated like broadcasting.

In the 1960s and 1970s, many cable operators began to move out of the business of simply retransmitting broadcast signals from the nearest large cities. They enticed viewers in major metropolitan areas to purchase their service by offering stations from around the country and by adding channels (the weather, Cable News Network) that were unique to cable. Nevertheless, the FCC continued to regulate the cable industry under the "ancillary" justification. Many cable TV executives viewed the regulatory link to broadcasting as a hindrance. Gaining lobbying strength as it gained economic power, the cable industry began to fight this comparison with broadcasters and the restrictions that came with it. Cable executives believed the restrictions were aimed at slowing their industry's growth in order to protect over-the-air broadcasters.

The lobbying effort was helped by the deregulatory climate of the 1980s. One important result was the Cable Communications Policy Act of 1984, which divided the regulatory authority for cable. It gave the FCC overall jurisdiction but allowed state and local governments to control franchising — the process of drawing up contracts. In addition, the act stipulated that local franchising authorities could require systems to provide channels for public, educational, and government use.

Cable companies challenged this "must carry" provision in courts, and they won. The courts did not accept the commission's argument that cable's status as ancillary to broadcasting justified forcing systems to carry particular channels. Still, neither the act nor the court decisions refuted the idea that the cable business is a service ancillary to broadcasting. Some industry spokespersons, however, argued that the ancillary tag was outmoded. They went so far as to say that the government should view them as similar to newspaper companies, with all the First Amendment rights that apply to the print media.

Their position was bolstered by the 1996 telecommunications bill. As the *New York Times* noted, Congress intended it to "promote a free-for-all rivalry between local telephone companies, long distance carriers, cable television operators and even electric utilities."[11] Previously, the federal government had not allowed phone companies and electric companies to intrude on cable's turf, for regulators feared that the huge firms would overwhelm cable operators and stifle competition. By the mid-1990s, some cable companies had become so powerful that regulators believed the restrictions were no longer necessary. The 1996 bill therefore permitted phone and electric companies to compete with cable firms by providing audiovisual news, information, and entertainment services through their own lines. In return the bill allowed cable firms to enter long distance and local telephone businesses.

With that kind of potential competition over the provision of news, entertainment, and information programming, some observers wondered why the government was not viewing cable through a newspaper rather than ancillary-to-broadcasting model. It seemed, in fact, that in shifting from government regulation of cable to regulation by the marketplace, federal officials were quietly moving toward accepting the notion that the cable business ought to fall under a different regulatory philosophy than broadcasting, with a latitude in content much closer to that of newspapers.

GOVERNMENT AND THE BUSINESS OF MEDIA

As this chapter has shown, the regulations that governments enforce in a mass media industry are generally the result of struggles by various groups in the industry to achieve conditions favorable to them within the broad context of mass media law and tradition. In societies torn by political turmoil — in Africa and Eastern Europe, for example — the regulations may vary from month to month as the shifting fortunes of those in power are reflected in the shifting fortunes of people in the media who support them. Stable societies tend to have more predictable media rules.

In the United States, two forces operate to ensure that regulations and the organizations in power do not change dramatically. One force is the **self-perpetuating activities of the groups that benefit most from the regulations.** Successful media organizations typically channel some of their profits into making certain that the rules that have allowed them to become successful continue to guide the industry. Academic observers have described this activity as "capturing" a government agency. When it involves channeling resources into achieving goodwill with government circles or among the population at large, the activity is called **public relations.** When the work involves attempts to convince government officials on specific issues, it is called **lobbying.**

Often, public relations is itself carried out through mass communication. An example is the large-scale persuasive effort that commercial television broadcasters conducted in the 1950s to halt competition for their audiences by over-the-air and cable services that charged for access to additional programming. "Save Free TV" was the rallying cry that could be read and heard nationwide across several media. The hope was that rank-and-file Americans would pressure their elected representatives to quash any regulations that would encourage alternatives to broadcast television.[12]

Lobbying is a narrower and more direct activity. Nearly every U.S. media industry maintains a lobbying effort, most of which takes place at the federal level, in Washington, D.C. Sometimes, state and local lobbying is also necessary.

TALKING POINT 3.5   Movies, the Government, and World War II

Direct government control over entertainment has been rare in the United States. During World War II, however, the U.S. government, through its Office of War Information (OWI), exercised immense control over the images Americans received at their local theaters.

Technically, the OWI's Bureau of Motion Pictures was just a liaison office with the Hollywood studios. In practice, though, Hollywood's producers paid strict attention to the guidelines, since they supported using celluloid to help win the war at home and abroad. They found their instructions in a thick manual distributed in August 1942. Called *The Government Information Manual for the Motion Picture,* it advocated the casual insertion of a constructive "war message" in a picture whenever possible. For example:

> At every opportunity, naturally and inconspicuously, show people making small sacrifices for victory — making them voluntarily, cheerfully and because of the people's own sense of responsibility, not because of any laws. For example, show people bringing their own sugar when invited out to dinner, carrying their own parcels when shopping, traveling on planes or trains with light luggage, uncomplainingly giving up seats for servicemen or others traveling on war priorities; show persons accepting dimout restrictions, tire and gas rationing cheerfully, show well-dressed persons, obviously car owners, riding in crowded buses and streetcars.
>
> In crowds unostentatiously show a few wounded men. Prepare people but do not alarm them against the casualties to come. . . . Show colored soldiers in crowd scenes; occasionally colored officers. Stress our national unity by using names of foreign extraction, showing foreign types in the services.

The OWI suggested that each filmmaker ask himself seven questions before undertaking a movie, especially, "Will this picture help win the war?" Thinking of the office and its guidelines makes viewing all sorts of movies made from late 1942 through 1945 especially interesting.

SOURCE: Richard R. Lingeman, *Don't You Know There's a War Going On?* (New York: Putnam; 1970), pp. 221–222.

We have already seen the power of lobbyists in defining the regulatory position of cable television. Another example is the attempt by the Direct Marketing Association to exclude out-of-state catalog goods from being taxed. Prior to 1980, taxes had not been levied. However, with the boom of the catalog business in the 1980s, local merchants, who must charge state tax because they are located in the state, began to lose business to catalog firms. When these merchants tried to change the law, direct marketers and their allies worked to persuade legislators in several states not to impose taxes on goods bought by citizens of those states from mail-order firms outside their boundaries. As of the mid-1990s, they have remained successful in holding back taxation that would harm most of their business.

The second force operating to ensure the stability of fundamental operating principles for U.S. media is the logic of the American judicial system. It places high value on rules of the past, or **precedents,** established by English common law, the U.S. Constitution, and U.S. court decisions. An Expression for this approach is well known in legal circles: *stare decises et nonquieta movere,* which means "to stand by past decisions and not disturb things at rest." In other words, a judge should resolve current problems in the same manner, or along similar lines, as other problems were resolved in the past.[13] This approach, like lobbying and public relations, guides governments toward behavior that is conservative, predictable, and imbued with support for the business of media.

Such predictability means governments typically set conditions for the operation of mass media industries that producers can work into their approaches to content. Governments can therefore become minor considerations in producers' day-to-day profit-and-loss decisions. Of course, discontented groups may launch challenges to the regulatory status quo. Those benefiting from it will then have to use public relations, lobbying, or the courts — or all three — to defend their traditional claims on the authorities' resources.

Lobbying, public relations, and legal efforts for a production firm are usually carried out by personnel or organizations that specialize in dealing with governments. Their contentions with regulators and others who want to change things may stretch over a period of several months or even years. These defensive approaches hold a number of advantages for production firms with regulatory challenges before them.

First, the approaches give production firms maximum opportunity to redirect rule making in their favor. Second, people involved in the actual creation of mass media material by and large continue along traditional paths, though sometimes a few government-pleasing modifications are engineered by the firms' most important policymakers. Third, if the rules are against the production firm, the approaches provide the time the firm's policymakers need to plot long-term changes that conform to the rules and to integrate them into the organization's creative activities with as few disruptions as possible.

The ability of mass media production firms to integrate regulators' expectations into the fabric of decision making about content is generally a stable element in the production process. Less predictable, and therefore more crucial, subjects in daily production decisions are the expectations and activities of organizations that can withhold or provide critical resources to support individual products on a daily basis. It is to the influence of these organizations — those who take on the client power role — that we turn in Chapter 4.

CONSIDER THIS

1. What might be some dangers to U.S. society if the federal or state government had taken on both the "authority" and "client" power role in the media system?

2. A requirement instituted in 1927 continues to hold that the major holders of a U.S. broadcast license be U.S. citizens. Do you think this is still a good idea? Why or why not?

3. Go to a major library and browse through the collection of old magazines from the nineteenth and early twentieth centuries. The articles and ads will give a fascinating sense of a bygone era. Comparisons with contemporary ads will, in addition, see our own era in a new light.

NOTES

1. Among the sources for the facts presented in this chapter are J. Herbert Altschull, *Agents of Power: The Role of the News Media in Human Affairs* (New York: Longman, 1983); Edwin Emery and Michael Emery, *The Press and America* (Englewood Cliffs, NJ: 1978); Daniel Pope, *The Making of Modern Advertising* (New York: Basic Books, 1983); Erik Barnouw, *The Sponsor* (New York: Oxford University Press, 1978) and *A Tower in Babel* (New York: Oxford University Press, 1968); Garth Jowett, *Film: The Democratic Art* (Boston: Little, Brown, 1976); Christopher H. Sterling, *Stay Tuned: A Concise History of Broadcasting* (Belmont, CA: 1990); and Joseph Dominick, Barry Sherman, and Gary Copeland, *Broadcasting/Cable and Beyond* (New York: McGraw-Hill, 1990).

2. Quoted in Altschull, p. 11.

3. Quoted in Altschull, p. 24.

4. Quoted in Altschull, p. 23.

5. Quoted in Emery and Emery, p. 97.

6. Quoted in Emery and Emery, p. 95.

7. Quoted in Emery and Emery, p. 96.

8. Quoted in Emery and Emery, p. 97.

9. See Albert E. Smith with Phil A. Koary, *Two Reels and a Crank* (Garden City, NY: Doubleday, 1952).

10. Jowett, p. 119.

11. Edmund Andrews, "Communications Reshaped: The Overhaul," *New York Times,* February 2, 1996, p. A-1.

12. Erik Barnouw, *The Image Empire* (New York: Oxford University Press, 1970), pp. 246–247.

13. Don R. Pember, *Mass Media Law* (Dubuque, IA: William C. Brown, 1977, pp. 3–4.

CHAPTER 4

Media Support
Paying the Piper, Calling the Tune

This chapter

- discusses the importance of the "client" power role.
- shows how production firms get money to create movies, magazines, books, television shows, and so on.
- reviews the importance of the advertising industry, which provides the dominant support of media in the United States.

"Money talks." Perhaps this well-worn phrase is the best way to explain this chapter's subtitle. The relationship mass media production organizations (film studios, book publishers, newspaper firms) have with their client organizations is typically the most important relationship they maintain with their environment. Of course, all the power roles discussed in Chapter 3 influence the output of producers. Authorities are unquestionably crucial, because, as we saw in the previous chapter, they set the basic terms under which all mass media in the society operate. Once the most basic of the authorities' conditions are set, however, interactions between clients and producers take over as the most pivotal interorganizational forces shaping mass media materials.

The reason for this contention lies in what client organizations do. Recall that clients make purchases in support of existing products before these products reach the public. Clients help producers accomplish certain activities. For example, advertisers purchase space in newspapers and magazines in the hope that readers will buy their products. Bookstores purchase books from publishers with the aim of retailing them for a profit. Record stores buy discs and tapes to sell profitably to the public.

In acting as clients, these organizations provide production firms with the cash flow that is most directly responsible for their survival. Examination of the producer-client relationship shows that while the phrase "money talks" may be a rough indicator of clients' importance to producers, a better way to describe it is that money starts a key interorganizational conversation. That is, influence in the producer-client relationship runs both ways—from producers to clients as well as from clients to producers. Also, the influence runs deep, extending even to the decision-making structures of production organizations and to the images producer and client executives hold of their audiences.

THE VARIETY OF PRODUCER-CLIENT RELATIONSHIPS

The examples of clients to be found in the newspaper, magazine, book publishing, and record industries show that there is no uniformity in the kinds of organizations that take on the client role. In fact, even within an industry, one sector may have different kinds of patrons from another sector. Consider the book industry. Although bookstores as a broad class are important to the solvency of many publishers, there are also many publishers that rarely turn to bookstores as key monetary supporters of their products' public release. For example, libraries are crucial to publishers of certain technical monographs, digests, encyclopedias, and other volumes. By contrast, school boards and schools are essential in the elementary and high school ("el-hi") market.

The complexity does not stop there. Even within a sector of an industry, different kinds of clients may exist, and they may hold different levels of importance. Trade book publishers with bookstores as their major clients may also sell a fair amount to public libraries. Similarly, children's book publishers that aim mostly at the library market may, at times, find that stores are also profitable clients for some titles.

It is useful, then, to speak of **primary** and **secondary** producer-client relationships. A client is primary in a producer's scheme of things if it contributes more than any other type of client to the solvency of the production firm. For example, if libraries contribute more than bookstores to the profits of a particular publisher, libraries are the primary and bookstores the secondary client organizations for that publisher.

As the preceding examples suggest, clients become supporters of mass media producers with the aim of using them to carry out other activities. In the United States, these activities relate most often to one of three forms: exhibition, distribution, and advertising. In the general trade sector of book publishing, the primary clients are exhibitors (stores). The mainstream U.S. movie industry is different. There, a group of major distributors, rather than exhibitors (the theaters), take on the primary client role.

Clients in the Movie Industry

The "majors" are eight powerful distribution firms — Sony Pictures, Paramount, 20th Century Fox, MGM-UA, Universal, Warner Brothers, New Line, and Buena Vista (Disney) — that are owned by movie production firms. The majors control about 90% of Hollywood's product that ends up in American movie theaters.[1] Drawing on money made on previous films and on long-term bank financing arrangements, the major distributors provide cash for making films to their own production firms. Other revenues used by production firms to make movies come from two other types of distribution subsidiaries: those that direct product to theaters in foreign countries and those that direct films to the homevideo market, cable television, and broadcast television markets.

The high cost of distributing movies to the mainstream market typically means that independent production companies (those that do not own distribution firms) must persuade one of the majors to carry their output if they wish to reach huge audiences. Such arrangements can benefit both parties. A major might be interested in taking on an independently produced movie because it adds to the inventory the distributor will have for theaters, while it frees the major's parent company from the high cost of making a greater number of its own films in a given year. Moreover, the cut of the box office gross the distributor receives for the film is substantial, typically around 47%.[2]

For their part, independent producers forego this large royalty for the privilege of plugging into the most powerful and efficient method of theatrical distribution available. In addition, the distributor often finances a portion of the film for a higher cut of the profits. The distributor's power as a client is frequently indirect. When a bank finds out that a major has agreed to carry a film by an independent producer, the film's success becomes more plausible and the bank is more willing to extend credit for making the film.

Advertisers as Clients

The third form of media clients — advertising — is without question the most pervasive form in the United States. Advertising involves payment for calling attention to a product, service, or need. Whether the subject is Coca-Cola, a cleaning store, or the United Way, the goal of advertising is straightforward: to persuade people to purchase or otherwise support the product, service, or need.

Advertising is itself a media production activity. In fact, it is sometimes carried out by itself, separate from other kinds of mass media materials. Mass-produced billboards, handbills, catalogs, audio cassettes, records — even video cassettes — are part of myriad media that carry only advertising messages. At the same time, advertisers find it useful to place their announcements alongside material that does not carry overtly persuasive intent, material such as newspaper and magazine articles, radio programs, and television shows. Their

TABLE 4.1 NATIONAL ADVERTISING SPENDING BY MAJOR MEDIUM, 1994

Category	Total Spending (in millions)	Percent of Spending Represented by Top 100 Advertisers
Magazine	8,463.0	44
Sunday magazine	999.9	41
Newspaper	11,744.6	23
Outdoor (billboard)	909.8	32
Network TV	11,893.2	77
Spot TV	12,718.8	38
Syndicated TV	2,358.1	67
Cable TV networks	2,970.2	57
Network radio	599.8	56
Spot radio	1,272.3	28

SOURCE: Advertising Age, *September 27, 1995, p. 62.*

This table gives a snapshot view of the comparative value different mass media hold for advertisers trying to reach audiences across the United States. It also shows how critical the 100 leading national advertisers are to national media spending.

These figures represent spending to reach nationwide audiences, not ad spending confined to local areas. **Syndicated** TV deals are advertisements on particular TV or radio programs that are placed individually on stations around the country, rather than through a single network buy. If a company creates a show, gets an advertiser to sponsor it, and then places the program on stations around the country that may show it at different times, it is considered a syndicated TV deal.

Spot purchases are national purchases made during network programming as a result of deals with local station representatives, not through TV or radio networks. Time for spot ads exists because networks typically allow their affiliates to sell a few minutes an hour to advertisers during network programming. Some advertisers may buy spot ads because they want to advertise in just a few localities, not on the entire network. For example, a supermarket chain might get involved in a spot deal because it wants to advertise during prime time, but only in the five cities in which it has stores.

hope is that people using these media will also attend to the commercial messages and act favorably in response to them.

Clearly, then, advertisers' client relationships with mass media production firms are a direct outgrowth of their desire to reach people who may respond favorably to their messages. In 1994, the 100 leading companies in U.S. advertising spent an estimated $42.7 billion on this activity. Most of that money was used to purchase time or space among attractive nonadvertising material on broadcast television, on radio, in magazines, or in newspapers. For example, in the same year, the twenty-five top newspaper advertisers spent $2.5 billion, the twenty-five top magazine advertisers, $2.6 billion; the twenty-five top network radio advertisers, $348 million; and the twenty-five top network TV advertisers, a little over $5.9 billion.[3]

These numbers do not reflect the thousands of companies that spent much smaller amounts supporting media through advertising. Still, it is worth paying attention to the largest mass media customers, because the amounts they spend may be of particular significance to the survival of production firms within a media industry, or even to the health of the industry as a whole. It is difficult for broadcast television executives to ignore Philip Morris, for example, which spent about $2.4 billion on advertising in 1994, 17% of it on broadcast network TV and 10% on local stations. Similarly, newspaper executives might find it difficult not to consider the May Department Stores Company, which placed about 76% of its $418 million ad budget in that medium. Even more difficult to ignore are classes of advertisers — food firms, airlines, tobacco companies, and the like — that pack a lot of financial clout in certain mass media industries. For example, only five department stores (May, RH Macy, Sears, Campeau, and Dayton Hudson) together contributed about $1.6 billion to newspaper coffers in 1994. And just four auto companies (General Motors, Ford, Chrysler, and Toyota) provided about $1.1 billion of support to magazines in the form of advertising space purchases.[4]

Less obvious, but even more concentrated in their ability to direct the flow of cash to mass media, are the leading advertising agencies that service the national advertisers. These organizations clarify, crystallize — even create — the advertising plans for their clients. They produce advertising material based on these plans, purchase media space or time for the material, and evaluate the success of their efforts with the aid of market research firms (which they sometimes own). In the process, they direct hundreds of millions of dollars toward, or away from, various mass media industries. In 1988, fourteen advertising agencies each paid over $1 billion to various American mass media firms for carrying their commercial announcements. The range of manufacturers whose cash the agencies controlled was quite broad. For example, Young and Rubicam, with $1.8 billion in ad placement billings, operated in support of firms as diverse as Bell Atlantic, Kodak, Nestle, Ford Dealers Association, National Yellow Pages, Connecticut Mutual, Health and Tennis Corporation, and Cellular One. The agency allocated 34% of its billings to network television, 23% to local ("spot") television, 5% to radio, 14% to consumer magazines, 6% to newspapers, 6% to direct response (mail order) advertising, and 3% to cable television. The rest went to business publications, medical journals, farm periodicals, billboards, and transit advertising. Other agency leaders doled out money in similar proportions.[5]

The interconnection of advertisers, advertising agencies, and market research firms in supporting the production of newspapers, magazines, television programs, and other mass media material indicates that when it comes to advertising, the client can be seen as an industry in itself, rather than a single type of organization. While advertisers put up the money to proclaim their products or services, ad agencies often set the agenda for using the funds. Small wonder, then, that many production firm executives see the major advertising agencies collectively as the key forces to influence for support.

TABLE 4.2 TOP ADVERTISERS IN FOUR MEDIA, 1994

	Dollars (in Millions)
Network Television	
Procter & Gamble	880.9
General Motors Corp.	509.4
Philip Morris Cos.	424.3
Pepsico	349.6
Ford Motor Co.	349.0
Newspapers	
Federated Department Stores	299.8
May Department Stores Co.	279.2
Circuit City Stores	239.3
Dayton Hudson Corp.	137.1
Magazines	
General Motors Corp.	379.5
Philip Morris Cos.	294.0
Ford Motor Co.	241.9
Proctor & Gamble	197.3
Chrysler Corp.	148.9
Outdoor (Billboards and Related Activities)	
Philip Morris Cos.	68.6
B.A.T. Industries PLC	36.7
RJR Nabisco	19.3
McDonald's Corp.	18.0
Anheuser-Busch Cos.	16.2

SOURCE: Advertising Age, *September 27, 1995.*

The largest producers and sellers of consumer goods are often the largest advertisers. Marketers may use different mass media for different purposes. Note, for example, that three of the top five outdoor advertisers are firms that create and sell cigarettes.

Don Lachowski, a vice-president of sales at Turner Broadcasting System, reflected this idea somewhat bitterly in 1980, when his company's advertising-based cable TV channel was struggling for recognition and support from Madison Avenue. Speaking to a group of advertising industry executives, Lachowski complained that major advertising agencies had been deliberately understating the movement of audiences to cable from broadcast TV because they did not want to change their media buying patterns. The prevalent attitude, he said, had been that "if we ignore it [cable as well as other new technologies] and pretend it doesn't exist, maybe it will go away."[6]

THE PRODUCER-CLIENT RELATIONSHIP
AND MASS MEDIA MATERIAL

Lachowski's concern about the flow of advertising dollars into the cable TV industry points to the clearest influence of the producer-client relationship on mass media content. Simply, if there is no money to create the material, it will not be created. Lachowski's comments came at a point in cable TV's history when the advertising industry was still unsure of how broad and deep a commitment it was willing to make to the medium. Things have changed since then; in 1994, the top 100 advertisers spent $1.69 billion on cable TV commercials, many times the amount of a decade earlier.[7]

Still, the general tension Lachowski was addressing is not unusual. Every year, book publishers, magazine publishers, record producers, and newspaper publishers go out of business because not enough clients exist to support them. Once in a while, entire niches within mass media industries see their client resources dry up. Overall, though, many mass media producers thrive. It is to the influence of the producer-client relationship on mass media output that we now turn.

The Relationship as a Communication System

As a first step, it is useful to learn what it means to talk about a relationship between production and client firms within a mass media industry. Throughout this book, dealings between organizations are described as exchanges between faceless entities. Here, however, it pays to be more systematic about this point, because it bears strongly on the knowledge of how producer-client links operate in the media on a daily basis.

The key to understanding the influence of the producer-client relationship lies in seeing it as a communication system involving **boundary personnel** from the client and production organizations in a mass media industry. Boundary personnel are workers who communicate with workers in companies other than their own.

To understand the function of the communication system in each organization in the relationship, consider sociologist Howard Aldrich's proposition about executives and resources. The major goals of organizational leaders, Aldrich said, "are avoiding dependence on other [organizations] and making others dependent on one's own organization."[8] For planners in both production firms and client firms, this means dispatching people to find out about other organizations in the environment so that concerns about resources can be identified and dealt with successfully.

Mass media production firm executives worry particularly about their firms' primary clients because they affect the solvency of the production firm directly. These clients become what sociologist William Evan has called **normative reference organizations.**[9] That is, they become entities that production executives see as generating requirements they must contend with if they are to bring in the cash necessary for survival. The clients' needs depend on the kind of client organizations involved. Sometimes their overall goal is the profitable retailing of products, as with book or record stores. Other times the goal is to reach people who will respond favorably to certain messages, as with advertisers.

To learn of specific client aims, and to help shape them, production firms assign salespeople, marketing executives, and other employees the task of contacting people in client firms. Client firms, in turn, assign people to work with production firm representatives in order to clarify client needs. In view of the desire of production executives for predictable cash flow, we would expect that their boundary personnel will use talks with their counterparts in the client firms to negotiate expectations about output that will be profitable for the production firms.

TABLE 4.3 THE MAY DEPARTMENT STORES COMPANY'S MEDIA SPENDING

Medium	Ad Spending (Thousands of Dollars)
Magazines	4,475
Sunday magazines	8,566
Newspapers	317,229
Outdoor	131
Network TV	20,487
Spot TV	14,142
Syndicated TV	3,853
Cable TV networks	1,395
Network radio	325
Spot Radio	5,694
Total	**376,295**

SOURCE: Advertising Age, *September 27, 1995, p. 54.*

Department stores tend to advertise locally, where their stores are, and not nationally. Therefore, they are important clients for local advertising media, particularly newspapers, as this chart shows. The May Department Stores Company, the case in point, is based in St. Louis. It owns different chains in cities around the country, from L. S. Ayres in Indianapolis to Foley's in Denver.

Note that these data, adapted from *Advertising Age,* break out only certain media and not others. For example, not listed here are monies spent for direct mail letters, catalogs, and business publications, to name a few places ad monies can go. May Department Stores spent 10% of its approximately $418 million ad budget on these "unmeasured" media and 90% on the above media.

At the same time, we would assume that client executives would instruct their boundary personnel to make it clear that they expect certain sorts of performance from the production firm that will be profitable for the client organizations. The influence of the producer-client relationship, then, would flow from the continual interactions of the boundary people who make up the relationship. The influence would go in both directions; each side would negotiate its expectations of the other.

Two important insights into the producer-client relationship derive from the idea that the relationship is continually being created:

- Knowing the history of a producer-client relationship is relevant to understanding its current situation.
- Every relationship involving one production and one client organization must necessarily be different from relationships involving any other producer-client pair. This is because the perceptions of a given organization's executives on their environment will be at least somewhat different from the perceptions of executives in other organizations. The differences are simply due to the different people involved, their history together, the tradition of their organization, and the history of their organization's interactions with other organizations.

Yet it would be incorrect to make too much of the differences between the relationships that involve the same types of established producers and the same kinds of established clients in a particular area of an industry. Although there are differences among the producer-client relationships within an industry's niche, there are also important similarities, which stem from organizations' needs to compete for the same resources. Exploring these similarities leads to useful generalizations about the influence of the producer-client relationship over the creation of mass media content.

SETTING LIMITS FOR THE PRODUCTION FIRM'S ACTIVITIES

The producer-client relationship limits what a mass media production firm can do in its day-to-day activities. The limits affect the production firm in three broad areas:

The kinds of people who are the targets of the company's media output

The frequency at which the material is released to those people

The amount it costs to produce and release the material

These limits are set as a result of competition between producers over the resources (usually money) that clients can provide. The number of clients and the amount of money they want to devote to mass media are limited at any point in time. In exchange for spending their money, clients want the media they support to provide them with certain benefits. For instance, a bookstore chain wants to be confident that it will sell the copies of a book about antiques it ordered. Or, an airline that purchases space in a newspaper's twice-weekly "business review" section to promote lower fares wants to feel secure that the cost of the ads will be more than regained by the number of seats booked because of the ad.

In the case of the antiques book publisher, the satisfaction of bookstore chains with the speed and number of sales determines whether the company can continue to target antiques collectors through that type of outlet. Response from the bookstore chains also determines how many new titles about antiques the publisher can profitably turn out each year, as well as how much it should expect to charge for each title.

The cases of the newspaper and the airline differ in that the newspaper will probably not cease publication if the airline withdraws future advertising. Nevertheless, if all airlines decide to pull their ads, and if other travel-related firms follow, the monetary shortfall may lead the paper to institute strategies to attract business travelers to their business section. Alternatively, it may give up on getting travel clients and look to other markets for support, such as producers of copying machines and computers. If it cannot convince enough advertisers that it is meeting their needs, the newspaper may need to cut the section's frequency to once a week or implement other measures that would make the section profitable for the newspaper despite the decrease in advertising revenues.

The newspaper example highlights the value of a **resource-rich** environment to a production firm. A resource-rich environment is one that offers a large number or variety of interchangeable elements that can help a producer survive. When executives in a newspaper firm confront a large number or variety of potential clients interested in a broad range of publics, they find it a lot easier to support their venture than when this diversity is absent. Even facing such an environment, though, production firm executives still have to present clients with products that yield the benefits they are seeking at a price they are willing to pay.

For example, if the people reached by a media production firm begin to be of no interest to clients, the firm will have to fold its operation. Similarly, if the cost of reaching a target audience begins to be considered too high by relevant clients, the producers will not be able to continue their approach. Too, if the producer can interest only a few clients to sustain a frequent production of material for a target audience, the producer will have to release its material less often.

Even when the environment is relatively rich, a production firm may feel compelled to court clients. Poor relationships with clients may lead many firms to look for other options, which may encourage more competition with the production firm and lead the firm to experience a scarce resource situation. This situation befell the *Philadelphia Inquirer* newspaper in the early 1990s. Advertising agencies, which had often accused the prestigious regional daily of not paying attention to their needs, began to drop their sponsorship as the economy took a downturn.

In 1991, the director of media services for a local ad agency noted the change: "Two years ago, the *Inquirer* had a very definite mentality of 'We're the only game in town, and if you don't like it, tough.' They woke up because of the economic situation. They're getting hurt tremendously in retail lineage, and classified and real estate are down."[10]

"Waking up" meant trying to be more helpful and accommodating to advertising agencies. The *Inquirer* simplified its ad rate charges and assigned a sales manager to be the contact person for each of the top twenty agencies it deals with. It also assigned someone to the new post of manager of agency relations to answer clients' marketing and research questions. Moreover, it began a hotline and a quarterly newsletter to acquaint ad people with new sections of the paper they might want to sponsor and new market research findings that might help them get new business.

There are times when even the kinds of activities the *Inquirer* implemented do not hold clients. Basic client demands may actually change to the point that they can no longer support certain kinds of mass media. This loss of support, by extension, can affect the kinds of mass materials produced.

THE CASE OF MAGAZINES

The link between changing client demands and mass media output can be illustrated by looking at changes in the U.S. consumer magazine industry. **Consumer magazines** are the segment of the magazine industry aimed at the general reading public. "They are called consumer magazines because their readers buy and consume products and services that are sold at retail and may be advertised in those magazines."[11]

Advertising is a crucial vehicle of support in the great majority of these magazines, although an increasing amount of money is earned through reader subscriptions and, sometimes, newsstand sales. Consumer magazines generally derive about half their revenues from advertising and half from readers. Judging by the number of consumer magazines in the United States, the environment for supporting this activity is rich indeed. According to the editorial department at *Folio,* a trade magazine for magazine publishers, about 3,300 magazines were distributed in the United States in 1992.[12] To be considered a consumer magazine by *Folio*'s staff, a publication must be aimed at nonbusiness users, be released at least three times a year, have a circulation of at least 3,000, and contain at least sixteen pages of editorial (as opposed to advertising) matter.

The fields of interest of consumer magazines are diverse — from "girlie" magazines to periodicals about boxing, wrestling, and karate; to those dealing with sewing and crafts; to news magazines. Still, the environment for support by advertisers and readers is not unlimited. *Folio* reports that only 10% of the approximately 300 magazines started each year in the late 1970s survived a year.[13]

The Move to Specialization

If one trend could be said to encompass the consumer periodical area in the early 1990s, it would be the increased movement toward specialization in subject matter and readership. This trend is clearly associated with the movement of advertisers away from supporting large general interest magazines from the mid-1960s through the 1970s.[14]

Up until that time, consumer magazines with large, heterogeneous readerships (such as *Life, Look, Coronet,* the *Saturday Evening Post*) had been very attractive to national advertisers. Magazine publishing firms had tried to build huge circulations by offering readers very low subscription rates. Advertisers were satisfied with this situation, because it allowed them to use just a number of magazines to reach the kinds of widespread audiences that only network radio could duplicate — and radio could not carry pictures.

To satisfy producers and clients, magazine circulation figures were systematically audited by an independent agency, the Audit Bureau of Circulation (ABC). In addition, to facilitate cost comparison of two periodicals, both parties used an efficiency measure, **cost per thousand** (CPM). CPM is the price an advertiser pays to reach 1,000 people through a full-page, black-and-white ad.

With the advent of television, however, the situation changed. By the late 1950s, 86% of all U.S. homes had at least one TV set; the number jumped to 93% in 1965.[15] Advertisers, attracted to the audiovisual capabilities of TV, realized that the new medium reached basically the same heterogeneous audience as the general consumer magazines, and at about the same CPM. This was the beginning of the end for these periodicals, despite their large readerships. For example, the 1963 *Coronet* ceased publication while carrying a circulation of 3.1 million.[16] *Life, Look,* the *Saturday Evening Post,* and others also died a little before or during the 1960s.

Magazine publishing began to surge again in the late 1960s, but it was in a new relationship with advertisers. Many advertisers saw that television filled their need to reach giant, diverse segments of the population quickly. Magazine executives, recognizing that the head-on battle with TV was lost, tried to convince advertisers that certain kinds of periodicals were still worth their advertising dollars: the ones that helped them reach narrower social segments (often the wealthy) with specially tailored messages.

Magazine executives noted that quality-looking magazines could be produced much more cheaply than prime time television programs. CPMs, therefore, could be reasonable, even if subscribers numbered only in the tens of thousands. This was particularly true if the magazine passed more of its costs along to readers in subscription fees. In addition, magazine executives contended that passing more costs on to readers indicated that subscribers would read the magazine (and its ads) more seriously, because they had paid a significant sum to receive it.

J. W. Click and Russell Baird reflected the advertisers' point of view on this trend: "The efficiency of carrying advertising within a specialized area to persons obviously interested in that activity appeals to advertisers catering to such an area and makes these magazines ideal media for their ads at lower overall cost and with minimal waste circulation."[17]

Rethinking Audience Research

Many magazine executives, recognizing the needs of advertisers in a TV age, took the initiative to establish a new relationship with their clients based on a new perspective. As a result, the advertising industry supported special interest consumer magazines that could prove the worth of their readership, and this area of the business grew tremendously. From *Psychology Today, Essence,* and *National Lampoon* to *Smithsonian, Money,* and *Omni,* the 1970s saw magazines with circulations in the hundreds of thousands (instead of the several millions) get strong support on Madison Avenue. As the key to this producer-client relationship became efficient specialization, leading magazine publishing firms, advertising agencies, and the Magazine Publishers Association began to devise more studies and measures that reflected the value of a magazine to sponsors. Magazine executives wanted to present their periodicals to advertising agency people as better buys than other periodicals or other media (especially television). Agency executives, for their part, wanted to justify their media-buying decisions in quantitative, "scientific" terms that would be difficult for their bosses to question.

Consequently, during the 1970s and 1980s, both parties joined forces to develop various measures that go beyond circulation and CPM to chart various characteristics of their readers. Many magazine executives decided they had to tell potential advertisers such facts as how many children their readers have, how many cars they own, how often they take vacations, sometimes even what wines they buy. The emphasis on targeting specific readers that advertisers want also led publishers to sharpen and focus their editorial product.

George Green, president of *The New Yorker,* noted the change this way: "Magazines today are often designed around the advertising, particularly with specialized magazines. [Research] studies are getting so specific that you can

TABLE 4.4 LEADING MAGAZINE REVENUES, 1993 (DOLLARS IN MILLIONS)

Magazine	Total	Ads	Subscribers	Newstand
1. *TV Guide*	$997	$322	$399	$246
2. *People*	722	367	157	198
3. *Time*	614	344	243	27
4. *Sports Illustrated*	546	302	228	16
5. *Reader's Digest*	500	131	346	23
6. *Parade*	411	411	0	0
7. *Newsweek*	408	260	123	25
8. *Better Homes & Gardens*	321	189	121	11
9. *Good Housekeeping*	303	207	66	30
10. *PC Magazine*	300	250	39	11
11. *U.S. News & World Report*	298	202	88	8
12. *Business Week*	263	217	40	6
13. *Family Circle*	247	163	34	50
14. *National Enquirer*	235	28	19	188
15. *Ladies Home Journal*	234	128	88	18
16. *Woman's Day*	227	146	27	54
17. *Forbes*	218	174	39	5
18. *Cosmopolitan*	217	141	16	60
19. *National Geographic*	215	47	168	0
20. *Star Magazine*	197	16	14	167

SOURCE: Advertising Age, *January 2, 1995, p. 15.*

In this table, total revenues of a magazine equal money from advertisers plus money from subscribers plus money from newsstand sales.

While many magazines are drawing increasing amounts of money from subscriptions and single-copy sales, a crucial part of a magazine's revenues usually still comes from advertising. Note that three of the top four periodicals (*Time, People,* and *Sports Illustrated*) are owned by Time Warner.

design magazines around readers so you can have more clearly defined target audiences for the advertisers."[18]

The Lesson Beyond Magazines

The power of clients to set the general conditions of production can be seen across media industries. In network TV, for example, journalist Les Brown claims that "programs come into being to deliver . . . [an audience] to advertisers."[19] One can see how changes in client demand over the years have influenced:

The **number and kinds** of people whom the four major commercial broadcast networks have targeted as viewers

The **amount of television time** the networks take up with their programming

The **costs** of programs that networks show at different times of the day

Similarly, in the movie industry, analysis of the relationship between the major production companies and their clients (the major distributors) reveal how financial interests of the distributors have guided studies regarding costs, audience requirements, and the number of films they should produce. Garth Jowett and James Linton conducted such a survey in the 1970s. They found that distributors' requirements led the major production firms to create "a smaller number of blockbusters (with higher production costs and larger audience requirements) rather than . . . a larger number of 'lesser' movies (with lower production costs and smaller audience requirements)."[20] With pay-per-view cable, pay cable, VCRs, video discs, and a much larger international audience, the movie industry of the 1990s has many more distribution "windows" to consider. As a result, there is a good deal of argument among production and distribution executives regarding whether it is best for their firms to pursue a strategy of primarily blockbuster, medium-cost, or low-cost releases. Nevertheless, the proposition still holds that the distributor has much say in the nature of the output.[21]

The popular recording industry stands out as a fascinating exception to this pattern of client influence. As noted earlier, record producers' primary clients are record stores. Thus, one might expect the stores to collectively exert a dominant influence on the kinds of people targeted, the approach to titles released, and the cost of each recording. By all accounts, though, radio stations and cable music outlets such as MTV and Black Entertainment Television exert the influence we have attributed to clients, even though they provide no money to the recording firms.

The reason for their clientlike clout is apparent. Traditionally, record stores have not provided people with ways to hear all the albums and singles on their shelves. Nevertheless, they expect customers to be familiar with the popular records they carry. This expectation encourages producers to publicize their output so that stores will want to carry it. Purchasing advertising time on television and radio to play all new songs would be prohibitively expensive. Popular music formats on radio allow recording company boundary personnel to do the next best thing: to persuade radio station programmers to play the songs. Records played often and widely have a better chance of being carried in record stores than those that are not. In a sense, then, stores have handed over much of their client-based influence to the radio stations.

Over the past several years, an increasing number of record stores have installed listening bars where customers wearing headphones can listen to CDs they are thinking of purchasing. Moreover, music firms are advertising some of their new CDs on cable TV networks that target their prime customers. So far, these developments do not seem to have affected the importance of radio and cable music playlists in increasing sales. This may change in the coming years.

CLIENTS AND MASS MEDIA CONTENT

Setting general limits for the production of mass media material is often only the beginning of the client system's impact. In many cases, client needs affect producers' specific decisions about the ideas presented in the material — the kinds of arguments made, the types of topics covered. Although the potential for this kind of influence exists in all kinds of producer-client relationships, it is most common when the advertiser is the client.

Direct Interference by Advertisers

Interestingly, many American media creators have contended that interference by advertisers in their work is nearly immoral. They even consider it unprofessional to create messages that blatantly attempt to help and attract advertisers. For example, the editor of the *Ladies' Home Journal* said flatly that her colleagues should not plan editorial matter (the nonadvertising matter in a magazine) to interest advertisers. She claimed that neither publishers nor major advertisers expect such interference because it detracts from the editorial credibility with which advertisers want to identify.[22]

The reality, however, is that it is difficult to find a mass media product supported by advertising that does not carry an imprint of the sponsors in its content. Moreover, a portion of that influence sometimes involves direct negotiation of editorial support for a product, service, or idea in exchange for an advertiser's commercial support.

A particularly startling example comes from the declining days of the *Saturday Evening Post.* In order to secure $400,000 of Ford automotive advertising for the periodical's October 5, 1968, issue, *Post* executive Martin Ackerman promised the client that Henry Ford would grace the cover of the issue.[23]

Advertising executives agree that such activities are uncommon among large advertisers and mainstream media. They claim that clients and producers understand that such editorial-advertising deals become obvious and weaken the credibility of a medium as both an advertising and editorial vehicle. Nevertheless, anecdotes continue to pop up about media production firms that ensure editorial coverage for an advertiser in exchange for ads. In the magazine industry, research indicates that direct advertiser influence on editorial matter is more common among trade magazines than among consumer magazines. **Trade magazines** are periodicals that target readers in particular occupations with information about their workplace.

In 1990, an article in *Folio,* a trade magazine for the magazine industry, stated that "advertising pressure on editors is the skeleton in the closet of the magazine publishing industry: Everyone knows it's there, but no one wants to talk about it." According to the article, several editors of trade periodicals admitted in private that the pressure to give in to sponsor demands to trade advertising for editorial coverage can be intense. The message to keep advertisers happy is constant, said one source: "I simply go along with the system because it's the only way I know to hold my job.[24]

This situation does not appear to have changed in the late 1990s. The reason seems to be the precarious monetary situation in which many small trade journals find themselves. As two academic observers of the trade magazine industry have noted, "Editorial integrity is much easier to maintain if the

TABLE 4.5 TOP TEN WEB PAGE ADVERTISERS

1. AT&T	$567,000
2. Netscape	556,000
3. Internet Shopping Network	329,000
4. NECX Direct	322,000
5. MasterCard	278,000
6. American Airlines	254,000
7. Microsoft	240,000
8. c/net	237,000
9. MCI	231,000
10. Sportsline	218,000

SOURCE: Advertising Age, *December 11, 1995, p. 8.*

In 1995, advertising on the World Wide Web, the graphical portion of the Internet, was beginning to develop. These are estimates of spending in the final three months of that year. The survey was conducted in October and November 1995.

[magazine] is in solid financial condition and does not need to desperately woo advertisers."[25]

Structural Influence by Advertisers

Although less startling than direct pressure, the most common impact of Madison Avenue on editorial material is **structural.** Structural influence does not involve bending to demands by individual clients. Rather, it means that creators respond to their perceptions of the client structure's needs as a whole. This typically involves creating media materials that are supportive environments for the commercial messages. The activity is driven by the idea that target audiences pay more attention to ads when they are surrounded by noncommercial matter that relates to the ads in a positive way.

Typical of this approach is the newspaper that publishes weekly articles about science and computers with the aim of attracting computer advertisers. A similar tack is the use of food recipes in the *Ladies' Home Journal* to serve as the appropriate environment for salad dressing and other components of meals.

Of course, one can argue that this kind of activity benefits readers as well as advertisers and producers. The purpose here is not to dispute that conclusion, but rather to point out that material is often created in response to sponsors, not necessarily or even primarily in response to readers.

Inserts and sections that do not tie in with advertisers' needs would likely not be created. It is difficult to imagine, for example, that a series of articles about deceptive labeling by major food brands would show up in a homemaker-oriented women's magazine that relies on food sponsorship for support. Similarly, it would be surprising if a newspaper routinely initiated stories exposing abuses in price and quality in area food stores.

Moreover, to ensure that advertisers feel comfortable with their commercial placements, editors often deter writers from directly criticizing sponsors or their product policies in articles that get printed. For example, one editor of a magazine for young parents admitted to modifying an article about toddler's shoes so as not to alienate key shoe advertisers. The original article had told parents to avoid purchasing shoes with stiff soles. This is a suggestion that pediatricians often offer but that can be construed as advising against the purchase of the sponsors' shoes. As a result, the passage was changed to say that the shoes should not be too tight, a caution the editor thought would offend no one.[26]

Censorship and Advertisers

The influence of advertisers on editorial content is not considered to be censorship. **Censorship** is the active attempt by an organization or group to suppress material that a production firm has already composed. By contrast, tailoring editorial material to create an attractive environment for ads constitutes an active, willing attempt on the part of the production firm to reflect the needs of clients. Production executives understand that "many agencies and corporations consider it an endorsement of an editorial product if you advertise in a magazine."[27]

How far a production firm is willing to shift its editorial environment to attract certain types of advertisers depends on

The nature of the firm
Its need for certain kinds of advertisers
Its perception of demands from those advertisers

For example, a newspaper's editors might not initiate a critical investigation of supermarkets in the area for fear the paper will alienate a key class of revenue-providers. At the same time, editors' commitment to journalistic professionalism may lead them to print balanced stories about supermarket problems if these stories have originated outside the papers. Moreover, through interaction between marketing and salespeople of the different firms, the newspapers may even convince the stores it is acceptable to do so.

Some producers actually go out of their way to alienate certain types of advertisers in order to maintain — even show off — their editorial points of view and readership. The politically left *Mother Jones,* the scandal-mongering *National Enquirer,* and the sexually and politically provocative *Penthouse* magazine are just a few of the many magazines that do not win the support of conservative mainstream advertisers such as General Motors, General Mills, and General Electric. They survive because they have found enough clients who find their editorial environment acceptable for reaching the audiences these media vehicles claim to reach.

THE CASE OF TELEVISION

The wide-ranging influence of the producer-advertiser relationship over the creation of mass media material can be shown through a brief sketch of that relationship's effect on prime time commercial network television in the early 1990s. Prime time network TV programming involves two levels of client relations. On one level, advertisers purchase time during shows on the four major networks — ABC, CBS, Fox, and NBC. On the other level, the networks use much of the money to support production firms that create programs, which become the building blocks of the networks' schedules.

The Importance of Ratings

The influence of advertisers occurs on both levels. To understand how, one need only begin with that basic viewership gauge, the Nielsen ratings. Over the years, broadcasters and advertisers have encouraged the development of Nielsen measurement categories that directly reflect the specific marketing concerns of sponsors. During TV's first two decades, companies that bought time on TV were interested almost exclusively in attracting huge numbers of people to their commercials. In the 1970s, their goals in reaching TV audiences began to shift toward targeting certain large segments within the TV audience, especially women or men aged 18 to 49. The 1980s saw an insistence by marketers on knowing more precisely than before how and when those age and gender segments watched TV. Moreover, the four networks, feeling competition from cable TV, home video, and independent stations, were increasingly eager to show advertisers that they could meet advertiser's needs for reaching huge, but well-understood, audiences.

As noted in Chapter 5, Nielsen and a few competitors have been working hard to create instruments that will give marketers a wide variety of information about TV viewers. At the present stage of ratings technology, though, standard Nielsen reports list findings on just a few basic categories: the number of viewers at any particular moment and their age and sex. These data are sold to advertisers, ad agencies, and networks and become the basis for advertiser-network negotiations over the cost of air time. These negotiations affect not only the profits of each network but also the amount of money that networks can pay production firms for programs.

The Importance of Time Periods

Network television is often the medium of choice for advertisers trying to reach tens of millions of people at a time. As a result, the number of viewers a network reaches with its shows is extremely important to TV advertisers and the networks. Both groups have tended to make capturing extended blocks of viewers' time, rather than winning a half-hour slot here and there, an important criterion for network success. Winning the year in a time block (whether morning, afternoon, evening, or late night) means being able to charge substantially more for commercials during that block at the start of the next year.

For many national advertisers, however, the age and sex of viewers during these time blocks are also very important. The most attractive target has been 18- to 49-year-olds, because they hold more discretionary spending money than younger and older people. **Prime time** — the 8:00 – 11:00 P.M. block that is generally the most popular viewing period — presents the networks with the best opportunity to reach 18- to 49-year-olds, because most of them are home from work during these hours. Consequently, each network's executives try to create a prime time schedule that will attract the largest possible number of households while they try to grab the highest percentage of 18- to 49-year-olds of the three networks.

Programming to Win

Explaining how network executives try to program to win reveals to a considerable extent the shape and content of the prime time schedule. For example, with the aim of "winning the night," ABC, CBS, Fox, and NBC programmers set up their schedules to maximize audience flow from one show to the next. How they did so differed according to the advertisers they wanted to serve. Fox, a network that received its sustenance from clients interested in reaching young adults, scheduled programs aimed at these groups beginning at 8:00 P.M., the start of prime time.

ABC, CBS, and NBC executives shifted their programming strategies during the 1990s in response to competition over advertisers from Fox as well as to what they saw as viewers' changing habits. In 1990, the Big Three networks were still following a longtime pattern of placing programs designed to lure both children and their parents, because children were thought to control the set during prime time. After 9:00 P.M., they would schedule shows more "adult" in theme, because by that time many children were considered to have relinquished set control to parents.

In the mid-1990s, however, the children-to-parents strategy changed. The networks began to worry that they were alienating people aged 20 to 30 without TV-watching children by starting off with "family" fare at the start of prime. These twenty-somethings, or Generation-Xers (as marketers call them), were becoming increasingly important to advertisers; ABC, CBS, and NBC executives worried that Fox might grab them — and the ad money that followed — at 8:00 P.M. Moreover, network research found that more and more homes were using several TV sets during prime time; children might be viewing videos or cable channels while parents were watching the broadcast networks.

As a result, the Big Three began to air *Friends, Mad About You,* and other series clearly aimed at twenty-somethings, not families, at the start of their evening blocks. They scheduled family-oriented programs primarily on Friday and Saturday evenings, when twenty-somethings were not as likely to be near the sets. But the effects of the Big Three networks' rethinking of prime time strategies did not end there. The implications of their programming shifts were not lost on executives of cable services, who were more than willing to pick up advertisers aiming at the audiences that ABC, CBS, Fox, and NBC were leaving behind. For example, the Nickelodeon children's service made it clear that it would beef up its family programming at the 8:00 hour. Similarly, A&E and Discovery, which aim their shows at the older end of the 18–49 spectrum, reminded advertisers and their audiences that they were the place for people who felt deserted by the broadcast networks.

In the late 1990s, the prime time approaches of TV networks increasingly vary, depending on the advertisers they think they need and can attract. Whatever basic programming strategy is chosen, the entire evening schedule is set up to maintain an overall tone that encourages audience flow across time periods. For example, a network might schedule an evening of situation comedies, or it might run sitcoms until 10:00 P.M. and then move on to dramatic fare in its last prime time hour.

Because of advertiser interest in 18- to 49-year-olds, with a skew toward the lower end of that range, the executives choose programs they believe, or determine through research, will primarily attract that group. **Counterprogramming** may occur if a competitor is stubbornly successful at holding on to one segment of the desired audience. For instance, when ABC uses a football game on Monday evening to attract a large percentage of 18- to 49-year-old males, CBS and NBC sometimes counterprogram with "women's" movies and series to lure 18- to 49-year-old females and advertisers interested in them.

CBS was also involved in a different sort of counterprogramming strategy in the late 1980s. The network found that it was not competing well for the most desirable slice of the 18- to 49-year-old segment — those at the younger end. As a result, instead of trying harder, network strategists began to tout the importance of 45- to 55-year-olds to advertisers and to skew their program buys in that area.

Ad people were not convinced that the older audience offered as good a target as the younger one, however, and CBS marketers were unable to change their minds. CBS found itself suffering monetarily under the weight of relatively low ratings and an undesirably old audience. In the mid-1990s, the network desperately tried to change its image and lure age groups that would please more TV advertisers.[28]

The meaning of this example should be clear: Equally important as the material ABC, CBS, Fox, and NBC schedule during prime time is the material the networks have learned not to schedule as a response to their clients' requirements. Programs aimed exclusively at youngsters are unacceptable, as are programs for people over 60. The reason is that the networks can attract much more advertising money during prime time by luring 18- to 49-year-olds. Similarly, programs that are not upbeat, or are too provocative or controversial, are frowned upon by network executives, because most advertisers feel that such programs do not provide the best environment for their commercials. Program production executives have picked up on this criterion, as they have the general advertiser-oriented network perspective.

Production Rules

Over the years, production executives have negotiated specific rules with the networks that make their ideas for shows much more likely to be accepted. These guidelines extend to the very structure of the programs.

- The plot must be created with natural breaks about every ten minutes so that commercials can be inserted.
- The regular characters of a series should reflect (or attract) viewers whom the networks are hoping to draw for advertisers. An 8:00 P.M. twenty-something situation comedy must have the kind of young-adult ensemble that *Friends* has: a motley group of bright young men and women, often living together (or nearby) platonically. At least a few of them should be unemployed or have jobs for which they are overqualified—a circumstance that some have said is currently the fate of that age group. If the program is "family" situation comedy, the recipe is different. It must have at least a couple of children for the youngsters of the house to like, a good-looking male lead for the parents to ogle, and at least one pretty woman for male encouragement.
- If the sitcom is due to be broadcast on Saturday, the requirements are even more specific. Saturday evening is a period of high VCR use and out-of-home activities among white young adults. An unusually high percentage of network viewers during this time are African-Americans and senior citizens. They tend not to be as mobile or own VCRs in as great a percentage as other groups. In attempting to attract these audiences to their channels, network executives ensure that their Saturday evening programs are populated with blacks, older people, or both. As a result, the census of blacks and older people is higher on Saturday evening than at any other time of the week.

This sketch conveys only some of the ways that producer-client relationships affect the creation of material in network television. Changing circumstances in the industry and in the world may influence the way the relationship is played out on a daily basis. During the 1991 Persian Gulf War, for example, network news producers began to feel pressure from national advertisers to de-emphasize their coverage. Sponsors, they said, were afraid their upbeat, consumption-oriented commercials might not look good shown next to images of dead or maimed soldiers. At NBC, the pressure led to decisions to refrain from offering special reports if possible. Even though the network received high ratings, it sold only about 20% of its commercial time, making the specials economically infeasible for the network. "Commercials need to be seen in the right environment," explained an advertising executive. "A war is not an upbeat environment."[29]

WHEN CLIENTS ARE NOT ADVERTISERS

This kind of widespread influence is not confined to media in which advertisers are the clients. Consider elementary and high school (el-hi) textbook publishing. The primary clients for el-hi textbook publishers are various state and local school systems around the country. Often, a central administration will periodically create a list of the only books that educators throughout the area can choose; teachers will then pick from that list.

Naturally, textbook publishers are eager to get their textbooks on the approved lists in as many places as possible. As a result, editors and marketing executives pay close attention to the educational and moral guidelines that school board members voice, as well as to the public controversies that swirl around particular issues or titles and the positions of school boards on those controversies. They try to please advocates of change as well as traditionalists. They even pay attention to the way that school board members inspect the books.

A popular inspection technique is the "flip test." This involves flipping the pages of a text to note the kinds of activities that are illustrated, as well as the number of whites, African-Americans, Hispanic-Americans, Native Americans, and Asian-Americans who are named or drawn. From this feedback, editors draw up guidelines about what school systems will accept, which they pass along to authors of the texts.

Because publishing firm executives want to remain under consideration by as many school boards as possible, they tend to urge authors and illustrators toward materials that will be acceptable everywhere. The lists of dos and don'ts are typically long and specific. Prohibitions include such possibly controversial topics as divorce, mixed marriages, and religious observances. Requirements include representation of various minority groups in specific numerical quotas, often so that they will be noticed in a flip test.

The result, say many educators, are homogenized textbooks that are acceptable to everyone but that present material in so predictable and bland a manner that students are not challenged to think about their surroundings; in fact, students may become bored. Authors and illustrators are often exasperated with the process, because they feel this least-common-denominator approach to textbook publishing robs them of any opportunity to be creative. Irene Trivas is one person who stopped accepting assignments to illustrate children's readers in the late 1980s. According to the *New York Times,* she was frustrated with publishers' efforts to "be everything to everybody," as she put it.[30] Here is her account of the instructions she received for one book:

> It's etched in acid in my mind. They sent 10 pages of single-spaced specifications. The hero was a Hispanic boy. There were black twins, one boy, one girl; an overweight Oriental boy, and an American Indian girl. That leaves the Caucasian. Since we mustn't forget the physically handicapped, she was

born with a congenital malformation and only had three fingers on one hand.

One child had to have an Irish setter, and the setter was to be female.

The Hispanic had two parents. The father has a white collar job. The mother is an illustrator and she works at home. At one point, they are seen through the kitchen screen door making dinner, having spaghetti and meatballs and a salad. The editor appended a note that said, "Make sure it's not iceberg; it should be something nice like endive."

They also had a senior citizen, and I had to show her jogging.

I can't do it anymore.[31]

Trivas and others in and out of the el-hi industry fault textbook publishers for not trying hard enough — or not being brave enough — to use the producer-client relationship to influence school boards to use less formula-ridden approaches. The result, they argue, is that American schoolchildren are being taught with books that make little attempt to acknowledge that youngsters, like adults, want materials that will interest and excite them.

TALKING POINT 4.1   A Confidential Guidesheet

In order to make their books acceptable to as many school boards as possible, elementary and high school textbook publishers often give their authors confidential lists of dos and don'ts. Here are a few policies from a confidential guide sheet that a major textbook publishing firm expected all its authors to follow during the early 1980s. Anecdotal evidence suggests that many of these are still in force.

- Brand names, commercial identification: Do not use or show.
- Death: Do not include except in anthologies and only if well balanced by other materials.
- Divorce: Do not include.
- Evolution: Avoid, except in science texts where it is a necessary part of the curriculum. Make sure all reference is to theory, not fact. Include statement required by Texas in front matter.
- Mixed marriages, religious or racial: Do not show.
- Religion: Do not show symbols of. Avoid all references to unless it is the theme of a story or exposition. If it is central to the piece, consider leaving the piece out. Avoid topics considered by some to be antireligious — for example, evolution, witchcraft, secular humanism.
- For materials in preparation this year, represent minorities in the following minimum percentages — whites 68%, blacks 15%, Hispanic-Americans 10%, Asian-Americans 1%, Native Americans 1%.

SOURCE: Confidential.

A PROFOUND IMPACT

Neither this el-hi textbook example nor the network TV case — nor any of the examples in this chapter — covers all the implications the producer-client relationship holds for the output of mass media systems. Clearly, though, the relationship's impact is profound. When working in media organizations, reading industry trade magazines, or merely being an aware media consumer, it is useful to trace the links between production firms and their clients. Learning about their influence on one another can lead to a better understanding of the forces that guide media output.

One key purpose of the producer-client relationship has so far only been hinted at: its role in defining the audience. It may have occurred to you during the discussion of schoolchildren, or while reading the other examples in this chapter, that notions of the audience loom large in any producer-client relationship. Yet the concept of audience, and the part the producer-client relationship plays in it, are not as straightforward as they may seem. Yet, targeting audiences is a major activity of mass media producers and clients. This activity is so important, and so fascinatingly complex, that the next chapter is devoted to it.

CONSIDER THIS

1. What do executives at major urban newspapers mean when they say that their main competition for advertising is not primarily other newspapers?
2. How many TV programs do you and your friends watch at the same time with the help of a remote control? Do you use it to miss the commercials? How do you think advertisers try to get around the problem?
3. Investigate one of the numerous controversies concerning how history should be taught in elementary school. How has it affected the way school boards define acceptable texts and the way individual publishers have fashioned their books?

NOTES

1. See also Garth Jowett and James Linton, *Movies as Mass Communication* (Beverly Hills, CA: Sage, 1980), pp. 25–64; and Janet Wasko, *Movies and Money* (Norwood, NJ: Ablex, 1982).
2. Telephone conversation with Bruce Snyder, president, Domestic Distribution, 20th Century Fox Film Corporation, June 20, 1991.
3. These figures are from *Advertising Age,* September 25, 1995.
4. *Advertising Age,* September 27, 1995, p. 1.
5. *Advertising Age,* March 29, 1989, p. 82.
6. Quoted in *Advertising Age,* November 24, 1980, p. 68.
7. *Advertising Age,* September 27, 1995, p. 1.
8. Howard Aldrich, *Organizations and Environments* (Englewood Cliffs, NJ: Prentice Hall, 1979), p. 267.

9. William Evan, *Organization Theory* (New York: John Wiley, 1976), p. 123.

10. Laura Loro, "Philadelphia Papers Appeal to Agencies," *Advertising Age,* January 28, 1991, p. 12.

11. J. W. Click and Russell N. Baird, *Magazine Editing and Production,* 2nd ed. (Dubuque, IA: William C. Brown, 1979), p. 4.

12. *Folio,* March 15, 1994, p. 193.

13. Cited in Leonard Mogel, *The Magazine* (New York: Spectrum Books, 1981), p. 2.

14. Mogel, p. 3.

15. Christopher Sterling and Timothy Haight, *The Mass Media: Aspen Guide to Communication Industry Trends* (New York: Praeger, 1978), p. 372.

16. Click and Baird, p. 2.

17. Click and Baird, p. 24.

18. *Advertising Age,* October 19, 1981, p. S-6.

19. Les Brown, *Television: The Business Behind the Box* (New York: Harcourt Brace Jovanovich, 1972), pp. 49–50.

20. Jowett and Linton, p. 39.

21. See Leonard Klady, "Movies' Mangled Margins," *Variety,* October 23–29, 1995, p. 1.

22. Jennifer Howland, "Ad vs. Edit," *Folio,* December 1989, pp. 92–100.

23. Click and Baird, p. 33.

24. Howland, p. 92.

25. Click and Baird, p. 263.

26. Howland, p. 95.

27. *Advertising Age,* October 19, 1991, p. 20.

28. Rick Dubrow, "Fall TV Schedules Aim at the Young and the Restless," *Los Angeles Times,* May 30, 1990, p. D1.

29. Bill Carter, "Few Sponsors for TV War News," *New York Times,* February 7, 1991, p. C1.

30. Susan Chira, "Writing Textbooks for Children: A Juggling Act," *New York Times,* January 17, 1990, p. B8.

31. Chira, p. B8.

CHAPTER 5

Targeting the Audience

This chapter

- explains how an audience is a label, a construction of reality.
- examines the way media organizations and advertisers think about audiences.
- discusses the research techniques that media firms use to ensure they are reaching the right people and to learn more about them.

All of us use the word *audience* nearly every day of our adult lives. We talk about the audience for a TV show, the audience for a movie, the audience for a concert. A movie review we read might discuss the audience's reaction. A parent might tell us about the audience's response to a child during a public performance at school. We might worry about how the audience will receive a speech we are giving.

Rarely, though, do people stop to think of the meaning of the word *audience,* or its implications. Simple as it sounds, and as commonly as it is used, *audience* is a complex, often misunderstood term. As it relates to mass communication, it means a variety of activities that profoundly influence the way media creators see society and the way members of society see themselves and the world. The aim of this chapter is to explore the activities that lie behind "the audience" and to tease out their significance. To begin, it is useful to introduce the most important point about an audience: that it is a concept, a construction of reality.

THE AUDIENCE AS A CONSTRUCTION OF REALITY

To explain this concept, consider the following nonmedia example.

Imagine a professor's audience in a university lecture course. The professor faces a collection of individuals. Each individual sees himself or herself as embodying certain attributes — friendly, selfish, religious, and the like. Friends, enemies, strangers, and mere acquaintances may think about these individuals in other ways.

The professor, however, looks out at the individuals in the lecture hall and thinks of them not as individuals whom he knows separately and personally in very different ways, but rather as a *group of students.* This collection of students is the professor's audience. He thinks of them as students because the university pays him to think of them that way. The professor will not be rewarded — he may even lose his job — if he thinks of the people in front of him as volleyball enthusiasts and invites them out for a game in the gym.

As straightforward as it sounds, this approach to the individuals in his class has major consequences. The professor talks to the people he faces in the lecture hall according to his understanding of the way professors are supposed to talk to their students. The categories he thinks about when he creates his lectures are student-related categories: how bright they are, how interested they are, how knowledgeable they are about the subject, and what most students around the country are expected to know about the subject.

His lectures are not likely to be guided primarily by whether people in his class are parents or whether they practice certain religions. If, however, the professor were facing those same people at an abortion rights rally, categories such as their religious beliefs and parenthood would be quite relevant.

The purpose of this example is to make the following points:

- First, although individuals are real, audiences are not. **Audiences are abstractions.** They are ideas about groups of people.
- Second, **audiences are constructed.** That is, an audience is created when certain categories are chosen over other categories to describe a group of people.
- Third, **the categories people use to construct their audiences flow out of the reward systems that guide them.** Recall that the professor defined his audience as students because his employer (the university) expected him to see students in that classroom. All audiences are constructed in this way, whether those creating the audience know it or not.

Constructing Mass Media Audiences

These generalizations apply to the mass media as well. In theory, there is an infinite number of ways that executives of mass media production firms can discuss the people who come into contact with the materials they release. Audiences can be constructed with categories that range from eye color to religious preference and beyond — and the categories can change.

In practice, though, the executives tend to discuss their firm's audience along much narrower, very predictable lines. It is no surprise to someone working in television that commercial network executives speak primarily of the age, gender, and race of their viewers. Nor would it cause a stir in the consumer magazine industry to state that executives emphasize incomes and acquisitive spending in addition to age and gender when building images of their readers. In neither case are such items as their grandparents' countries of origin, their kissing habits, or their religiosity likely to play a part in audience construction.

To understand how the basic categories of audience become established in a media production firm, it is important to recall the producer-client relationship discussed in Chapter 4. Clients are organizations — advertisers, bookstores, movie distributors — that pay producers for the creation of media products before those products reach the public. As shown in Chapter 4, clients exert powerful influences on the guidelines producers adopt regarding their output. At the same time, production firms often take part in negotiating the demands their clients make of them.

It is through this ongoing interchange between producers and their population of clients that the categories of people the clients wish to reach through the producer's media output are established. Production firms receive money from their clients for creating materials that attract these audiences. In turn, the producers may lose support — or even go out of business — if they cannot provide materials that satisfy enough clients to keep the enterprise alive.

The Case of Children's Books and TV

To make this interorganizational construction of audience more concrete, consider the contrasting forces that affect the way an audience called "children" is constructed in the library market as opposed to the television market. The children's library marketplace is comprised of publishers who sell most of their books to children's libraries. The children's television area is comprised of TV production firms and networks that support programming by selling air time to advertisers (mostly toy, candy, and cereal companies).

The two sets of relationships are drastically different. Children's libraries are run by librarians, who have gone to school to learn about children and their development. They have been taught to view youngsters as aesthetically inclined, intellectually developing beings whose diverse interests need to be cultivated. Categories such as age and gender are starting points for asking what can and should stimulate creativity at different ages. Abstract designs, illustrations that reflect artistic individuality, stories that have emotional tension and that, for older children, display moral difficulties — these are among the characteristics that librarians feel describe the best children's books.

Practical considerations also enter into librarians' purchasing approaches. For example, branch librarians typically want to encourage children to borrow many books from the library because when their branch's circulation statistics increase, they receive more book-buying money from the library system. The result may be that certain types of books librarians dislike but that they know children and their parents enjoy — Richard Scarry picture books, for example — are ordered for the shelves as a nod to circulation concerns. In general, though, librarians are convinced that they can and should help shape what is popular among their borrowers. They learn to point youngsters toward what they feel are fascinating books that also help them grow aesthetically and intellectually.

On the producer side of this producer-client relationship, editors of publishing firms who want librarians to buy their books pay careful attention to the criteria librarians use to decide what constitutes a good book. Generalizing from the large population of librarians they know, the editors construct images of children and priorities of children that are compatible with those of their primary clients. In addition, they choose authors and manuscripts that fit these images and their associated criteria.

They may even try to influence librarians' criteria in directions they feel are useful for their firm. For example, the acceptability of adolescent "problem" novels by authors such as Judy Blume might get a boost among librarians through editors' initiatives. Such a decision has to be framed within the boundaries the library field has set regarding children's needs and capabilities at certain ages.

Contrast the library market approach with that of commercial network television. Network officials commission programs for children in response to the needs of their clients: advertisers and ad agencies. Cereal companies, toy companies, and candy companies that advertise to children face requirements that lead them to construct their audience very differently from the way librarians do. Their mandate for reaching children is to persuade them to buy certain products or nag their parents to buy them.

The categories through which advertisers see children are, therefore, related not to broad concerns about youngsters' aesthetic and intellectual development but rather to an interest in children as little consumers. To attract advertisers, network officials select TV programs and construct their children's TV schedules with the same goals in mind. Challenging children's creativity and responding to a variety of individual interests take a backseat to capturing the greatest number of possible juvenile viewers so as to make it efficient for advertisers to buy time to reach them. Along the same lines, a child's age and gender are not so much indicators of capabilities and broad interest areas (as they are with publishers) but rather tags that imply purchasing habits, knowledge of consumer culture, and commercial persuadability.

One result of this thinking is different guidelines for selecting "children's" material. For example, librarians typically reject TV-based books, such as those about the *Animaniacs* and *Goof Troop* cartoon series, that are sold in department stores and supermarkets. They dislike the books' predictable plots, flat illustrations, and their function as advertisements for the many other *Animaniacs* and *Goof Troop* products.[1] To advertisers, however, sponsoring programs around these characters — using the same style of plots and illustrations of the books — is not considered a drawback if they reach enough of their targeted audience. Moreover, the link between the programs and related items that children can buy might be considered a benefit to advertisers, because they believe it reinforces in young viewers the idea that commercially driven popular culture is acceptable.

The point here is not to make the library market publishers look good and the network executives and their producers look bad. Rather, it is to show how the categories that media production firms use to describe the audience they need to reach serve the interests of the marketplace in which they work and affect their content selection guidelines. In this case, very different constructions of children and their needs emerge. So do very different attitudes toward the acceptability of certain kinds of content.

The same process of audience construction occurs in other media situations. It takes on particular day-to-day intensity when producers compete vigorously with one another for advertisers' cash. Looking for market niches that will help them draw the money clients may otherwise spend on competitors, producers often choose to focus on **narrowly specialized attributes** they feel will appeal to advertisers.

Audience Construction in the Magazine Business

The magazine business is a good example of such **targeting** or **narrowcasting.** Consider, for example, the way *Popular Mechanics* and *Rolling Stone* magazines portray themselves and their audiences to the advertising trade in their own ads.

Rolling Stone often reaches out to potential clients who shy away from advertising their products in the magazine because of an image that the audience is made up of holdover hippies from the 1960s who shun material goods and reject commercialism. *Rolling Stone*'s marketing department wants to actively discourage this idea. Its job is to point out that the magazine provides an environment to successfully reach leisure-oriented *consumers*.

An example of their work is a two-page spread in the October 23, 1989, issue of *Advertising Age*. The left page shows the face of a young, curly-haired blond woman. She is made up to look like a 1960s "flower child," and her eyes are closed as if she is meditating. The caption above the photo reads "Perception." On the right page, under a caption that reads "Reality," is the face of an older woman. No longer flowered, she is impeccably made up, with streaks of suntan lotion on her lower lip and nose. Her eyes are closed not for meditative reasons but so that she might tan in the sun. The paragraph below the photo makes the point clearly:

> When the moon was in the seventh house and Jupiter was aligned with Mars, the readers of *Rolling Stone* were painting their faces to keep out of the establishment. Now, they're painting their faces to keep out of the sun. Last week, *Rolling Stone* readers established themselves as users of sun protection and skin care products more than 62 million times. If you're looking for one of the best markets under the sun, you will find plenty of exposure in the pages of *Rolling Stone.*

In the same *Advertising Age* issue, *Popular Mechanics* constructs a different audience, but with similarly commercial inclinations. The magazine claims it is designed to attract "the must-know man," an active, intelligent adult male whose inquisitiveness ignites acquisitiveness in himself and others. *Popular Mechanics* says that it has succeeded in becoming a "must read" for this important advertising target, and then proceeds to add particulars to the image:

> The Must-Know Man comprises a huge 25% of American males over 18 with a substantial household income. That's 13.3 million Americans. A very special breed of Americans, the doers, the men who make things work.
>
> The Must-Know Man is a very different type of man. He's the man who isn't content to read the news about technology; he must know what it is and how it works.
>
> The Must-Know Man is equipment intensive. He buys power tools, electronics, automobiles, boats, and much more. He is the consumer willing to buy the best, whether it's a computer or a power drill, or a life insurance policy for his family.
>
> The Must-Know Man also influences the purchases of many other men and women. When you reach The Must-Know Man, you're reaching an expert.[2]

Note that both *Popular Mechanics* and *Rolling Stone* back up their visions of the people they try to attract with specific information about the buying habits of those people. The information they present fits perfectly with the audience visions they are creating. Characteristics that are irrelevant to the audience image the magazines want to present to advertisers — their church-attending records, for instance — would not be included in their appeal to clients.

In the examples presented, *Rolling Stone* constructs an audience of leisure-oriented consumers of the good life; that image is extended by trumpeting the amount of suntan lotion its readers purchase. *Popular Mechanics* portrays its constituency as confident men whose take-charge style extends to buying the very best products to get the job done. The list of products its readers purchase fleshes out this image and becomes an essential part of it.

The underlying message of these ads is clear: Magazine firms are acknowledging that to attract advertisers they need to do more than construct an audience image and build an editorial environment to suit it. Producers know they must prove to their potential clients that their media vehicles actually reach people with those attributes. This requirement raises three major questions about the construction of audiences in mass media industries:

- How does a production firm go about trying to prove to its clients that its media output will, in fact, reach people who have the desirable characteristics of the promised audience?
- To what extent can such proof be considered a genuine reflection of the characteristics of the individuals who actually make up the producers' audiences?

TABLE 5.1 TOP TWENTY NATIONAL PUBLICATIONS AMONG ADULTS WITH HOUSEHOLD INCOME OF $60,000 OR MORE (1990)

Title	Circulation (in Thousands)
National Geographic	9,251
Better Homes & Gardens	8,990
Reader's Digest	8,610
TV Guide	7,426
People	7,281
Time	7,165
Newsweek	5,739
Sports Illustrated	5,480
The Wall Street Journal	5,037
USA Today	4,526
HG	4,166
Money	3,974
U.S. News & World Report	3,824
Smithsonian	3,526
Travel & Leisure	3,411
The New York Times (Sunday)	3,179
House Beautiful	3,015
Country Living	2,910
Bon Appetit	2,873
Architectural Digest	2,783

SOURCE: Advertising Age, *July 9, 1990, p S1.*

Relatively wealthy segments of the population attract many marketers. Consequently, many magazines try hard to attract the relatively wealthy.

- What might be some social consequences of labeling certain segments of society according to images created as a result of producer-client relationships?

"KNOWING" THE AUDIENCE

The short answer to the first question, and the beginning of an answer to the others, is that media production firms commission **audience research.** Audience research involves systematic investigation to determine if the numbers and kinds of people the producer has decided to reach with certain media materials are attracted to the output.

This answer is only a partial one, though. While many firms do rely on a good deal of audience research, others find it either too expensive, or impossible to accomplish when it is most relevant. Before exploring the variety of projects that are included in audience research, it is useful to examine when audience research is conducted and when other ways of "knowing" the audience are used by producers to convince clients that they do, in fact, draw the people they say they draw to their media materials.

The emphasis here is on the role played by audience research and other forms of knowing the audience in a production firm's interactions with its clients. Audience research is primarily aimed at *reducing the risk* that these relationships will fail and that the clients will leave. It should not be surprising, however, that audience research conducted for external organizations is also used *within* media production organizations to reduce the creators' risk of failure and to guide them toward certain types of output. This function of audience knowing is taken up in Chapters 7 and 8.

Deciding to Conduct Research

To examine how audience knowing works for producers and clients, consider a newspaper firm involved in developing ideas for a new weekly section on science. Newspaper executives might commission research to determine if the section will be read by a sufficient number of individuals who are attractive to the target advertisers — computer, camera, and business equipment stores. The executives realize they are dependent on advertisers and their agencies for support. Before spending large amounts of money, these parties might demand research to back up the newspaper's audience-reaching claims.

In this example, both producers and clients consider audience research a useful way to come to terms with the question of audience — to see if people with the categories the advertisers and producers want to reach will, in fact, say they will read the new section. Yet audience research is not always conducted at the point of creation in every area of the mass media. There is a spectrum of attitudes toward this kind of exploration. Some media producers consider audience research on individual products critical to their success. Others use it sparingly, and still others hardly use it at all.

The trade book segment of the book industry lies at the end of the spectrum, where audience research is minimal. **Trade books** are hardcovers directed mostly to bookstores and general libraries. When asked why they refrain from conducting market research on their titles, publishers typically point out that every book title is a unique product, not directly related to the other titles they publish. Conducting audience research on the concept of the book before it is created will not, they feel, give an accurate gauge of consumer response to a particular manuscript.

Publishers also do not typically conduct audience research after the book is created. Their reason is that a book is not like a bar of soap the manufacturer wants to sell in standard form for many years to come. It is, rather, merely one of a continual stream of new publications the publisher hopes will find a place, usually temporary, in the market. Trade publishers contend that spending time and money to test every new title when it is ready to be shipped to the stores would be too expensive an activity, and come too late in the process.

Alternatives to Audience Research

The trade publishers' reluctance to conduct audience research on individual titles does not, however, mean that they ignore considerations of their ultimate consumers. To do so could be deadly, especially from the standpoint of convincing bookstores that their works will sell. Instead, they have developed other methods for supporting the position that the proposed product matches their audience's likes and dislikes.

One is to use sales figures that are stored on their computers. If a submitted manuscript has a topic similar to that of titles the firm previously sold for $19.95, at an average of, say, 10,000 copies, marketing personnel might inform the editorial staff that expected sales will be in that ballpark. Decisions about the potential book's shape, length, marketing program, price — sometimes even its publishability — would proceed from there.

Also used to make presumptions about the audience are generalizations from sales figures that large bookstore chains such as B. Dalton and Waldenbooks sometimes share with publishers. Conversations between key store executives and publisher representatives may lead publishers and bookstores to construct ideas about emerging interests in segments of the audience. This, in turn, could encourage the creation of certain books to fill the clients' perceived need.

Related but nevertheless distinct techniques for claiming knowledge of the audience in the absence of systematic research are **the use of track record talent and track record content.** A **track record talent** is a creator who has a list of proven recent successes and a strong reputation in his or her field. To trade publishers and their bookstore clients, an author whose book made the *New York Times* best-seller list last year is a good bet for success this year. The assumption is that the author has a feel for the interests of a considerable number of readers.

As a result, the manuscript generated by the creator becomes a way to define the concerns of the audience — at least until sales of the next book drop drastically. For instance, a manuscript about a group of amateurs competing for a place on the U.S. Olympic rowing team might not draw the attention of a top trade editor. Submitted by popular author David Halberstam, however, the book's possibilities suddenly seem greater, because Halberstam has shown over time that he attracts a large number of readers. Halberstam also has a better chance than unknown writers to appear on a television talk show or to garner a newspaper review of his book. This fact, too, can help sell books and thus persuade bookstores to carry the title.

Track record content works in ways similar to those of track record talent to reduce perceptions of risk and crystallize impressions of audience interests. Track record content refers to subjects and approaches that have enjoyed success in media material in the recent past.

If, for example, books about hobbies have been profitable, a publisher may feel that a book in the same general area will be attractive to distributors and garner good sales. Of course, there is always the danger that following what many others have done will place a production firm on the downward side of a trend. For firms interested in exploiting track record content, the trick is to seize upon subjects that have not yet reached the peak of their popularity. Adapting ideas that are making their mark in other media is one strategy to use.

For example, an editor who notices an interest in sensational murders among newspapers and broadcast organizations may alert the sales force that it can help convince bookstore agents that an audience exists to support a book on this subject. Tying into popular topics is also a good way to generate publicity for books in other media — and this, too, can persuade booksellers to allocate store space for the title.

The Case of the Movie Industry

We have noted that executives in book publishing and their clients are accustomed to using track record considerations as a primary way to predict what an audience will like. Trade publishers have felt that the individualistic nature of their materials makes it either impossible or too expensive to quantitatively study audience response to a work before it is fully created. This perspective is shared in several publishing areas — for example, scholarly periodicals and children's books. Many more areas of the mass media, though, place a premium not so much on individual products as on research-based predictability of success with the consumer.

On the spectrum from little to much audience research, the Hollywood movie industry is in the middle. Hollywood takes an approach to knowing the audience that is both similar to and different from that of trade book publishers. As in the book industry, producers of theatrical films must justify the selection of individual projects to their clients.

In the motion picture business, clients are often major movie distributors or banks that lend producers money for individual projects (see chapter 4). Like trade book editors, movie producers traditionally have contended that they create individual products that are not amenable to proper audience response testing before they are made. They argue that people cannot judge whether they want to see a film based on a short description of a story; people might respond positively to the description and negatively to the finished product, or vice versa.

Preproduction Research

As a result, audience research has traditionally not been conducted as a prelude to creating a particular film. Instead, the other techniques of knowing the audience come into play. Like trade book publishers, movie producers have used general numerical profiles of their customers (the makeup of moviegoers in terms of age, sex, and race) along with track record talent (successful directors, writers, actors) and track record content (clearly popular themes and subjects) to guide their project choices and convince their clients that the product will succeed.

Since the mid-1980s, though, movie executives have become more research-oriented when looking at new projects. Movie studios might test promising plotlines on samples of moviegoers to see which draws the most interest. Even the script might be analyzed quantitatively. A company called Emotional Response Index System (ERIS) claims it can forecast whether a movie will be successful even before it is completed. Based on a sampling of thousands of people, ERIS concludes that it can analyze scripts to see if they have the qualities wanted in theatrical films.[3]

Preproduction research such as this is still fairly uncommon in the movie industry, but it may increase. Part of the reason is the new generation of executives who arrived when conglomerates took over the major studios during the 1970s and 1980s. These executives are more trained in consumer goods and advertising research than their predecessors. They are accustomed to conducting consumer research at the earliest stages of product development, and they see no reason that movies should be treated differently.

Another part of the reason is the skyrocketing cost of movies. The cost of generating a typical trade book is not likely to go above a couple of hundred thousand dollars, including marketing expenses.[4] By contrast, the cost of creating an average American film exceeds $28 million, plus almost half that much for marketing expenses.[5]

Although the book publishing cost is by no means low, publishers seem to feel that combining track record considerations with numerical figures of popularity from their own records and those of bookstore chains can reduce the risk of failure across their slate. Audience research would increase the cost of the enterprise to a level where the final price of each book would be far above the going rate for books. Moviemakers, however, are dealing with much more money in the entire venture. Spending on research to ensure the optimal potential of a title is considered acceptable because it amounts to only a small portion of a film's total cost.

Postproduction Research

Once their product is completed, the movie studios' approach to their audience is more aggressive and systematic than that of book publishers. Studios commonly use three types of audience research: title testing, previewing, and tracking.

Title testing involves conducting interviews with filmgoers in shopping malls and other public places to determine which of a number of possible names for upcoming films is most likely to reflect the nature of those films in such a way as to draw people to the theaters. The belief is that the first wave of people who choose to see a new film will be attracted by its name and cast.

If that first group likes the film, they will talk favorably to friends about it, a phenomenon called **word of mouth.** Executives believe that strong word of mouth is a key to a release's success, often even more than positive newspaper, TV, and magazine reviews. If, however, the title is boring or draws an audience expecting to see a different kind of picture, it can severely damage the word of mouth and cripple the movie's chances.

Consider the movie *Field of Dreams,* a romantic comedy with a baseball backdrop. Originally, the creators proposed naming it *Shoeless Joe,* a reference to a legendary baseball player. Title testing revealed, however, that potential moviegoers thought that a film with such a title was a baseball biography or a comedy about a hobo. Producers feared that these perceptions would bring the wrong group of initial moviegoers into the theater, with a resulting poor word of mouth. They changed the title to *Field of Dreams* because they felt it communicated the film's romantic inclinations more clearly.[6]

Previewing takes place after a film is completed but before it is formally released. The studio shows a preliminary **(rough-cut)** version of a movie to an audience of theatergoers. Sometimes, the director and producers attend the screenings and note reactions at certain points. More often, researchers give the viewers cards to fill out that ask what they liked and disliked about the movie.

The reactions can be used to reedit parts of the film. The original sad ending of *Fatal Attraction,* for example, was changed to make it happier after negative audience reactions during previews. Preview audience answers also guide studio marketing departments and ad agencies toward themes that would most likely encourage people to see the movie.

Tracking takes place from about two weeks before the movie is released through the first month of release. Its purpose is to determine the effectiveness of publicity and word of mouth the producer and distributor have been trying to stir up over the film. Three times during each of those weeks, a company named National Research Group surveys a random sample of Americans by phone. National's operators read a list of current or soon-to-be-released films to people who say they have recently seen theatrical movies. For every film on the list, they are asked (1) if they are aware of it and (2) if they want to see it.

National Research Group sells the results to major movie producers and distributors. These findings arrive too late to change the movie or its pattern of release to the theaters. Nevertheless, the film's marketers see this way of knowing the audience as indicating whether revisions to their publicity and advertising plan are needed to help draw optimal ticket sales.

If, for example, people are aware of a new movie but do not want to see it, marketers will conclude that the **weight of publicity** and advertising has been fine, but the **creative approach** to informing people about the product has been poor. They may then take steps to correct the problem. In the worst case, marketers feel that a tracking study can help indicate what *not* to do when they try to entice certain groups of consumers to particular films.

FORMAT-DRIVEN AUDIENCE RESEARCH

Recall that it is the individualistic, stand-alone nature of trade books and (to a lesser extent) Hollywood movies that leads producers and their clients to feel reluctant or unable to rely on audience research, especially before the product's release in the marketplace. There are, however, other areas of publishing and moviemaking where there is little concern with one-shot creations. Think of juvenile adventures such as those based on Nancy Drew and the Hardy Boys; the groups of books about home repair or World War II marketed by Time-Life Books; the *Baby Sitters Club* aimed at teenage girls; the *Little Rascals* movies of the 1930s; and the various *Star Trek* films of the 1970s and 1980s. These are just the tip of the iceberg of materials in publishing and moviemaking that rely not on new products every time for their money, but rather on the continuation of previous themes, characters, and even plots.

Such a consistent arrangement of symbolic material—the layout, tone, and general approach—across two or more versions of a cultural product is called a **format.** When a succession of products is associated with a particular format, that group of items is called a **series.** The Hardy Boys, Nancy Drew, and James Bond formats are all connected with series—in books, film, and TV. The term *format* can also be used to describe the consistent approach that a specific mass media channel—a particular TV station, magazine, newspaper—takes to its material. The format creates what people think of as the "personalities" of those channels.

For example, radio stations typically act out their particular formats through the songs they play and the sounds of their on-air personalities. WMMR-Philadelphia, a radio station with an "album-oriented rock" format, carries a mix of certain kinds of music, news, and features designed to lend a character to the station even though the songs played change from week to week.

Magazines and newspapers have easily detectable formats, too. The *New York Times* is recognizably the *New York Times* every day, while *People* magazine follows a very different, yet consistent, style.

In regard to television, the term *format* may apply to both the channel and the series carried by the channel. *Nick at Nite,* a nightly cable service filled with TV shows and movies chosen to attract people who grew up during the 1950s and 1960s, is one example of a TV channel format. *Leave It to Beaver,* one of the several hit 1960s situation comedies *Nick at Nite* sends over the wire, is an example of a series format. Week after week, the program carries the same setting, characters, and approach to plot.

When this kind of long-term approach is intended from the start (and it often is), producers and their clients agree that it makes research on the target audience's reactions a good deal more feasible than with stand-alone creations. One reason is that producers view the cost of research as relating to a stream of future products, not just a single item. Just as important, producers believe that formats make audience research practical from a logistical standpoint.

They feel a format provides them with a completed product to test that will be similar to forthcoming products.

ADVERTISERS AND AUDIENCE RESEARCH

It is no accident that virtually all media sponsored by advertisers are organized by formats. Advertising executives are rooted in a package goods marketing tradition where quantitative evidence rules. They demand research-based evidence that the media they use will attract individuals with characteristics matching their marketing needs. The creation of media materials as part of a format satisfied the quantitative research demands of advertisers much more easily than if the materials were fully distinct from one another.

From the production firm's standpoint, use of formats allows producers to construct audiences that particular advertisers will like, to create materials that will attract those audiences, and to hold on to them over time. For their part, advertisers accept the idea that if one takes a sampling from a format — say, two issues of a magazine or a week of a radio station's broadcasts — one will get material that is representative of the format at other times as well. They also accept the proposition that if a stable format can be shown to attract a certain audience at one point in time, it will likely attract that audience at other points in time. This reasoning makes audience research more economically feasible than studying readers of every issue of the magazine or viewers of every episode of the TV series.

What advertiser-supported media firms sell to their clients, then, are formats that can be used to reach audiences of predictable sizes and types. Just how much audience research a company commissions to prove this predictability varies widely. Magazines catering to narrow audiences, for example, often cannot afford to conduct the kinds of readership audits, tests, and surveys that large mass market magazines can. That such small media often thrive within their niches indicates that advertisers, too, vary in their insistence that research backs up their media buys.

Audience research on advertiser-supported media falls into two broad categories:

Research on the vehicle's format before it is introduced to the marketplace

Research on the format after it is introduced

Concept Testing in Ad-Supported Media

Research on a format before it is introduced often involves trying out ideas on potential audience members, a procedure called **concept testing.** As an example of concept testing, consider the way Time Inc. Magazines tried to find out if there was a lucrative market for an entertainment guide conceived by two of its employees. The two were given money to find out whether the proposed periodical had the potential to draw the number and kind of subscribers who would be attractive to advertisers. An advertising packet was mailed to 500,000 people who had been culled from Time's magazine subscriber lists. This packet described the periodical, included mock-up cover pictures, and asked the recipients if they would like to subscribe.

Enough people said yes for Time to set the projected circulation base at 500,000. More important, Time associated the ones who wanted to subscribe with audience characteristics that typically draw strong advertiser interest: main age group 25–45, 72% college educated, about 50:50 male/female, and median income $40,000. In addition, Time learned that 85% of those responding owned VCRs, 51% owned CD players (versus 15% nationwide), and 66% regularly bought hardcover books. This suggested strong potential in home electronics, alcohol, automotive, TV programming, and mail-order book, video, and music-club advertising. Impressed with these results, Time's management proceeded to give the go-ahead for the magazine, which came to be known as *Entertainment Weekly.*[7]

Concept testing is not confined to the magazine industry. A radio station owner toying with a major format change, a television station concerned about the look of its local news hour, and a television network interested in mounting popular series all place the viability of their ideas to the target audience among the points they need to discover before they move ahead. Concept testing typically involves interviews in one or more of the following settings:

Over the phone

In an auditorium

In a focus group

Via a cable television channel

The first three methods are used regularly in the radio industry. **Telephone calling** is a common way to test and refine radio formats. Radio station staff or personnel from a hired research firm phone people who match the characteristics of the intended audience. These people can be chosen in a number of ways. They may be drawn from the telephone directory, they may be contacted from a list of known listeners; or they may be selected through dialing numbers generated by use of a **random numbers table.** The random numbers technique starts with the first three digits of prefixes assigned by the telephone company to the listening area. The last four digits of the telephone number are taken from a list of random numbers found in statistics books or generated by computer.

Once they contact individuals over the phone, radio station representatives first ensure that the person fits the characteristics their firm wants to attract. If, for instance, the target audience is 18- to 35-year-olds, the callers will not care to explore the opinions of someone older or younger who answers the phone. When they reach someone appropriate, the interviewers play short portions of songs the station intends to use as part of its format. They ask the people to rate the songs, and then ask a variety of other questions aimed at getting a picture of their respondents' radio listening habits throughout the day.[8]

Unlike the one-to-one nature of phone interviews, **auditorium testing** takes place in large groups. An example of concept testing in auditoriums can be drawn from commercial network television's testing of series. One-paragraph descriptions of the series formats are read to viewers who, typically, have been invited to the auditoriums — often called "preview" theaters — to evaluate programs and commercials. These viewers are asked if they would watch the series based on the descriptions. If a producer's concept receives high marks from appropriate audiences (i.e., audiences the network and its advertisers are pursuing), the network interested in commissioning the series will pay for the creation of a pilot.

A **pilot** is the first show of a proposed series. It is designed to illustrate the possibilities its format has for attracting an audience and holding it through a succession of weekly episodes. **Pilot testing** means showing the pilot to groups of viewers, either on specially rented cable TV channels or in preview theaters. When cable TV is used, the individuals selected are asked to view a movie or series on the channel at a certain time.

After the program has ended, the viewers are asked questions over the telephone about what they saw. In the theaters, viewers sometimes sit in chairs equipped with dials that are used to indicate how much they like what they see on the screen. These responses, along with their written comments, help network executives decide whether or not to commission the series.

Pilot testing is simply another term for audience research that evaluates a completed version of a format before it is released to the marketplace. This kind of evaluation takes place in a number of media industries, both print and electronic. Although the auditorium is a popular site for pilot testing by network TV and movie firms, those in the print area tend to prefer individual interviews with consumers or focus groups.

A **focus group** is a collection of six to twelve people who have been chosen to match the media producers' (and advertisers') preferred audience profile. Lured by cash or free food, these people are encouraged by a specially trained moderator to comment on a variety of topics related to the format and its competition.

Local television news formats are often the subject of focus groups. Local news is a potentially highly profitable part of a station's operation, but is also a very expensive area involved in a tight battle for audiences and advertising dollars. Stations often use focus groups to explore how target audiences evaluate aspects of their formats compared to those of the competition.

TALKING POINT 5.1   Mapmaking and Market Research

Most people realize that psychology, sociology, computer programming, and statistics can be applied to the targeting of audiences. Cartography — the science of making maps — is not a skill one is likely to think of when considering the brainpower that firms apply to learning about and reaching potential customers.

Nevertheless, mapmaking is increasingly important for helping marketers, particularly direct marketers (those who advertise via the telephone and the mail). They use a variety of maps to organize, and make sense of, the welter of geographic and demographic data the U.S. Census Bureau and other huge data bases present to them. Following are examples of four efforts under way in the 1990s to map out the year's national census for the benefit of those who sell:

- The R. L. Polk market research firm and Geographic Data Technology were developing an address coding guide that would enable marketers to match postal addresses on a map of part of a community with census data. The work takes advantage of the U.S. Census Bureau's file of computer-generated maps of all U.S. roads and addresses. Polk's aim was to sell marketers the ability to flexibly zero in on large or small groups of homes to find out the median household income, median age, percentage of minorities living there, and other data.

- The Strategic Mapping research firm was developing a software package similar to Polk's, but with the ability to allow marketers to combine census data with information in its own proprietary data bases.

- CACI, another research company, was marketing a consumer market segmentation program named Acorn. For a fee, it would enable marketers to draw maps of each of 250,000 neighborhoods defined by the census. Through the use of census data, the neighborhoods would be classified into forty-four distinct consumer types, such as "high-income suburban families with young children" and "mainstream Hispanic-Americans."

- Similarly, the firm Claritas was selling a well-known market segmentation system called Prizm, which stands for Potential Rating Index by Zip Markets. Prizm classifies all U.S. neighborhoods into forty basic lifestyle segments, or clusters. Claritas intended to match the 1990 census data, transformed into its clusters, with postal zip codes.

SOURCE: *Advertising Age*, December 10, 1990, p. 46.

Moderators encourage participants to express opinions about the news anchors and reporters on the stations, as well as about the stories covered and the newscasts' images. Responses from several focus groups are among the considerations of the station manager and news director when they are making decisions regarding their station's approach to news.

Persuading Advertisers to Support a Format

Let us assume that a format has passed concept and pilot testing and has been released into the highly competitive media environment. Now the production firm's challenge is to convince advertisers that they are reaching the size and type of audience they desire. This is accomplished through research that zeroes in on four features of the audience: circulation, demographics, lifestyles, and psychographics.

Circulation research involves determining the number of individuals who are consumers of the producer's media output. In the case of newspapers and magazines, the actual numbers of subscribers and single-copy sales are verified by an independent firm, the Audit Bureau of Circulation (ABC), which is paid by the publishers. Audited circulation is impossible with the three major electronic media that typically carry ads—radio, broadcast TV, and cable TV. The reason is that consumers do not subscribe to specific ad-supported programming channels (as they do, for example, to the unsponsored Home Box Office pay cable service). Instead, in about 98% of American homes, people can receive over-the-air material free through their radios and television sets. In well over half of American homes, they also purchase the right to watch any of a number of advertiser-supported channels. Auditing the amount of time that everyone spends with those media would clearly be unrealistically expensive.

Over the years, however, the advertising industry has accepted as standard a number of ways to provide circulation figures for the electronic media. All these approaches are based on the proposition that the TV and radio habits of Americans can be estimated accurately by contacting a statistically random sample of the U.S. population. Sizes of the sample are determined by careful mathematical calculation and vary depending on the specific goals of the research. The research methods used to estimate circulation differ in how they elicit information from the individuals in the sample. One approach is to use a diary, another is to conduct interviews, and still another is to use a meter to monitor media use.

A **diary** is a notebook in which an individual radio listener or TV viewer is asked to record radio listening or TV viewing information. Typically, the notebook contains a grid that lists stations on one axis and time (by quarter hours or half hours) on the other. **Interviews** elicit this information directly, by telephone or in person. The interviewer may draw on the individual's memory (e.g., "Did you listen to the radio yesterday between 6:00 A.M. and 10:00 A.M.? If so, what station?") or may ask what the person is doing at the time ("Are you listening to the radio now? If so, what station?").

Meters are the major measurement tool in the TV industry. In the United States, the A. C. Nielsen Company, a huge marketing research firm, has a virtual monopoly on its use of meters in a sample designed to reflect national viewer patterns as well as in samples aimed at tracking habits in each of the nation's largest metropolitan areas. For its research on metropolitan areas,

Nielsen installs a meter on every television in the several thousand households sampled. This meter measures whether a TV is being viewed and notes the channel (over-the-air, cable, or VCR).

Since only the sets, not the people, are metered, the results allow the company to generalize about TV use for the household, but not for specific individuals. Nielsen derives generalizations about the habits of individual viewers by comparing its meter data with diary entries from another sample of viewers.

A newer strategy, which Nielsen has installed in the approximately 4,000 homes that comprise its national sample, is the **people meter.** This small box, connected to the TV sets of the sample households, holds a preassigned code for every individual in the home, even visitors. The research firm asks each viewer to push his or her button at the start and at the end of viewing. These individual actions, transmitted to Nielsen computers through telephone lines, are the basis for the firm's conclusions on national television viewing habits.

Whether they gather media use information by diary, interview, or meter, research firms combine their findings to get a measure of circulation — how many people watched or listened to what programming at what time. Circulation numbers from electronic and print media are the most basic figures used by **media buyers** at advertising agencies. Media buyers are responsible for helping advertising agencies choose the most efficient media vehicles for their advertising message.

To a media buyer, the most fundamental measure of a mass medium's efficiency is **cost per thousand** (cost per mil, or CPM). A medium's cost per mil is the amount of money an advertiser must pay to reach 1,000 people in its audience. With print media, the number is usually based on the price of an entire black-and-white page. For instance, if a newspaper has a circulation of 100,000 and charges $1,000 for a page, the CPM would be $10 ($1,000/100,000 × 1,000). This would be considered a more efficient media buy than a newspaper in the same area with the same circulation that charges $1,500 per page, because its CPM would be $15.

But CPM based purely on circulation can be a misleading measure of efficiency. Neither magazine nor newspaper publishers, for example, are content to have advertisers think that their periodicals' readership is limited to the Audit Bureau of Circulation figures. They point out that individual copies are often shared among a number of readers, especially in places such as physicians' offices and beauty salons.

To support this claim with quantitative data, they commission additional research, often from MediaMark (MRI) or Simmons Market Research Bureau (SMRB), to come up with the average number of people who read an issue of their periodical. This figure, called the **pass-along rate,** is particularly high when a periodical is placed in physicians' offices or beauty salons. The number is meant to convince media buyers that the actual circulation of the periodical makes it an even better buy than audited circulation indicates.

But pass-along possibilities are not the only limitations that producers and their advertisers find in basic circulation figures. An even more important one has to do with the inability of raw circulation numbers to say anything about the kinds of people who use particular print or electronic media.

Imagine that you are a media buyer trying to find the most efficient medium with which to reach physicians in a city with two newspapers. It would be nonsense to suppose that your actual CPM would be $10 and $15, respectively, because you really have no information about how many physicians read the two papers.

If, for example, 1,000 physicians were among the 100,000 readers, the relevant CPM would be $1,000 for the first newspaper and $1,500 for the second. These high rates might make you think twice about using the general circulation papers to reach such a narrow audience. You might be inclined, instead, to advertise in a newspaper or magazine directed squarely toward physicians in the area. You would, therefore, reach more of them, and it is likely that the relevant CPM would, by comparison, be quite attractive.

Targeting Narrow Audience Segments

This kind of thinking is not at all unusual. Over the past few decades, marketers in the United States have been trying to tailor products to increasingly narrow segments of the audience. "Doctors" may, in fact, be considered too broad a category by many companies. To them, specific kinds of doctors (surgeons, obstetricians, dermatologists) or doctors with specific kinds of hobbies (cars, travel, skiing) might well make up the relevant audiences. Clearly, media firms that cater to advertisers interested in reaching such segments of the population cannot use circulation figures alone to prove their value. Instead, they commission research to bring out the characteristics of their consumers that will attract their advertisers. These investigations take three basic forms:

Demographic

Psychographic

Lifestyle

Demographic characteristics are the most common traits gauged by audience researchers. These are basic social features used to distinguish people from one another. Examples of such categories are age, gender, geographic location, occupation, and race.

Advertising executives are typically interested in reaching segments of the population that have substantial **disposable income** — that is, money for items beyond the bare necessities of life. This interest in disposable income leads them to pursue demographic categories they believe clearly predict spending ability. As a result, such items as age, gender, occupation, race, and profession typically take importance over favorite color, ability to swim, and height. (Of course, if the latter categories can be shown as predictive of buying habits, they are used as well.)

BOX 5.1 Affluence and Values

Advertisers and their agencies are continually exploring new ways to understand segments of society that are made up of attractive consumers. Affluent consumers are particularly attractive, because they have more disposable, or discretionary, income than others. One way to understand affluent consumers is to ask them about their values and tie these values to purchasing habits. Such information helps advertisers decide which consumers to target, what media to use, and how to speak to them.

For example, in 1995 the Conde Nast magazine firm commissioned the Roper Starch Worldwide research firm to study the values and shopping habits of 1,000 adults with household incomes of $100,000 or more. Here are some of the findings:

- Only 29% of the affluents consider themselves "better off than most."
- Only 13% consider themselves "very well off."
- 55% said that "the material things people own aren't the best indicator of their success."
- But 18% said they "admire people who own expensive homes, cars, and clothes."
- And 16% said they "like to own things that impress people."

The researchers found they could divide the affluents into five groups:

- Luxury Lovers, representing 29% of the group, who are young and image-conscious;
- Savvy Affluents (23%), who are the most price-conscious and save money;
- Strained Affluents (13%), who have the "lowest" incomes and strive to reach more luxurious lifestyles;
- Contented Affluents (14%), who are older, married, and least appearance-conscious; and
- Trail Blazers (21%), who are heavy travelers and most interested in new media and computers.

SOURCE: Leah Haran, "Chevy Tastes Persist on Cadillac-like Income," *Advertising Age,* September 18, 1995, p. 3.

The past few decades have seen many attempts to construct audiences with characteristics that go beyond demographics, because fierce competition among marketers has led them to look for other features of the population they can target to encourage consumption of their products or services. At the same time, fierce competition among media firms for advertisers has led them to claim that although their audiences are small, they possess characteristics that make them especially desirable to particular advertisers.

To do so, media producers pay for research on their audiences and store it in computers. These **data bases** allow producers to sift through large amounts of information that could make the audience attractive to particular advertisers.

An example comes from the newspaper industry. In the early 1990s, newspaper companies began to use data bases to halt their eroding share of the ad market in their communities. Executives believed they could use targeted lists of readers to attract advertisers and discourage them from turning to other media such as catalogs and other direct mail products. In one case, Cowles Publishing Company's *Spokane-Review* and *Spokane Chronicle,* both in Spokane, Washington, used contests, questionnaires, and promotions to build small data bases of readers with special interests such as computers and hunting. The company then tried to attract advertisers interested in targeting such readers.[9]

As this example suggests, marketers and the media producers who try to appeal to them pay particular attention to their personality characteristics and lifestyles. **Lifestyles research** ties media users to recreational or buying habits. Often, the activities are quite specific — for example, the number of trips readers take or the number of homes they own. In touting the lifestyles of their audience, media firms often combine them to create a kind of composite personality. *Popular Mechanics*' "Must-Know Man," described earlier in this chapter, is an example of an attempt to combine demographic and lifestyle attributes into a character that would appeal to male-oriented advertisers.

Actual research on the personalities of audience members is called **psychographic research.** The aim is to attach traits such as leadership, sociability, independence, conformity, and compulsiveness to the people who use a magazine, cable channel, newspaper, or other media vehicle.

In the mid-1980s, for example, SRI International used its popular VALS (Values and Lifestyles) survey to argue that people it called "belongers" are heavy commercial TV viewers, while "inner-directed" individuals are the heaviest public TV watchers. Radio stations, TV stations, magazines, newspapers, and other media use these data to convince advertisers that they reach people who have the temperament to purchase certain kinds of products.

The use of specialized research to segment consumers into specific audiences is growing and has an impact on the way advertisers use media. Since the mid-1980s, there have been growing complaints by advertisers that their ads are getting lost amidst the barrage of commercial messages hurled at consumers by the most popular media.

Concern about such **commercial clutter** has been strongest in the broadcast media, though it has been voiced about certain print organs, too. Advertisers have also indicated growing problems in sponsoring print media for the wealthier segments of the population. Although these busy people may well subscribe to a substantial number of publications, it is not at all clear that they have the time to read much of what is in them, especially the ads.

In Search of New Ad Vehicles

In response to these concerns, a variety of major advertisers have begun to re-think their approaches to media support. Ad-supported cable television chan-nels have been one collective beneficiary of their intention to sometimes look away from over-the-air broadcasters in an attempt to reduce clutter. Nick-elodeon, Lifetime, ESPN, and Cable News Network, among the more popular channels, have been quite successful in convincing certain advertisers that, along with reducing clutter, they construct audiences in a way that could be more effective for some sponsors than are certain broadcast TV purchases. Commercials in movie theaters and on videotapes of recent films have also be-come more popular.

Three other ways to reach consumers that have gained strength among marketers in recent years are:

Promotion

Direct marketing

The use of captive-audience media

Promotion involves payment by a marketer to be associated with an event or individual. Consider Nike's payment of professional basketball players to wear Nike shoes, Virginia Slims' sponsorship of tennis matches, and the placement of products from the Spiegel catalog on the *Wheel of Fortune* tele-vision game show.

Direct marketing is the activity of using the mail or the telephone to convince consumers about products and services. Clothing catalogs, automatic phone dialers (where a machine conveys a message and invites information), and the blizzard of brochures people typically call "junk mail" are a few of the categories that characterize this arena.

Also growing rapidly is the **captive-audience** approach to mass media. A mass medium with a captive audience is one in which the people exposed to it have nowhere to go when they encounter the medium and few (if any) alter-native media to distract them. POP Radio Corporation, which broadcasts cus-tomized music and commercials to supermarkets, is a typical player in this area.[10] Another is Turner Broadcasting's Airport Channel, which customizes news programming for travelers who watch it on monitors while waiting for flights. Probably the most controversial captive-audience medium is Channel One, which brings ads with news to students in classrooms.

By building projects around the long-term sponsorship of a number of "participating advertisers," companies such as POP and Turner aim to solve the problem of clutter and allay advertisers' fear that consumers will ignore the media they sponsor.

None of these forms of salesmanship — promotion, direct marketing, and attempts to find captive audiences — is new. What is different about their con-temporary situation is the growing amount of money marketers have been

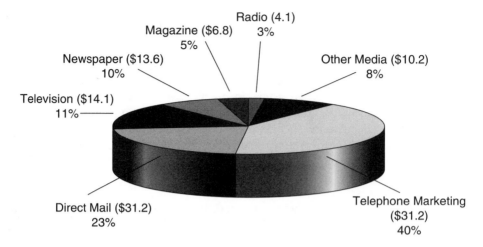

FIGURE 5.1 Direct marketing impact. (SOURCE: *Advertising Age,* October 9, 1995, p. 34.)

This pie chart shows the percentage of total 1995 direct marketing ad expenditures by medium (dollars in billions). Of the $234.5 billion in total advertising expenditures in the United States in 1995, direct marketing accounts for $134 billion, or 57.1%. Telephone marketing accounts for the bulk of direct marketing spending.

committing to them. One potential consequence if they continue to grow is that large advertisers will siphon off substantial advertising support from traditional broadcast and print media.

Even more likely is that, to remain attractive, traditional newspapers, magazines, and broadcast outlets will bend their editorial materials to fit the interests of major advertisers even more than in the past. This possibility concerns observers who already worry that American media are guided too often by business pressures of which their readers, listeners, or viewers are ignorant.

RELIABILITY, VALIDITY, AND THE CONSTRUCTION OF AUDIENCE

The increasing desire of marketers to target ever more specific audiences in the ways and places that most persuade them to buy is being fed by data base companies. These firms collect huge amounts of information about individual consumers through credit card purchases, loan application disclosures, periodical subscriptions, and similar behaviors. Marketers tend to believe that information about people's previous purchases is an important indicator of their future consumption activities. As a result, many pay high prices to extract from data bases a wide variety of surprisingly personal information about individual American consumers: how much they earn, how much they

TABLE 5.2 "WHAT'S IN IT FOR ME?"

	Definitely Agree				Definitely Disagree
	5%	4%	3%	2%	1%
Better protection against fraud	28	13	20	12	25
A lower finance charge on your credit card	25	11	17	14	32
No annual fee for your credit card	25	12	14	12	37
Cash back on purchases	19	11	21	13	35
Discounts on products you buy	18	15	19	14	34
Special services or better treatment as a preferred customer	18	12	20	14	35
Notification of sales	17	11	20	16	35
Information about new products on the market	15	11	18	18	37

Percentages are rounded to the nearest whole number; therefore, responses may not total 100%. (SOURCE: Advertising Age, *October 2, 1995, p. 32.*)

"Suppose an organization were to offer you [list of incentives] in return for the right to use information about you and your family for other business purposes. Are you likely to agree to this or not?"

paid for their house, what cars they own, how old their children are, and a good deal more.

Research and Privacy

The computer data base is an important contributor to direct marketing's swift rate of growth. It has given advertisers the confidence that they can narrow their focus to special consumers, particularly affluent ones.

Direct marketers contend that the cutting edge of merchandising lies in using data bases to target potential customers with information specially dedicated to their interests. They claim they can use demographic and lifestyle categories from data bases to target people who are most likely to purchase certain kinds of products. They also believe that because this identification of prospects is so efficient, it pays to pursue them with handsome catalogs, audio cassettes, and even video cassettes in addition to (and even instead of) advertising in newspapers, magazines, or on TV.

Sometimes, direct-marketing materials are adjusted to the needs of specific individual consumers using information derived from the data bases. The Volvo auto company can personalize a brochure to John Jones with the year John bought his most recent car, for example.

Access to this kind of information raises many concerns regarding citizens' right to privacy. In fact, as time goes on, a growing number of voices have been expressing concern about the marketing and use of data bases with information on Americans. We might also ask whether these information banks are accurate. For that matter, we might ask how accurate are any of the approaches to audience research noted in this chapter.

Research and Accuracy

The question of accuracy in audience research is a complex one. Over the past several decades, certain audience research procedures have come to be accepted as standard in particular areas of the media. This means that both producers and clients in those media consider the procedures to be the best available mix of reliability, validity, and economy.

Reliability refers to the ability of two researchers using the same methods to arrive at results that are the same from a statistical standpoint.

Validity means that the results can be considered truly representative of what goes on in the population as a whole, outside the survey situation.

Economy points to the need to pay attention to the costs of audience research.

Research that raises to intolerable levels the price producers must charge advertisers or consumers will not be commissioned by either party. It follows that the need to economize on audience research could introduce problems of reliability and validity. If, for example, a telephone survey based on random digit dialing finds that 25% of those called do not answer, the accepted procedure would be to phone again. Experience has shown that with many repeated attempts, it is possible to get a completion rate on calls of over 90%.[11] Calling a number several times, however, is an expense that most marketers do not want to incur. If the callback procedure is not carried out carefully, though, problems of reliability will result. Yet standardizing enough callbacks to get a 90% completion rate is expensive. Typically, research firms content themselves with only one extra attempt to complete a call. The result is that the validity of the sample of people considered to be a statistical representation of "the audience" is suspect.

Enduring Problems with Validity

In many cases validity problems remain even if no cost considerations are involved in determining the research approach. One reason is that drawing a truly representative sample of users of certain media has proved to be nearly impossible.

In the television ratings business, for example, Nielsen has often had a difficult time drawing a statistically random sample from the nation as a whole. Some families may refuse to allow people meters in their homes; others may demand that they be taken out after they have been installed. Nielsen has had a particularly difficult time auditing poor areas of the country, where theft and breakage of meters are not uncommon. The firm also finds that to persuade poor people to be part of the sample, it must pay them a good deal more than the token amount it gives to most families in the sample.

In Nielsen's case, and in the case of much audience research, another major problem of validity arises. Following people's activities and asking them to declare what they do on a daily basis causes them to speak and act differently than they would if no one were tracking them. It is a common joke in the industry that Nielsen families turn on the TV even when they go out for the evening because they want to help their favorite shows. Similarly, people who fill out radio diaries often put down the station they would have listened to if they had been listening. The same kind of problem exists with newspapers and magazines. When people are interviewed about the periodicals they read, it is difficult to separate wishful thinking from accurate recall.

Many of the inaccuracies become part of the data bases sold to advertisers who are deciding what media to sponsor. Magazine-selling companies compound the inaccuracies, in effect, by providing customers with incentives to lie about themselves in order to get lower rates.

For example, nonstudents who receive "student discounts" on *Time* magazine become part of a student data base group that *Time* uses for its own internal marketing plan as well as to sell to other firms. Small inaccuracies such as these are repeated many times over with respect to a wide variety of demographic and lifestyle categories. The result is a multitude of data sets with questionable validity regarding American consumers.

The most sophisticated of audience researchers, advertisers, and media producers are well aware of these drawbacks. Their reply is that they do the best they can with what they have. Attempts to correct the most controversial problems often take up the energies and development costs of research firms. Nielsen and a few other firms, for example, have been working on what is called a **passive people meter.** The idea is to have a computer recognize individuals in the television room so that they do not have to push buttons.

No audience research system will ever be totally free of problems, though. From a practical standpoint, audience research methods typically reflect attempts to achieve results that both sides of the producer-client relationship consider valid and reliable and at costs acceptable to both advertisers and producers. People in the media business require audience numbers to justify their actions and lower their risks. As a result, media executives act as if their research procedures and audience numbers were basically satisfactory, even if a little reflection could show that the problems connected to gathering the numbers make their generalizations highly suspect.

THE LARGER POINT

There is an even larger point to make, however, and it is the underlying theme of this chapter: Even if all questions of reliability and validity could be brushed aside, it still remains that every media audience is a construction of reality.

This does not mean that the categories used by production and client organizations to construct audiences have no basis in fact. Audience research is aimed at ensuring that those categories can be related to real individuals "out there."

It bears repeating that the questions asked in audience research are designed by the organizations asking the questions for their own purposes. In mass media industries, producers and clients, not consumers, control the basic terms on which audiences are defined. Sometimes this causes problems. Individuals or groups of consumers do not like the way mass media industries are defining them. They want to be thought of differently, so that the media will deliver different mass media materials to them. What this means, and how it is resolved, is the subject of the next chapter.

CONSIDER THIS

1. Does the idea that a magazine constructs an audience necessarily mean that the information it uses is not true?
2. Compare the advertisements in two cable channels or magazines that you know are aimed at different audiences. How different are the ads?
3. Radio station executives program their stations with different formats, depending on the audiences they are trying to attract. Can you identify and describe several radio station formats in your area?

NOTES

1. See Joseph Turow, *Getting Books to Children: An Exploration of Publisher-Market Relations* (Chicago: American Library Association, 1979).
2. *Advertising Age,* October 23, 1989, p. 21.
3. Joseph R. Dominick, *The Dynamics of Mass Communication* (New York: McGraw-Hill, 1990), pp. 496–498.
4. Edwin McDowell, "Publishers Experiment with Lower Prices," *New York Times,* May 8, 1989, p. D10.
5. *Motion Picture Almanac, 1991;* telephone conversations with Bruce Snyder, president, Domestic Distribution, 20th Century Fox Film Corporation, June 20, 1991, and with Leonard Klady, film reporter for *Variety,* November 2, 1995.
6. Interview with Perry Katz, Universal Pictures marketing, March 6, 1990.
7. Alfred Balk, "The 'Entrepreneurs' Behind *Entertainment Weekly*," *Folio,* November 1989, pp. 79–83.
8. Joseph Dominick, Barry Sherman, and Gary Copeland, *Broadcasting/Cable and Beyond* (New York: McGraw-Hill, 1990), pp. 342–343.
9. Janet Meyers, "Papers Study Data-base Marketing," *Advertising Age,* November 5, 1990, p. 60.
10. Allison Fahey, "Actmedia Is Ready to Fight Back, *Advertising Age,* March 19, 1990, p. 18.
11. Hugh Malcolm Beville Jr., *Audience Ratings: Radio, Television, Cable* (Hillsdale, NJ: Lawrence Erlbaum, 1985), p. 96.

CHAPTER 6

The Power of the Public

This chapter

- explores the circumstances under which members of the public can influence the media.
- suggests a framework based on the resource-dependence model that can explain and predict those circumstances.
- draws examples from the newspaper, children's book, textbook, radio, and television industries.

We can all recall moments when we were annoyed at a newspaper we read, a radio station we listened to, a TV station we watched. For some people, this annoyance turns to anger, and the anger turns to action. One need only flip through the pages of major newspapers or trade magazines to find cases where people's rage about what is presented by mass media firms explodes into demands for change. In organized groups or individually, people may insist on changes in the images they present, in the people who control the media materials, or even in the government and corporate policies that set the structure of media industries in the first place. Consider a few of the controversies that have received attention in the recent past.

A group of physicians tried unsuccessfully for years to persuade the *New York Times* to ban cigarette ads from the newspaper. They also demanded that the paper increase coverage of their anti-*Times* viewpoint, and this, too, was rejected.[1]

During the early 1990s, people from a variety of quarters expressed concern about "gangsta rap," a form of music with lyrics they claimed encouraged violence against women, the police, and other groups. One target of their anger was Time Warner, which owned half of Interscope, a major producer of gangsta rap. Many in the music industry defended the right of rappers to express themselves, saying that their ideas reflected an important, neglected portion of society. Prominent on the other side were Senator Bob Dole, former U.S. Education Secretary William Bennett, and the National Political Congress of Black Woman, headed by C. Delores Tucker. This vigorous opposition seems to have convinced Time Warner's chairman, Gerald Levin, in 1995 that it was in his company's best interest to sell its interest in Interscope. The latter continued to release gangsta rap songs, however.[2]

Days of Rage: The Young Palestinians, a documentary about Palestinian–Israeli hostilities from a Palestinian viewpoint, became the center of controversy in 1989. Critics of the program, which was partially funded by the Public Broadcasting Service, argued that not only was the documentary stridently anti-Israel but it also received hidden support from Kuwaiti and other Arab interests. The critics demanded that PBS not air the show. PBS did air it, but added a panel discussion on the program's pros and cons immediately after the telecast.[3]

These incidents represent just the tip of an iceberg of recent attempts by people outside mass media industries to influence them. Sometimes they succeeded; sometimes they did not; and sometimes there were compromises. The purpose of this chapter is not to catalog these attempts, or even to list the most important ones, but rather to create a framework for understanding such incidents and to confront a basic question: **Under what circumstances can individuals or organized groups exert influence when they want to change mass media materials?**

OUTSIDE PRESSURE ON MEDIA FIRMS

To begin answering this question, it is helpful to build upon ideas introduced in previous chapters. One is that a mass media production firm must rely on its environment for survival. The environment provides the resources — money, supplies, people, information, permission — that a production organization needs in order to create and release mass media material to the public.

Previous chapters have also made clear that the resources mass media producers need are not distributed randomly throughout the environment. On the contrary, organizations taking on the power roles of authorities, clients, exhibitors, and distributors hold key resources and make important demands on producers in exchange for them.

Recall, too, that production firm executives are not passive about their environment. Typically, their intention is to avoid becoming too dependent upon specific entities that provide them with money, supplies, people, information, and permission. They maintain their independence by hiring specialized boundary personnel to shape the demands that outside groups make on them. For example, lobbyists for broadcasters try to ensure that government regulation of radio and TV stations does not become burdensome. Similarly, marketing executives from newspaper firms try to shape their clients' perceptions of their papers' ability to deliver desirable audiences.

Media production executives are, in other words, people who respond actively to pressures in their environment. They try to deal with those pressures in ways that benefit them. At the same time, they realize that in order to take resources from the environment, they must give in to certain demands. Not all demands are equal. For example, if the cash of a particular advertiser is crucial, or if the permission of a government agency is necessary and unchangeable, the executives are more likely to accommodate the needs of these organizations than if the power of those outside organizations were negligible.

Generally speaking, production firm executives are likely to respond to outside pressure with three major considerations in mind:

> The **importance** of the resources that particular organizations offer
>
> The **substitutability** of those resources
>
> The **negotiability** of the demands on them

These considerations are evaluated together. The money of an advertiser may be important to a newspaper, but not *that* important if substitutable advertisers can be found. A compromise might be worked out if the advertiser were willing to negotiate. From a producer's standpoint, it is best if a client can be accommodated while not affecting the producer's control over organizational policies.

The concerns of media executives about the importance of resources, their substitutability, and the negotiability of demands on them can help us understand how they deal with demands for change by individuals or organized groups. The questions for our consideration here are: How seriously do executives evaluate demands by public or public advocacy organizations? How far are they willing to go to negotiate compromises with them that satisfy demands on both sides? The answers have much to do with the relative value of the resources that various constituencies bring to the producer's table.

PRODUCERS AND MEMBERS OF THE PUBLIC

It is logical to start at the most basic level: the response of production firms to comments or suggestions of members of the public about mass media material. Such offerings are certainly not rare. Moreover, for the most prominent media firms, the stream of reader, viewer, and listener phone calls, postcards, and letters can be very large indeed.

A staff member in the *New York Times* Letters to the Editor department estimated in 1990 that 70,000 people write to the newspaper each year.[4] Of course, the hope that a letter will be printed on the editorial page may have been a strong incentive for some readers to write. Still, the count appears to be high even when people know they will not see their names in print or on screen. In the late 1970s, Herbert Gans counted 351 letters to NBC TV news anchor John Chancellor in one month.[5]

The Influence of Individuals

What influence do members of the public have on the creation and release of the materials they are calling or writing about? A better way to phrase the question is, What resources can an individual member of the public offer to production firms that they cannot get elsewhere without giving up independence of action to that person? It would seem that the answer varies depending on the situation. All else being equal, the more production personnel perceive an individual's comments to be in sync with organizational policy, the greater the likelihood they will respond positively.

Organizations may actually welcome certain types of comments. As noted in Chapter 5, one consideration that goes into forming organizational policy is ongoing concern about the audience's likes and dislikes. Remember, though, what media executives mean when they talk about audience interests. Chapter 5 stresses that mass media production firms view audiences through lenses that reflect business needs. That is, they pay close attention to categories of their target consumers that they and their clients (for example, advertisers) find useful.

Based on market research, these categories often become a part of media executives' assumptions about the environment, which lead them to generate the organization's routines — that is, its daily patterns of activity. Successful routines typically result in output satisfactory to clients and many consumers. Still, even successful production personnel constantly try to improve their performance. They are likely to welcome suggestions for change that fit their basic assumptions about their audience and environment, even if the suggestions imply changing some of the routines based on those assumptions. The reason is that acting positively on suggestions that flow with organizational plans involves giving up only a little organizational independence in the service of ideas that may yield profit.

However, the more an individual's demands require the production firm to depart from its basic policies, the less likely it is that production personnel will respond positively to the individual claimant. Instead, the demands will probably be rejected as irrelevancies, nuisances, or threats. This is because assumptions, policies, and routines are developed with reference to the resources held by powerful sets of forces in the environment: competitors, clients, distributors, exhibitors, authorities, and the like. Production personnel will likely feel that one person who threatens not to view, attend, or purchase a media product can do little harm compared to the resources that an important advertising client or regulatory agency can remove from the production firm.

Precisely how does a media production firm respond to contacts from members of the public? How do members of the organization channel the comments, positive and negative, in useful ways? Recall that in order to manage the environment efficiently, production firm executives develop routines for themselves and for specialized boundary personnel. In line with this understanding, we would expect any producer regularly receiving comments from individuals outside the organization to develop a set of responses to them. Organization researchers James March and Herbert Simon have called this kind of routinized response pattern a **performance program.**[6]

Performance Programs

The performance program that a media organization develops for public contacts may be simple, involving a couple of steps and people, or it may be elaborate. An important difference between print and broadcast media in the United States must be noted. As explained in Chapter 3, print has traditionally been free of prepublication regulation through safeguards dating to the earliest days of the republic. The broadcast industry has not been so lucky. There, regulation mandates an individual's right to usurp air time under certain limited circumstances.

Specifically, the **Equal Time** provision of the 1934 Federal Communications Act requires broadcasters to allow announced candidates who are qualified for public office "equal opportunities" to state their views at the same rates.[7] Moreover, broadcasters, unlike print firms, operate as public trustees of the airwaves and must renew their licenses every few years. Radio and TV executives therefore have a strong incentive to develop performance programs that protect their money-making routines and at the same time limit the number of citizen complaints to government officials.

The routines they develop, then, will probably depend on the kinds of demands brought by members of the public, the executives' fear of government regulation, and the public relations goals of the company. In the case of letters to the *New York Times,* it is clear that management does not see this kind of input as a threat to the firm's autonomy or as a problem that can spark government regulation. Instead, the editor is expected to turn it to the *Times'* own benefit.

In describing his department's routines for dealing with public input, Kalman Siegel, the *Times'* letters editor in the early 1970s, explained that his organization keeps total control over the use and disposition of the material it receives. Siegel suggested that the letters section has long served several company goals at the same time: journalistic, marketing, and public relations goals. On the journalistic front, he pointed out that *Times* management believes the letters section "is one of the paper's great responsibilities in helping to form public opinion."[8]

He noted that marketing is in sync with journalism here: The letters section is popular and is usually among the most widely read parts of the paper. Siegel pointed out that in addition to journalistic and marketing purposes, the letters section fills a public relations function. He gave the distinct impression that famous or powerful people will have easier access to the letters section than will members of the public without such influence. The reason is obvious: Prestigious letter writers give prestige to the paper.

The *Times'* policy of controlling the public's access to organizational activities while using public input for the company's benefit can be found in many media organizations. Consider the way a major market radio station dealt with letters that were not written for public consumption but, rather, to complain about station programming and urge change. Like many media managers, the station's executives did not consider individual complaints to be representative of the audience; they saw only their market research as tapping into that.

Their treatment of complaint letters, therefore, was to handle the comments quickly without affecting the organization's efficiency. However, because they also were concerned with maintaining a good public relations posture and not having problems at license renewal time, they wanted to dispose of the complaints without alienating the correspondents.

The Case of a Radio Station

A study of the station's handling of the letters revealed a clear-cut performance program.[9] Although every letter received a personal answer (the letter writer's name was mentioned and the subject noted), the reply was patterned after a standard form. The station's editorial director, writing in the name of the sta-

---

TABLE 6.1 FEEDBACK LETTER TOPICS AND A RADIO STATION'S REPLIES

Topics

I.	Favorable remark about the station's on-air personality
II.	Nonstation-related request
III.	Opinions and proposals relating to current events
IV.	General complaint about a personality's actions
V.	Specific complaint about a personality's actions
VI.	Complaint about station policy
VII.	Complaint about a specific station action

Association of Topics with Replies

Topic	Reply
I.	"Always happy to hear from a satisified listener."
II.	"Here is some information that may help you . . ."
	"Write to this government agency to get information."
III.	"Why don't you call our talk shows and present your ideas on radio?"
	"Since we feel that your idea is most interesting, why not present it as a rebuttal to our editorial? Contact our editorial director . . ."*
IV.	"Our moderator is among the best informed in the country."
	"Thousands of listeners feel different from you."
V.	"Our moderators often take positions they don't really believe for the sake of stimulating discussion."
	"You may be assured the problem will not be repeated."
VI.	"It is a practical truth of broadcasting that high commercial content is necessary to maintain high quality service to listeners."
VII.	"We have no obligation under Federal Communications Commission regulations to provide equal time . . ."

*This response was evoked by two complaints against the rudeness of a talk show host and by one complaint against the rudeness of a producer. (SOURCE: Joseph Turow, "Another View of Citizen Feedback to the Mass Media," Public Opinion Quarterly 41 (Winter 1977–78), pp. 535–543.)

tion manager, followed a systematic procedure. He answered the letters efficiently while insulating the comments from the station personnel they discussed so as not to upset organizational routines. These responses followed a formula. Sandwiched between a fixed introductory thanks for the writer's comments and a fixed final hope that the writer would continue listening to the station were remarks that attempted to deal with the particulars of the complaint, demand, praise, or question.

The packaged replies to complaints were aimed at defusing threats to the station by associating station policy with basic principles with which the plaintiff was unlikely to argue. As Table 6.1 shows, in reply to a negative opinion of a station personality, the "station manager" said that "thousands of listeners feel different from you." A commitment to intellectual excellence and superior performance was the defense used in the comment that a talk show host was "among the best informed in the country." A charge of bias or racism on the part of a talk show host was countered by an invocation of the principle of diverse and free-flowing ideas. And a complaint against too many commercials was met by a statement about the need to recognize the connection between good business and good service.

Interestingly, when a feedback letter invoked a rule—the Equal Time rule, for example—the station responded by saying that the writer had misunderstood its meaning and applicability: "Until [one of two men who are both obviously running for public office] announces his candidacy, we have no obligation under Federal Communications Commission regulations to provide equal time to either man."

PRODUCERS AND PUBLIC ADVOCACY ORGANIZATIONS

It is very likely that in the great majority of cases, production organizations do not have to go beyond this kind of containment when dealing with critical comments and demands by members of the public. One reason is that it probably works most of the time. In the study just described, analysis of questionnaires that were sent to, and answered by, eighty letter writers indicated that the station's pattern of replies was quite successful at accomplishing the station manager's objective of not alienating them. Moreover, the little evidence that exists about people's knowledge of media operations suggests that most individuals will not take the time or trouble to find out what further steps they could take to successfully pursue their demands.

Strength in Others

When individuals do pursue their complaints and demands, it is often because they have found strength and ammunition in other individuals who share an interest in the issues they raise. They might tap established organizations with broad-ranging activities — for example, the NAACP, the American Civil Liberties Union, or the Ku Klux Klan. They might seek organizations that pursue specific interests or deal with specific media — for example, Fairness and Accuracy in Reporting (FAIR) and the Media Access Project. Or they might even start their own organization.

In any of these cases, the media-related complaints may be part of a larger agenda for society that the group wants to implement. Consider an organization interested in combating ethnic and racial prejudice. Its leaders might protest against commercial TV's portrayals of certain ethnic groups because of their concern about the medium's power to circulate negative images throughout society. A more politically attuned reason for focusing attention on television could be that it provides a pool of images that many people already know, can label as negative, and can mobilize around. In other words, organizations sometimes choose to pick fights with commercial TV because the medium can easily be used as a rallying point on which to recruit new members and keep old ones.

Production firm executives do not like to discuss their arguments with advocacy groups publicly because they do not want to encourage other complaints. Advocacy group leaders, for their part, sometimes like to sound as if their challenges were more successful than they really are in order to hold on to their followers. Despite the reluctance of the parties to divulge details, some generalizations can be made.

One is that a large number of organized protesters is in a better situation to encourage change than are individual plaintiffs. The reason is that production personnel would likely be more concerned about the strong public relations damage that large protest groups can wreak compared to unknown individuals. This intimidation would be particularly felt in a media organization not accustomed to such protests. Executives might be uncertain how to preserve their independence of action.

At the same time, we would expect executives in a media organization familiar with protests to have worked out a set of routines for evaluating and handling angry demands. As usual, the goal of such a **performance program** is likely to be organizational autonomy in the production of messages. This means maintaining the firm's efficient production routines as well as the flow of the resources the organization needs from its environment to continue those activities.

Four considerations will probably enter into determining how to respond to outside demands.

> The greater the change the group proposes, the more difficult it will be for the producer to accept it.
>
> The greater the probability that the change will alienate major resource providers, the more difficult it will be to accept it.
>
> The less critical the resources that the group can marshal against the producer, the less likely the producer will listen.

Even if the group's resources are important, the greater the ability of the producer to get those resources (or substitutable ones) elsewhere, the more likely the producer is to refuse to give in to the demands.

The Whittle Communications Case

A comparison of the outcomes of two producer-directed activities illustrates these points. The cases involve different special interest publics: teacher groups and public health advocates. The one involving teachers was a protest against Whittle Communications in the late 1980s and early 1990s. During that period, Whittle Communications embarked upon a program to bring an advertiser-supported TV news channel to junior and senior high schools.[10]

Whittle's plan was to provide all the equipment needed to receive satellite programming in a large number of classrooms per school. In return for doing so, the schools would agree to show all students in the classrooms a daily twelve-minute news program, with two minutes of commercials. The commercials, paid for by advertisers interested in reaching youngsters, would recompense Whittle for the cost of the technology. Whittle's expectation was that over time, Channel One would yield the firm handsome profits.

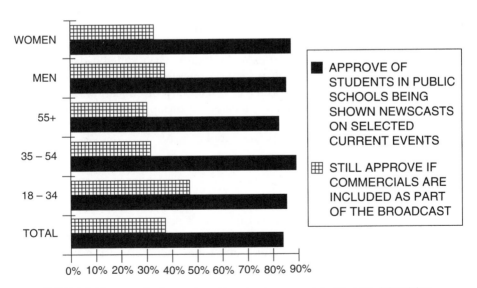

FIGURE 6.1 Most people disapprove of in-school commercials (SOURCE: *Advertising Age,* August 14, 1989, p. 4.

A national survey by the Gallup organization for *Advertising Age* revealed that most adults did not want TV commercials in school. Despite such evidence and public outcries against Channel One, Whittle Communications went ahead with it.

When Whittle's plan for advertiser-supported TV in schools was announced, it drew angry protests from the American Federation of Teachers, a
large teacher's organization, as well as from parent-teacher groups around the
country. They argued that forcing students to watch commercials was contradictory to the aim of education. They also contended that education involves
critical evaluation, which does not mesh with the forced feeding of advertising
messages. Whittle should drop the whole idea, they insisted. The groups
gained support from the Board of Regents of New York and the Superintendent of Public Instruction in California, which represented all the public
schools in these two states. The protesters hoped that with the organizations
representing the resources of two large school regions on their side, Whittle
would give up.

That did not happen. Whittle management calculated that a very profitable number of schools around the United States was willing to trade showing Channel One for the merchandise the company was offering. School budgets were hurting and many principals saw the deal as a way to acquire
technology that could be applied to many useful educational purposes. Just as
important, major advertisers still agreed with Whittle that Channel One could
be an efficient way to turn a high-spending yet elusive demographic group —
American teenagers — into a captive audience.

Whittle saw the public attacks against Channel One as an unacceptable attempt to infringe on its profit-making autonomy. With an adequate number of
schools willing to sign on and the resources of major advertisers behind them,
the firm was eager to show that the groups militating against it did not represent the collective opinion of educators. As a result, Whittle formed a board of
twelve educators and public figures to provide what it called "advice and direction" for Channel One's programming. Consisting of two university presidents, well-known authors, a former U.S. secretary of education, and others,
the panel was clearly designed to deflate the groups' claim that education
would be ill-served by Channel One's arrival. The project moved forward, and
Channel One is still running in the late 1990s.

The Harvard Alcohol Case

Place this episode next to a very different kind of bid to influence production:
an attempt by professors at Harvard University's School of Public Health to insert themes about the perils of drinking and driving into TV programs. Over
the years, many activists, researchers, and other members of the public have
condemned broadcasters for irresponsibly portraying the consumption of alcohol as a comfortable, upscale thing to do or as the basis for drunken humor.

Noting that alcohol is one of America's major highway killers, Jay Winsten, director of the Harvard Alcohol Project, began a campaign in 1988 to do
something about TV's handling of the issue. His initial meetings were set up
with the help of the former heads of NBC and CBS. These contacts helped
him connect with many of the industry's writers and producers. Winsten

prodded them to be careful about the manner in which they portray drinking. He suggested particularly that they mention in their programs the "designated driver" — the person appointed by a group of friends as the nondrinker for the evening who will drive the others home.

By spring 1990, Winsten had met with more than 160 writers and producers. He claimed that more than eighty series episodes had carried some reference to the dangers of drinking and driving since he began his campaign. Hollywood TV producers confirmed that the Alcohol Project had made an impact on programming. "They are extremely effective lobbyists," noted a producer from a firm with a number of popular sitcoms. "They have a way of making you feel bad if you don't get involved."[11]

In comparing the Alcohol Project with the anti-Whittle campaign, a number of resource-based reasons for the Alcohol Project's success and the anti-Whittle activists' failure become apparent. For one, the difference in the media involved gave advocacy groups more leverage in the network TV case than in the Channel One case. TV broadcasters operate as public trustees and must renew their licenses with the Federal Communications Commission at regular intervals. Channel One, by contrast, is essentially a closed-circuit satellite-to-cable service that does not fall under the FCC's broadcast station licensing rules.

Although production firms technically do not come under government regulation, the valuable stations that networks own do, as do the stations of their affiliates. Broadcast station owners are sometimes concerned that FCC regulators will interpret rules and license renewal petitions in ways that reflect the public indignation directed at broadcasters. Because they are not responsible to a federal agency, Whittle executives may feel less need than their broadcasting counterparts to satisfy large or prestigious segments of the public that are not directly relevant as audiences to their advertisers.

But the different reactions of the network TV producers and Whittle were not based only, or even primarily, on the regulatory sensitivities of the firms involved. As the earlier comment of the sitcom producer implied, the reactions seem to have related mainly to the way the activists approached the thorny issue of organizational autonomy and established routines. The anti–Channel One groups forced Whittle Communications into an uncomfortably public all-or-nothing position in the face of a potentially lucrative program.

The Harvard Alcohol Project, by contrast, was content with limited goals. Its members did not insist, for example, that the TV networks eliminate beer commercials from their airwaves or alcohol from their shows. They ignored critics who claimed that giving the networks an excuse to justify the presentation of alcohol (by showing a designated driver) was not helpful to the anti-drinking cause. Instead, they pragmatically accepted the needs of producers, networks, and advertisers and offered to work with them to create pro-social messages that would fit into established routines and make the creators feel good.

"They are already depicting alcohol use in many instances," Winsten told the *New York Times,* "and we just ask them to use sensitivity in how they portray the issue. They can save lives with a line or two of dialogue." He added his belief that part of his group's success stemmed from its nonconfrontational approach.

"There are advocacy groups that are prepared tactically to bring pressure to bear and then there are efforts to recruit writers and producers voluntarily," he said. "The programs that are successful are those that had at their origin or very quickly developed support from within the industry."[12]

Winsten's comments suggest that all-or-nothing demands are very risky even in the broadcast arena, where sensitivity to public demands may be greater than in other media. It is, in fact, difficult to think of a single program that ABC, CBS, NBC, PBS, or Fox has removed from its schedule as a result of public advocacy group protests. Network executives actually like certain types of controversy because it encourages viewers to tune in. According to some in the trade press, ratings-tweaking seemed to be behind ABC's airing of a 1994 *Roseanne* episode in which two women kissed passionately and CBS's airing of an interview with Julie Andrews on *60 Minutes* during which the singer bared her breasts. Moreover, flare-ups over TV programs as diverse as *Days of Rage: The Young Palestinians, Beulah Land* (a miniseries in which protesters zeroed in on what they considered to be unfavorable portrayals of blacks) and *Dateline NBC*'s decision to interview O.J. Simpson after his murder trial indicate that when pressure to remove a program or an episode becomes public, the networks will refuse to do so, even when it is clear that the show will lose money. Their fear is that caving in will set a bad precedent and invite an avalanche of similar protests.

This does not mean that all-or-nothing pressure by movements on media organizations is totally futile. One example of successful collective pressure is the "flaming" of the Cantor & Siegel law firm on the Internet in April 1994. Cantor & Siegel decided to use e-mail to advertise their services to a large number of Internet users. The receivers of the ads, however, were incensed that a firm would send what they considered junk mail under the guise of a bona fide message. The apparently spontaneous response was to swarm the law firm with angry replies and condemnations. This "flaming" (some call it "spamming"), which was repeated in other cases, startled marketers with its ferocity. It helped to establish a norm against using e-mail for advertising.[13]

Also to be considered is the possibility that a succession of advocacy group protests will give executives pause before releasing material that will bring another storm of petitions. They may fear that continual protest by powerful constituencies will ultimately embarrass them publicly, cause advertisers to hesitate in their sponsorship of material, and invite agencies of the federal government to hold regulatory hearings. This seems to be what happened when Time Warner chairman Gerald Levin decided to sell the firm's portion of Interscope. C. Delores Tucker, head of the advocacy group, had bought Time Warner stock and had used a stockholder meeting to angrily denounce the company's hand in gangsta rap. Moreover, Levin was well aware that U.S. government officials would soon be ruling on the acceptability of his firm's purchase of Turner Broadcasting from an antitrust standpoint.

Still, the refusal of media companies to yield to public demands causes great frustration among advocacy groups. As a result, they often turn for help to powerful go-betweens: legislators, regulatory agencies, courts, and advertisers.

PRESSURING PRODUCERS THROUGH AUTHORITIES

Organizations and individuals have a straightforward purpose in looking to legislatures, regulatory agencies, and courts in their bids to reform mass media material. Lacking the leverage to influence producers directly, they hope to persuade the authorities to join forces with them and, through the increased leverage they would achieve, carry out their goals of making changes in the media. Two major assumptions underlie such advocacy activity:

Authorities truly do have substantial leverage with producers.

Public advocacy organizations can enlist the authorities to help them by using that leverage.

An examination of the forces at work in such situations shows that these assumptions are not always warranted.

The Range of Pressure Points

The territory covered in this discussion is large. Public advocacy groups may be interested in virtually any government decision affecting the **structure** of a mass media industry or the industry's **relation to other industries.** They may voice their arguments at the **federal, state,** or **local** level. Moreover, at each level they may choose **courts, legislatures,** or **regulatory agencies** as arenas in which to make their arguments.

Advocacy groups often choose the courts to appeal for changes in media when they believe that current laws are unconstitutional or that the courts' interpretation of existing law will support their interests. When activists decide that lawsuits are not the best vehicle to implement change, they may resort to legislation by elected representatives or rule making by regulatory bodies such as the Federal Communications Commission, the Federal Trade Commission, and a city's cable commission. Members of those bodies are typically chosen by the chief executive at the federal, state, or local level (the president, the governor, the mayor) with the approval of the relevant legislature (Congress, the state assembly, the city council).

Mark Nadel, in his general study of "the politics of consumer protection," notes that a public advocacy group's success is based on its ability to make politicians believe that it has a major **constituency** — that is, a large following among the voters. The successful advocacy organization, he says, "takes phenomena defined as problems and lifts them to the point where they become political issues — a larger public becomes aware of the problems, and governmental participants feel pressure to take action on the problem."[14]

Nadel also points out that "the public's knowledge of government hearings and records comes from the media." Mass media are, therefore, important in expanding the constituencies of all sorts of pressure groups, whether their targets are media firms or other areas of life.[15]

Ironically, though, an advocacy group's difficulties in reaching potential members are compounded when mass media industries themselves are the group's target. One difficulty is that media executives may oppose the aims of the activists and therefore hinder their use of media to get public support. Another problem is that attempts to change media through the government are often stifled because of the First Amendment to the U.S. Constitution, which guarantees freedom of speech and the press from government control. As such, it strongly limits the ability of government representatives to join advocacy group members in forcing media organizations to create certain types of content.

These difficulties, together with the constituency-expansion challenges faced by all types of public advocacy organizations, mean that any influences on mass media materials through government pressure will typically be complex and limited. Space here does not permit examination of the many paths that lead out of this subject. The following sections describe some consequences of the two most intentional sorts of attempts made by activists to shape content:

Pressuring authorities to provide **access** to a production firm's mass medium

Pressuring authorities to **eliminate** certain materials created by mass media firms.

PRESSURING AUTHORITIES TO PROVIDE ACCESS

A. J. Liebling, the writer and journalism critic, once quipped that in America there is freedom of the press for the person who owns one. It is true that people who own media vehicles have tremendous freedom to decide who and what gets represented through them. As noted earlier, the First Amendment protects the rights of most producers of mass media material to deny people the use of a medium to express views contrary to those of the people who control it.

When speaking of this kind of access, though, an important distinction must be made between the regulated and unregulated media. Broadcast television, radio, and cable television are regulated. Newspapers, magazines, books, audio recordings, and video recordings are unregulated.

With respect to unregulated media, the U.S. Supreme Court has strongly implied that governments have no right to force the insertion of content. In the 1974 case of *Miami Herald Publishing Company v. Tornillo,* the Court declared that laws requiring newspapers to allow individuals they have attacked in the press to reply are unconstitutional. Writing for the Court, Chief Justice Warren Burger's position was uncompromising: "A responsible press is undoubtedly a desirable goal, but press responsibility is not mandated by the Constitution and like many other virtues cannot be legislated."[16]

This perspective gives *New York Times* editors the belief that they have a legal right to refuse space to the anticigarette activists mentioned at the beginning of this chapter. Legal observers have generally interpreted the Court's discussion of the press to include all unregulated media. In relation to regulated media, however, the government has reserved a greater right to intervene in favor of citizens desiring a direct voice. A major U.S. Supreme Court decision in *Red Lion Broadcasting v. the FCC* (1969) justified this difference. The Court allowed that the distinction between broadcasting and most other media hinges on the idea that broadcast frequencies comprise a "scarce resource."[17]

Although there is no law of nature that prevents anyone from starting a newspaper, the justices said, there are simply not enough broadcast frequencies to go around. That being the case, it is permissible for the federal government to regulate the use of airwaves by issuing licenses. The airwaves belong to the people, not the licensees, the Court asserted, and "it is the right of the viewers and listeners, not the right of the broadcasters, which is paramount." Consequently, "there is no sanctuary in the First Amendment for unlimited private censorship operating in a medium not open to all."[18]

In regard to the public's access to broadcasting, federal regulators have claimed the right to intervene in two areas:

The acquisition and use of channels

The right to reply and debate

The Acquisition and Use of Channels

The allocation of rights to use the electromagnetic spectrum is a federal power that dates to the Radio Act of 1927 (see Chapter 3). This **allocation of frequencies** has sparked struggles among companies that want pieces of the lucrative broadcast and cable pies. It has also sparked the interest of advocacy groups who express concern that minorities — mainly blacks and Hispanics — will not be represented as licensees.

Not until the 1970s did the FCC feel enough pressure to agree that minority ownership of broadcast stations is an important way to encourage the airing of minority ideas. The FCC thus reserved the right to consider minority applicants as one of its priority concerns in awarding new licenses, in allowing the transfer of existing licenses from one broadcast company to another, and in bidding on radio and television licenses. In 1995, though, the U.S. Supreme Court held that minority preferences in government contracts must withstand strict scrutiny. This decision caused the FCC to revise its rules that gave minority bidders credits in spectrum auctions and other areas relating to licenses.

Pressure to Reply and Debate

Authorities' claim on the second access area — the right of reply and debate — has focused narrowly on the **rights of candidates for a political election** as well as broadly on the **rights of all individuals or groups to debate controversial issues** over the broadcast media.

As noted earlier in this chapter, the rights of candidates were spelled out in the so-called Equal Time rule of the 1934 Federal Communications Act. This rule has withstood the test of time. The right of members of the public to use broadcast and cable media licensed to others as platforms for debate has had a more stormy history.

The Federal Communications Commission set forth this right in 1949 through a regulation called the **Fairness Doctrine,** which states that broadcasters had to "afford reasonable opportunity for the discussion of conflicting views on issues of public importance." The FCC later extended the ruling to program originators on cable television systems.

In the landmark 1969 *Red Lion Broadcasting case,* the Fairness Doctrine was challenged before the U.S. Supreme Court. The justices upheld its legality; invoking the natural scarcity argument, the Court ruled that a federal requirement of citizens' access, though not acceptable in print media, can be applied to broadcasting.

Although the High Court used the *Red Lion* decision to validate citizens' rights to demand "fairness," in later cases it developed a line of reasoning that made access to the broadcast medium difficult to achieve. The justices suggested that notions of "fairness" should not be interpreted too literally. They felt an obligation to protect the commercial nature of the broadcasting system. Supreme Court Justice William O. Douglas expressed the fear that a radio or television station that was constantly forced to disrupt its programming to be a forum for public debate would find it difficult, if not impossible, to create an attractive, predictable environment for advertisers. As such, the station would probably cease to function. Because the purpose of the First Amendment is not to interfere with but to encourage free speech, he said, any such result runs counter to the nation's best interests.[19]

By the late 1980s, support for even a limited Fairness Doctrine had diminished among regulators. An increasingly conservative Federal Communications Commission decided it was in broadcasting's best interest to do away with the rule, and it was abolished in 1987.[20]

The regulatory history of other attempts to allow citizens more access in broadcast media has seen similarly narrow openings. For example, although the FCC has touted its interest in promoting minority ownership of licenses, the actual number of stations transferred to black and Hispanic interests under this program has been very small. Moreover, the commission has slowed the growing trend of **citizen-licensee agreements** to force access. These are pacts with station owners to air certain types of programming under the threat that if they do not air, the activists will drag the station through an expensive challenge to its license at renewal time.

When the idea of such pacts became popular in the early 1970s, broadcasters voiced alarm over the loss of autonomy and ad revenues that such forced programming implied. Still, those targeted for the agreements often felt they must yield to such pressure for the sake of hassle-free license renewal. In the late 1970s, the FCC came to the industry's rescue. The commission stated that it would sanction no agreement in which a broadcast licensee delegated its programming decisions to people outside its organization.[21] In the 1980s, the FCC made citizen-licensee agreements even more irrelevant by allowing the renewal for most broadcast outlets to be so predictable and unchallengeable that broadcasters no longer felt much of a need to even consider activists.[22]

Cable TV and Access

The regulatory climate has worked against broad citizen access to cable TV as well. Local communities select the cable systems they want, but they could choose to give franchises to minority-owned firms as a matter of policy. In the matter of program content, however, the Cable Communications Policy Act of 1984 freed cable operators from most rules covering the programs they carry. Some provisions in the act called for various kinds of local "access" channels for school, government, and public use. However, even as the act was passed, many argued — correctly, as it turned out — that these requirements would be overturned by the courts as running counter to the First Amendment.[23]

Three access requirements in the 1984 Cable Television Act have not been challenged by the cable TV industry, possibly because they seem to pose little threat to industry profits or autonomy. One mandates **leased access,** which means that a channel on which individuals or groups willing to pay a set fee can present any programming they wish so long as it is not "indecent." A second demands the same equal time considerations to candidates for public office that apply to broadcasting. The third extends the Fairness Doctrine to cable. Interestingly, though the latter was negated by Congress for broadcasters, it was never dissolved for cablecasters.[24]

Cycles of Regulation

It should be clear by now that regulation of access is a political process, with the desires of the broadcast and cable lobbies making their imprints on decisions by the FCC, the Congress, and even the courts. Although activists have never found access rights to the electronic media generous, certain periods have seen regulations that are more forthcoming than others.

In the 1980s, for example, the FCC went quite far in closing off access. At that time, Republican President Ronald Reagan, his appointees to the Federal Communications Commission, and many members of Congress were convinced that cable television, radio, and over-the-air TV stations were overregulated. They pointed to the growing number of media channels in the United States, and to the many local requirements that cable television operators offer public access channels, as evidence that the public would be well served if broadcasters were allowed to compete in the marketplace according to their own desires.

Following this logic, the FCC responded to the pressures of the cable and broadcast lobbies to allow them more control over their programming operations than ever before. The dissolution of the Fairness Doctrine is a case in point.

Radio and TV station executives had never liked the doctrine, which cut into their decision-making autonomy. In lobbying against the ruling, they claimed that the requirement was leading stations and networks to inject less controversy into their medium than would otherwise be the case. They argued that news producers were avoiding controversy as much as possible so as not to be accused of leaning toward one side and being forced to give up valuable commercial time — and decision-making independence — to contentious individuals.

The increasingly conservative FCC (aided by Reagan administration appointees) agreed. However, commissioners were unsure whether the doctrine was simply an FCC rule, which they could then repeal, or a law, which Congress would have to invalidate. They decided to try Congress first.

Twice during the 1980s, the FCC asked Congress to abolish the doctrine. Twice, a Congress divided on the issue did nothing. Finally, a federal court cleared up the legal ambiguity by ruling that the Fairness Doctrine was not a part of statutory law but simply an FCC regulation. Seeing its chance, the FCC killed the rule.[25]

The political maneuvering did not end with the FCC's 1987 action. Many in the Democratic-controlled Congress disagreed with the FCC's abandonment of the Fairness Doctrine. Not allowed by law to override a commission decision directly, Congress formulated a version of the doctrine and mustered enough votes to pass it into law. President Reagan vetoed it twice, however, and the FCC's approach stood firm.

Still, as the 1980s turned into the 1990s and the Reagan era gave way to the Bush and then the Clinton era, observers were remarking that new FCC appointees as well as the Republicans in Congress were taking hard looks at whether the broadcast and cable industries were meeting their public responsibilities. Optimists saw Clinton-appointed FCC chairman Reid Hunt as pushing more "responsible" programming by broadcasters, especially with regard to children. Pessimists saw Hunt's decision to auction the public airwaves off to the highest bidders and the Republicans' attempts to "deregulate" telecommunications, halt funding for the Public Broadcasting Service, and allow cable firms free reign over their fees as signs that trends were shifting even further away from advocacy perspectives and toward industry viewpoints.

PRESSURING AUTHORITIES
TO ELIMINATE MATERIALS

Although U.S. regulatory authorities have been reluctant to give public advocacy organizations access to mass media except in limited situations, over the years they have been more willing to help certain activist groups try to *eliminate* certain mass media material. Some of this willingness to narrow the boundaries of acceptable content undoubtedly is due to the emotional and political weight of the topics often involved — sex, violence, and misleading advertising. When these issues have come up, the rhetoric on all sides has usually been high-pitched and the battles rough-and-tumble. Often, too, pressure through authorities has been carried out in tandem with direct pressure on producers or other organizations in the targeted industry. Many times these activities have had important consequences. Yet even the most significant results of activists' pressure through authorities to eliminate mass media materials have not always been the ones activists expected. The reasons are based on a number of factors:

First Amendment concerns

The desire by courts to define terms clearly

The ingenuity of media firms to stick to the letter of restrictions while sabotaging their spirit

The Case of Sexually Explicit Literature

The influence of the first two considerations is readily apparent in the case of militancy against sexually explicit literature. This militancy both changed its nature and gained momentum in the nineteenth century. Until the 1800s, antagonism to such works in America was based mainly on religious grounds; people saw the writers as sinners against God. After that, public advocacy group opposition to sexually explicit literature increasingly showed up in courtrooms as cases of obscenity, not religion.

The 1821 Massachusetts court decision banning *Memoirs of a Woman of Pleasure* (*Fanny Hill*) was the first U.S. judicial case in which sexual content was the sole issue. Court cases were few until the last quarter of the nineteenth century, however. At that time, groups of citizens began calling for censorship. They targeted fiction of all types, classics as well as dime novels.[26]

Space does not permit even the briefest sketch of the ways such advocacy organizations as the Watch and Ward Society, the New York Society for the

Suppression of Vice, and the National Organization for Decent Literature have tried to use federal and state courts, as well as legislatures and police, to prohibit the publication or sale of sexually explicit material throughout the country. Here our purpose is to point out that although those organizations scored some impressive victories, particularly in the first half of the twentieth century, the lasting product of their labors was quite the opposite of what they expected. Rather than encourage censorship, their work led to elimination of the threat of censorship over the majority of books with sexual themes.[27]

The sequence of events that started the ball rolling in this direction was a series of court challenges between about 1910 and 1930 by antipornography organizations. Their targets were Greek, Roman, and French classics with erotic motifs, which were being imported or produced in the United States. It was assumed by most judges (and upheld by the Supreme Court in 1957) that obscene publications are not protected by the First Amendment.

The difficulty, however, was in defining "obscene." Vigorous defenses by publishers and importers of the historical importance and enduring qualities of the classic works targeted for censorship led various judges to develop specific criteria for obscenity. These criteria indicated much greater leeway for newer books that were being called obscene. Historian Felice Flanery Lewis captures the point well: "In challenging the classics, censors ironically precipitated the birth, in a very restricted form, of the concept that literature with social value was outside the scope of censorship laws, a concept that would eventually do much to defeat the banning of literature."[28]

Jawboning

Ironies like this also weave through the history of movies and television. There the contested range of topics has been much broader than in the trade book industry. Sex and sexual innuendo have stirred much controversy, to be sure. But so have violence; racial, gender, and ethnic stereotyping; the quality of material for children; and a number of other issues.

A major difference between battles over obscenity and battles over other aspects of movie and television content has been use of the courts. Although lawsuits have been the preferred path to force elimination of obscenity, they have not been nearly so common a path with respect to other areas of content. With a few important exceptions, the most popular advocacy group tactic has been to apply pressure to government regulatory or legislative officials so they, in turn, will bully (**jawbone**) producers into making changes.

Politicians so pressured will probably respond along the lines outlined in this chapter. They will likely assess the size of the group, the sophistication of its public relations apparatus, and the ways it can help them gain reelection. Then they might place their perceptions of the group's power against that of the industry they are urged to attack.

Industry leaders, too, are likely to conduct a formal or informal cost-benefit analysis, in which they compare the power of the pressure group with the potential revenues the company will realize from the material causing the fuss. They will also consider the possibility that key politicians will be persuaded to drop anti-industry positions. Failing that, they will assess what long-term political and economic damage they could bring on themselves if they ignore calls for changes in content.

If producers feel harm will be minimal, they may do nothing. In certain situations, though, they may well conclude the damage would be great. This could set into motion performance programs aimed to pacify the legislators and advocacy groups while keeping control over the production process. Two typical ways to do that are self-regulation and lobbying.

Self-Regulation

As the term suggests, **self-regulation** is an activity through which firms police their own activities in an attempt to discourage government interference in industry affairs. Mass media practitioners generally prefer self-regulation because it allows them more flexibility than government legislation to respond to rapidly changing demands of the marketplace while they quiet the anger of various public constituencies.

Recall from Chapter 3 that fear of government censorship led early Hollywood producers down the path of self-regulation. The movie industry's approach became a model for the National Association of Broadcasters (NAB) code when radio (and later TV) executives moved to head off government/advocacy group pressures. The NAB has abandoned its code, but the American Association of Advertising Agencies and the Public Relations Society of America still have codes of ethical practice.

Sometimes, severe threats of government interference lead firms to cave in on particular issues. This happened in the music recording industry in the early 1990s. Outcries were issued by a number of conservative groups against rock lyrics they considered harmful to young people. They persuaded legislators in more than two dozen states to consider bills requiring warning labels for parents on albums. Record manufacturers, fearing government regulation, voluntarily complied.[29]

Advertisers have particular reason to fear restrictive legislation or rulings by the Federal Trade Commission (FTC) because they practice what the courts call **commercial speech** — the use of language in the service of commerce. Over the decades, several U.S. Supreme Court decisions have indicated that the advertising industry's guarantee of free speech is not equal to the guarantees given to noncommercial materials. Although ruling that certain aspects of advertising do come under the protection of the First Amendment, the justices have made it clear that government is free to regulate commercial speech that is "false," "misleading," or "proposes illegal transactions."[30] As can be imagined, advertisers would like to have the ability to control how such terms as *false* and *misleading* are understood. Self-regulation would give them the room to create definitions of *false* and *misleading* that would quiet critics but at the same time not be as restrictive as government regulations.

TALKING POINT 6.1   Indecency and the FCC

Because obscene or indecent language is not protected by the First Amendment, the Federal Communications Commission has the right to penalize stations that air indecencies. Indecency is defined by the FCC as "language or material that, in context, depicts or describes, in terms patently offensive as measured by contemporary standards for the broadcast medium, sexual or excretory activities or organs." The difficulty, of course, is knowing what is "patently offensive" by community standards. Therein lie the seeds of battles that have ebbed and flowed with the power of conservative political movements in the nation.

Several of those battles were fought at the turn of the 1990s. Responding to complaints by radio listeners from around the country, the Federal Communications Commission began cracking down on "indecency." Those opposing the FCC insisted they were not defending "smut" for the sake of smut. Rather, they argued, government involvement in taking messages off the air was worse than the messages' offense. They insisted that battles to protect civil liberties are always fought at the borders of good taste, because those borders define the limits of individuals' freedoms.

People who thought the FCC was moving in the wrong direction pointed to "obscenity" cases that were not nearly as clear-cut as the FCC judged them to be. In October 1989, for example, the commission fined KLUC radio in Las Vegas $2,000 for playing Prince's "Erotic City," and fined WTZA radio in Miami $2,000 for playing "Penis Envy" by Uncle Bonzai. Defenders of the first song argued that it contained the phrase "we can *funk* until dawn," not the four-letter word the FCC considers obscene. No listener had complained in four years of radio airplay. In May 1988, however, someone with a tape recorder heard the song on the air and tracked down the sheet music — which does contain the dreaded word. The individual alerted the FCC, which condemned the piece.

"Penis Envy" contains the following line: "If I had a penis, I'd still be a girl/But I'd make much more money and conquer the world." Defenders of the song contended that it is jokey, and that the offending line is really a feminist political point. They lost their case. In summer 1995, a U.S. District Court of Appeals reaffirmed the basic constitutionality of the FCC's indecency regulations in *Action for Children's Television v. FCC.*

SOURCES: Jon Pareles, "Outlaw Rock: More Skirmishes on the Censorship Front," *New York Times,* December 10, 1988, p. 32; Kevin Zimmerman, "Yo! Rap Zapped by Lyrics Flap," *Variety,* March 7, 1990; Denis Wharton, "Media Groups to FCC Back Off on 'Indecency,'" *Variety,* February 28, 1990, p. 40; "DC Circuit Upholds FCC Limits on Airing of Indecent Programs," *Entertainment Litigation Reporter,* August 18, 1995, p. 1.

Lobbying

Lobbying is often used to justify self-regulation, to argue that the latter is enough and that legislation is not needed. When the cycle of regulation is on the upswing, a media industry's response is often to beef up lobbying defenses. In the ad industry's case, for example, the upswing in regulatory interest was met by the banding together of several trade groups that typically do not work together — the American Advertising Federation, the Association of National Advertisers, and the American Association of Advertising Agencies — to support coalitions that lobby for particular causes.

In rare instances, none of the lobbying is successful and laws are passed prohibiting certain media materials. Much more often, the combination of lobbying and self-regulation brings about conclusions that are frustrating to advocacy groups. Citing the First Amendment or other key philosophical principles, authorities refuse to enact legislation that imposes prior restraint on production firms' creation of media materials.

In such situations, politicians try to appease all sides by negotiating compromises with the producers who are under fire. Politicians may jawbone the producers to bow somewhat to government pressures. Therefore, the producers will appear contrite to members of the public, and the politicians will look tough. At the same time, producers may pursue a self-regulatory course that appears to surrender to their opposition but, on closer inspection, does not — or creates new problems. This is because mass media practitioners often believe that content elements disliked by activists (sex, violence, cartoons) are essential to their firm's survival in the marketplace.

Pressure on the Movies

One example of this ironic turn of events is a movie case that harks back to the early days of the Motion Picture Producers and Directors Association (MPPDA), Hollywood's self-regulatory arm, which began to develop its first movie code in the 1920s. The code muffled many of the organized voices calling for government regulation of the movies. With state and federal legislators calmed, film executives began to see the MPPDA and its director, Will Hays, as instruments by which they could test — and define and slowly expand — the limits of movie respectability. Producers and writers learned quickly that it was easy to get around the spirit of the code's mechanical morality.

Consider the MPPDA's requirement of **compensating values** as an example. It asserted that virtue had to be rewarded, and sin punished, in movies because, "if good eventually triumphed and evildoers perished miserably, the laws of God, man, and the drama would be simultaneously satisfied." Movie historian Arthur Knight notes the ironic consequences of this approach:

> The studios were quick to perceive that what this meant, in effect, was that they could present six reels of ticket-selling sinfulness if, in the seventh reel, all the sinners came to a bad end, and they could go through all the motions of vice, if, at the last moment, virtue triumphed. Censors around the country might continue their snipping of occasional scenes, but who could object to movies in which "morality" was so eagerly espoused.[31]

Certainly, public advocacy groups did not expect the Motion Picture Code to lead to such films when they pushed the industry toward self-regulation. But this was the consequence of forcing media practitioners to give in to advocates' demands without considering marketplace demands and routines, which generally get first priority. Similar patterns of response can be cited regarding the many episodes of legislative and FCC jawboning of network officials over the years in response to advocacy group outcries over violence; sexual innuendo; racial, ethnic, and gender stereotyping; and the need to eliminate objectionable plotlines and characterizations in children's television.

When violence has been a major issue, the producers have replaced it with sexual innuendo or "action comedy," where the fighting is softened with laughs. When sexual innuendo has raised major legislative eyebrows, TV producers have switched to violence. When advocacy groups have joined with authorities to rail against racial, ethnic, and gender stereotypes, these have been replaced by more subtle stereotypes of the same groups, or by other groups who may evoke similar audience responses. And children's television has incorporated elements that mollify some advocacy groups while not really changing the fundamental plotlines and characterizations that stirred the opposition in the first place.

All this implies that when advocacy groups have been powerful enough to pressure legislators and regulators toward action, production executives have moved to eliminate certain types of content, sometimes greatly. The point to underscore, however, is that what has resulted from the battle has often not been what the advocacy group members or the government officials expected. Because media practitioners have held business imperatives above government pressures, what sometimes emerged was simply another version of the same problem.

PRESSURING PRODUCERS THROUGH CLIENTS

Advocacy group members frustrated with the runaround they get when they appeal directly to producers, and with the maddening snail's pace, hesitation, and unpredictability they encounter when they try to change material by working through legislatures or courts, have been increasingly turning their energies toward the organizations that sponsor mass media content. Their reasoning is straightforward: Because buying patterns of primary client organizations are crucial to mass media producers' survival, successful advocacy pressure on clients should create powerful leverage to make the desired changes in the producers' material.

In reality, though, the situation is not so straightforward. Like producers and authorities, organizations that take on the client role are continually faced with many competing interests in their environment. This makes their sensitivity to advocacy groups not at all clear-cut.

The probability is that, like their counterparts in production and authority organizations, the leaders of client firms will conduct cost-benefit analyses to decide whether they should give in to advocacy group demands—and if so, how, when, and to what extent. Of course, media clients can be very different from one another, and it is impossible to make blanket statements about the outcome of such cost-benefit calculations. It appears that government organizations that act as the clients (as opposed to regulators) of producers may be quite responsive to activist pressure. This is because public officials up for re-election are well aware that in supporting mass media producers, they are spending public money and are therefore open to public scrutiny.

An example at the federal level can be drawn from the early 1990s, when the National Endowment for the Arts (NEA) was attacked vigorously by conservative groups for supporting a photographic exhibition with homosexually erotic works. The protesters succeeded in getting U.S. Senator Jesse Helms to push a proviso through Congress that the NEA should not use its funds for purposes that could cause sexual, religious, or ethnic offense. Helms's requirement was watered down substantially a year later. Nevertheless, advocates of government support of the arts argued that the result was a distinct warning about the kinds of materials the NEA might not support in museums, broadcasting, movies, and print.[32]

The Case of Textbooks

The power of advocacy groups to manipulate government funders of mass media producers and, by extension, to influence media producers is found most commonly at the level of state and local governments. The targets there are elementary and high school textbooks. Because textbook selection is an activity conducted by state and local agencies and controlled by elected officials, it is susceptible to many pressures from public advocacy organizations. Moreover, the belief in the United States is that parents have the right to help guide curriculum development in their children's schools. There is also an undercurrent of concern about the texts chosen by officials. Incidents of extreme public unrest over texts chosen by schools seem to occur in cycles.

A rash of textbook controversies erupted in the mid-1970s, for example. The chairperson of the American Library Association's Freedom to Read Foundation warned that "a nationwide, persuasive, anti-intellectual movement is developing that can be compared to the McCarthy era."[33] Advocacy groups such as the Citizens for Decent Literature, the Hard Core Parents of Louisiana, the Ku Klux Klan, the John Birch Society, and the National Parents League raised objections to textbook content, thereby creating a climate of fear among book selection committees around the country.

One of the centerpieces of protest was a book selection conflict in Kanawha County, West Virginia, in 1974. The tension was instigated by one member of the Kanawha School Board, the wife of a fundamentalist minister, who objected to the method of textbook selection. She was joined by thousands of protesters against the board's adoption of 325 books they believed "denounced traditional institutions," paraded the notion of cultural relativism, and in general subscribed to an ideology of secular humanism as a substitute for orthodox conceptions of the rule of God and the Bible.[34] Tempers flared as antitextbook protesters organized, held marches and rallies, circulated petitions, appealed to elected officials, and boycotted the school system. Violence broke out as vandals destroyed school property, and a picketing protester was shot. After the majority of a special citizen review committee recommended that all but thirty-five of the books remain in the classrooms (a minority report recommended that many more be banned), the Kanawha Board of Education building was bombed and partially destroyed.

By the end of 1974, it appeared that the protesters had won a number of concessions from the county school board. However, the revised guidelines were declared illegal by the state superintendent of schools. In the meantime, many parents had begun to send their children to newly created private Christian schools, which siphoned off much of the core of the protest movement, and the situation calmed down a bit. Sociologists Ann Page and Donald Clelland, commenting on the event four years later, noted that "although the vehemence of the protest has subsided, the anger lingers on."[35]

The Kanawha incident and others like it mobilized teachers and librarians around the country in preparation for further textbook battles. Professional publications such as the *American School Board Journal* and *Library Journal* suggested performance programs its readers could follow in order to minimize the damage created by the fiery groups. "Don't *you* get scalded," warned one article.[36]

Nevertheless, books in several communities were altered in response to public protest and renewed interest in school board elections. More important, into the 1980s a climate of fear and caution spread over many textbook committees that were not embroiled in controversy and did not wish to be. Reflecting on such self-censorship, legal scholar Paul Goldstein contends that "the public's greatest influence [in textbook selection] lies in its silence, and in [school professionals'] decisions to reject materials that will spark controversy and rouse the public from its silence."[37]

Book marketers and their editors know this, says Goldstein, and they create textbooks that are likely to fit the least controversial common denominator of acceptance among certain school systems. As one textbook company executive noted, the dominant concern of a supervising editor has become

> to achieve a compromise between the controls necessary for national acceptance and the originality of the author's contribution to education. In the el-hi field, particularly, he must balance skillfully the demands of contradictory curricular material, of "progressive educators" and traditionalists, of exponents of the science-centered culture and the humanists, and above all of the majority and minority pressure groups.[38]

One indication of this influence was the guidelines a major publisher of elementary school texts gave to its authors in the early 1980s. The pages advised against depicting death, divorce, and games of chance, among other activities. In addition, they cautioned that the authors had best "avoid topics considered by some to be antireligious, e.g., evolution, witchcraft, and secular humanism."

Advertisers and Pressure

From the example of advocacy group pressures on publicly sponsored client organizations we move to one relating to private clients: large television advertisers. The biggest threat advocacy groups seem to hold over TV advertisers is a widespread boycott of their products. Big companies that turn out a multitude of consumer goods are sometimes quite skittish — even more skittish than the producers or networks — about getting on a major advocacy movement's hit list.

One can make a strong argument that it was advertisers' fear of a boycott — a fear reinforced by research reports from giant ad agency J. Walter Thompson — that in 1977 forced the U.S. television networks away from its years-long violence-oriented action programming. Similarly, it seems that threats by the Coalition for Better Television and the Moral Majority to finger sponsors that supported sexually and ideologically "immoral" programs in the early 1980s created a climate of fear among advertisers and led network programmers in directions more sensitive to the activists' complaints.

Of particular significance to their cause was the public endorsement of its aim to "improve" television by the giant consumer goods firm and the then-largest TV advertiser, Procter & Gamble. Word in the trade press was that Procter & Gamble executives had been nervous about reports that the Coalition for Better Television was planning to list their firm among companies that sponsor unacceptable prime time programs. They were even more worried that the coalition might later attack Procter & Gamble's ownership of six sultry daytime soap operas, a huge and important investment for the manufacturer. "P&G was afraid the soaps would be a problem down the line," said a television network executive. "By focusing [the coalition's] attention on prime time, I guess they figured they'd get them off their backs."[39]

This comment reflects an awareness of the intricate strategies sometimes involved when advertisers and advocacy groups meet head-on over commercial TV. On the other side, television distributors and producers generally try to convince advertisers and ad agencies that the particular advocacy organization or movement is not representative of the public at large and that, in any case, product boycotts tend to be ineffective. Moreover, in the 1990s, networks, syndicators, and producers have special interests in sometimes pushing programs past conventional TV limits. They feel that in an era when videotapes and pay-TV movies cross those limits regularly, conventional TV must take risks to attract the attention of certain audience segments that advertisers desire. As a result, conventional TV may risk alienating certain advertisers if the audiences it attracts can draw other sponsors.

In the early 1990s, this posture was adopted by the Fox Television network, which aggressively targets high-spending young adults, and by Tribune Entertainment, which competes furiously for the lucrative market of women at home during the day. The Fox show that especially drew anti-advertiser fire was *Married with Children,* a Sunday evening situation comedy series that turned the traditional family sitcom on its head. Far from being amused, a concerned woman from a Detroit suburb managed to convince advertisers that *Married with Children* insulted family life and was filled with immoral conversation and allusions. As her campaign progressed, it became clear that many people around the country agreed with her.

In the Tribune Entertainment's case, opposition arose separately in several areas of the country to *Geraldo,* the popular daytime talk show distributed by Tribune Entertainment. Activists, including local Parent-Teacher Associations, were angry because Geraldo was routinely highlighting such subjects as "Women Who Date Married Men," "Girls Who Can't Say No," "Campus Rape," and "Parents of Slain Prostitutes." They protested to local stations and advertisers that the topics were beyond the pale of good taste, especially when aired in the late afternoon, when children might be watching.

TALKING POINT 6.2   Making Parents Angry

Advocacy-group anger over *Geraldo!* in the early 1990s was surpassed in the mid-1990s by even greater vehemence over a large number of television talk shows. Consider three topics of the November 1995 episodes of the *Jerry Springer Show*: "I'm Having Your Man's Baby," "I'm a 13 Year Old Prostitute," and "Wild Teens." *Ricki Lake* weighed in with "Surprise! I Want You to Be the Father of My Baby," while *Jenny Jones* had "Makeovers for Transvestites," "My Daughter Is Too Promiscuous," and "Jenny, Fix Me Up with Your Hottest Guest."

Concern about such programs, which had been mounting for years, seemed to overflow during Fall 1995. Advocacy groups turned to advertisers for leverage to tone down the programs. At first, many sponsors were hesitant to act, since they were afraid that by moving to less controversial programs they would lose the relatively large audiences of these tabloid-talk programs. Eventually, companies such as Procter & Gamble and AT&T decided to act, possibly because they were embarrassed by revelations that they were continuing to support such daytime fare quite heavily. P&G, for example, had spent $28.3 million on the programs from January to July 1995 — up 53% from those months during the previous year.

The firms did not leave these shows altogether, however. Company executives argued that to do so would not allow it to reach the audiences it wanted and also not encourage change for the better in daytime talk television. Instead, they entered into conversations with the programs' producers, letting them know which kinds of episodes they would sponsor and which they would not. "In the end," said *Advertising Age,* "they hope to genetically engineer a new breed of TV talk show that is interesting, attracts sizable audiences, but is socially palatable."

SOURCE: Joe Mandese, "Talk Show Stalwart P&G Pans 'Trash,'" *Advertising Age,* November 20, 1995, p. 1.

Fox and Tribune handled the cases differently, in tune with their perceptions of the benefits and costs of losing advertisers or forcing the producers to make the changes desired by activists and sponsors. Fox representatives publicly refused to back down from their support of the show. Instead, they tried to turn the publicity about the series to their benefit, denying that *Married with Children* was immoral while playing up its attraction to young, hip audiences. If word was sent to the producers to be more cautious with certain themes in the future, it was certainly not communicated widely.

Tribune executives, on the other hand, expressed public alarm at the stream of large advertisers (General Motors, Coca-Cola, Weight Watchers, Kroger Co.) that were deserting *Geraldo.* They also acknowledged that several TV station program directors, reeling from the controversy and losing some local sponsors, were considering whether they should place the show in a less desirable time slots or drop it altogether.

The result was a public admission by *Geraldo* creator and host Geraldo Rivera that he had gone too far. In interviews with the advertising and electronic media trade press, meetings with TV station executives, as well as a videotaped address sent to station managers around the country, Rivera spoke of "walking a tightrope between exploitation and sensible balance." He promised that his program would often deal with issues that were socially responsible, which advertisers could be proud of and sometimes even tie into. He was, he said, "a reasoned voice, a businessman and a lawyer," who was now seeking a balance of topics that would be more acceptable to all the parties involved.[40]

"I'm my own best salesman," he told *Advertising Age.* "Part of my ethic is that if there is a problem, I want to fix it."[41]

It is doubtful that the changes Geraldo planned to institute would satisfy all the program's detractors. As Rivera himself suggested, the purpose of "remixing" the elements of his show was primarily to reduce the controversy enough that advertisers would return, but not so much that his core audience of viewers would stop watching. Ultimately, calming the concerns of advertisers, local station managers, and (potentially) regulatory agencies was of greater immediate importance than making the advocacy groups happy.

Such a result was to be expected. As this chapter has shown, public demands are constantly transformed within mass media production firms by organizational and interorganizational demands that receive greater priority. The bridge that sometimes connects producers and the public is long and scarred by holes, broken planks, and weird passageways.

CONSIDER THIS

1. Have you ever written an angry letter to a media firm? Did your experience gel with the predictions of this chapter?

2. Most large cities have one or two major daily newspapers and tens of radio stations.

By law, radio stations must give political candidates equal time on their airwaves because of the scarcity of airwaves and presumably the limited competition this scarcity causes. Is this fair, however, when major daily newspapers, which are much scarcer, are not forced to give equal time?

3. If you were to form a media advocacy group, what issues would you champion?

NOTES

1. See Loren Ghiglione, "Newspapers Should Stop Cigarette Ads," *Christian Science Monitor,* October 4, 1989, p. 19; and Alan C. Miller and Myron Levin, "Smoking Critics Seek Sweeping Restrictions on Ads for Cigarettes," *Los Angeles Times,* June 15, 1990, p. D1.
2. Brooks Boliek, "Anti-Rap Coalition Trains Sights on TV Talk Shows," BPI Entertainment News Wire, October 28, 1995.
3. See Walter Goodman, "How PBS Handles Mideast Viewpoints in Two Documentaries," *New York Times,* December 5, 1989, p. C19; and Steven Emerson, "Days of Rage: Journalism or Propaganda?" *New York Times,* September 6, 1989, p. A23.
4. Telephone conversation, October 15, 1990.
5. Herbert Gans, "Letters to an Anchorman," *Journal of Communication* 27 (Summer 1977), pp. 86–91.
6. James March and Herbert Simon, *Organizations* (New York: John Wiley, 1978), p. 141.
7. Sidney Head, *Broadcasting in America* (New York: Houghton Mifflin, 1972), pp. 347–350.
8. Kalman Siegel, *Talking Back to the New York Times* (New York: Quadrangle Books, 1974), p. 8.
9. See Joseph Turow, "Another View of Citizen Feedback to the Mass Media," *Public Opinion Quarterly* 41 (Winter 1977–78), pp. 534–543.
10. See, for example, Susan Chira, "Whittle Says Channel One Is on Target," *New York Times,* February 16, 1991 p. D 17; Scott Hume, "Channel One Ads Bug Adults, Survey Shows; News Programs Backed," *Advertising Age,* August 14, 1989, p. 4; and Bill Carter, "Whittle Names a Board to Advise Channel One," *New York Times,* August 28, 1989, p. C8.
11. Richard Stevenson, "And Now a Message from an Advocacy Group," *New York Times,* May 27, 1990, sect. 2, p. 26. Quote is on p. 29.
12. Stevenson, "And Now a Message."
13. Stephen McGookin, "FT Review of Business Books," *The Financial Times,* September 27, 1995, p. ix.
14. Mark Nadel, *The Politics of Consumer Protection* (Indianapolis: Bobbs Merrill, 1971), p. 211.
15. Nadel, p. 213.
16. Quoted in Jethro Lieberman, *Free Speech, Free Press, and the Law* (New York: Lothrop, 1980), p. 123.
17. Christopher H. Sterling, *Stay Tuned: A Concise History of American Broadcasting* (Belmont, CA: Wadsworth, 1990), p. 427.
18. Quoted in Lieberman, p. 126.
19. Oscar G. Chase, "Broadcast Regulation and the First Amendment," in Michael

Botein and David M. Rice (eds.), *Network Television and the Public Interest* (Lexington, MA: Lexington Books, 1980), p. 143.

20. Joseph Dominick, Barry Sherman, and Gary Copeland, *Broadcasting/Cable and Beyond* (New York: McGraw-Hill, 1990), p. 411.
21. Ronald Garay, "Access: Evolution of the Citizen Agreement," *Journal of Broadcasting* 22 (Winter 1978), p. 103.
22. Sterling, pp. 523–526.
23. Sterling, p. 530.
24. Dominick et al., p. 412.
25. Dominick et al., p. 411.
26. See also Felice Flanery Lewis, *Literature, Obscenity, and the Law* (Carbondale: Southern Illinois University Press, 1976), p. 7.
27. Lewis, p. 45.
28. Lewis, p. 45.
29. *Variety,* March 14, 1990, p. 47.
30. Don R. Pember, *Mass Media Law* (Dubuque, lA: William C. Brown, 1977), pp. 351–352.
31. Arthur Knight, *The Liveliest Art* (New York: Signet, 1958), p. 112.
32. Allan Parachini, "Senate Defeats Attempts by Helms to Cut Art Funding," *Los Angeles Times,* October 25, 1990, p. A1.
33. "Textbook Battles," *American School Board Journal* (July 1975) p. 21.
34. Ann Page and Donald Clelland, "The Kanawha County Textbook Controversy: A Study of the Politics of Life Style Concern," *Social Forces* 57 (September 1978), p. 268.
35. Page and Clelland, p. 278.
36. *American School Board Journal* (July 1975) p. 21.
37. Paul Goldstein, *The Changing American Textbook* (Lexington, MA: Lexington Books, 1978), p. 38.
38. Goldstein, p. 57.
39. Colby Coates and Bob Marich, "P&G's Rap at TV Laid to Fear of Boycott," *Advertising Age,* June 22, 1981, p. 85.
40. Craig Endicott, "Geraldo Remixes 'Heat, Light,' " *Advertising Age,* January 15, 1990, p. S-2.
41. Endicott, p. S-2.

CHAPTER 7

The Production Process

This chapter

- examines the process through which media firms create TV programs, newspaper stories, and other materials.
- explains how ideas about social power are often built directly into this process.
- sketches the way social power relates to media production in the kinds of people who are hired as well as in the content they create.

Americans who pay even casual attention to radio sounds, television images, and print materials that surround them daily see and hear a welter of different claims, opinions, and arguments. A manufacturer advertises that one product is better than another. A politician quoted in a newspaper opposes a presidential action. Two psychologists on a radio talk show scream at each other about the best way to solve interpersonal problems. A TV movie acts out conflicting views on mercy killing. A hit record revels in the joys of love, while another mourns that "love stinks."

The list could go on and on. To casual observers it may seem that there are no limits to the number of topics mass media can raise, the ways they can raise them, or the people who can state their viewpoints. But this is an incorrect assumption. As this book has shown, the firms that create mass media materials are limited in what they can do. Clients such as advertisers, authorities such as federal and state governments, distributors such as the TV networks, and other organizations taking on various power roles in a mass media industry make important demands on production firms, even to the point of defining the audiences they ought to pursue. These influences lead producers to limit the kinds of arguments and depictions they generate.

When forces with substantial leverage are displeased with a production firm's content, the result can be severe harm to the production firm. Aware of the demands on them, production companies develop courses of action to satisfy their own needs as well as those of the outside forces. These courses of action, or **policies,** attempt to shift organizational activities in directions that respond to outside demands. Production firms may make changes in the audiences they target, the types of materials they create, and the values they portray in the materials.

In this chapter we discuss how this process works. Exactly how does power over resources in society at large become channeled into power over what media personnel do and, as a result, into the media images they create? How, for example, do resource-related pressures influence the storytelling approaches that editors and reporters rely on? How do pressures from outside and inside organizations affect the way magazine columnists, movie producers, and sitcom writers get their work done without going crazy? This chapter and Chapter 8 explore these and a bundle of related questions.

RESOURCES, IMAGES, AND LEGITIMACY

To begin our exploration, we should review a few basic ideas from Chapter 1. Remember that mass media bring cultural models to huge numbers of people through fiction and nonfiction stories or other performances. These cultural models depict conduct, and the consequences of that conduct, by individuals and institutions. Recall that institutions are loosely knit groups of organizations that exert control over key aspects of social life: education, health care, law, the military, business, and more.

The organizations that make up institutions do not always agree on the best way to approach key issues. In the medical institution, for example, major arguments about health care policies have erupted between nursing and medical physician organizations, between medical physician and osteopathic physician groups, and between physician organizations and government departments that control many of health care's purse strings.

The most powerful organizations within an institution make up its **establishment.** These organizations have the clout to guide the most common practices in the institution's domain of social life. The American Medical Association, for example, has historically been such a powerful force in representing physicians that it qualifies for an "establishment" label.

Mass Media and Institutional Legitimacy

The notion of an institution is important in discussing mass media production firms because media producers portray institutional practices whenever they depict aspects of society in fiction or nonfiction stories. Many in the audience probably accept the presentations as "common sense" or "the way it is"—for others if not for them. But for some people the media images may provoke discontent and a desire to place their version of society alongside the others they see or hear. They may want to call attention to themselves in order to gain legitimacy for their cause in the institution and in society at large.

Are all versions of reality equally likely to find a place in the most important mass media? Scholars from a variety of backgrounds say the answer is no.[1] What they mean is that the most common versions of reality presented in news, entertainment, and advertising are those that accept the authority of the most powerful organizations in every institution. Another way to say this is that the mass media tend to uphold the **legitimacy** of the established economic, political, educational, artistic, religious, and military organizations of society.

When writers make this claim, they mean that the media justify the organizations' authority—their right to exist as powerful elements of the society's institutions. Production firms tend to create cultural models that actually portray the right of these organizations and the institutions to which they belong to remain powerful in the society, to control resources and hold leverage. Police shows on television portray honest police as rightfully in charge. Situation comedies show going to school as a necessary part of growing up. Discussions of religion in major newspapers affirm the right of major religious denominations to exist. Movies about illness accept the importance of hospitals in society.

The scholars who make these points are not implying that the mass media are always unquestioning and bland with respect to these organizations. Certainly, in glancing through newspapers and magazines, watching television dramas, or listening to the radio, we often come across arguments that attack the dominant political parties, articles that criticize large corporations, songs that make fun of teachers, stories that demand military reform. Moreover, we see that intellectual fashions change, that social divisions occur, and that these and other tensions find their way into the media. It is clear, too, that some mass media materials often displease members of an institution's elite (for example, business leaders) as well as other portions of the public.

Recognizing that mass media materials often display social tensions and conflicts does not, however, sweep away the argument that mass media content tends to legitimize the establishment. Despite their depictions of social problems, most mass media in a society rarely challenge the nation's dominant institutional forces to the point of raising realistic alternatives. Rarely, for example, do U.S. television programs seriously portray solving the nation's economic problems by doing away with the capitalist banking system, reducing the nation's armament problems by completely dismantling the military, or decreasing a viewer's own monetary difficulties by stealing and then mocking the police. To the contrary, in all but the most unstable societies, the legitimacy of established institutional setups and their values is a theme weaving through the bulk of mass media.

Certain mass media production firms are more likely than others to be concerned about pleasing the establishment. The difference is in where the firms get their resources. Production companies that rely on getting a great many of their most important resources (money, authority, personnel, services, and the like) from the mainstream of society (governments, giant advertisers, powerful advocacy organizations such as mainstream religious denominations, necessarily huge and diverse audiences) will likely arrange their activities so as to offend as few of these entities as possible. Production firms that rely on resources from areas of society outside the mainstream (nongovernment bodies, specialty distributors and exhibitors, rather small and homogeneous audiences, small advertisers interested in reaching those specific audiences), however, might have no fears about attacking the mainstream.

The distinction lies between what can be called **mainstream** and **peripheral** media output. For example, in the United States it is possible to produce novels extolling communist ideologies as a solution to social problems; the First Amendment to the U.S. Constitution prohibits government interference. However, it is doubtful that such peripheral material would be highlighted on network television or considered attractive by major movie studios such as Paramount, Columbia, and Fox, which have solidly mainstream approaches to their products.

Legitimacy and the Price of Entry

Fear of advertisers, distributors, exhibitors, and other forces in the production firms' environment is not, however, the only reason mainstream production organizations legitimize the establishment. The price of entering mainstream media business is another factor. Gone are the days when near-indigent entrepreneurs could found daily newspapers or magazines aimed at "the masses" and succeed. The costs of technology and labor for the industrialized production and distribution of messages are such that financing even mid-size media ventures can cost millions of dollars. These costs can generally be met only by wealthy firms. Because they want to keep their wealth and power, such firms have a vested interest in the society's basic economic and political ways of doing things.

Consider the newspaper industry. The price tags of three newspaper acquisitions in 1987 reflect the wealth needed to manage the descendants of the penny press: The Media News group bought the *Houston Post* for $150 million; Ingersoll Publications acquired *The Daily Record* of Morristown, New Jersey, for $100 million; and, in one of the most expensive newspaper purchases ever, the Hearst Corporation took over the *Houston Chronicle* for $415 million.[2] Such costs tend to limit entry to the daily newspaper industry to the already well-heeled, to people and companies with vested interests in the establishment and, by extension, in the established ways of depicting institutional reality.

In other areas, too, entering the mainstream usually presupposes being part of at least the economic establishment. Television and radio licenses regularly trade for hundreds of thousands, even tens of millions, of dollars. Foreigners and convicted criminals are not even allowed to obtain licenses. As for the costs of producing and distributing movies, they can easily shoot into the tens of millions. Buying an ongoing film studio or TV network and its diverse holdings requires stratospheric sums; Sony Corporation paid $2 billion for Columbia Pictures Entertainment in 1989.[3] Six years later, Time Warner paid $7.5 billion for Turner Broadcasting System, Disney invested $19 billion to buy Capital Cities' ABC, and Westinghouse spent $5.5 billion for CBS.[4]

Even in the magazine business, where technology and labor expenditures need not be astronomical, launching a periodical economically but wisely costs at least several hundred thousand dollars. The reason is that in the magazine industry, as in the recording and book industries, the key to success lies not just in producing material that will attract the public. If that were the case, magazines, records, and books could be produced at very low costs by nearly anyone.

The trick lies in also building distribution and exhibition channels for the product. With a magazine, this means promoting the periodical strongly to advertisers, subscribers, and a viable number of distributors and exhibitors to get them to feel that supporting the product will bring them money. This many-sided promotion can be very expensive, in time as well as money. Previous experience (a **track record**) in the business is crucial, because it makes it easier to cultivate the trust of wholesalers, retailers, advertisers, investors, and banks.

Buying an already successful magazine can cost millions. In 1988, for example, McFadden Holdings bought *The National Enquirer* for $412 million.[5] In the biggest magazine publishing deal of the 1980s, Rupert Murdoch paid $3 billion for Walter Annenberg's Triangle Publications (including *TV Guide, Seventeen, The Racing Form* newspaper, and a powerful magazine distributing operation).[6] A deal that turned heads in the mid-1990s was the sale for $2.1 billion of Ziff-Davis, publisher of highly successful computer magazines, to Japan's Softbank Company.[7]

The costs and connections for setting up a production firm that has a chance of being successful in the mainstream generally demand that the owners themselves be part of the establishment. But a number of questions arise:

> How do the people who work in firms oriented toward mainstream resources actually learn what it means to create portrayals that legitimize established institutional structures?

> Do production companies that tilt toward the economic and political mainstream develop explicit policies that guide their employees to uphold the establishment? If so, how have these policies developed, and how do media personnel learn how to translate them into content?

> If not, how do such portrayals get established? Do news reporters, TV fiction writers, magazine columnists, and radio talk show hosts intend to

uphold the establishment when they carry out their work? What happens to them when they disagree with certain ideas they are working with?

What about media workers who belong to minority groups in the society? To what extent do they get involved in creating output for mainstream organizations? When they do, how much freedom do they have to portray their ethnic identities as separate from the majority? How do they learn acceptable portrayals of society's institutions?

THE IMPORTANCE OF ROUTINES

In searching for answers to these questions, one point becomes especially clear: Many of the people who create mainstream news and entertainment have little daily sense of a duty to reinforce fundamental institutional norms in these materials. Their bosses do not regularly emphasize this idea. Nor do the firms' boards of directors exhort employees about the importance of respecting the pillars of society's institutions: the church, the presidency, the law, medicine, or capitalism itself.

To the contrary, those who create mass media materials have much more specific requirements to think about. A congressional reporter for a newspaper, for example, is likely to focus on writing good summaries of the government rivalries he or she is covering. A songwriter wants to find a combination of lyrics and music that will grab listeners. The writers of a TV situation comedy episode will probably be centrally concerned with getting laughs from the audience. Moreover, many of the people who work in mass media production firms consider themselves intelligent, critically aware individuals. They might be insulted to think that they spend their time trying to "propagandize" for the establishment.

As it turns out, the most powerful engines for supporting established institutional approaches in mass media are the activities that people think about least: the standard procedures, or **routines,** that become part of their professional working lives. Routines have much in common with habits. They guide people through procedures they need to follow without forcing them to think too deeply about them. This helps an organization get work done quickly. Of course, when the routines employees carry out lead them toward products that fail in the marketplace, they pose a problem. When they are successful, however, routines keep an organization's activities efficient and on track.

But routines do more than help media producers create efficient content. They also are a major force in leading the people who work for mass media production organizations to generate materials that mirror the legitimacy of established institutional power. Without realizing it, people who use these routines are following guidelines that media practitioners created many years ago to solve very practical problems in getting their work done. At the same time — and probably without realizing it — those people built into these routines ways of portraying the world that harmonize with the establishment.

THE ORGANIZATION OF NEWS ROUTINES

Consider an example from the news business. Ask a journalist for the most important concept that guides reporting, and he or she is likely to answer **objectivity.** Nowadays, the journalist may quickly add that of course there is no such thing as absolute objectivity, and that objectivity in journalism means being as fair as possible.

Ask how one writes an objective story, and the person will probably list a number of criteria, including the following:

- The piece should proceed according to the **inverted pyramid** form. That is, its first paragraph should note the story's essentials — the who, what, where, when, how, and why of the incident — and then expand on details as the article unfolds.
- The piece should be written in the **third person;** the reporter should not intrude into the article or color it with his or her personal opinion.
- This "objective voice" should be accompanied by **quotes** from the individuals involved as well as from credible observers.
- Care should also be taken to include at least *two* sides to the story.

News people are typically very careful about writing their stories according to the guidelines of objectivity. They believe that in most cases the approach leads to stories that are free from political preferences. Scholars who write about news work, however, insist that news very much reflects the preferences of the most powerful groups in society. Gaye Tuchman, for example, has argued that "news both draws upon and reproduces institutional structure."[8] And Phillip Tichenor, George Donahue, and Clatice Olien have observed that "where there is diversity in social power, media tend to reflect the orientations of those segments that are higher up on the power scale."[9]

How can such seemingly neutral approaches to writing a news story perpetuate patterns of seeing the world that mesh with the establishment? To answer this question, we must look at history.

Origins of News Objectivity

Present-day requirements that news reports be objective trace their origins to the emergence of the penny press in the late 1830s. The papers were responding to major changes taking place in the United States as a new, restless population of urban workers ("artisans" and "mechanics") emerged on the scene. These city laborers became increasingly angry with what they saw as the control held by the established merchant class over American institutions. Their anger was not reflected in the mainstream daily newspapers of the big cities. These "sixpenny" papers, supported as they were by the dominant political parties and by expensive subscriptions, followed their wealthy readers in looking down on the working class.

By contrast, Benjamin Day of the *New York Sun,* James Gordon Bennett of the *New York Herald,* George Wilkes of the *National Police Gazette,* and others positioned their penny products toward "the great masses of the community."[10] They chastised the sixpennies for their alliances with "cliques and parties" and not with the general public's good.[11] The penny paper entrepreneurs claimed to speak for all, both worker and merchant. A newspaper costing only a penny would give all citizens equal access to knowledge, they argued, and the commonsense reports in the paper, controlled by no party and no class, would benefit democracy.

In their editorials, these papers managed to blend a concern with traditional American institutional values — individual property rights, the market system, and the power of the state — with a concern for the rights of workers to move upward in society. This approach led to the development of objectivity as the key criterion of good journalism. The reason was quite practical: Newspaper publishers needed to appeal to readers of all political and economic stripes with stories that the readers would believe. Their solution for attracting both workers and owners, both rich and poor, seemed easy: Present them with "the facts" — the objective reality — and let them make up their own minds.

The idea of an objective reality was accepted easily in the United States at that time. People felt that facts represented truths everyone could agree with. Science could discover the absolute truth; photographs would not lie. Today, many people do not accept such notions so easily. They believe that photos *can* "lie" — or, at any rate, they can present one of a number of perspectives on the same scene. But nineteenth-century journalists, like most people of their day, were sure it was possible to reveal the world impartially, to separate fact from fiction. Publishers, editors, reporters, illustrators, and photographers worked hard to establish routines that would allow them to present factual, objective accounts of events.

Slowly over the years, and in response to a variety of technological, economic, and political demands on newspapers, the procedures that represent objective journalism developed.[12] Today, journalists and their audiences take for granted such conventions as the inverted pyramid, the third-person objective voice, the use of quotes from credible sources, and the telling of more than one side of a story. They usually consider these practices neutral tools that, when used professionally, can reveal "the facts" about situations.

Closer examination, however, reveals that the routines of objectivity are not the neutral recording instruments journalists like to believe they are. As this historical sketch suggests, a particular view of reality was built into these procedures. This view was a middle-of-the-road approach that tried to balance the interests of both merchants and laborers, of upper and middle class, while upholding the traditional institutional structure. On the one hand, journalists chose stories that showed the workers that the journalists stood with them against unscrupulous wealth. On the other hand, the objective methods of reporting what they found led journalists to uphold the wealthy class even as they exposed its problems.

Objectivity and Authority

To see how objectivity works to present an establishment view, consider one guideline: Quoting credible sources is evidence that a report is objective. The commonsense logic of journalism is that the most credible sources are those who hold legitimate positions of authority. These tend to be government leaders, police officers, corporate executives, and keepers of official statistics rather than alleged criminals, admitted nonexperts, or people with no special knowledge of a complex situation.

As a result, the facts and perspectives of people in authority are dominant in objective news reports. Their presence in stories about corruption within the establishment thus quietly supports those who claim that the problems are due not to the system but to a few rotten apples.

Sources that journalists consider authoritative can also **manage the news** in many instances. This means they can guide reporters to certain topics and not others so as to erase or obscure threats to their powerful positions within the established system.

The requirement to present more than one side of a story is another objectivity guideline that can be viewed as legitimizing the establishment. Being "balanced" in this way obliges the journalist to be evenhanded. It also forces the journalist to sound uncommitted, and it allows people in power the opportunity to defend themselves, even if the journalist knows they are being inaccurate and insincere.

This posture of neutrality was purposefully built into the role of the journalist over the past century. Editors took pride in the adversarial relationship that had developed between the newspapers and the government (see Chapter 4), and in the support they offered the laboring American classes. Many news organizations prided themselves, and continue to pride themselves, on uncovering social problems that suggest the need for correcting society.

Yet the key word here is *correcting,* not *destroying.* This **remedial** role of journalists became so clear, in fact, that many writers began to refer to the press as the **fourth branch of government,** which reflects the understanding that an "objective" press does not stand in opposition to the established order of things. To the contrary, it exists to participate in the growth of that order.

THE ROUTINES OF FICTION

Many of the same points about the legitimizing role of routines in mainstream U.S. journalism apply to other mainstream mass media activities. A large number of writers have argued that the most widespread fiction tends to accept the established institutional setup of the society as a given. Certainly there are areas of popular culture with a tradition of expression that stands opposed to mainstream values.

The American music industry has always accommodated groups that oppose the establishment. In the early 1990s, the rap segment of the recording industry witnessed obscenity trials of music groups such as the Dead Kennedys and 2 Live Crew along with widespread indignation that the lyrics of a number of rap groups were racist and sexist. Music stores tended to carry the groups' albums, especially when huge conservative outcries against them made them into money-making celebrities. Radio stations, afraid of alienating advertisers and the Federal Communications Commission, tended to stay away.[13]

Fiction and the Establishment

Writers on mainstream popular culture stress that even mainstream material is sometimes critical of the establishment. Popular fiction, they note, often exposes tensions between different classes or groups in society and holds certain elite types up for laughter or even scorn. Think of unfavorable images you have seen recently of bankers, bosses, strict parents, or government bureaucrats.

Yet, these observers point out, even when the materials focus on problems of the society, whether in comedic or serious ways, the portrayals should not be considered anti-establishment because they tend not to support radical breaks with traditional ways of doing things. Love of one person at a time is still the standard romantic appeal in songs; the nuclear family is considered the most desirable living condition for adults with children; government agencies are regularly depicted as crucial to the functioning of society; jobs — bosses and all — are shown as facts of life that must be endured and can even be enjoyed; robbing a bank is rarely condoned. This tendency is clear on TV, in the movies, in comic books, in songs played on the radio, and elsewhere in mainstream mass media.

Communication researcher George Gerbner suggests that fiction can portray institutional values and prejudices much more clearly than news[14] because journalists must be guided by "the facts" and thus cannot make up endings to their stories. If a gang of drug addicts robs a bank, a reporter who knows nothing about them cannot portray them as mean and ugly and say that they have been caught. A writer concocting a bank robbery for a movie plot can, by contrast, do just that. The producer, director, and casting director can also make sure that the robbers are of an age, sex, ethnicity, and race that will suit the needs of the story and not offend large numbers of people in the audience.

The selection of particular types of people over others for roles in mainstream materials often reflects institutionally accepted notions about who belongs in what positions in society. When grade school teachers are portrayed mostly as women and truck drivers mostly as men, it reinforces notions that people have learned to accept as the commonsense values of society. Violence in storytelling also depicts social values. Violent criminals are bad but violent heroes are good, mainly because they use their power to catch criminals, who threaten society. Fiction emphasizes the need for law enforcement to protect society's values, even if the enforcer has to be a special arm of the law (James Bond or Dick Tracy), a vigilante cop (Bruce Willis in *Die-Hard*), a private detective (Mike Hammer), or Batman.

Storytelling Formulas

Fiction writers, like news writers, often have no idea that they are legitimizing established institutional practices when they create their works. Like news, however, these ideas are built into the storytelling routines. No one has traced the roots of these routines, partly because it is difficult to know how far back in time to go.

Storytelling is as old as humankind. Folklore from around the world contains themes of institutional legitimacy and the celebration of social values that foreshadow some of those in mass media material. Even supposedly home-grown American mass media forms have roots in other societies. Research on the Western, for example, indicates its origin in the folklore of early colonial settlers, in published memoirs of Indian captivity and the westward movement, and in the popular books of knights in shining armor that Sir Walter Scott turned out in the early nineteenth century. To trace the historical creation, perpetuation, transformations, and interconnections of a large number of fiction forms in much the same way that people have traced the development of objectivity in American journalism would be a prodigious undertaking.

It seems clear, though, that part of the reason for institutional legitimacy in mainstream fiction lies in routines involving the basic starting point for fiction making in many mass media production firms: the **formula.** A formula is a set of widely recognized principles for selecting and organizing material. In fiction, formulas consist of certain types of **settings, characters,** and **plots.**

In a cowboy tale, for example, the setting may be the "Wild West" (a frontier on the edge of "civilization"). Typical characters would be the cowboy, the sheriff, the bank robbers, and the female schoolteacher. A typical plot would involve some kind of tension between the characters.

For example, a number of movies and books adopt the following plot structure: A cowboy who was once a bad guy but has reformed is being blackmailed by the bad guys who want him to return to their side. In the face of a weak sheriff, the bad guys threaten the town. The cowboy (aided by his romantic involvement with the schoolteacher) must decide whether to risk exposure as a former criminal or let the town fall to the marauders.[15]

Writers can vary this basic plot structure to come up with a multitude of seemingly different stories. Combining elements from two or more formulas may result in new formulas that appear more creative and sophisticated than older ones. At the same time, the variations involve characters, plot patterns, and even settings that reflect certain ways of looking at the world. The tension noted in the cowboy formula, for example, almost always leads to an emphasis on the traditionally American importance of masculine individualism and the correctness of using force to solve problems. Pacifism is not a theme that can coexist easily with a cowboy tale.

Formulas and the Rise of the Movie Industry

Popular formulas provide mass media production firms with models for easily manufactured output that seem to have a good chance of success with large numbers of people. At the same time, because mainstream social values are part of their building blocks, creators can use formulas to thwart complaints by the mainstream that their material is institutionally unacceptable.

Movie historian Robert Sklar shows how the use of formulas protected Hollywood production firms in their early years. After World War I, the film industry was attacked by groups that feared movies were their enemies in a battle they were waging over American values. In short, their aim was to maintain a conservative, "small town" perspective in the face of an increasingly urban, industrial, and ethnically diverse society. They saw American movies, with their vivid portrayals of crime and salacious behavior, as directly opposing this goal. To these spokespeople for the traditional middle and upper classes, the direction of the movies was particularly worrisome because power over the photoplay rested largely in the hands of foreign-born Jewish producers who, they felt, could not be trusted to promote traditional American values.

The producers' response, Sklar says, was to steer a middle course through the warring factions in American society. The film executives presented new lifestyles on the screen, but in such a way as to "clearly avoid breaking away from the fundamental economic and social mold." One of the ways they protected themselves was to base their films on time-tested formulas, varied in style and minor detail to fit the period.

> Faced with an audience more divided, more defensive, and yet increasingly avid for visions of alternative styles and behavior, moviemakers not unnaturally sought the subjects and treatments that pleased the most and alienated the fewest. The noisy and well-organized opposition and their own settled beliefs and filmmaking practices kept them from straying too far beyond the remaining stereotypes and formulas of the middle-class order. What they became adept at was reformulating older conventions; only when the need was obvious and overwhelming did they dare to generate a new formula. The re-

sults were not so different from traditional culture as reformists and censors sometimes made it appear.[16]

Sklar makes another point about the movie moguls that resonates with what has been said about journalist-entrepreneurs. These men were, despite fears of the defenders of middle-class culture, "deeply committed to the capitalist values, attitudes, and ambitions that were part of the dominant social order."[17] They cared about their businesses and about the society that had allowed them to prosper. And though they may well have wanted to point out its problems and encourage people to solve them, they had no interest in tearing the establishment down.

JOINING THE ORGANIZATION

It is clear, then, that legitimation of established institutions through mainstream mass media materials has deep roots in the history of production activities. In addition, the huge cost of engaging in mainstream media production makes it likely that the organizations involved will align themselves with the establishment.

What of the people who work in those organizations? Do *they* accept those values, or do they simply follow formulas and other approaches to content without caring? How, in any event, do they learn what is involved in creating acceptable materials?

Hiring Patterns

Studies of the people who join mainstream U.S. production firms to help create material suggest that most of them accept the institutional views that get into their output. This seems particularly true for news people. Studies of journalists consistently reflect what John W. C. Johnstone, Edward Slawski, and William Bowman call "the fact that in virtually any society those in charge of mass communication tend to come from the same social strata as those in control of the economic and political systems."[18] In the 1970s, for example, Johnstone and his associates found U.S. journalists to be overwhelmingly from solidly middle-class or upper-middle-class backgrounds."[19]

Among entertainment performers, this generalization does not hold. A high percentage of the nation's most successful singers and comedians are African-Americans from disadvantaged backgrounds. Sociologists point out that nonblack entertainers are likely to come from religions — particularly the Jewish and Catholic faiths — that have generally been considered socially disadvantaged. Apart from performers, though, it appears that hiring throughout both the journalistic and the nonjournalistic mass media has tended to reflect patterns of racial, class, and gender dominance in U.S. society as a whole.

Numbers tell only part of the story, but they can be startling. For example, government agencies, women's groups, and labor guilds have presented much evidence of the low representation of women as directors, producers, and performers in television and the movies. The Screen Actors Guild found that only 19% of all 9,440 parts in theatrical films in which guild members worked in 1989 went to females.[20] Socially disadvantaged men and women of color have found even greater difficulty getting roles. In 1989, for example, fully 82% of all 9,353 parts in theatrical films went to whites.[21]

Economic and political changes in the society at large *have* affected hiring. The prominence and power of blacks as performers in the recording industry over the past few decades, for example, have encouraged firms to hire blacks for the mid-level executive positions with which the performers work. This, in turn, has encouraged other types of minority hiring throughout the industry.

Often, though, changes at the performer level do not radiate very far. Network television provides a case in point. During the 1980s, more black entertainers starred in network TV programming than ever before. A number of factors contributed to this situation. First, the black middle class had grown to become an attractive market for national advertisers. At the same time, ratings companies reported that blacks spend 40% more time watching broadcast TV than do whites. Moreover, it became clear that shows with certain black personalities (Bill Cosby, Arsenio Hall, Oprah Winfrey) appealed to "crossover audiences" of whites and blacks. In view of these considerations, network executives, trying to fight a decline in their general audience numbers, decided to coax black heavy viewers to these shows with the aid of black stars. This approach was especially apparent at the Fox network, which tried hard to lure young blacks and Hispanics to its programming.

Black TV stars hired some black actors, writers, and administrators to work with them. Although the number of key African-American players increased on screen, by 1990 the increase had only a small ripple among TV writers or in the network decision-making suites. According to the Writers Guild of America, West, less than 2% of the Writers Guild members working in television in each year from 1982 through 1987 were black.[22] In network executive suites, the absence of black men was particularly noteworthy. Of the eight network vice-presidents or programming directors who were black, only one was a man.[23]

Minorities have been rare in journalism organizations as well. In the early 1980s, only 10% of their employees were nonwhite. As for gender, the insistence of feminist groups in the 1970s that women be given equal occupational opportunities seems to have had a significant impact. Professors David Weaver and Cleveland Wilhoit found that the proportion of women working as journalists in the early 1980s was substantially higher than in the early 1970s (33% as opposed to 20%). It did not approach the percentage of women in the total full-time work force (43%), however.[24] In this respect, journalism was still ten years behind the times.

TALKING POINT 7.1   Unequal Access, Unequal Pay for TV Writers

In 1993, the Writers Guild of America, West, released a report detailing the job experiences of its members who are women, members of minority groups, and people over 50 years of age. The findings reflected the difficulty these writers have experienced in becoming a part of the Hollywood establishment. For minority writers, especially African-Americans, the report noted large gains in membership and in TV employment. The report spoke of these increases as "pockets of promises." Women, it noted, were making "limited gains."

The situation seemed to be going downhill, though, regarding writers over the age of 50. In the decade from 1982 to 1991, the percentage of employment accounted for by this group declined in both television (from 26% to 18%) and feature films (from 21% to 14%). In fact, the percentage of Writers Guild members who were actually employed was found to decline steadily after age 40.

The writers of the report noted that "older television writers appear to be 'typecast' in a variety of ways. For example, they are less likely to write for situation comedies than for dramas and television movies, and they are less likely to write for network series than for syndicated or cable series." Much of this discrimination clearly relates to the interest that television producers have in reaching people 18 to 49 years old. Producers believe that writers not in that age group cannot speak to the interests of people who are. The report states, for example, that "writers over 50 have practically no presence on series aired on the [youth-oriented] Fox network, where they account for just 3% of those receiving teleplay credits."

SOURCE: William T. Bielby and Denise D. Bielby, "The 1993 Hollywood Writers' Report: Unequal Access, Unequal Pay" (West Hollywood, CA: Writers Guild of America, West, 1993), p. 3.

Hiring Patterns and Media Content

Reflecting on the "mainstream" characteristics of the creators of society's mainstream news and fiction, some researchers have contended that those mass media perpetuate institutional legitimacy because the people involved impose their personal values on the content. Johnstone and his associates convey this impression. After sketching the typical background of journalists, they conclude that it is "perhaps more than accidental that . . . news in large measure reflects men's rather than women's definitions of newsworthiness . . . and that the establishment groups in the society are virtually always defined as more newsworthy than those of minority or disadvantaged groups."[25]

Political researchers Robert Lichter, Linda Lichter, and Stanley Rothman take this line of thinking to its logical conclusion in their study of the beliefs of journalists who work for newspapers that reach the nation's elites: the *New York Times,* the *Washington Post,* and the *Wall Street Journal.* They found that the newsworkers in these firms were far more likely than the rest of the U.S. population to describe themselves as politically left of center. They concluded that the liberal tendencies of these workers were the primary reason for the newspapers' tendency to be liberal in their approach to political affairs.[26]

Lichter, Lichter, and Rothman's conclusions can be challenged, however. For one thing, the *New York Times,* the *Washington Post,* and the *Wall Street Journal* are not that ideologically different from the rest of U.S. journalism. Although they have adopted the historical role of "the fourth estate" more vigorously than many other daily papers, their approach to the world is still fundamentally one of supporting the nation's dominant institutional structures.

Moreover, it can be argued that these researchers' logic is backward. Instead of interpreting their findings as meaning that the so-called liberal employees influence the news organizations, it would have been at least as sensible to say that the newspapers' policies led to hiring those types of people. That is, the practice of investigative, relatively challenging journalism attracted — even demanded — people with those interests and characteristics, idealistic people who were interested in working within the system, but not altogether happy with the status quo.

Sociologist Herbert Gans uses this kind of analysis to disagree with the Lichter, Lichter, and Rothman position. He argues that the world of newswork ends up dictating the values of people who can work in it, rather than the other way around. Gans states that neither the personal values nor the upper-middle-class background of most journalists really gets to the heart of why they write what they write on their jobs. Surely, as explained in the next chapter, personal likes and dislikes influence what appears in print or on the home screen. But, Gans asserts, the "basic shape of news" would not be different if a journalist came, for example, from a working-class or a middle-class home. The reason is that the mainstream perspectives guiding newswork are built into news work activities; the work guides the person, not the other way around. Gans suggests that working-class people would have a hard time filling the employment prerequisites for news work. Even when they could, in order to act as journalists they "would likely have to shed their working class values and reality judgments."[27]

Having a background that reflects dominant values, then, helps a prospective employee in two ways. First, it makes it easier to obtain a position in a major mass media organization. Second, it allows the new employee to adapt to media work more easily than a person without that background.

But how does one "adapt" to media work? What is involved in getting recruited to an organization and learning its ways? How does this mesh with the twin acts of getting production work done and legitimizing the establishment? To answer these questions, we must examine the subjects of recruitment and socialization to mass media production organizations.

FORMS OF RECRUITMENT

Mass media firms typically hire some creative personnel as permanent staff members and others for short periods of time. Permanent, or **staff,** recruitment therefore means hiring people to be regular members of the firm. The second approach involves freelance work. Management hires creative person-nel to carry out specific tasks. They are relied on to do the job according to the best of their knowledge, and they leave when they finish.

Creative personnel who take on a **selector** role in their organization are quite likely to be recruited on a staff line. Selectors are members of an organi-zation who make decisions about accepting or rejecting certain materials for production. Examples are newspaper editors, movie producers, and advertis-ing account executives.

It is useful to use the term **artist** to describe people who actually gener-ate ideas for the materials selectors have chosen. In everyday language, the word *artist* means that the work performed is of especially high quality. Here it simply refers to the range of activities that certain types of employees carry out. Writers working on book manuscripts, actors playing movie parts, TV ex-ecutives creating the schedules for their networks' prime time shows, and journalists creating news stories all serve as artists.

These examples raise two important points. First, selectors sometimes also act as artists. The network TV executives are artists in their creation of the lineups, but they are also selectors in choosing the shows that will appear in those lineups. Similarly, some book publishers require their editors to write books as well as move them through the production process.

Second, while selectors who are also artists typically enter organizations through staff recruitment, artists who are not selectors may be recruited ei-ther permanently or on a freelance basis, depending on the industry and the circumstances. Journalists, for example, are generally recruited for a bureau-cratic approach to production, while trade book writers are mostly hired freelance, one book at a time. A newspaper editor, an advertising copywriter, and a television news anchor typically are recruited in the staff track. By con-trast, when a movie studio hires stuntpeople to perform in a movie, it is usu-ally understood that the company will stop paying them when the filming is over. Screenwriters and novelists are also generally picked up on a freelance basis.

Reasons for Different Hiring Forms

The reasons for these different approaches to hiring vary. Many companies simply cannot support a permanent lineup of highly paid artists. It may be (as in the stuntpeople's case) that their specialties are infrequently used. Or it may be (in the case of screenwriters or novelists) that the artists need a long time to complete their work and the firm cannot afford to keep paying them while they are not contributing directly to profits.

Some movie companies do keep actors and writers on staff. Publishing firms may have long-term contracts with writers. Whether a firm hires artists on a continuing basis will depend to a large degree on the financial health of the company, the firm's tradition, and the losses the company could incur if the artists went to competitors. Sometimes, production executives need artists they can rely on for daily work.

Illustrators in an advertising agency fit this description, as do newspaper reporters. A daily newspaper typically uses its reporters' work every day. At the same time, some papers find it prestigious and ultimately profitable to support a few bureaus and investigative reporting units even if they prepare publishable stories only every few weeks or even months.

However, a small scholarly publishing company, a struggling monthly magazine firm, or a new recording company may not be able to afford such delayed gratification; some newspapers may not want to. Thus, circumstances would probably dictate that these firms recruit freelance artists when selectors believe the artists have something specific to contribute, and only for the length of time it takes them to contribute it.

Another case in which it is likely that artists will be hired for short periods at a time is an industry where popularity and acclaim are unpredictable from one work to the next. Selectors in areas ranging from scholarly book publishing to network television know that the value of particular artists may rise while the value of certain others may plummet. They realize that by hiring artists for brief periods, they may be forced to pay more money to highly desired recruits than if they locked them into permanent contracts. In many situations, though, this added expense is more than made up for by the selectors' ability to choose creators quickly and efficiently so as to meet current fashions and production workloads.

The differences in the ways artistic personnel are brought into the creation of mass media materials suggest that they learn the routines of the organizations they work for in various ways. How does this process take place? Do different learning situations mean that some types of artists are trained in routines that legitimate the established institutions whereas others are not? The answers require understanding how the socialization process works in freelance and staff hiring styles.

FREELANCE SOCIALIZATION IN MEDIA INDUSTRIES

Socialization is one of the most basic activities of humans in human communities: learning to fit in. It is an active process that takes place in the normal course of daily life, in organizations as well as elsewhere in society. As people move through social situations, they and the people they work with negotiate rules about their interdependent behaviors (their **roles**).

Power — the use of resources to guide someone else's behavior — is a key ingredient in the process. People use resources (knowledge, money, willpower, status) to advance their positions within their organization, and they use their status to garner more resources. Increased power gives them increased control over the organization's activities.

These points apply to both craft and bureaucratic production styles. Socialization occurs differently, however, if an artist is a full-time, long-term member of a particular production firm than if he or she works freelance and is recruited stop-and-go by various organizations. For permanently hired artists, much of the learning to compete for status and resources takes place in the "home" organization where they work full time. The continuation of employment and promotability is daily judged primarily by people within that firm. Freelance artists, on the other hand, must not only convince the companies they work for to hire them again, but must also develop power bases outside those companies to continue to generate more work in other places.

Doing this effectively generally requires admission to a community of similar artists — of writers, musicians, stunt actors, and the like. It is a community where a complex hierarchy, an elaborate system of contacts, and an often ritually prescribed gauntlet of competition strongly influence the artists' ability to enter production organizations, as well as the artists' market value.

The Case of the Hollywood Musician

Robert Faulkner refers to many of these issues when he writes about the Hollywood studio musician's search for freelance work:

> When he seeks to enter studio work, the unestablished recruit sees his career as contingent upon his ability to develop the proper web of contacts with those who control access to jobs. Sponsorship is the major social mechanism which brings him to their attention, allows him to establish a reputation as a solid and dependable performer, and prepares him to cope with the various pressures of the work itself. From the viewpoint of the sponsors, several important conditions must be attended to: (1) the young musician must be sponsored in such a way that established colleagues are not threatened with loss of power and prestige; (2) contractors and leaders [who recruit and work, respectively, for the studio] must be convinced that the recruit is competent and can be depended upon; (3) the appropriate timing and pacing of the candidate's introduction into the division of studio labor must be determined and implemented; and (4) the candidate must learn the subtle etiquette of the referral system and, most importantly, that sponsorship is a process of reciprocal exchange.[28]

Although Faulkner uses the pronoun *he* in describing the importance of sponsorship in craft socialization, his remarks apply equally to women. In fact, they reflect the fact that women have not broken into studio musicianship as easily as men. Part of the reason undoubtedly is their difficulty in making the connections that Faulkner stresses are so important. Women and members of minority groups have long pointed out that in mass media industries, as in other areas of business, their inability to join the circles that provide connections and sponsorships have hindered them from being considered for attractive freelance jobs.

The reasons for not making contacts may have to do with activities that seem irrelevant to the talents required. Playing baseball or golf, drinking in bars, and gambling in card games have little to do with musicianship or any other artistic talents. Yet these friendly diversions serve to increase the chances of networking and cementing professional relationships. People who cannot get in on them may well be left out of the sponsorship process.

A Delicate Power Struggle

Memoirs of artists from a variety of mass media industries confirm this view. Such accounts indicate that a delicate power struggle occurs over the recruitment of unknown freelance artists. This struggle involves people in a variety of roles, and chief among them are the neophyte artists themselves. They must learn to convince the right people of their talents. Among the most important of these people are artists and talent agents who already belong to an "inner circle." They decide whether to introduce particular artists or their agents to key selectors in production organizations. These selectors—the people who do the hiring—often expend great effort to get to know new talent and help the best along. What constitutes "the best" of the new talent becomes part of the complex negotiations that go on within artistic circles.

The pressure felt by freelance artists to meet one another in order to get hired typically makes it difficult for them to distinguish social occasions from business meetings. The sense of community then takes on overtones of both comradeship and social control. Ideas are shared, stolen, and exchanged. Rules are formulated, changed, and reformulated. Expensive deals are initiated by the shake of a hand.

Through it all, there is a strong awareness that what counts at the end is satisfying executives in the production firms who hire them for particular jobs. Musicians who will work at Fox have a keen idea what the person hiring there expects. This may be different from the approach taken by the selector at Universal. The artists' thoughts of the audience—the people "out there"—fade in importance as the desires of production firm selectors become more immediately crucial.

The extent to which selectors are willing to take chances on new artists varies. The editor of a "little magazine" might be willing to publish a writer who has not yet appeared in print, but the editor of a large-circulation magazine will probably not. Established artists and agents learn these preferences and approach new artists with them in mind. In general, these inner-circle members are likely to feel ambivalent about suggesting new names. On the one hand, they know that selectors want to learn about good new faces and are likely to be grateful to artists who can help in their search. On the other hand, sponsoring an artist who ends up failing can be worse than not suggesting someone at all. It must also be acknowledged that established artists sometimes see newcomers as threats to the current generation of talent.

Dues and Track Records

Fear of competition combines with awareness of the needs that selectors face in their production organizations. As a result of these conflicting tendencies, sponsorship systems tend to be conservative. The people involved take few chances on relatively few people. Artistic circles promote the idea that members should not suggest artists for important jobs unless they have **paid their dues** in related work and begun to establish **track records.** A person establishing a track record is someone who, in paying dues by creating perhaps less widespread or expensive material, has shown that he or she is reliable, talented, and ready for more responsibility.

This emphasis on paying dues and accumulating a track record ensures that a relatively small number of newcomers will move through the recruitment gauntlet, which in turn ensures that most members of the inner circles will continue to find jobs. This approach also tends to weed out artists who could disrupt a production organization's routine activities and profits. Word gets out among freelance artists regarding what different companies expect.

Freelancers learn quickly that they will be rehired only if their talent comes without disruption in organizational routines and profitability. Selectors may reject even geniuses if they develop reputations for being inefficient. As a member of the Hollywood television community said in the late 1960s, "A script by a genius may contain a scene twenty-five minutes long that can't be edited." To avoid this trouble, a producer or story editor who recruits writers will look not for geniuses but for people "who can meet their deadlines and give him material that he can shoot in six and a half days, within his budget, and without any trouble [from network censors].[29]

Proving oneself to an artistic community usually means becoming part of that community's establishment. When the establishment is involved in producing mainstream mass media materials, this system of craft socialization tends to act as yet another insurance that portrayals will not challenge the legitimacy of institutional structures. The legitimation operates even when the artists are members of a socially disadvantaged minority group, who might be expected to have some very different views from those who typically create content.

The Case of Minority Writers

A good way to illustrate this is to describe the position in which Latino, African-American, Native American, Eskimo, and Asian-American writers find themselves when they want to work on the most mainstream of mass media materials; network television programs. TV writers with these ethnic backgrounds are quite scarce. According to several industry sources, a large number of minority writers are interested in applying their skills to this lucrative field, but their efforts have been stymied.

In 1991, only 125 of the 3,657 members of the Writers Guild, West, who found TV work were members of the previously mentioned minority groups. In the same year, only 309 certified members (4%) of the Writers Guild, West, were minorities.[30] Actually, these numbers are a substantial improvement over those of previous years. In 1988, only 180 members of the Writers Guild, West, were minorities; in 1991 the number was 309, a 40% improve-

TABLE 7.1 DIVERSITY IN HOLLYWOOD

	Actors	Writers	Directors	General U.S. Population
Female	35%	24%	20%	51%
Black	12%	3%	2%	12%
Latino	3%	1%	2%	9%
Asian	2%	0.5%	0.6%	3%
American Indian	1%	0.2%	0.1%	0.8%

SOURCE: Los Angeles Times, *December 7, 1995, page 1.*

Three major Hollywood unions have compiled figures on racial and ethnic diversity within the TV and movie entertainment industry. It should, perhaps, be noted that these categories represent only the tip of an iceberg of ways to determine whether the movie and television industries provide opportunities for different types of people. Geographical background, sexual preferences, and political ideology are examples of other categories that could be investigated.

ment over 1988. Moreover, some important studios increased their hiring of minority writers substantially. Reeves Entertainment and Spelling hired no minority writers in the 1990–91 season. But at Warner Brothers Television, minority employment increased from 4 writers in 1987 to 28 in 1991. The 28 accounted for 6% of television writers employed at Warner-TV, second highest among the majors. Fox-TV led in minority employment, at 8% of those employed.[31]

The availability of these writers for sitcoms may, to some extent, be traced to efforts that several organizations within the television and movie industries had made to initiate minority writer training programs with the stated goal of placing them in the creative mainstream. The Writers Guild had a training program in which a minority writer was given a chance to work with an established writer who had been recommended by a producer "as someone in tune with that producer's series." According to a Writers Guild executive, the program allowed an inexperienced writer to be "shepherded through the system — from initial story conference through finished script — while deriving inside knowledge about a particular show."[32]

A somewhat different approach was taken by Walt Disney Studios, whose record of employment of women and members of minority groups in creative positions was one of the worst in Hollywood throughout the 1980s. Intent on changing this, a new Disney management started a fellowship program for African-American, Latino, Asian, and female writers. In 1990, 27 writers selected to take part in the program were culled from more than 2,000 applicants throughout the country. Each was to be paid $30,000 over the course of the year. "We're trying to develop these writers into first-rate commercial screenwriters," said a Disney executive. She added that "each writer will be assigned to work with [an established] creative team."[33]

These people were given the opportunity of a lifetime. They were escorted into the inner circles and operations of an artistic community that they would find difficult, if not impossible, to enter under normal circumstances. But the benefits for minorities were not distributed uniformly. The greatest increase with African-Americans, whose membership grew 50% over that of 1988. One reason for this progress had to do with the interest that broadcast networks, particularly Fox, showed in sitcoms with African-American characters. Advertisers had indicated they would support programs that drew this audience, and the word among network executives was that teens and young adults were not turned off by programs with predominantly black casts.

With the opportunity for African-Americans to make these connections came two catches, however. One was that while the recruitment programs opened up the writing field to a broader area of society, the minority writers hired often worked on sitcoms with characters of their own ethnicity. Most of the minority writers employed in TV were African-Americans who worked on sitcoms that featured African-American actors.

What the Writers Guild report called the "severe typecasting" of minority writers was reflected in statistics based on the types of network series on which they worked. Minority writers accounted for 7% of those receiving credit for sitcoms. However, no minority writers received credit for writing serial dramas (such as *Beverly Hills 90210*) or action dramas (such as *Hunter*), while minority writers accounted for just 2% of the writers receiving credit on episodic dramas.

The second catch was that the recruitment programs tended to ensure that the newcomers would adopt TV's established approaches to reality. The writers were encouraged to fit in. Practically speaking, in the late 1980s and early 1990s, TV production firms needed savvy black writers for the growth of black sitcoms. These recruitment programs were aimed at finding and training such writers, not encouraging new perspectives on life for the home tube or big screen. This made it quite unlikely that the writers would generate stories that expose unexposable tensions in society and seriously challenge the legitimacy of established institutional structures.

Staff Socialization in Media Industries

The same statement could be made about writers recruited for staff work, even though the process by which their socialization takes place is likely to be different from that followed by freelance writers.

A key difference between freelance and staff artists is the areas in which they compete with other artists for privilege and prestige. Freelance artists fight for privilege and prestige both as full-time members of artistic circles trying to get jobs and as temporary members of production organizations. Permanently employed artists, by contrast, need to direct much more attention to one source; the production organization that hires them on a long-term basis.

A magazine writer working full time will probably pay less attention to cultivating job-related contacts outside his or her firm than will a freelance writer who is continually looking.

Still, it should be clear that the differences between the two types can be exaggerated. Staff magazine writers, public relations practitioners, advertising copywriters, and journalists are by no means hermits confined to firms. They get involved with members of their fields outside their organizations, and these involvements contribute to their socialization in ways that parallel the influences that communities of freelance artists exert on their members.

Learning Outside the Organization

We can identify five particularly important avenues of involvement outside their current firm by bureaucratically employed artists:

School training
Job mobility
On-the-job contacts
Participation in professional associations
Subscriptions to professional media.

Not every avenue holds equal importance in every mass media industry. Specialized school training is important in cinematography, but not in casting. Moreover, the formal requirements for particular occupations may change over time.

Take U.S. journalists as an example. For them, college training has been gaining in importance. While journalists who started their careers before World War II tended not to be college graduates, by the early 1980s most working journalists were college-educated. Still, being college-educated did not necessarily mean that their degree was in journalism. In the early 1980s, fewer than one in three working journalists actually majored in journalism.[34]

Another mechanism for sharing journalistic values and routines outside current news organizations is job switching. In their sample of 1,001 various journalists throughout the United States, David Weaver and G. Cleveland Wilhoit found that 75% reported working previously for one or more different news organizations. We might suspect that news people who work in different organizations tend to bring some of the practices and perspectives of their previous employment to their new situations.[35]

Another study found that journalists tend to conform to general trends of the labor force at large in terms of the timing of their job switches. That is, they more commonly change jobs in early rather than late stages of their careers. Therefore, as a journalist grows older, he or she is likely to be involved with counterparts from other organizations less through job switches and more through on-the-job contacts and participation in professional associations.

TABLE 7.2 FROM WHOM DO REPORTERS REGULARLY RECEIVE COMMENTS ABOUT THEIR WORK?

	Medium						
Source of Comment	Dailies	Weeklies	News Magazines	Wires	Radio	TV	All Combined
Superiors	29%	28%	41%	42%	49%	42%	35%
Peer	38%	41%	20%	42%	46%	45%	40%
Journalists outside own organization	15%	16%	17%	33%	17%	16%	17%
News sources	48%	32%	33%	21%	33%	36%	39%
Audience	48%	56%	40%	13%	50%	55%	49%
	N = 254	N = 118	N = 30	N = 24	N = 90	N = 288	N = 589

SOURCE: *David Weaver and G. Cleveland Wilhoit, The American Journalist (Bloomington: Indiana University Press, 1986), p. 79. Reproduced by permission.*

Even people who work full time for mass media firms, as reporters typically do, discuss their work with people outside their organizations. Outside colleagues and news sources, in addition to audiences, may play a role in how a newsworker approaches his or her work.

The data in this table come from a nationwide study of journalists conducted during 1982–83. The percentages do not add up to 100 because respondents mentioned more than one source of comments.

On-the-job contacts are very common among working reporters. Journalists from different papers meet one another often in the course of assignments. They file similar stories after viewing the same events, speaking to the same sources, reading the same press releases, and sharing ideas about it all.

This phenomenon is called **pack journalism,** and it has been cited as a key reason for the similar subjects and angles used by reporters covering the same event. Often, too, reporters get ideas of what is important by reading the same newspapers (the *New York Times,* the *Washington Post*) and tuning to the same wire services. Robert MacNeil made this point through an anecdote from his years working for NBC news:

> In 1963, when Governor George Wallace tried to prevent the integration of Alabama's schools with his "stand in the schoolhouse door," NBC correspondent Tom Pettit, covering the story there, phoned a producer in New York, who started telling Pettit how to handle the story.
> "There's a good story in the *New York Times* this morning," he said.
> "We don't get the *New York Times* down here," Pettit said.
> "Well, the night lead of the AP says — "
> "We don't have the AP."
> "Never mind. The UP's got a pretty good angle on it — "
> "We don't have the UP either," Pettit said.
> The producer said, "You don't have the UP?"
> "No."
> "You don't have the AP?"
> "No."
> "You don't have the *New York Times*?"
> "No."
> "Then how do you guys know what's going on down there?"[36]

Professional associations (such as the American Newspaper Association and the Association for Education in Journalism) and professional media (such as *Editor and Publisher,* the *Columbia Journalism Review,* the *American Journalism Review*) also tend to bring journalistic heads together on both large and small issues — from gossip about people in the field to canons of journalistic ethics to the proper way to cover certain types of events. In so doing, they provide umbrellas of public precedent to protect journalists who may feel forced by their organizations to carry out activities they consider unprofessional.

The trade magazines also reinforce the principles of objective journalism among the corps of journalists in mainstream news organizations throughout the country. They do this by singling out practices that deviate from journalistic norms ("The Failure of Network News," revealed the *Washington Journalism Review*), by showing how new problems can be corrected through accepted routines ("Sex in the News: Some Guidelines," suggested the *AP Log*), and by celebrating the accomplishments of those designated the best and brightest (through, for example, the Pulitzer Prizes).[37]

TABLE 7.3 WHAT PROFESSIONAL PUBLICATIONS DO JOURNALISTS READ?

Publication	Frequency of Readership (%)		
	Regularly[c]	Sometimes	Never
Editor and Publisher[a]	29	34	37
Columbia Journalism Review	20	36	44
Quill	18	32	50
Washington Journalism Review	13	30	57
Journalism Quarterly	6	28	66
APME News	7	12	82
ASNE Bulletin	6	13	81
Journal of Broadcasting	6	11	84
Nieman Reports	3	17	81
Editor's Exchange	4	8	89
Wirewatch	4	7	89
ANPA News Research Reports	3	10	87
presstime[b]	3	8	90
Journal of communication	2	7	92
Newspaper Research Journal	2	8	91

[a]Of daily newspaper journalists, 39% regularly read and 40% sometimes read *Editor and Publisher*.
[b]A publication of the American Newspaper Publishers Association, *presstime* was a new journal at the time of interviewing. It is likely the journal is read by a larger audience now.
[c]Regular readership is defined as reading "almost every issue." *(SOURCE: David Weaver and G. Cleveland Wilhoit,* The American Journalist *[Bloomington: Indiana University Press, 1986], p. 110. Reproduced by permission.)*

The reading of journals and trade publications is one way people who choose careers develop professional identities and keep in touch with what is going on within their field. This table reports the findings from a national sample of print and electronic journalists conducted in 1982–83. The researchers asked them about their use of 15 magazines and journals that are published on subjects having to do with news.

In-House Training

Aside from formal schooling, job mobility, on-the-job contacts, professional associations, and trade magazines, the primary training ground for journalists — in fact, the primary training ground for all bureaucratically employed artists — is still the organization in which they work.

Learning what to do and how to do it is often the result of explicit instruction, learning by example, and learning from mistakes. Organizational resources serve as incentives for newsworkers. Superiors control resources — permissions, salary increases, special benefits, authority to make decisions independently — which they can release to artists carrying out "good" work.

Colleagues also control resources. They are likely to be more friendly and helpful to artists who do good work than to those who do not. Like every mass media artist, a journalist learns that good work means activities that fit well with superiors' policy regarding what the organization should create and how it should create it. As noted, the norms that make up the basic policy of a mass media production firm have built into them perspectives on the meaning of legitimate social power, authority, and justice, as well as on the limits to questioning them. By extension, then, a mainstream journalist who does good work legitimates the dominant institutional values of the society.

VALUE CONFLICTS

In his classic study of the way journalists learn their organization's policy, Warren Breed describes many of the learning avenues just mentioned. He calls what takes place "social control in the newsroom." By invoking the notion of social control, Breed raises another idea: the possibility of clashes between creators' personal values and the values of the organization as expressed in the firm's journalistic policy.[38]

Note that Breed's approach to the idea of journalistic policy is very different from the one used so far in this chapter. The two approaches do not contradict each other. They simply get at two different aspects of an organization's policy. One aspect, which we have already dealt with, is the organization's core policy. **Core policy** represents the fundamental perspective that an organization follows regarding the legitimacy of dominant institutions in the society. The second aspect, the one concerning Breed, is the organization's general policy. **General policy** is built on top of core policy. It represents perspectives that the organization follows in portraying areas of life about which executives set guidelines.

An example is in order. Consider two newspaper firms that conduct their creative activities so as to legitimate society's institutions. They can be said to have common core policies. But at the same time, say, one paper reflects a Democratic point of view, the other a Republican one. Also, one encourages investigative reporting and the other does not.

Beyond their core policies, then, the news organizations diverge in the general policies through which they represent the world. As noted in Chapter 2, such variation among mass media production firms is typical. It stems from differences in the firms' environments and from differences in executives' perceptions of the environments. However, this chapter shows that many firms are likely to share the same core policies even when they draw on different resources. One reason is that different as the resources are, they still come from mainstream sectors of society. A related reason is that in using these resources, the organizations often follow similar production routines — for example, routines that carry out the ideas of objectivity and formula.

The Commonness of Conflicts

Little is known about the nature of value conflicts among creators in mass media organizations. It is probably safe to suggest, though, that most conflicts that occur relate to general policy, not to core policy. This conclusion seems logical in view of the high degree of selectivity that goes into the recruitment of creative personnel in any area of the mass media, whether mainstream or peripheral. The selectivity ensures that creators who are admitted to responsible positions have paid their dues, carved out track records, and plugged themselves into social circles that make acceptance of their production firms' core values simply part of their lives.

Herbert Gans was reflecting this idea when he wrote about the middle-class core values of the mainstream news organizations he studied. Gans noted that "relatively few journalists came from working-class homes, and those who did lost touch with their origins long ago."[39]

The same idea holds true outside the mainstream. When William Bowman interviewed journalists from anti-establishment publications during the social upheavals of the early 1970s, he found that they shared negative opinions about the legitimacy of the dominant institutions. They welcomed radical change in the society at large. They viewed mainstream news media as "centralized managers of public consciousness . . . devoted to the preservation of the public order." Consequently, they saw their role as "opposition to the status quo, with a readiness to question the legitimacy of any social institution and a commitment to involvement rather than detachment as journalists."[40]

Dealing with Conflicts

There is also little known across the broad range of media regarding the value conflicts that seem to be more common — those involving a production organization's general policy. In the news business, studies of journalists that ask for their opinions about the news process are fairly common. Similar surveys of other industries are rare. Nevertheless, virtually every interview with a creator and every investigation of a mass media organization uncover at least some clash between what a person thinks the production organization should be creating and what it actually is creating.

Warren Breed's concise summary of the options an artist has for reducing this value conflict is worth quoting.

> At the extremes, the pure conformist can deny the conflict, the confirmed deviate can quit. . . . Otherwise, the adaptations seem to run this way: (1) Keep on the job but blunt the corners of policy when possible ("If I wasn't here the next guy would let all that crap get through . . ."); (2) Attempt to represent conflict morally and anti-intellectually ("What the hell, it's only a job; take your pay and forget it . . ."); (3) Attempt to compensate, by "taking it out" in other contexts: drinking, writing "the truth" for liberal publications, working with action programs, the Guild, and otherwise.[41]

What is most relevant here are the implications of Breed's options for the mass media materials that firms create. It would seem that option 2 would lead to a near-apathetic approach to work. Consider a TV writer disenchanted with the refusal by series producers to accept scripts about psychological conflicts of the characters; all the producers want is "action." Working under option 2, the writer may give up on that unusual theme and simply pitch ideas that he or she knows fit time-tested action-adventure or sitcom formulas. That, the writer might say, is the meal ticket, the way to pay the mortgage. If the writer followed option 3, he or she would also generally follow the path of least resistance. At times, though, the writer may also contribute work to organizations holding policies more consistent with his or her values. For example, while proposing traditional plots to most producers, the writer may also try to convince a prestige-oriented TV production firm that the network would be attracted to a special based on this "special" notion. Failing that, the writer might get a movie, novel, or magazine short story out of the idea.

Only option 1 would seem to encourage attempts to get around the expressed policy of a production organization. Following that line, the disenchanted TV writer would propose plots according to accepted formulas. In the scripts, however, he or she might include one or two scenes where characters reflect the issues the writer really wanted to highlight. Of course, consistent failure to get such scenes accepted could lead the writer to fall back on option 2 or 3.

One option Breed's list ignores is head-on confrontation on an issue with the help of other members of the organization. Written as they were in the 1950s, his "adaptations" do not take into account the increased tolerance for argumentation over policy that has existed among executives of many mass media organizations since the 1960s. The rise of women's rights, gay rights, Hispanic rights, black rights, and other civil rights movements has led to the hiring of members of previously excluded groups by mainstream mass media firms. Although those employees typically accept the core values of the organizations, they may quarrel at times with particular policies relating to the groups they most care about. Groups of similarly inclined employees may come together around these issues and complain to top management when they perceive a problem in the content produced.

University of Minnesota professor Leola Johnson has been studying such "coalitions" of black journalists in major newspapers around the United States. These loosely formed groups do not do much on a day-to-day basis, but spring into action when one of the members learns of an impending management or editorial decision that could run counter to the interests of the group. Then, using the news firm's electronic mail system as well as the usual forms of talk, the members may plan ways to stop the actions they oppose. Johnson finds that the coalitions are often not terribly powerful within their organizations. In fact, members whom the top brass sees as too opposed to general policy are not promoted or given good salary increases — indications that they should, perhaps, leave. Still, she concludes that the coalitions have an important role to play in sensitizing the editorial and business sides of mainstream newspapers, which are typically white and male, to black's concerns.[42]

Power and Policy

In general, we can suggest that the more powerful a creator is within an organization, the greater will be that creator's ability to get around general policy and to mobilize others around it. Steven Bochco's status as creator and executive producer of highly rated network TV shows such as *Hill Street Blues* and *NYPD Blue* gave him much clout in network executive suites. Similarly, the huge worldwide profits reaped by Sylvester Stallone's *Rocky* movies gave him a lot of power to dictate changes on the set or in the script.

There are limits to how far these talents can deviate. Clearly, network executives would allow no one, not even Bochco, to embark on a series so expensive and obviously insulting to traditional tastes as to put the network's ability to turn a profit at risk. Moreover, TV and movie executives often link the success of their creators directly to the formulas they have worked with, and no further. Stallone, for example, found it very difficult to persuade studios and banks to invest in movies that allowed him to depart significantly from his macho, Rocky-like image.[43] Such roadblocks cause much tension as creators try to persuade the organizations in which they work to allow them to exceed normal boundaries of general policy.

Still, the possibility of getting around policy should alert us to the idea that executives in production firms sometimes do allow, even encourage, changes in guidelines for creating mass media materials. *The Simpsons, In Living Color,* and *Murder One* are recent network television series that reflect alterations of this sort. This chapter has mapped the forces that discourage basic changes. Particularly in the case of mainstream material, these forces are powerful and deeply rooted. Moreover, they generally ensure that creators will select and shape output that legitimizes the ways institutions do things in society. Within boundaries set by those forces, however, many modifications occur, and they sometimes represent important shifts in the way mass media portray the world. Those changes, and the pressures that encourage and discourage them, are the subject of the next chapter.

CONSIDER THIS

1. Television programs and newspapers often criticize and mock the government and other institutions. In what way, then, can it be said that they legitimize them?
2. How many "peripheral" media do you use? What are they?
3. What is your favorite storytelling formula? Analyze it in terms of setting, characters, and plots. To what extent does the formula have ideas about society built into it?

NOTES

1. The literature on this topic is broad and deep. It ranges from writings on political economy and sociology of the mass media to linguistic and literary analyses of

media text. For accessible summaries of key issues, see Michael Gurevitch, Tony Bennet, and Janet Woollacott (eds.), *Culture, Society, and the Media* (London: Methuen, 1982); John Fisk and John Hartley, *Reading Television* (London: Methuen, 1978); and Raymond Williams, *Marxism and Literature* (New York: Oxford University Press, 1977).

2. Jennifer Lawrence, "Newspapers: Hot Properties in a Cool Economy," *Advertising Age,* January 25, 1988, p. S14; and *New York Times,* August 7, 1987, p. D3.

3. "Sony-Columbia Deal," *New York Times,* November 8, 1989, p. C18.

4. Diane Mermigas, "Levin's $8B 'Fresh Start,'" *Advertising Age,* October 9, 1995, p. 1; and 1995 YEAR IN REVIEW," *Advertising Age,* December 18, 1995, p. 19.

5. Andrea Rothman, "Peter Callahan: An Acquiring Mind," *Business Week,* May 15, 1989, pp. 139–140.

6. David Lieberman, "Murdoch Adds a Few Megatons to His Arsenal," *Business Week,* August 22, 1988, p. 39.

7. 1995 YEAR IN REVIEW, *Advertising Age,* December 18, 1995, p. 19.

8. Gaye Tuchman, *Making News* (New York: Free Press, 1978), p. 210.

9. Phillip Tichenor, George Donahue, and Clarice Olien, *Community Conflict and the Press* (Beverly Hills, CA: Sage Publications, 1980), p. 224.

10. Dan Schiller, *Objectivity and the News: The Public and the Rise of Commercial Journalism* (Philadelphia: University of Pennsylvania Press, 1981), p. 48.

11. Schiller, p. 48.

12. See Michael Schudson, *Discovering the News: A Social History of American Newspapers* (New York: Basic Books, 1978).

13. "Rap Band Members Found Not Guilty in Obscenity Trial," *New York Times,* October 21, 1990, p. 1.

14. George Gerbner, "Teacher Image in Mass Culture: Symbolic Functions in the 'Hidden Curriculum,'" in David Olsen (ed.), *Media and Symbols,* pt. 1 (Chicago: National Society for the Study of Education, 1974), p. 474.

15. See John Cawelti, *The Six-Gun Mystique* (Bowling Green, OH: Popular Press, 1975).

16. Robert Sklar, *Movie-Made America* (New York: Random House, 1975), p. 91.

17. Sklar, p. 91.

18. John W. C. Johnstone, Edward Slawski, and William Bowman, *The News People* (Urbana: University of Illinois Press, 1976), p. 26.

19. Johnstone et al., p. 28.

20. Amy Dawes, "SAG: Women Shortshrifted," *Variety,* August 8, 1990, p. 3.

21. Interview with Rodney Mitchell of the Screen Actors Guild, September 7, 1990.

22. William Bielby and Denise Bielby, *The Hollywood Writers' Report: Unequal Access, Unequal Pay* (West Hollywood, CA: Writers Guild of America, West), p. 1.

23. David Kissinger, "Blacks' Gains on TV Aren't Reflected in Networks' Executives Suites," *Variety,* May 30, 1990, p. 1.

24. David H. Weaver and G. Cleveland Wilhoit, *The American Journalist* (Bloomington: Indiana University Press, 1986), p. 54.

25. Johnstone et al., p. 100.

26. Robert S. Lichter, Stanley Rothman, and Linda S. Lichter, *The Media Elite* (Bethesda, MD: Adler and Adler, 1986).

27. Herbert Gans, *Deciding What's News* (New York: Vintage, 1979), p. 213.

28. Robert Faulkner, "Hollywood Studio Musicians: Making It in the Los Angeles Film and Recording Industry," in Charles Nanry (ed.), *American Music: From Storyville to Woodstock* (East Brunswick, NJ: Transaction Books, 1972), pp. 205–206. See also Robert Faulkner, *Music on Demand: Composers and Careers in the Hollywood Film Industry* (New Brunswick, NJ: Transaction Books, 1983). For a sociological discussion of job-seeking by actors in Hollywood, see Ann Peters and Muriel Cantor, "Screen Acting as Work," in J. Ettema and D. C. Whitney (eds.), *Individuals in Mass Media Organizations* (Beverly Hills, CA: Sage Publications, 1982), pp. 53–68.

29. Thomas Baldwin and Colby Lewis, "Violence: The industry Looks at Itself," in George Comstock and Eli Rubinstein (eds.), *Television and Social Behavior,* vol. 1 (Washington, DC: United States Printing Office, 1972), p. 362.

30. Bielby and Bielby, p. 61.

31. William Bielby and Denise Bielby, "1993 Hollywood Writers' Report" (West Hollywood, CA: Writers Guild of America, 1993).

32. Len Riley, "Writing for Television: All White or All-American," *Emmy Magazine* (Spring 1980), p. 39.

33. "Disney Picks 27 for Fellowships," *Variety,* August 27, 1990, p. 22.

34. Riley, p. 54.

35. David Weaver and G. Cleveland Wilhoit, *The American Journalist* (Bloomington: Indiana University Press, 1966).

36. Robert MacNeil, *The People Machine: The Influence of Television on American Politics* (New York: Harper & Row, 1968), p. 30. A particularly interesting discussion of pack journalism of a specialized sort is found in Sharon Dunwood, "The Science Writing Inner Club," in G. C. Wilhoit and William De Bok (eds.), *Communication Yearbook* (Beverly Hills, CA: Sage Publications, 1981), pp. 351–360.

37. David Altheide, "The Failure of Network News," *Washington Journalism Review* (May 1981), pp. 28–29; and Lou Boccardi, "Sex in the News: Some Guidelines," *AP Log,* June 28, 1976, p. 1.

38. Warren Breed, "Social Control in the Newsroom," in Wilbur Schramm (ed.), *Mass Communications,* 2nd ed. (Urbana: University of Illinois Press, 1972), pp. 178–194.

39. Gans, p. 210.

40. Johnstone et al., pp. 176–177.

41. Breed, p. 193.

42. Leola Johnson, personal communication, May 1991. A classic study of conflicts that Hollywood TV producers experience in their interactions with network executives is Muriel Cantor, *The Hollywood TV Producer* (New York: Basic Books, 1971).

43. Cameron Smith, "Requiem for a Heavyweight," *American Film* (January 1990), p. 24.

CHAPTER 8

Coping with Risks of Production

This chapter

- explains why a continuing tension must exist in media organizations between taking risks and shying away from them.
- explores what taking risks means to creators in different media industries.
- Describes how creators balance risks with activities they believe will have more certainty of success.

In terms of the production process, what is the difference between newspapers and soap? The question may spark some indignation. "How can the two be compared?" you might sneer. "Newspapers are symbolic creations. They tell us about crucial events in the life of humankind. Soap, on the other hand, is, well, simply an object."

Soap companies might object that calling one of their creations "simply an object" misses the profound importance that soap has had for civilization, both as a preventer of disease and as a symbol of cleanliness. Be that as it may, put aside any personal feelings you have about the relative social values of newspapers and soap, and you will see that making distinctions between soap and newspapers regarding the process of production is not as easy as it seems.

For one thing, the makers of soap and the makers of newspapers are both involved in the business of creating products for a marketplace. Both types of organizations compete with other organizations for resources. And both need the personnel, the equipment, the distribution clout, the retail savvy, and the public acceptance to maintain a successful, growing share of the audience.

With little effort, in fact, the power roles laid out in Chapter 2 as a framework for the process of creating mass media materials can be altered to apply to the manufacture of soap or any other product.

In what way, then, does the making of soap diverge in concept from the making of newspapers? The answer lies in the need of soap companies and newspaper companies for **product innovation.** *Innovation* means changing something that exists, creating something new. It is a complicated word, because different people have wildly different ideas of what "new" is, as later portions of this chapter show.

Still, comparing soapmaking and newspaper publishing in terms of the frequency with which the firm needs to make changes in the product reveals a striking difference. Over a short period of time, turning out a brand of soap involves no innovation. Once the soap has been designed and the production process set up, the manufacturer will turn out exact copies of the bar day after day. Any changes made in the soap would come rather slowly, as a result of competitive pressures and careful research and development.

A newspaper publisher could not exist that way. Nobody would want to buy exactly the same newspaper day after day. Newspaper dealers and readers expect new stories with each edition. "New" events must be covered, "new" ads displayed, "new" crossword puzzles presented. Research and development may plan long-term changes for the paper, but they could not take the place of the firm's need for a product that is altered daily.

This need for continual innovation, then, sets newspaper publishers — in fact, all mass media producers — apart from the producers of other goods. Still, like their counterparts in other types of business, the leaders of mass media firms want to turn out products they *know* will be successful. In other words, although the continuing need for newness is part of their business, so is the need for predictability. The problem is that no matter how powerful the firm is in its marketplace, it is impossible to predict success with certainty if content must keep changing. As a result, executives' impulses are often toward copying what was most recently successful, to continue to do what has been done. Yet copying something exactly is not acceptable, and it is never clear what kinds of changes will be successful. Clearly, there is a good deal of tension here: The need for change and the desire for continuity often stand in conflict with one another.

This tension over continuity and change exists in one form or another among all creative personnel in all media industries. It also exists among executives who choose creators as well as among the creators themselves. Newspaper editors and reporters, television producers and TV writers, book editors and authors all understand that they risk failing in the balancing act they must maintain between the need to search for novelty and the need to limit that search in the interest of efficiency and success.

This chapter is about how people in mass media production firms perform this balancing act.

What kinds of risks are mass media production organizations willing to take with their songs, movies, books, newspapers, or TV shows?

How do creators find out what degrees of innovation, what kinds of "newness," are acceptable to the mass media organizations in which they work?

When are they and their organizations likely to be most daring, and why?

RISKS AND ROUTINES

One way people control their search for newness so that they do not go dangerously offtrack is to use routines. **Routines** are patterned activities that people learn to use in carrying out certain tasks.

Routines are connected to every aspect of our lives. We all have routines for the way we get up in the morning, balance our checkbook, and choose radio stations in our car. Without routines we would have to think carefully about everything we do all the time. Because of routines, we can develop solutions to certain problems that repeat themselves, and we can respond to those problems quickly, almost reflexively, next time they arise.

The usefulness of routines carries over to work. Individuals in organizations generally try to develop routines in their work. These give them predictability and speed up certain repetitive aspects of the process.

Chapter 7 explores the way routines lead mass media creators to portray the world in a way that harmonizes with the established power structure in society. From that standpoint, routines reinforce institutional continuity; they block change that leaders of the society would consider fundamental. But routines play another role, too. They help creators deal with the need for change in mass media without causing problems in either institutional acceptability or organizational profits. To understand how this works, we can draw upon an area of sociology that investigates the strategies people in many different occupations use to cope with change.

Sociologist Everett Hughes suggests that the need for routines in work is particularly strong among physicians, fire crews, and other rescue personnel who deal regularly with what we would generally call emergencies. Hughes notes that when several unexpected events happen at the same time, these workers must be prepared to quickly call upon certain routines for getting the job done efficiently and in order of priority. The physician must play one emergency off against the other. For instance, a case of the black plague must take priority over Johnny's measles.[1]

RISKS, ROUTINES, AND NEWSWORK

Gaye Tuchman points out the relationship of Hughes's ideas to what she observed when conducting a scholarly examination of newswork. She notes that newsworkers confront "emergency" situations all the time. Dealing with unexpected events is a large part of their job. Every day, journalists are required to go out into the world, confront a wide variety of ongoing activities, pay special attention to some of them, and write stories about them by certain deadlines.[2]

Clearly, there are risks involved in this kind of work. Say the journalist covered a riot. One danger is that the journalist might focus on the "wrong" aspect of the riot. That is, the journalist's editor might not consider that facet of the riot to be interesting news, or the editor might not consider it news at all. Another potential difficulty is that the editor might not like the perspective the journalist used in writing about the disturbance. A third risk is that the journalist will write about someone taking part in the riot in a way that will place the newspaper in jeopardy of being sued for libel.

Yet another risk is that the journalist will be so worried about these and other problems of depicting the riot that he or she will not complete the story in time for the next day's paper. This would mean one fewer story possibility for the editor, and one day of wasted salary from the standpoint of the organization's management. Multiply one reporter's problem by similar risks confronting all the journalists in the organization, and it is apparent that the difficulty of getting a handle on what should be reported could have a paralyzing effect on a news organization.

Tuchman points out that journalists have solved the problem by shaping their work according to routines. These routines guide them toward dealing with the world quickly and acceptably. Consider the problem of knowing what events make "interesting" news. Reporters constantly negotiate this point with superiors and colleagues within their news organizations. As a result, when they decide to cover something, they usually have a good idea that either (1) the people they work with would have done so too or (2) they can persuade their colleagues and superiors that they would have done it. For example, an argument between the president and the chair of Congress's Ways and Means Committee about a new tax bill would likely be recognized as news by everyone in the newsroom. Whether the event deserves to be placed on the front page could be a subject of argument among selectors in the newsroom.

The News Net

For efficiency's sake, newsworkers set up a news "net" to ensure that reporters are monitoring areas of society that are likely to yield interesting or important news. The areas with the most potential (such as the White House and the Congress) will get the most coverage. Other areas will have sparser coverage, sometimes only with a "stringer" hired when something newsworthy does happen. And many areas will simply not be covered at all.

Laying out the news net means placing "news gathering" equipment and personnel in certain areas of the nation or the world and not in other areas. The way news organizations allocate resources reflects a complicated series of assessments that their executives make about news and society. For example, countries the executives believe are most relevant to the political and economic concerns of Americans will get the bulk of attention. Ability to gain access to these countries is also crucial for coverage. American politicians' interest in discussing the issue is also a factor. The resulting picture will necessarily ignore large parts of the world while accentuating others. One result is a media "politics of death." Twenty Palestinians who are killed as the result of riots in the Occupied Territories grab several days of coverage on TV and in newspapers, while the forced starvation of hundreds of thousands of people in Sudan hardly makes it into the news net at all.

Inside the News Net

The creation of news nets is not, however, the only way journalists make the handling of changing events in their world more predictable. Once the news nets are established, newsworkers approach the events that take place inside them in patterned ways, too. They generate expectations of the way news events happen that allow them to decide immediately what human and technical resources to allocate to such events, and what difficulties they will face in doing so. Tuchman calls these expectations **typifications** and shows how they affect the way events get reported.

Consider an event that a reporter typifies as **spot news** — news that is unscheduled and must be processed quickly. An example is the assassination of a national leader. Designating an event in this manner activates routines that place many other members of the news organization on special alert, calls for use of the fastest communication technologies, and allows for the immediate reallocation of resources (such as pulling reporters off other stories) if and when necessary.

A contrasting case is when a reporter or her or his newsroom boss dubs a circumstance as **continuing news,** meaning that it is important enough to be followed as a series of incidents occurring over a number of days, weeks, or months.

An example of this is the movement of a legislative bill through Congress. Not every bill is defined as continuing news by reporters and editors. Some bills are noted only as they are being passed or defeated. Once a bill is defined as continuing news, though, reporters and editors get certain routines into gear.

For instance, seeing a bill's passage as a chain of prescheduled events means that the reporter should plan. This might involve conducting research on topics related to the bill, anticipating problems in covering debates over the measure, and taking corrective action in advance to avoid those difficulties. This sort of planning also assures editors that acceptable news stories will be available at certain times even if enough interesting spot news stories do not materialize. It also allows them to plan their use of resources efficiently. As Tuchman points out, "at the very least, it enables a city editor to state 'Joe Smith will not be available to cover spot news stories a week from Tuesday because he will be covering the Bergman trial!'"

Recording News Acceptably

Imagine that a journalist's place on a news net has reduced the problem of being where "interesting" news will happen. Imagine, too, that the reporter and others in the news organization have used typifications to determine their strategies for covering the event as well as the resources in time, people, and equipment they will need. The next problem is how to record this in ways that are acceptable to superiors by deadline.

Gaye Tuchman suggests that what journalists call "objectivity" comprises the most important set of routines journalists have developed to deal with this problem. There are many angles to the idea of telling a story "objectively."[3] As noted in Chapter 7, the most well known are use of the "inverted pyramid," reporting in the third person, not injecting personal opinions into the tale, concentrating on verifiable facts, quoting those involved, and presenting more than one side of the story.

Video journalists follow some camera-related objectivity rules that their print counterparts need not consider. For example, an objective way of presenting a person on camera is to place the camera at the same level as the person, as opposed to a view from above or one made with special effects.

Journalists know very well that there are ways to express their personal biases while using the techniques of objectivity. Nevertheless, a story told in an objective manner has an aura of political neutrality in the mainstream news business and throughout society. Consequently, a reporter using the objective method can be confident that his or her story will not run the risk of rejection by an editor as biased or libelous. More generally, in following the canons of objectivity, a reporter carries out an invaluable series of routines that help him or her frame events acceptably and in time for deadline.

COPING WITH DEGREES OF RISK

Gaye Tuchman's examination of the manner in which journalists cope with the risks of their occupation alerts us to the roles that routines and risks play in different kinds of mass media organizations. To best understand the use of routines in several media contexts, we must speak of the degree of risk that creators face.

Degree of risk means the extent to which creators in certain media sectors place themselves in **economic** and **political jeopardy** if they fail. Economic risk refers to the possibility of financial loss, while political risk refers to the possibility of losing government support. The higher the possible loss, the higher the risk. Potential for economic loss can be considered low when the amount of cash needed to generate an individual product is relatively small. The potential political loss is relatively low when the product is not likely to fall under the critical scrutiny of organizations that take on authority or public advocacy roles. Potential for relatively high economic and political loss — and thus high-risk loss — can be found in situations where product development costs and public concern are high.

Contrasting TV and Books

Contrasting the creation of prime time network television programs with the creation of scholarly books illustrates these points. A television program is a relatively high-risk venture both for its production company and for the network that orders the show. An hour of prime time typically costs a little over a million dollars. The fee paid by the network to the producer for two airings of the program often barely covers expenses. In addition, all expenses represent costs that cannot be changed whether the people who ultimately view the program in its first showing number 10 million, 30 million, or 50 million. Production and network personnel become nervous when rating figures hover at the lower end of this range, because it means advertisers have not reached enough audiences by prime time standards.

Because the charges a network can demand of advertisers are based partly on the ability of the network's past and present shows to draw audiences, a low-rated program can cause network profits (and the production firm's reputation) to suffer. Bad ratings for one program may also have a negative impact on a network's profit picture that goes beyond a single time slot, because low viewership at one point in a network's evening schedule may reduce the audience flow across all that network's programs that evening.

Coupled with this high economic risk is the great political liability a prime time program can incur. Because of network TV's ability to consistently reach a very large number of U.S. households, including the children in those households, the medium draws the special attention of groups sensitive to what they feel are improper depictions of parts of society. Despite the enormous changes that have multiplied the number of media channels in people's homes, prime time commercial network TV is at the center of U.S. media in the eyes of government and public advocacy organizations. Consequently, there is a good chance a new prime time show will draw scrutiny by those groups.

Whereas the creation of network TV shows lies at the high end of the spectrum of economic and political risks in mass communication, production of scholarly books, called **monographs,** is a low-risk venture on both counts.[4] Manuscript acquisition and book production costs for individual titles are typically thousands of dollars, as opposed to hundreds of thousands and even millions in other media sectors. Book marketing, aimed mostly at libraries through librarians and academics, can often be carried out through mail-order ad campaigns that are inexpensive by media advertising standards.

Book reviews, which cost only the price of mailing review copies, can also help a title along. These rather low economic costs go along with low political liability, because the output of scholarly publishers is generally considered by forces outside the academic world to be beyond the day-to-day concerns of ordinary citizens. Few advocacy groups exert energy against narrowly distributed scholarly tomes.

The degree of risk that creators in mass media production firms confront influences the way they orient their routines to cope with risk. In general, the greater the risk involved, the greater the chance that creators will do two things: (1) move toward creating highly predictable, highly patterned mass media content (**content-based techniques of coping**) and (2) develop routines that involve **administrative techniques of coping,** techniques that are not so obviously reflected in the content itself. When risks are not so great, creators will tend to orient their routines only toward administrative techniques of coping.

ADMINISTRATIVE TECHNIQUES OF COPING

Administrative techniques of coping are routines designed to help creators seek out information or personnel that will maximize the chance of a particular product's success. Two broad forms of these techniques stand out — the use of **track record talent** and the use of **market research.**

Track Record Talent

A track record talent is a creator who has a list of proven successes and a strong reputation in his or her field. This term was introduced in Chapter 5 to describe a way production executives try to convince client organizations such as networks (for TV production firms) and libraries (for scholarly books) that the material they have created is in sync with audience interests. Production firms assure their clients that if a creator has succeeded in the past with targeted viewers, listeners, or readers, there is a strong chance the audience will accept him or her once again.

Actually, production executives use track record talent to minimize a *wide variety* of risks they confront when trying to balance continuity and change in their materials. Not only is using the same (previously successful) authors considered a way to be reasonably sure of an audience's reaction to new works, it often means it is a way to ensure the organization will be working with people who can be relied upon to complete the work within a particular time frame, in a manner that will not cause the production firm unexpected financial or political grief. Celebrities who are difficult to work with may be hired despite the grief they create because of the cash they bring in. Even in these situations, however, familiarity with the "misbehavior" of needed artists will allow the company to arrange its activities to expect such problems and thus minimize their costs.

Not all track record talents are celebrities, however. Sometimes, such a person supports the main artists in one way or another, is known to relatively few among the audience for the product, but still has a reputation within the industry of being crucial to the artistic success of a product. An illustration in the television industry is the team of producer Gary Smith and director Dwight Hemion, known for more than two decades for putting together successful musical variety programs. In the record industry, producers often develop reputations for eking out the greatest possible chance of success in a group's work through careful selection, arrangement, and editing of material. At different times, John Hammond, Leiber and Stoller, "Shadow" Morton, Phil Spector, George Martin, Hugh Padham, and Quincy Jones were considered among the ablest and most important record producers in the business.

A variation on this kind of behind-the-scenes use of track record talent is the employment of stars to search out and champion people with the potential for success. This happens frequently in scholarly book publishing. Academic publishing houses rely on well-known professors to point them toward new manuscripts. Sometimes, these **academic brokers** give their advice for free. Sometimes the publishing company pays them for evaluating manuscripts, searching for potential authors, and even serving as editors of book series they feel warrant attention.

The expectation is that a reputable scholar in search of manuscripts can plug into the various **artistic networks** discussed in Chapter 7 better than company editors can, who generally hold fewer long-term ties to the academic community. Publishers hope the result will be discovery of manuscripts that hold great chances of success. Also, they expect the academic brokers reputations' to rub off on the authors they back.

Market Research

Market research, the second administrative technique for coping, involves a very different approach to the problem of risk. Whereas the search for track record talent looks to past success as an indicator of future profits, market research probes the firm's contemporary environment for ways to reduce a product's chance of failure.

We can speak of two kinds of market research: (1) the kind that searches out ideas for new products, and (2) the kind that evaluates products that already exist or are under development. Both approaches are discussed in Chapter 5 in relation to a particular kind of market analysis: audience research. Audience research searches out attributes of the final consumers that can be targeted. By contrast, other types of market research survey the organizations that help bring the products to the consumers. This could involve checking with representatives from advertisers, exhibitors, or distributors about the kinds of material they would like to but cannot find.

In the trade book business, such advice is often solicited by marketing personnel, who are constantly on the lookout for trends they can report to their editors. Particularly helpful is advice from major clients such as the B. Dalton and Waldenbooks chains. Their computerized sales lists often provide management with book-buying trends, which can lead to suggesting that book publishers emphasize certain kinds of titles over others.

At times, trade publishing executives even ask the store executives' opinions about titles under consideration. Sometimes publishers' representatives show buyers from bookstore chains manuscripts of forthcoming books even before they are set in type. Most of this kind of activity is directed not toward changing the content of a book but rather toward judging its marketability and determining the number of copies to print. In certain special cases, however, a book publisher will contact some of its major clients to ask whether they would be interested in purchasing a title or **line** (a group of titles with a similar format) that is still only on the drawing board.

Marketing executives in Random House did this when they created their highly successful line of children's paperback picture books in the mid-1970s.[5] They wanted to release colorful books based on characters that would be familiar to both children and their parents (for example, the *Berenstein Bears* and the *Sesame Street* cast), and at the same time far less expensive than most children's books sold in bookstores. Random House executives were concerned that bookstore chains would consider the books too inexpensive to warrant carrying them, because their profit margins would be so low. They also worried that bookstores would resist allowing Random House to install the freestanding racks that marketing executives had determined would be necessary to draw attention to the books. Therefore, before proceeding with production, the executives showed some prototypes to executives of major bookstore chains. Only when they received enthusiastic reception and even a commitment by the chain to stock the books did the new "pictureback" line get the full go-ahead.

This cautious checking of development ideas that production personnel carry out with members of powerful organizations in their firm's environment goes on in virtually every sector of every mass media industry. Such research will probably not take place with respect to all products — for example, every issue of a magazine, every book title, every TV episode. It is likely to occur when new ventures demand long-term organizational commitment.

For example, when planning the introduction of a new monthly magazine, it is standard for executives to contact major advertising agencies to gauge their interest in supporting the periodical. The same is true with college texts aimed at introductory courses. Because such products cost a lot to produce and must sell in large quantities to be profitable, research on the environment becomes crucial. Accordingly, write three observers of the industry:

> Major text houses know which texts have leading positions in the market and which lag behind: that X has 6 percent of the relevant market, and that Y has only 2 percent. Close analysis of the successful texts and the laggards alerts the publishers to the topics and styles currently in or out of fashion. Then instructors are polled about any changes they would like to see in a particular text. These data are supplemented by information gathered by college travelers. The final result is a text that is usually bland and "safe" but profitable, since it has been tailored to the demands of the market.[6]

Note that here, assessing "demands of the market" does not include polling the ultimate audience: the students. In textbook publishing, as in other areas of the mass media, production personnel understand that the all-important first step toward success is getting the material in front of the audience through organizational intermediaries. The college instructor serves as an agent for the bookstore. He or she decides which titles students should buy and then presents the list to the store's purchasing manager. Students typically hold only an indirect influence on the decision to change the required book in a course. If they find a text boring or difficult to understand, classroom feedback may sway the instructor from assigning that book. Generally, the students have no choice but to read what is required.

CONTENT-BASED TECHNIQUES OF COPING

Sometimes, as in the case of certain introductory texts, market research results in the creation of material considered acceptable but not innovative by any of the parties involved. The same can be said for the use of track record talent. Still, these administrative coping techniques also allow for situations in which a production firm's environment demands materials that are clearly considered different from what came before.

An example is scholarly book publishing. Academics place great emphasis on ideas that extend or challenge previous scholarship in interesting ways. Another example is works of fiction. Newspaper and magazine book reviewers often judge such works according to criteria that emphasize arresting style, a distinctive "voice," or fresh thinking about life.

The problem for production firm selectors who work in these areas of mass media is that although they must constantly look for materials that are substantially different from previous output, they still wish to reduce the risks involved in doing so. Administrative techniques help them. For example, fiction editors can contract with John Updike, John Grisham, or Joyce Carol Oates to write novels, fully expecting that the book will get substantial serious critical attention in addition to earning money in advance of release through sale of paperback and other rights.

There are, however, areas of the mass media where creators do not expect that forces in the environment require them to speak through an individual voice or emphasize unusual approaches to the world. In many areas of the mass media, too, creators perceive their responsibility as simply to make money and not at all to advance the cause of art. High-risk products such as network television programs and Hollywood movies tend to fit this description. Yet, there are some areas of the mass media where product costs are low and individual artistry is not emphasized. Paperback romances, pornographic novels, and pornographic films belong in this category.

The point is that in most high-risk situations and in some low-risk ones, creators try to generate highly patterned mass media material that has a record of success. In these situations, administrative coping techniques become only first steps in trying to reduce the risks of production. Risk reduction through previously tested **formulas** and **stereotypes** plays an important part as well.

FORMULAS AS TECHNIQUES OF COPING

Recall from Chapter 7 that formulas are widely recognized principles for selecting and organizing material. The concept of formula is linked to the routines that make creators' work efficient and, at the same time, reflect the continuing legitimacy of the most powerful elements in society. Here it is relevant to point out that formulas not only encourage broad boundaries of institutional **continuity** but also help creators efficiently come up with ways to change content within these boundaries. In this sense, formulas are risk-reducing approaches to content. They provide creators with patterned approaches to content that many parties in a mass media industry agree contain the elements of success.

One of the tasks that creators in many media organizations set for themselves is to recognize the principles of particular formulas and the ways in which they can be varied profitably. Often, their understanding of formulas derives from immersing themselves in lots of mass media materials. Or it comes from being part of an artistic community, listening to colleagues and competitors talk about the way they created certain movies, books, TV programs, magazine articles, or whatever.

It is easy to uncover some of the basic components of a formula and ways in which it can be varied. For example, consider a list of "the best" and "the worst" of just about anything that one can see just about anywhere. Such lists reflect a popular formula that magazine and book editors have been scrambling to copy and vary. *TV Guide*'s J. Fred Muggs Awards and *Esquire* magazine's Dubious Achievement Awards are just two of the many lists released by media organizations.

A nonfiction formula is characterized by subject, point of view, and the sequence in which the argument is developed. Using these categories for orientation, we find that the basic concoction for nonfiction lists seems straightforward: Find a subject that many people confront every day — restaurants, the thought of moving to another city, the need for trivia in conversation, places to live — and find items to represent the best and/or worst examples of that subject. Quantify the results, if possible; a numerical index for the best and worst American cities, for example, is preferable to a simple listing. Stir well with a point of view that bespeaks absolute certainty and, often, urbane cynicism regarding the matter at hand. Bruce Felton and Mark Fowler describe the tone of many of these works in their introduction to *Felton and Fowler's Best, Worst, and Most Unusual*:

> The judgments offered in this book are both subjective and objective, rational and hysterical, serious and sardonic. In assessing their validity, you should bear in mind the words of Leonardo da Vinci: "I take no more notice of the wind that comes out of the mouths of critics than of the wind expelled from their backsides."[7]

This same knowing cynicism and sarcasm seem to be the standard point of view writers took up in magazine discussions of political and social trends during the 1980s and early 1990s. The approach did not apply to nonfiction formulas that reflected more personal aspects of the target audience's life. How-to articles on cooking, building, repairing, gardening, and coping with divorce, unemployment, sex, parenting, and dating seemed to require a more empathic tone.

A still different tone seemed to belong in another formula: a Hollywood star's autobiography (often written with someone else). Whether such works carried insight or merely vanity, it seemed *de rigueur* for them to fit the following mold: Start with a key incident from the height of the star's career. Slowly ease back toward stories of birth and upbringing. Then move the story along through tragedies and disasters to triumph or, at least, to a better world today.

Formulas exist in fiction as well. Fiction formulas can be characterized in terms of setting, character types, and patterns of action. In Chapter 7, the Western is discussed as an example of a storytelling form with built-in enduring American values, such as the importance of masculine individualism and the appropriateness of using force to solve problems. Here it is relevant to stress that the Western—as well as the detective, superhero, family sitcom, and other formulas, for that matter—is useful to production personnel because it helps reduce the risk of change. Popular formulas provide creators with comfortable molds that suggest how stories can be altered while the essence of characterization, setting, and even patterns of action remain the same.

The Western Formula

John Cawelti, who has studied the Western formula, provides a good example of this standardized approach to change. The plot of a Western, he says, comes from having three central character types bump up against one another within a predictable setting. This setting is some kind of frontier, some "meeting point between civilization and savagery."[8] The central character types are townspeople, who are the agents of civilization; the savages or outlaws, who threaten this first group; and the heroes (often cowboys), who are above all "men in the middle." That is, they possess many qualities and skills of the savages but are fundamentally committed to the townspeople. Cawelti notes that this three-way tension built into the Western points the way toward concocting a variety of plots.

For example, the simplest version of all has the hero protecting the townspeople from the savages, using his own savage skills against the denizens of the wilderness. A second, more complex variation shows the hero initially indifferent to the plight of the townspeople and more inclined to identify himself with the savages. However, in the course of the story, his position changes and he becomes the townspeople's ally.

This variation can generate a number of different plots. There is the revenge Western: Hero seeks revenge against an outlaw or Indian who has wronged him. In order to accomplish his vengeance, he rejects the pacifistic ideals of the townspeople, but in the end discovers that he is really committed to their way of life (John Ford's *The Searchers*). Another plot based on variation of character relations is that of the hero who initially seeks his own selfish material gain, using his savage skills as a means to this end; but, as the story progresses, he discovers his moral involvement with the townspeople and becomes their champion (Anthony Mann's *The Far Country*).

It is also possible, while maintaining this system of relationships, to reverse the conclusion of the plot, as in stories where the townspeople come to accept the hero's savage mode of action (John Ford's *Stagecoach* or, to a certain extent, Wister's *The Virginian*). A third variation has the hero caught in the middle, between the townspeople's need for his savage skills and their rejection of his way of life. This variation, common in recent Westerns, often ends in the destruction of the hero *(The Gunfighter, Invitation to a Gunfighter)* or his voluntary exile *(Shane, High Noon, Two Rode Together)*.[9]

BOX 8.1   Milestones in the Evolution of TV's Doctor Show Formula

ER and *Chicago Hope*, two hit TV programs of the mid-1990s, emerged from television's long interest in the doctor show formula. A popular culture formula is dynamic. That is, its setting, characters, and patterns of action change over time.

Below is one analyst's list of the TV series that marked significant changes in the doctor show formula from the vantage point of the 1980s. For a look at the forces behind the changes in the formula, see Joseph Turow's *Playing Doctor: Television, Storytelling, and Medical Power* (New York: Oxford University Press, 1989).

Medic: NBC, 1954–56; starred Richard Boone

Doctor Kildare: NBC, 1961–66; starred Richard Chamberlain, Raymond Massey

Ben Casey: ABC, 1961–66; starred Vince Edwards and Sam Jaffe

The New Doctors (segment of *The Bold Ones*): NBC, 1969–76; starred E. G. Marshall and David Hartman

Marcus Welby, M.D.: ABC, 1969–76; starred Robert Young and James Brolin

Medical Center: CBS, 1969–76; starred Chad Everett and James Daly

Emergency: NBC, 1972–77; starred Robert Fuller and Bobby Troup

Medical Story: NBC, 1975–76; anthology series (no continuing star)

Quincy, M.E.: NBC, 1976–83; starred Jack Klugman

Lifeline: NBC, 1978; documentary (no stars)

Trapper John, M.D.: CBS, 1979–85; starred Pernell Roberts and Gregory Harrison

St. Elsewhere: NBC, 1982–89; starred an ensemble cast of numerous actors

SOURCE: Robert S. Alley, "Medical Melodrama," in Brian G. Rose (ed.), *TV Genres: A Handbook and Reference Guide* (Westport, CT: Greenwood Press, 1985), pp. 73–90.

Formulas in Pornography

Clearly, combining the three elements of the Western formula in different ways can yield a multitude of "new" stories. Cawelti points out that the people producing the Western in any mass medium are quite conscious of the formula. In some mass media organizations, though, selectors are not content to rely on their artists to pick up the most effective approaches to certain kinds of material. Here, from the mid-1970s, are notes by a writer of pornographic novels on the approach his publisher expected him to take:

> It [the pornography] is aimed at the male market and is written to formula. There are seven basic story categories: incest (the single most popular genre), lesbianism, Lolita plots, domination, older woman/younger man, career girl plots, and straying from the marriage.
>
> The publisher's style sheet advises: "The plots of our stories should involve a sexual problem of some sort . . . the denouement, a solution. How the characters get there is what it's all about. . . . What this means is that we don't want detective stories with a lot of sex [or] Westerns with a lot of sex. . . . We want explicitly written, highly erotic novels of real people's experiences. . . . We CANNOT consider the following themes: male homosexuality, child molestation, bestiality, excretion, violent sadomasochism, or murder as part of the sex act. ALL CHARACTERS INVOLVED SEXUALLY MUST BE AT LEAST FIFTEEN YEARS OF AGE.[10]

Formulas in Music

Our discussion of fiction formulas has revolved around books and movies. But the use of formulas has long been a standard way to reduce risk in many areas of the mass media. American music publishers in the 1860s and 1870s, for example, tended to divide the types of songs they accepted into eight categories: love, family, reform or moral, religious, comedy, minstrel, tragedy, and topical. By helping them evaluate ups and downs in the sales of particular categories of sheet music (the main way songs were sold back then), the classification provided publishers with a way to choose songs and songwriters who matched the trends of the day.

Since that time, the mainstream music world has become much more stratified. Some areas, such as parts of the progressive rock scene, place greater emphasis than others on idiosyncratic artistry and unusual approaches to the world. We would expect that in such areas, producers would turn primarily toward administrative routines (in particular, the consideration of track record), not formulas, to cope with risk. There are, however, many areas of the music industry where selectors and artists try to spring toward success with minor variations on tried-and-true approaches to words and music.

This is especially the case with respect to singles. Singles are typically songs that recording companies release with the hope they will get aired on radio stations with formats that play hits. Video versions of singles are directed toward the MTV cable music video channel and its broadcast TV imitators. Because of the importance of singles for album sales in many cases, and because of the high risk of failure in getting airplay (most releases do not get significant exposure on radio), singles are the most formularized of all cuts on an album.

Recording producers are well aware that program directors and music hit predictors receive an enormous number of songs to sample. As a result, they sometimes listen to only the first three seconds of a song to decide whether they should select it as "hit bound." Formulas are considered crucial; the artistry lies in creative variation of the formula so it appears different and compelling. Clive Davis, a powerful executive at CBS and then Arista Records from the 1960s into the 1990s, has described the general singles formula:

> A hit single is a question of musical ingredients — they've all got to complement each other. You start with the "hook," a basic repetitive melody or lyric line that grabs hold of the listener. In lyrics, the safest theme, naturally, is love or lost love. . . . Ideally, the lyric and melody combine within the hook to make this line something nearly impossible to forget. But hooks come in all sorts of rhythmic, melodic, and lyrical shapes and sizes. . . . When I hear a song, my mind works like a computer. The "hit" ingredients register in it, and they are shunted off to various preprogrammed compartments for analysis. Voice is terribly important. Certain kinds of voices don't lend themselves to Top Forty play.[11]

Formulas in Series and Serials

Two ideas that creators generally recognize as related to the formula are the series and the serial. A **series** is a collection of individual products (books, magazines, movies, TV shows) that have the same key characters moving through separate adventures in each product. A bit different is the **serial,** wherein the same key characters move through continuing episodes of adventures across the products; the serial is a kind of chapter play.

We see series and serials all the time. The *Peanuts* newspaper comic strip is a series, while the *Doonesbury* strip is a serial. TV's *Star Trek: Voyager* is a series, while the *Star Wars* odyssey is a serial. Interestingly, during the past decade, the concepts of series and serials have been intermixed in television. *ER* is an example. It can be called a series, because most of what happens in each episode begins and ends with the episode. Often, however, a subplot continues across a number of episodes. Writers and producers call this serialized part of a series an **arc.**

It is easy to understand why creators in high-risk media industries consider series and serials useful to their work. For one thing, start-up costs of episodes in an ongoing series or serial are lower than those in a new project. Continually thinking up new heroes, villains, and ways to inject life into old formulas is more time-consuming than tinkering with one basic set of characters, setting, and plot pattern. In television, having the same actors, crew, locations, and props for every episode makes production a lot less expensive than producing a new program from scratch every day.

Sometimes, stand-alone products do so well that creators cannot resist the opportunity to turn them into series. Consider the *Halloween, Nightmare on Elm Street,* and *Police Academy* movies. This activity is not new. In 1950, Universal Pictures' *Francis the Talking Mule,* based on a book by David Stern, was a runaway success. This movie begat *Francis Goes to the Races* (1951), followed by *Francis Goes to West Point* (1952), *Francis Joins the Wac* (1954), *Francis in the Navy* (1955), and *Francis in the Haunted House* (1956). The first five films were directed by Arthur Lubin, who went on to create a similar TV series called *Mr. Ed,* about a talking horse.

There is an ironic flip side to the efficiency and risk reduction possibilities in series and serials. When the cost of several episodes must be allocated in advance, failure may involve a much greater cost than would any particular product that stands alone. Television program producers face this problem on a continual basis. When a series "hits," it can be a huge, consistent moneymaker for many years, but when it fails badly, the cash and airtime already committed to it can drain network resources badly. Consequently, the commercial net-

FIGURE 8.1 The popularity cycle of a TV formula (SOURCE: Joseph Turow, *Playing Doctor* (New York: Oxford University Press, 1989), pp. 277–279.)

Like all forms of popular culture, formulas on network TV go through times when they are used often to times when they are used little. The reasons are complex and reflect a variety of considerations relating to the industry as well as audience interest. In any event, TV producers profit most when they work up the "right" formula in the "right" way at the "right" time. The trick, of course, is knowing when and what "right" is.

As an example of a formula's cycle of popularity with network programmers, consider the changing number of doctor series aired from the 1952 through 1989 TV years. A TV year runs from September, when shows debut, to the following September. The 1952 TV year, therefore, spans from September 1952 through August 1953.

works have evolved an elaborate chain of strategies to develop, test, and schedule series so as to maximize their chances for success.

When searching for a series idea, production firm executives and their network counterparts typically claim they are looking for material that is "refreshing," "exciting," and "different." At particularly honest moments, many also admit that the best ideas they find echo material already popular on TV or in other media. This contradictory approach leads them to combine a strong reliance on popular formulas with attempts to find interesting variations on those formulas that will stand up over many episodes.

Consider the spate of prime time TV sitcoms that worked off the formula of twenty-something buddies trying to find their way in the world. In fall 1994, NBC introduced *Friends* with this premise. The program's promising start led the network to introduce *Hope and Gloria* and *Pride and Joy,* both variations on the same idea. By the next year the TV world was awash with *Friends*-like sitcoms on all four networks, shows such as *Can't Hurry Love* (which *Entertainment Weekly* called "lower-middle-class *Friends*,") *If Not For You* ("Very confused *Friends,*" according to the magazine), *The Drew Carey Show* ("*Friends,* but with less attractive people"*), The Single Guy* ("mostly married *Friends*"), and *The Crew* ("flying *Friends*").[12] Some of these shows did better than the others in the ratings. Being part of a cycle does not guarantee success.

The Formula in History

The search for the right formula-based material with staying power to make a successful series is not new in television or the movies. The series was a part of American popular theater from the early 1800s, and it was used extensively in magazines and books of that time.

Here, for example, is a fascinating letter that Ormond Smith, head of the powerful Street and Smith publishing firm, wrote to Gilbert Patten. At the time, the 1890s, Patten was a well-known writer of juvenile dime novels. Smith's purpose was to hire Patten to write a new series (or "library") of juvenile books for the company.

> December 16, 1895
> Gilbert Patten, Esq.,
> Camden, Maine.

Dear Sir:

Replying to your favor of December 13, at hand today, we beg to state that the material of which we wrote you in our last letter is intended for a library which we propose issuing every week; something in the line of the Jack Harkaway, Gay Dashleigh series which we are running in *Good News* and the *Island School* series, all of which are expressed to you under separate cover, the idea being to issue a library containing a series of stories covering this class of incident, in all of which will appear one prominent character surrounded by suitable satellites. It would be an advantage to the series to have introduced the Dutchman, the Negro, the Irishman, and any other dialect you are familiar with. From what we know of your work, we believe you can give us what we require, and would be pleased to have you write one of these stories at once. Upon receipt of it, if satisfactory, we will be prepared to make a contract with you to cover twenty thousand words weekly for this library and a sufficient number of *Good News* stories to keep them running in the columns of *Good News,* if you believe you can turn out this amount of work.

It is important that the main character in the series should have a catchy name, such as Dick Lightheart, Jack Barkaway, Gay Dashleigh, Don Kirk [characters in previous series by Patten], as upon this name will depend the title for the library.

The essential idea of this series is to interest young readers in the career of a young man at a boarding school, preferably a military or a naval academy. The stories should differ from the Jack Harkaways in being American and thoroughly up to date. Our idea is to issue, say, twelve stories, each complete in itself, but like the links in a chain, all dealing with life at the academy. By this time the readers will have become sufficiently well acquainted with the hero and the author will also no doubt have exhausted most of the pranks and escapades that might naturally occur.

After the first twelve numbers, the hero is obliged to leave the academy, or takes it upon himself to leave. It is essential that he should come into a considerable amount of money at this period. When he leaves the academy he takes with him one of the professor's servants, a chum. In fact, any of the characters you have introduced and made prominent in the story. A little love element would not be amiss, though this is not particularly important.

When the hero is once projected on his travels there is an infinite variety of incidents to choose from. In the *Island School* series, published by one of our London connections, you will find scenes of foreign travel, with color. This material you are at liberty to use freely, with our hero as the central character, of course, and up-to-date dialogue.

* * *

This letter will, of course, be held as confidential. After you have fully examined the *Island School* material, kindly return to us.

Yours truly,
Ormond Smith[13]

STEREOTYPES AS TECHNIQUES OF COPING

Smith's reference to "the Dutchman, the Negro, the Irishman" brings up another content-based device that creators of mass media material use to cope with risk: the **stereotype.** A stereotype is the portrayal of an identifiable social group in such a way that members of that group are consistently invested with certain personality characteristics and social activities. The Dutchman (actually, *Deutschman* — the German), the Negro, and the Irishman were the butt of jokes in many turn-of-the-century novels, magazines, films, and recordings.

Much has been written about the nasty characterizations that racial, ethnic, and other groups in society have suffered in popular culture through the years.[14] Chapter 7 notes that such portrayals picture those groups' position in society from the vantage point of elites who want to retain power. Here the purpose is to point to an important *organizational* reason for the perpetuation of stereotypes. Simply put, stereotypes are vehicles for getting work done quickly, efficiently, and with a lower risk of individual failure than would otherwise be the case.

Not all stereotypes are useful. Today's mass media creators recognize that the clout of various public advocacy organizations, along with social changes, have turned some social types into liabilities. In the commercial television networks, censors routinely review scripts and completed programs to guard against consistently negative portrayals of individuals belonging to certain groups. African-Americans, Native Americans, Hispanics, homosexuals, senior citizens, and women have made the censors particularly sensitive to certain injustices over the past several years.

Despite the sensitivity and the pressure, many studies show that stereotypes are alive and kicking on TV and in other mass media. Often the offense is more subtle than it was before the advocacy groups complained. TV creators may, for example, shift away from depicting Hispanics as drunk and lazy, but may still show almost all of them as ignorant and holding low-paying jobs. Or the creators may choose to exclude them from the scene, even when the plots take place in Los Angeles, where Hispanics comprise a large percentage of the population.

Exclusion has often been the fate of Mexican-Americans, Native Americans, and homosexuals. When a social group does not have a strong advocacy body in its corner — for example, gypsies and, until recently, Arabs — media creators feel no need to be subtle. Using these groups as well as Nazis and extraterrestrial creatures, producers can dip into a storehouse of unfavorable cultural images — foreign, secretive, alluring, dangerous, deceptive — to evoke certain moods and accomplish certain plot goals.

Stereotyping is not limited to ethnic and racial groups. Some physical characteristics and occupational labels are frequently associated with personality characteristics and social activities. Overweight people, short people, people with glasses, blue-collar workers, private detectives, police, physicians, nurses, high school teachers, college professors — these and other labels often ignite standard characterizations on television, in movies, and in formula-based paperbacks.

In the early 1990s, commercial television's weekday afternoon and weekend cartoons for children were brimming with stereotypes in the way characters looked and sounded. People with messy hair and angular, lined faces were almost always bad, while people with neat hair and smooth, round faces were almost always good. Glasses implied nerdiness. And deep, raspy voices in men as well as high, shrieky voices in women were often associated with evil.

TALKING POINT 8.1   Good Girl/Bad Girl Stereotypes

Stereotypes are sometimes difficult to notice, because they are so much a part of people's thinking about the world; we accept them as "common sense." To become sensitized to stereotypes at work, it may pay to go back in time and look at the way groups in society were portrayed. Strange patterns will then become apparent.

Consider, for example, the following descriptions of women from two Western novels by Zane Grey that were written in the first quarter of the twentieth century. The first, from *The Lone Star Ranger,* describes the best kind of women. The second, of Ruby the dance hall girl in *The U.P. Trail,* refers to a dangerous, bad woman. As historian Russell Nye notes, such descriptions were common in the early 1900s:

> He stood holding her tight, with the feel of her warm, throbbing breast and the clasp of her arms as flesh and blood realities to fight a terrible fear. He felt her, and for the moment the might of it was stronger than all the demons that possessed him . . . , and now, with this woman in his arms, her swelling breast against his, he bent under the storm of passion and joy. . . . Their lips met in their first kiss. The sweetness, the fire of her mouth seemed so new, so strange, so irresistible. . . . She met him half-way, returned kiss for kiss, her face scarlet, her eyes closed, till her passion and strength spent, she fell back upon his shoulder. Presently she recovered, and she only drew the closer, and leaned upon him with her face upturned. He felt her hands on his, and they were soft, clinging, strong, like steel under velvet. He felt the rise and fall, the warmth of her breast. A tremor ran through him.

* * *

> Her arms were bare, her dress cut very low. Her face offered vivid contrast to the carmine on her lips. It was a soft, round face, with narrow eyes, dark, seductive, bold. She tilted her head to one side and suddenly smiled at Neale. It startled him. It was a smile with the shock of a bullet. The girl took hold of the lapels of his coat. She looked up. Her eyes were dark with what seemed like red shadows in them. She had white teeth. The carmined lips curled in a smile — a smile impossible to believe, of youth and sweetness, that disclosed a dimple in her cheek. She was pretty. She was holding him, pulling him a little toward her.
>
> "I like you!" she exclaimed.
>
> He felt her, saw her as in a dream. Her face possessed a peculiar fascination. The sleepy seductive eyes; the provoking half-smile, teasing, alluring; the red lips, full and young through the carmine paint. All of her seemed to breathe a different kind of power than he had ever before experienced — unspiritual, elemental, strong as some heady wine. She represented youth, health, beauty, terribly linked with evil wisdom, and a corrupt and irresistible power, possessing a base and mysterious affinity for man. The breath and the charm and the pestilence of her passed over Neale like fire.

SOURCE: Russel Nye, *The Unembarrassed Muse: The Popular Arts in America* (New York: Dial Press, 1970), p. 296.

Casting

The use of stereotypes extends to **casting,** the choosing of actors for shows. The casting of even small parts — roles in which actors say little — could be time-consuming if casting directors worked hard with producers, directors, and agents to think about the social and dramatic implications of their choices every time they hired people for an episode. Instead, they have developed shared beliefs about what types of people the audience will find credible in what roles.

They justify these "clichés" by claiming that they are used both to save time and to help the "look" of the show. Small parts, they stress, should function like moving wallpaper. Although these are crucial for populating the program, they should not call attention to themselves, because that would mislead viewers into believing small parts are relevant to main elements of the plot. Here, for example, are comments by a producer in the late 1970s about the approach TV people use to choose certain types for small parts:

> You have to recognize what the audience can buy instantaneously. Unless it's a plot point. Because if you have somebody walk in as a police officer, the audience should [snaps fingers] accept him as a police officer. So you look [at the script to find out] where he is walking. I mean, you could have a little more effeteness in a policeman in Beverly Hills than you could in Watts. By a damn sight, you would be far more likely to accept a white or Chicano policeman in Beverly Bills than a black policeman. . . .
>
> Why should I start arguments in a living room or den between husband and wife? I mean, why make a point out of something that's not a point? Carpenters are male. Telephone operators are female. Now, there are a lot of male telephone operators now. But not enough so that when you say "telephone operator," the immediate thought isn't female.[15]

Stereotypes such as these become part of the routines of casting so that the people involved can follow them even when they do not agree they are necessary. Talent agents, for example, know the "rules" of social typing when they scan TV scripts or script summaries called "breakdowns" while looking for parts for their clients. They are reluctant to break these rules. The following interview of an agent about age considerations in casting reveals how adherence to generally perceived rules often discourages nontraditional suggestions.

AGENT: Oh, they list [age in the script and breakdown] and they sometimes stick to it and sometimes don't. What I do when I make up my list [of actors to be sent to the casting director] — if they say 30, I'll give them anything from 25 to 35.

INTERVIEWER: Do you find most age requests stop at 35?

AGENT: For men, there are a great number of roles over 40. Women over 40 — not many, obviously.

INTERVIEWER: Why is that?

AGENT: Well, there's just not that much call for them. Because of the story lines. The story lines are always dealing with heavies, with troubles in situations. It's always men involved. Whether he's a banker, a doctor, or a lawyer, a Mafia chief, whatever.

INTERVIEWER: Under what conditions would you suggest a woman if the breakdown said "banker"?

AGENT: I wouldn't, because it would say "he."

INTERVIEWER: Do you see "he" as necessarily denoting a male?

AGENT: Oh sure; I even look down [the breakdown page] for the "he" or "she" to see which [part] starts with "he or "she." They say "all roles will be considered regardless of ethnic group, sex, et cetera." That's baloney. Well, sometimes you can take a role and if it's not in the script you can turn it from white to black.

INTERVIEWER: Will unusual casting notions affect your standing with casting directors?

AGENT: You don't send them in. What I do, if I have an offbeat idea, to protect myself. You say, "You know, I got an idea; you probably won't even like it. It's really off, far out. . . ." And you protect yourself. If they like it — "terrific!" If they don't, "Yeah, it really was offbeat."[16]

FORMULAS AND ARTISTIC PERSONALITY

Although they recognize the importance of standard approaches to characters, settings, and plots for managing risks in the creative process, mass media creators often try to establish their own artistic personalities within the formulas' boundaries. Horace Newcomb and Robert Alley point out, for example, that while television producers are "clearly aware of the limitations" the industry imposes on them, they "work within, around, and through them to achieve creative goals.[17]

Creators who become successful members of their artistic communities may develop reputations for working in a particular style or reflecting a particular view of life. In TV, Marcy Carsey, Steven Bochco, Steven J. Cannel, Linda Bloodworth-Thomason, Barney Rosensweig, Donald Bellasario, Fred Silverman, David Lynch, David Wolper, and Herbert Brodkin are just a few examples of executive producers whose programs reflect a particular style or view of life. These are individuals whose approaches resonated with the needs of their industry at the time they worked. Most, such as Silverman (*Matlock, Father Dowling Mysteries, Perry Mason* movies), Bellasario (*Magnum, P.I., Quantum Leap*), Bloodworth-Thomason (*Designing Women, Evening Shade*), Cannel (*The A-Team, Wiseguy, 21 Jump Street, Loose Cannon*), Rosensweig (*Cagney and Lacey, The Trials of Rosie O'Neil*), and Carsey (*The Bill Cosby Show, A Different World, Roseanne*) reworked standard formulas slightly in directions designed to match changing times. Others — Bochco *(L.A. Law, Doogie Howser, M.D., Cop Rock, Chicago Hope)* and Lynch *(Twin Peaks, American Chronicles)* come to mind — sometimes took greater risks by changing the tone and direction of established formulas more drastically.

The presence of Wolper and the late Brodkin in this list indicates that production companies exploit different niches in their industry. The heads of the majority of TV production firms choose to compete in the most popular areas of network programming, providing them with bread-and-butter material stamped with their track records and styles. Others choose to be more selective about their activities and contribute "prestige" fare that the networks need once in a while. Brodkin's *Holocaust* and *The Missiles of October* and Wolper's *Roots* are famous examples from decades past. Whatever their niches, however, all these people are keenly aware of industry demands on them that influence what they can do, how they can do it, and when they can show it.

INTEGRATING CHANGE INTO ROUTINES

The preceding interview implies that casting ideas considered "offbeat" sometimes get accepted. It is difficult to predict when some unusual recommendations will get picked up by production firms and others will not. One way to understand how much change is acceptable is to link it to the executives' perceptions of the political and economic risks involved. A suggestion that selectors consider politically dangerous or a huge monetary gamble will not be tried under ordinary circumstances. Instead, the changes that take place will be those fitting into the "low" or "mild" risk categories. The creative changes that they allow will typically mesh well with traditional approaches to formulas and stereotypes.

There are times, however, when executives of some mass media production firms, their distributors, and their exhibitors decide to take what they consider high risks in releasing new products. How they define high risk and when they take it vary by mass media industry and even by companies within particular industries.

The year 1990 provides an example. The talk in Hollywood then was that although much TV programming reflected formula-ridden business as usual, a number of television producers and networks had taken the plunge with drastically "unconventional" spins on formulas.[18] Particularly eyebrow-raising approaches being tried were the casting of a teenager with Down's syndrome as a regular cast member (in *Life Goes On*); the use of a bizarre, hauntingly unusual tone and photography in a dramatic serial *(Twin Peaks);* the scripting of previously unacceptable foul language (in *Against the Law* and *Uncle Buck);* and the merging of two seemingly incompatible formulas, the musical and the gritty cop show *(Cop Rock).* In the latter series, hardened police officers would suddenly burst into song.

TALKING POINT 8.2   Talking in Codes

When television producers pitch ideas for series to one another and to network programmers, the language they use is filled with shorthand references to the way their "new" ideas fit into series with formulas that have proven records of success. To get a feel for this code, consider the following excerpt from a piece about the cop series *Hill Street Blues* and its relation to the hospital series *St. Elsewhere,* two shows that appeared on NBC during the 1980s.

> *Hill Street Blues* had germinated . . . when Fred Silverman, then president of NBC television, suggested to Brandon Tartikoff, his chief programmer, and Michael Zinberg, the vice-president for comedy development, that what the network needed was "a cop show in a neighborhood with a heavy ethnic mix." Tartikoff and Zinberg, in turn, approached two producers from MTM, Michael Kozoll and Steven Bochco. The two had worked on police dramas a few years before. Police dramas had been out of style for a while because of an antiviolence swing against TV, but Silverman was convinced the form was coming back. MTM, with a good reputation among the critics as well as a track record for drawing audiences, might smooth the path.
>
> The NBC executives stressed that Silverman wanted a nervy, rough show from the viewpoint of police on a real-world frontier. Paddy Chayevsky's movie *The Hospital* was cited for its ragged, frantic style, its near-surrealistic depiction of the horrors of medical life, its mockery of the conventions of medical shows. David Gerber's *Police Story* TV show was cited because its police officers had personal lives. Most of all, to Bochco and Kozoll, the NBC executives mentioned *M*A*S*H* and ABC's sitcom *Barney Miller.* It came down to "a little bit of *M*A*S*H,* a little bit of *Barney Miller.* We'd like you to develop a show that has more to do with cops' personal lives."
>
> . . . Although [*Hill Street*'s] early ratings were dismal, Silverman and Tartikoff held on to it as a message from the then number-three network that it would support Hollywood creativity. They were rewarded after the first year when the series, after winning a gaggle of Emmy awards, began to climb sharply in popularity.
>
> According to some insiders, that is when Silverman said, "Now we can do *Hill Street* in a hospital."

SOURCE: Joseph Turow, *Playing Doctor: Television, Storytelling, and Medical Power* (New York: Oxford University Press, 1989), pp. 238–239.

Reasons Firms Take Risks

What conditions lead executives in a television production firm and a network — or, for that matter, in any mass media industry — to take risks they perceive as unconventional, while others do not? Industrial sociologists suggest that unconventional risk taking is more likely to occur in relatively small organizations within an industry than in its largest companies. This is because large organizations with lots of products tend to develop long chains of command to handle the daily business. The resulting bureaucracy tends to involve a rather rigid and time-consuming approach to innovation. Companies with just a few people and a few products, by contrast, often take a "we try harder" approach that makes them more daring.

Industrial sociologists also point out that a low-profit picture will move even the largest firms to consider previously undreamed-of risks. When revenues coming into the firm are acceptable and outside forces are acting on the firm in predictable ways, company leaders see no reason to take steps that could drastically disrupt the company's standing if they fail. But when unexpected problems arise outside the firm that diminish profits greatly, worried executives may decide that established routines are not working and that bold steps are required to get the firm on track again.

The Case of Newspapers

In the U.S. media scene, it is easy to show how circumstances such as those described have led executives to change their approaches to their products. The newspaper industry provides one example.

In the 1990s, many city papers continued to lose circulation and advertising revenues as young adults abandoned the major dailies in favor of suburban weeklies and electronic media. Extremely concerned about the situation, executives at some dailies and their parent organizations began to consider bold moves to make their products attractive again to readers and advertisers. Proposed solutions included drastically shortening stories to make them more quickly digestible and using computers to tailor newspapers to the specific interests of individual readers. Among the advertiser-luring strategies tested was the selling of space to sponsors for a long period of time in the most read parts of the paper — even the front page.[19]

Newspaper conglomerates often tried to reduce the risks of these and other drastic measures to improve newspapers' readership and profitability by testing the changes in a few of their smaller papers, where failure would not be disastrous for the parent firm. For example, the Knight-Ridder newspaper chain used its Boca Raton daily, rather than its *Miami Herald* or *Philadelphia Inquirer,* to test the leasing of advertising space.[20] By contrast, in commercial network television, unconventional attempts to raise audiences and advertising profits took place on a national stage. In television, the stakes appeared even higher than in newspapers. Executives at ABC, CBS, and NBC considered the first half of the 1990s a period of turmoil as audiences and profits plummeted because of increased competition by other broadcast interests as well as cable and home video.

The Case of Network TV

Part of the networks' problem was Fox Television. A subsidiary of a large media conglomerate, Fox had assembled a lineup of stations that allowed it to compete with the Big Three's prime time lineup a few days a week. Well aware of their underdog status, Fox's programmers decided to go out on a limb to commission quirky programs such as *The Simpsons, It's Gary Shandling's Show,* and *Married . . . with Children* that turned traditional approaches to their subjects (families, talk shows) on their heads.

When the series aired, reviewers hailed them as brash, innovative fare.[21] More important for Fox, these programs became the leading edge of shows that began to make Fox competitive in the ratings with the networks on nights when all four broadcast their programs. Also making Fox attractive to advertisers was its large percentage of viewers between 18 and 40 years old. This age group had been deserting Big Three network fare and had become increasingly difficult for advertisers to reach through broadcast TV.

Fox's success with unconventionally irreverent programming led its nervous network counterparts to follow suit. They began to accept suggestions from producers to move formulas in previously unthinkable directions. "Things have changed," said one producer. "*The Simpsons, Twin Peaks, Cop Rock* have pushed back the boundaries of what it is possible to do."[22]

Nevertheless, most observers agreed that the majority of programming on the three networks — as well as on Fox — would not be of the highly unconventional sort. For one thing, many advertisers expressed the concern that they did not want to be associated with anything they perceived as "shredding the envelope," in the words of Madison Avenue. And, while a crowd of small, independent producers was lining up at the networks to pitch series ideas with bizarre twists, executives from the largest production firms, with their eyes on long-term profits from syndication, were eager to follow more conservative interpretations of formulas. "We're not in the business of producing trendy TV," the head of Paramount TV's network programming division bluntly told *Variety.*[23]

The Big Three's acceptance of unconventional ideas in 1990 was short-lived. *Cop Rock, Against the Law, Twin Peaks,* and other heralded programs fared poorly in the ratings and were yanked off the air by summer. Network programmers, fearing a close ratings race in the year ahead, retreated to the tried and true when they chose ideas for the next year's programs. They reasoned that experimentation had by and large failed to draw large audiences for them, and felt it was too risky to take chances on the coming season.[24]

The perception by television industry personnel that *The Simpsons, Cop Rock,* and *Twin Peaks* were unconventionally innovative fare must be understood from the standpoint of the nature of the TV industry at that time. These programs were very clearly tied to enduring television formulas. Moreover, the individuals involved had no interest in questioning the system of programming or its basic value structure. On the contrary, those who created the shows had already developed at least some track record in the entertainment community. They indicated that they understood and were following many of the commonly accepted routines of popular entertainment. All of this suggests a larger generalization: that producers and distributors of mass media materials judge the importance of change in terms of what has been done before in that industry. From the vantage point of people outside the industry — intellectuals who view public TV, for example, or publishers of scholarly books — the change may not be very significant at all.

CONSIDER THIS

1. Compare the "news nets" of a local television station and a daily newspaper in your area. You can infer the news net by systematically viewing news programs and reading the paper so that you learn what reporters cover and where they are placed. How much do the nets appear to differ? Can you suggest or learn why?

2. Speak to professors about whether they perceive academic brokers as powerful influences on book publishing in their area of specialization. Learn how the process of scholarly publishing works.

3. Watch children's cartoons and try to understand how the animators use body types, voice, and costumes to signal "goodness" and "badness."

NOTES

1. Quoted in Gaye Tuchman, "Making News by Doing Work: Routinizing the Unexpected," *American Journal of Sociology* 77 (July 1971), p. 111.
2. Tuchman, pp. 110–131.
3. Gaye Tuchman, *Making News: A Study in the Construction of Reality* (New York: Free Press, 1978).
4. See Lewis Coser, Charles Kadushin, and Walter Powell, *Books: The Culture and Commerce of Publishing* (New York: Basic Books, 1982).
5. See Joseph Turow, *Getting Books to Children: An Exploration of Publisher-Market Relations* (Chicago: American Library Association, 1979).
6. Coser et al., p. 338.
7. Bruce Felton and Mark Fowler, *Felton and Fowler's Best, Worst, and Most Unusual* (New York: Crowell, 1975), p. viii.
8. John Cawelti, *The Six-Gun Mystique* (Bowling Green, OH: Popular Press, 1975), p. 35.
9. Cawelti, pp. 46–47.
10. Harry Steinberg, "The Porn Brokers," *New York Times Book Review,* November 28, 1976, p. 55.
11. Clive Davis and James Willwerth, *Clive* (New York: Dial Press, 1970), p. 312.
12. *Entertainment Weekly,* September 15, 1995, p. 20.
13. Quoted in Quentin Reynolds, *The Fiction Factory* (New York: Random House, 1955), pp. 88–89.
14. For examples, see Gaye Tuchman, Arlene Kaplan Daniels, and James Benet (eds.), *Hearth and Home: Images of Women in the Mass Media* (New York: Oxford University Press, 1978); Robert Berkhofer, *The White Man's Indian* (New York: Vintage, 1979); and Donald Bogel, *Toms, Coons, Mulattoes, Mammies, and Bucks* (New York: Vintage, 1973).
15. Quoted in Joseph Turow, "Casting for Television: The Anatomy of Social Typing," *Journal of Communication* 33 (Spring 1983), p. 19.

16. Turow, pp. 22–23.
17. Horace Newcomb and Robert Alley, "The Producer as Artist: Commercial Television," in J. Ettema and D. C. Whitney (eds.), *Individuals in Mass Media Organizations* (Beverly Hills, CA: Sage Publications, 1983) pp. 91–107.
18. Elizabeth Guider, "Off the Wall Gets You in the Door, If Not on the Air," *Variety,* August 15, 1990, p. 85.
19. Janet Meyers, "Knight Ridder Aims Young," *Advertising Age,* October 8, 1990, p. 38.
20. Meyers, p. 38.
21. Ronald Grover, "The Fourth Network," *Business Week,* September 17, 1990, pp. 114–120; and Cyndee Miller, "Hey Dudes: Fox TV May Have a Cash Cow in Its Licensing Deals," *Marketing News,* June 11, 1990, p. 1.
22. Squire Rushnell, quoted in Guider, p. 85.
23. Guider, p. 85.
24. Joe Mandese, "Big 3 TV Nets Play It Safe," *Advertising Age,* May 27, 1991, p. 1.

CHAPTER 9

U.S. Mass Media in a Global Economy

This chapter

- explores the international activities of U.S. mass media firms.
- examines different perspectives on the international role of U.S. media technology and content.
- considers major changes in the competitive environment for U.S. media in different regions of the world.

An American of the 1990s who takes a trip to another country might be surprised to finds signs of home all around. In most areas of the world, U.S. products such as Coca-Cola and IBM shout their familiar trademarks from billboards and magazines just as they do in the states. Movie theaters everywhere regularly unspool films from Hollywood. Foreign television stations air a parade of American series, from classics such as *I Love Lucy* and *Bonanza* to more recent fare such as *Miami Vice* and *Dallas.* Foreign radio stations play a heavy diet of music recorded in Los Angeles, New York, and Nashville. Major hotels in most of Europe and parts of Asia pipe the Cable News Network into guests' rooms. And for those with an inclination to read about the world from an American source, a wide array of periodicals, including *Time, Newsweek,* the *New York Times,* the *Wall Street Journal,* and *Business Week,* can be purchased in most capital cities.

The statistics that suggest this story are startling. In the 1990s, U.S. mass media materials account for 75% of broadcast and basic cable TV revenues and 85% of pay-TV revenues worldwide. Fully 55% of all theatrical film rentals and 55% of all homevideo billings worldwide are for U.S. products. American CDs and tapes account for about half of global recording revenues. And the United States commands 35% of the book sales market.[1]

Side by side with this "Americanization" of international mass media, though, are reactions against it. Some opposed to Americanization give broadly cultural reasons for disliking it. Others speak of intentions to gain political power. Still others speak of an interest in economic gain. Often, all these considerations are at play simultaneously.

What fuels the international Americanization of mass media?

What objections and limitations have people outside the United States placed in the way of American mass media power?

What trends indicate the outcome of this struggle between Americanization and anti-Americanization during the next quarter century?

This chapter tackles these questions. Guiding the analysis is the proposition that the global mass media business, like domestic U.S. mass communication, involves competition for symbolic and material resources. Understanding mass media power on an international scale therefore means understanding how companies and governments use resources to struggle over political, economic, and cultural concerns.

The following section presents an influential view from the late 1960s that criticizes American use of resources to this end. It is followed by an overview of some ways in which American power has been challenged during the past twenty years in both wealthy and poor nations. Much opposition has come from governments who want to protect their cultural values. Of rising importance are challenges from nongovernment bodies — large non-U.S. mass media corporations that have learned to beat U.S. firms at their own game. The chapter ends with a discussion of two areas of the world where the influence of international competition among media firms is only beginning to be felt: Europe and, ironically, the United States itself.

THE MEDIA ARE AMERICAN

Few people would disagree that Americans have dominated the mass media scene around the world during the second half of the twentieth century. There is much less consensus on how that has come about and precisely what it means.

The most sweeping and provocative approach to this question links the widespread Americanization of mass media outside the United States to the political, economic, and military goals of the nation's elite. In the late 1960s, communication researcher Herbert Schiller developed this perspective in an influential book titled *Mass Communication and the American Empire.*[2]

"The American Empire"

The theme of Schiller's work is as follows: An empire is a conglomeration of far-flung countries or territories acting under the direction of a particular nation. The Romans, British, French, Turks, and Germans are just a few of the peoples who exercised authority over large parts of the globe in past centuries. In the twentieth century, much of the world has been dominated by the American empire. This empire is, however, uniquely different from all those that came before it.

The difference lies in the resources through which the United States exercises its control over nations. Other empires have imposed and maintained their authority mainly through military force, subduing the locals and establishing armed outposts throughout their colonies. By contrast, the American empire projects its influence primarily not by the sword but through mass communication.

Schiller spends the bulk of his book detailing what he means by the projection of American domination through mass communication. He claims that over the decades, and especially since the end of World War II, the U.S. government has worked hand in hand with large U.S. corporations to provide an appropriate acceptance of American business throughout the world. This has involved much more than ensuring that trade agreements are in America's best interests. Many parts of the world have social systems that would not accept the American business ways of doing things or would not have needs for the kinds of products American firms produce. As a result, the long-term goal of the political-corporate partnership has been to transform much of the world along American capitalist lines, with an emphasis on the modern consumer marketplace.

In other words, Schiller says, making the world the oyster of American business and dominating it with American products has first meant making sure that as many nations of the world as possible adopt the American way of life. This sort of projection of cultural power is called **cultural colonialism.**

Schiller argues that American cultural colonialism takes place primarily through mass communication. His discussion points to three broad areas through which this spread of power takes place: mass media content, mass media structure, and mass media technology.

On the matter of content, he claims that the easy availability of American movies, music, and television programs subtitled or dubbed in foreign languages has been drowning the cultural voices of their societies. Foreign companies, with relatively little money, have often found it impossible to compete with their huge American counterparts in price, technical know-how, or distribution. The resulting Americanization of mass media has brought portrayals of life and enactments of values that, Schiller argues, do not match the needs and traditions of these societies.

For example, airing TV programs that parade urban wealth in an African nation where people are struggling to survive on the land teaches children and adults incorrect lessons on what to strive for in life. Schiller would say that in-

TABLE 9.1 GLOBAL TELEVISION PRICES FOR U.S. PROGRAMS (IN U.S. DOLLARS)

Region/Country	Cost for 50-Minute Program
Europe	
Germany	15,000–90,000
Poland	750–1,500
Far East	
Japan	15,000–120,000
Malaysia	1,000–2,000
Phillipines	1,000–1,700
Central and South America	
Bolivia, Paraguay	200–600
Chile	800–5,000
Middle East	
Israel	800–2,200
Jordan	600–800
Saudi Arabia	1,500–2,000
Africa	
Egypt	1,000–1,200
Kenya	200–750
South Africa	4,000–10,000
Zimbabwe	200–250

SOURCE: Television Business International, *October 1995, p. 122.*

These countries were chosen from among those listed in *Television Business International.* This table allows comparison between the prices that wealthy and poor nations pay. In general, the costs of these programs are far lower than those of similar technical quality that nations could produce themselves. Critics maintain that the low prices encourage cultural colonialism.

stead of being presented with TV programs that tempt them with capitalist gratifications, the people should be imbued with values that help them use their own traditions in ways that maximize their nation's welfare and deal with its special problems.

Mass Communication and the American Empire also discusses how mass media structures have been avenues for cultural empire building. **Structure** refers to the way mass media industries are organized in a particular society. Schiller points out that American ways of organizing and funding mass media have been copied around the world.

Consider the use of advertising to support print and broadcast media. Advertising, Schiller contends, is an inappropriate way to support mass media in many societies. He suggests that advertising champions materialist values, discourages saving, and, when foreign firms promote the wares, may weaken the economy of a nation by encouraging the purchase of imported products. Yet the U.S. government and large American mass media corporations have pressured the governments of many countries, both rich and poor, to adopt a media model that allows advertising. For Schiller, the benefits of this strategy for the United States are clear. The ads provide a platform for American goods while they favorably act out the materialist values that would encourage people to want those goods.

This spread of "the American way" takes on special concern for Schiller when it comes to America's control over the technologies that bring cultural materials to different societies. Technological power today is as one-sided as when Schiller wrote his book: No country other than the United States is a net exporter of mass media materials. To make Schiller's argument even more contemporary, one need only point out that, using the latest direct broadcast satellites, American programmers and advertisers already have the expertise to transmit their output to any country in the world, to be received by small, relatively inexpensive dishes. The day is at hand when corporations will regularly slide American mass media materials across national boundaries to billions of people without the cultural leaders of their countries being able to do anything about it.

The American Advantage

Schiller's theme, in short, is that American domination of content, structure, and technology of mass media has aided U.S. political and economic "imperialism" by weakening the indigenous values of countries around the world and making them more "American." His thesis was controversial when it appeared, and it fueled an enduring debate among people who care about mass media and culture.

Many intellectuals applauded Schiller for facing up to what they felt were the subtle ways that American capitalism was spreading its influence. Others insisted that spreading American news and entertainment values around the world was not all bad, because it could help encourage democratic ideals and concern for the rights of individuals. Still others contended that Schiller incorrectly assumed a power of mass media culture that it did not actually have. They argued that people from other countries do not interpret American programs as Americans do, nor will their values be changed drastically as a result of their viewing, listening, and reading.

Some thinkers who accept the notion that American culture is being spread throughout the world nevertheless reject the proposition that lies at the core of Schiller's book: that the United States is creating an empire. Instead, they see the issue in terms of international trade and the **comparative advantage** of nations with respect to certain products. The notion of comparative advantage claims that the collective wealth of all trading partners is maxi-

TABLE 9.2 TOP TEN U.S. EXPORT MARKETS (ALL MEDIA), 1994

Rank	Country	Sales (in Thousands)	Percent of Yearly Total
1.	Germany	$151,805	13
2.	United Kingdom	140,219	12
3.	Japan	136,003	12
4.	Italy	118,061	10
5.	France	85,078	7
6.	Korea	68,410	6
7.	Spain	57,221	5
8.	Australia/New Zealand	52,226	5
9.	Scandinavia	41,378	4
10.	Canada	22,272	2
	TOTAL	$872,714	77

SOURCE: Variety, *October 30, 1995, p. M28. Copyright,* Variety. *Reprinted with permission of Variety, Inc.*
Although 10 foreign territories continue to account for more than three quarters of all sales by American Film Marketing Association companies, growth in Asia/Pacific, Latin American, and Eastern European territories is altering the makeup of the remaining 25%.

mized if countries specialize in producing what they do best and trade with one another in order to secure the whole range of products produced between them.

By this account, the media dominance Schiller discusses came about simply because, compared with the rest of the world, Americans have excelled in devising mass media materials and technologies as well as the organizational structures that go with them. Economist Richard Collins argues, for example, that the U.S. preeminence in the international television program trade has come about because of certain characteristics of U.S. TV programs and certain realities of TV production in the United States. The most significant of these advantageous factors are:

- Language (English is the most commonly known language across nations)
- The large size and competitive structure of U.S. domestic markets (it encourages the creation of a lot of product aimed at broad audience tastes)
- The availability of a critical mass of competent creative personnel (this allows the United States a predictable flow of product)
- The availability of financial services and manufacturers of necessary equipment (which gives U.S. media producers the basic material resources to sustain their output).[3]

America's leadership in these areas, contends Collins, goes a long way toward explaining the country's leadership in international trade.

Helping to flesh out this comparative advantage approach to understanding the flow of TV programming is the notion of public good. A **public good** is a product or service for which consumption by one person does not reduce the amount available to other individuals. A TV show fits this description because once it is made, it continues to exist whether it is viewed by 100 people or 3 billion people.

This characteristic explains why American TV production firms find that most, if not all, of the costs of creating the public goods have already been recouped in the domestic U.S. market. In contrast to what firms in most countries can afford, American TV production budgets are large because of the competitive requirements of the American TV market and because the country's size allows successful shows to recover their high costs from advertisers. As a result, when Americans come to the international marketplace, most, if not all, of the costs of creating the public goods have already been recouped through their domestic sales. They can, therefore, offer to countries the most technically lavish programming at prices that are difficult to refuse.

Although those who advance the comparative advantage approach often use it as an alternative to the notion that the United States is building an empire, the empire-building and comparative advantage approaches to mass media need not be seen as opposing each other. It is quite possible to see America's comparative advantage in mass communication as both a contributor to its colonial reach and a result of its colonial power.

Whatever position one takes on the empire or comparative advantage theses, it is important to note that since the late 1960s, when Schiller's book was published, two major challenges to U.S. dominance have appeared that demand a refocusing of both approaches to its international role in mass communication. One is the entry of huge foreign firms into the international media scene. The other is the increased determination by governments around the world to restrict American mass media products. From the standpoint of U.S. firms, the challenges are greatest in the nations with the greatest resources: the countries of the First World.

THE FIRST WORLD AND AMERICAN MEDIA

When *Mass Communication and the American Empire* was written, U.S. firms did indeed have a corner on the transnational market for news and entertainment. Certainly, media firms such as Time Warner, Viacom, General Electric, and Disney still exert global reach and influence. Yet non-American global media powerhouses now exist as powerful competitors. In the 1990s, more than a few U.S. executives have stated that within the decade, the bulk of mainstream mass media production, distribution, and exhibition will be controlled by six or seven firms — not all of them American. Consider some of the foreign contenders:

Bertelsmann	A German company that started out in magazine publishing, it has branched out into a variety of mass media throughout the world. In the United States, Bertelsmann owns RCA Records and its record clubs, a chain of bookstores, and a couple of publishing firms.
News Corp	Owned by Australian-American mogul Rupert Murdoch, News Corp owns strings of highly profitable newspapers and magazines in Australia, England, the United States, and elsewhere. The firm also owns 20th Century Fox, along with Fox's various film and TV holdings (including the Fox TV network). Murdoch also has a major stake in the sky direct-broadcast satellite venture aimed at sending commercial programming directly to the homes of Britons and Europeans.
Philips	A huge Dutch electronics manufacturer that owns Polygram Records as well as Polygram Films.
Sony	This Japanese technology giant owns Sony music as well as Columbia Pictures and TriStar.
Seagram	In 1995, this Canadian liquor giant bought the American media conglomerate MCA from Matsushita, Sony's great rival in Japan. MCA owns successful theme parks as well as companies that make and distribute theatrical movies, TV shows, records, and videotapes.

Other non-U.S. players in the struggle for international mass media dominance are also noteworthy. They are not as powerful as the preceding firms, but their strategic importance in particular media makes them targets for either takeovers or joint ventures that would expand one of the other conglomerate's reach enormously. Here are a few:

Hachette	This huge French media conglomerate concentrates mainly on magazines (such as *Elle*) and European broadcasting.
Fininvest	Controlled by Italian mogul Silvio Berlusconi, its subsidiaries virtually manage Italian commercial broadcasting, have interests in French broadcasting, and place much of the advertising in Italy.
Springer Group	Owner of the influential news magazine *Der Spiegel* and other periodicals, this firm has been expanding into broadcasting, theatrical exhibition, and home video.

The Changes in Western Europe

Several factors have led to the rise of Western European and Japanese mass media firms as major competitors to the United States in the global marketplace over the past two decades. In the case of the Western European firms, three long-term developments had the greatest impact:

The general growth of the European economies

The privatization of broadcast media on the continent

The 1992 decision by the European Economic Community to eliminate
tariffs among its members

As for general growth of the European economies, it has been steady and
widespread, resulting in healthy advertising revenues for magazine and newspaper businesses across the region. Theatrical film exhibition has also pros-
pered. Some European companies, such as the initially print-oriented Bertels-
mann, have used their profits to evolve into large conglomerates with interests
in movie exhibition, video cassette distribution, cable TV, and broadcasting, as
well as books and magazines.

The movement of private companies into broadcasting, cable television,
and satellite distribution was a great departure from the historical policies of
most European countries. The broadcasting structure of Western European nations was founded on the notion of public service. Radio and TV stations were
established as public entities, ruled over by bodies established by the government. With few exceptions, the people in charge scorned the U.S. approach
of giving the airwaves over to private firms that funded their activities through
advertising.

This attitude began to change in the mid-1970s. With the appearance of
new technologies such as cable television and satellite broadcasting, companies throughout Europe began clamoring for the right to expand the number
of channels available to citizens' homes. Bowing to pressure, many European
authorities began to allow private firms into the broadcasting, cable, and even
satellite realm.

One reason was that the governments did not want to use their own tax
dollars to cover the huge amounts of money needed to establish a national
presence in these areas. This **privatization** — the introduction of private firms
into the broadcast arena — was accompanied by **commercialization,** the
transformation of radio and television into vehicles for marketers. Following
the American model, the firms realized that there were large numbers of advertisers who would pay handsomely to get their commercials into the homes
of European consumers. The lure of advertising monies quickly became the
engine driving the spread of broadcast and cable channels throughout Western Europe.

Europe 1992

The upward trend in advertising also reflected a keen awareness by international marketers that Europe 1992 was at hand. Europe 1992 was a shorthand
phrase meaning that agreements by the nations of Western Europe through
their European Economic Community (EEC) would transform the area into
one country from the standpoint of trade beginning in 1992. Previously, tariffs

had made it difficult to export goods among neighboring countries of Western Europe. With the EEC eliminating those tariffs, competition across the continent would be encouraged. Experts predicted lower prices throughout the region as a result. They also noted the effects of the EEC's decision on advertising.

The lure of a tariff-free market of consumers with a population size and wealth close to those of the United States was irresistible to marketers around the world. Traditional advertising vehicles such as magazines, movie theaters, and newspapers, as well as the newly privatized broadcast channels, elicited strong interest from companies that wanted to introduce their products to new parts of Europe or protect their brands in anticipation of the new marketing realities.

The privatization and commercialization of Western European mass media have been accompanied by the rise of powerful advertising conglomerates with international reach. Firms such as Eurocom (French), Cordient (British), and the WPP Group (British) grew by leaps and bounds in the 1980s as they voraciously bought ad agencies, market research firms, and media buying organizations in Europe, Asia, and the United States.

This growth was often fueled by relatively easy money available through "junk bonds." It was guided by the idea that multinational marketers expected their advertising agencies to be able to serve their creative, research, and media-buying needs across countries and across continents. Perhaps not surprisingly, some executives in these global agencies argued that in many cases it was useful to adopt the same persuasive strategy in every country in which a product was sold. Using the same campaign (with appropriate translation) in different countries of Europe, as well as in the United States and Asia, for products such as toothpaste and tampons would, they contended, give global marketers the best way to control the appeal and efficiency of their marketing efforts.

A number of major international marketers disagreed that global, or even pan-European, advertising was the way to go. Nevertheless, a number of mass media ventures were designed to cater to advertising across boundaries — for example, MTV Europe, which aims its ad-supported footprint at more than 16 million cable households in England and on the continent.[4]

The Japanese and Global Media

The rising power of Western European companies in all aspects of the international mass media scene during the 1980s and 1990s was paralleled by the major role that Japanese firms began to play. Sony and the Nintendo video game giant are perhaps their country's most visible representatives; they are not, however, the only ones. Companies such as Fujisankei (a major Japanese movie studio), Softbank (a huge computer software distributor that owns U.S. computer magazines), and Dentsu (one of the world's largest ad agencies) have all involved themselves in the international production realm in some major way.

In the early 1990s, there was even a Japanese-founded filmmaking company in Hollywood: Apricot Studios. At the same time, Japanese publishing firms were showing interest in buying minority or controlling ownership in American magazine and book publishing companies.

Unlike that of Europe, nearly all Japanese involvement in international media production activities has consisted not of creating new ventures from scratch but of financing or purchasing existing ones. Several considerations motivated the Japanese to join the global mass media bandwagon almost exclusively by purchasing it. One was the immense amount of money that many Japanese firms were earning in the world marketplace. The low value of the U.S. dollar and many European currencies in comparison to the yen has made U.S. and European media firms attractive to Japanese firms with media connections. The Japanese could afford to buy the best.

The second, probably more important, factor is that Japanese executives appear to believe that their indigenous production approaches are not well adapted to the international market. Japanese singing stars do not make the hit charts around the world, whereas U.S., British, and other European stars often do. Japanese TV shows and theatrical films do not travel well, even though Japanese movie studios have periodically tried to concoct a product that imitates American action films. Their solution: If you can't beat them, buy them, if you have the resources. The Japanese have the cash.

The most spectacular results of this thinking were Sony's and Matusushita's multibillion-dollar purchases of Columbia and MCA, respectively. By all accounts, the two electronic giants were intent on buying powerful American record and movie companies that would provide them with the "software" to encourage consumers to purchase new "hardware." Sony officials attributed much of their failure to succeed with their Beta-format VCR in the 1970s to an inability to tempt consumers with exclusive movie titles. Their American purchases were aimed at giving them programming clout.

These acquisitions also seem to have been designed to give the manufacturers leverage with the creators of programming. Throughout the 1970s and 1980s, it had become clear to industry observers that fundamental policy splits had developed between production firms and equipment manufacturers. U.S. recording companies, for example, vigorously opposed the Japanese manufacturers' digital audiotape (DAT) recorder on the grounds that it would encourage copyright violations. The Sony and Matsushita acquisitions represented attempts to close these splits by taking control of major forces in the production segments of their industries. It is no coincidence that a compromise on DAT was reached not long after Sony's purchase of CBS Records.

Continuing the American Connection

Two conclusions emerge from this sketch of the strong presence of Europeans and Japanese as international movers and shakers in mass media. The first is that Herbert Schiller's characterization of international mass communication as an almost exclusively American domain needs to be revised at the threshold of the twenty-first century. Rather than an American-dominated activity, global mass communication might best be described as a First World activity. That is, news and entertainment throughout the world are created by companies from several of the richest countries in the world to be shared by the richest nations, the less wealthy, and the poor.

That ownership of a substantial segment of transnational media activity is being shared more broadly now than previously reflects a decline of U.S. economic clout in the world economy. Yet, while companies from other parts of the world are more involved in global mass communication than ever before, the media remain overwhelmingly American in a number of ways.

For one thing, much of the information and entertainment material owned by non-U.S. firms is created by Americans. MCA, 20th Century Fox, Columbia Pictures, and MGM/UA (which is owned by the French bank Credit Lyonnais) may not be strictly American companies anymore. Nevertheless, Los Angeles is still the base for producing their movies, albums, TV shows, and theme parks. Equally important, the dominant model for internationally profitable content in the news, information, and entertainment realm is American, whether produced by Americans or not.

When Italian and Japanese producers attempt to create movies for the world market, they consciously try to emulate Hollywood's style — and they sometimes even do it in English. Similarly, when Hong Kong entrepreneurs decide to generate a Chinese-language magazine with news about business, *Forbes* and *Business Week* become relevant models. Atlanta-based Cable News Network has likewise become the standard for an all-news channel in the international cable TV and satellite-to-home business.

The American way does not predominate only in content. Japanese radios, televisions, VCRs, and video discs improve and miniaturize American-generated technologies. These technologies reflect a long-standing American philosophy of mass communication: that it is a good thing to multiply media channels so that people who can pay will have a variety of news and entertainment options. Much of this privatized and individualized (as opposed to collective and governmentally driven) approach to mass media technologies is still backed by the American model of mass media industries: profit-making production firms supported in the main by advertising. Although the persuasive appeals of ads may vary in different countries, the basic American pattern of using mass media as marketing vehicles remains constant.

Canadian Concerns

Not all First World governments support the global, privatized, commercialized, and Americanized direction that much of the mass media has taken, and they have marshaled resources against it. Canada provides a particularly interesting example. Politicians in the English-speaking parts of that country have lamented that their people are especially vulnerable to American influence on all media fronts. Artists, journalists, educators, politicians, and media executives have worried about the continuing flood of news and entertainment products emanating from their southern neighbor.

One problem they raise is that American films, videos, albums, and periodicals dominate their markets for those products, which makes it difficult for their local firms to survive. Increasing the American influence are TV and radio stations broadcasting from Buffalo, Detroit, and other U.S. cities near Canada. They attract a large percentage of the Canadian population, which is concentrated along its long border with the United States.

Alarmed educators and politicians have contended that as a result of American mass media, Canadian youngsters know more about current events in the United States than about Canadian ones. They have urged their government to work against what they see as U.S. cultural domination by encouraging Canadian mass media. Canadian entertainment companies, eager to grow, have supported their activities. Over the past few decades, Ottowa has urged Canadians to watch Canadian media.

One strategy to help their mass media has been to tax the advertising dollars Canadian firms use when they buy ads in foreign periodicals and broadcasts that reach Canada, while not taxing the ad monies they spend on Canadian media. This has helped news magazines such as *Maclean's* compete with *Time* and *Newsweek*.[5] Another tack has been to bolster the movie industry by providing government subsidies to films produced with a certain percentage of primary personnel (directors, stars, writers) who are Canadian citizens.[6]

Government grants have also supported production by firms who sell programs to either of the two television networks. The goal of the Canadian Broadcasting Corporation (CBC) is to have more than 90% of its prime time offerings made in Canada. The nongovernment network, CTV, has a prime time quota of about 60% Canadian content.

To discourage audiences from viewing American programs on U.S. networks (and losing ad monies as a result), the CBC and CTV have sometimes required U.S. production firms to send episodes of TV series across the border before the U.S. networks have aired them. More commonly, the Canadian networks have taken to broadcasting U.S. programs at the same time as their American counterparts. This has benefited the Canadians because of an advertising arrangement worked out with ABC, CBS, and NBC. As part of the arrangement, the Canadians get a separate feed of the shows, with commercials sold by the CBC or CTV inserted in lieu of American commercials. Also as part of the deal, Canadian cable systems carrying the American networks show Canadian commercials, so that the additional audience benefits the Canadian network, not the U.S. affiliate.[7]

Canadian government and industry officials realize that all efforts to "protect and encourage Canadian mass media" are politically touchy. One barrier to simply barring American media from entering Canada is that this would infringe on Canadians' rights to read what they please. Another is that hindrances to U.S. media products displease powerful industry lobbying groups in

Washington. Officials argue that Canadian logjams in the face of American media products would represent intolerable barriers to fair trade. Canada relies greatly on its commerce with the United States. Canadian officials must, therefore, tread a fine line between responding to their constituencies at home and not endangering larger U.S.–Canadian trade agreements.

European Tensions

Concerns about external mass media forces are being expressed throughout Western Europe, too. The concerns of some of the smaller countries are not just about American cultural products. Dutch leaders, for example, have worried that their public TV channels will lose a lot of viewership — and viewer support for funding — as citizens turn to commercial signals in the Dutch language that companies from elsewhere in Europe (especially Luxembourg and Belgium) have thrust across their borders.[8]

Generally, though, the greatest anxiety has not been voiced over border crossing by European-made products but rather over materials made in the U.S.A. European media executives and intellectuals know full well that American adventure movies capture some 70% of their countries' movie seats and that American shows saturate the airwaves on commercial stations.[9] They also know that what their own firms produce is not in the international league: In a typical year, 90% of European film and TV programs never leave their country of origin.[10] Not always in agreement on a solution to this problem, European intellectuals have nevertheless determined to come up with individual as well as collective responses to American mass media power.

Perhaps the most impressive pan-European attempt to encourage entertainment production on the continent was announced at the end of 1990. After a cliff-hanging series of postponements and hesitations, the Council of Ministers at the European Parliament approved a $250 million, five-year funding package for MEDIA, the European Community's attempt to develop its own TV and movie industries that can sell to the world. Boasting twelve programs based in various European capitals, MEDIA's mandate fell into roughly three areas: distribution, production, and training. Its programs provide seed money for everything in movies and TV production, from scripts and cartoons to feature film coproductions, multinational distribution, and the development of new audiovisual technologies. The goal was to encourage creation of a network of movie and TV professionals of all types so that an internationally competitive European infrastructure in audiovisual industries could emerge.[11]

Such actions frighten American film and TV executives. They fear that European government initiatives to develop theatrical and small-screen programming will be accompanied by trade regulations that strongly limit mass media products created in the United States. Some countries have already legislated quotas on the number of programs that can be aired on individual stations. A European Community directive effectively limits U.S. programming to no more than 50% of airtime in member countries. Although 50% is still a lot, American executives worry about the precedent of setting such quotas; 50% today could be lowered to 20% next year.[12]

As a result, lobbyists from U.S. audiovisual industries (representing movie, record, and TV interests) have worked hard in U.S. and European government circles to make sure that their products are well represented in general fair trade agreements with the United States. Jack Valenti, chairman of the Motion Picture Export Association of America, was among those in the early 1990s advocating that the U.S. government apply substantial material and symbolic resources to ensure that American mass media industries would not be locked out of Europe.

Valenti argued that the central issue was the economic health of the United States in an age of huge trade deficits. He described America's film, video, and TV entertainment industry as one of the country's "glittering trade jewels," responsible for an annual surplus of more than $3 billion in balance of trade. And he contended that those in the EEC who were imposing restrictions on U.S. media products were using the guise of protecting national cultures to boost their companies' revenues at the expense of American firms.[13]

By the mid-1990s, both sides had moved toward some rapprochement. The MEDIA program did not seem to have worked, though a new five-year MEDIA 2 was instituted in 1995. Its emphasis was less on making films than on developing distribution pipelines for them. Becoming more pragmatic, European filmmakers realized that they needed the money and advice of American film distributors if they were going to succeed across Europe and in the world market.

Americans, for their part, began to see that by developing alliances with European production firms, they could profit from films made on the continent and reduce concern about the overwhelming dominance of U.S. product. In 1995, Jack Valenti tried to get on the good side of the Europeans by persuading Hollywood studios to invest $2 million in helping train Europeans, particularly in marketing and distribution. Nevertheless, tensions remained in Europe and elsewhere in the industrialized world, as French government officials, among others, argued that the popularity of American films had brought about the collapse of national cinema industries in Italy, Germany, and elsewhere.[14]

Continuing U.S. Dominance

Despite the tensions and recognition of the need to ally with Europeans, American media firms have moved aggressively to distribute U.S. products during the late 1990s in two ways. One, the traditional path, has been to sell U.S. movies and television programs. The other, newer way has been to sell entire channels of programming.

The business of selling individual U.S. programs was booming because the number of free and pay-TV outlets was growing around the world. New pay-cable firms in Australia, new channels in Holland and Switzerland, and escalating competition in Germany and England were, by mid-decade, just a few of the places looking for programming that could give them high ratings and strong identities. Increase in channels has led to an increase in production in industrialized countries themselves. Low- and medium-budget dramas, sitcoms, and game and talk shows are filling prime time, often doing better than, and pushing out, U.S. products. Nevertheless, there is not enough indigenous product to fill the time. As a result, high-budget American dramas such as *Beverly Hills 90210, Picket Fences,* and *Baywatch* are still considered crucial for programmers.[15] Quotas are hardly an issue anymore, and the concern for product outweighs concern for "cultural autonomy."

The trade magazine *Variety* estimated in 1995 that U.S. exporters of series and films to those outlets would rake in a record $2.75 billion in revenues that year. Especially attractive to executives in industrialized countries are series and made-for-TV movies that have drawn large U.S. audiences. "Dogfights . . . are breaking out all over Europe for hot new [U.S.] series, TV movies and other A-tier fare," reported *Variety*.[16] Consider *Murder One,* the much-praised ABC series from Steven Bochco. In 1995, it fetched $250,000 per episode through a joint bid from the BBC and Sky satellite channel in Britain, about three times the average price for a U.S. series in that area. But it is not only the major firms, such as the BBC and Murdoch's Sky, that are putting down lots of money for "American" fare.

According to *Variety,* "even more junior players among foreign TV buyers are now making competitive bids" when they think a show can enhance their channel's recognition or draw viewers to it during a key time of day. To U.S. distributors, the opportunities were enormous. "With the expansion of TV in Germany and more opportunities than ever in the U.K., you are able to do more [TV deals] than at any time in the last ten years," said the head of Worldvision Enterprises, a major distributor of U.S. TV, in 1995.[17]

The expansion in Europe and Australia, as well as in relatively well-off parts of Asia and Latin America, also applies to the new side of U.S. program sales. In a growing number of cases, suppliers of content such as U.S. majors no longer just sell their shows individually, or even bundled together with a batch of feature films. Instead, the growth of these video delivery systems to the home has led major U.S. suppliers to offer entire around-the-clock programming services such as CNN, MTV, U.S.A, and HBO to the cable and satellite firms of different countries. The owners of these channels are the same U.S. major producers who create the majority of U.S. programming and distribute it around the world.

In most cases, the channels are advertiser supported, but in some, such as HBOs, customers subscribe and the money is shared by the carrier and the service. Although the basic formats are usually the same as their counterparts in the United States, the services are altered to suit regional tastes. MTV's several Asian services, for example, use less rock-oriented playlists than MTV Europe or America. MTV Europe, like most U.S. channels in Europe, uses the English language. In Latin America, by contrast, U.S. services such as Discovery and MTV have hosts who speak Spanish and often present dubbed or subtitled materials.[18]

TABLE 9.3 PROGRAMMING CHANNELS AIMED AT LATIN AMERICA, 1995

Channel	Genre	Ownership
Canal De Noticas NBC	news	NBC
Canal SUR	general entertainment	Panamericana Television
Cartoon Network	children's	Turner Broadcasting
Cine Latino	movies	Multivision, Mexivision
Cinecanal	movies	UIP, Multivision, 20th Century Fox, SACSA, Cablecinema
Cinemax	movies	Time Warner Ent., Sony, Ole Communications
CNNI	news	Turner Broadcasting
Country Music Television	music	Gaylord, Group W
Deutsche Welle	news/documentary	ARD
Discovery Channel	education/nature/history	Cox/TCI/Newhouse/ John Hendricks
E! Entertainment Television	general entertainment	Time Warner Ent., 5 other U.S. MSOs
ECO	news	Televisa
El Canal de las Estrellas	general entertainment	Televisa
ESPN International	sports	ESPN
Fox–Latin America	general entertainment	Fox
GEMS Television	women	Empresas/Cox
HBO Ole	movies	HBO/Warner Bros./Ole Communications
MTV Latino	music	Viacom
Much Music	music	CHUM TV
Nostalgia Television	general entertainment	Concept Communications
Prime Deportiva	sports	Liberty Sports (TCI)
RAI America	news/general entertainment	RAI
Sony Entertainment Television	general entertainment	Sony, HBO Ole
Tele Noticias	news	Reuters, Telemundo, Artear, Antena 3
Tele Novelas	novelas	Televisa
Tele Uno	general entertainment	Worldvision/Multivision
Telehit	music	Televisa
Television Espanola Int'l (TVE)	news/general entertainment	RTVE
The Travel Channel	information	Landmark Communications
Warner Channel (WBTV)	general entertainment	Warner Bros., HBO Ole
TNT	general entertainment	Turner Broadcasting
TV5	news/general entertainment	TV5–Europe, TV5–Quebec
USA	general entertainment	Viacom, MCA, Multivision, Telefe
Worldnet	news/information	U.S. government

SOURCE: Broadcasting and Cable International, *October 1995, p. 58. Copyright, Cahners Publishing Company.*

Latin America, which includes Mexico, Central America, South America, and Caribbean countries, has become a battleground among the programming services of media conglomerates.

Some U.S. executives see the American channels as a hedge against the increasing number of production firms in different regions of the world that can supply programs to their own countries. Moreover, they are confident that as cable systems and satellites expand their channel capabilities greatly by switching from analog to digital signals, they will have need for even more U.S. channels. "There are going to be digital platforms around the world in the next two or three years, and they will very much need channel providers like ourselves," said Kay Koplowitz, CEO of the joint venture of Time Warner and Paramount that owns U.S.A Network and the Sci Fi Channel.

THE DEVELOPING WORLD AND AMERICAN MEDIA

Anger about these sorts of developments emanates from leaders not only of industrialized countries but also of the poorest countries of the world. In many of these so-called Third World nations, the concern is directed as much toward general Western, or First World, media products as toward specifically U.S. mass media materials. Building from a perspective similar to that of Herbert Schillers, Third World intellectuals and politicians argue that the Americanized global mass media situation has been harmful to their nations.

The issues they raise are complex and varied. On the subject of imported entertainment, critics argue that broadcasting American and British programs for several hours every day is counterproductive to societies where survival and running society are the main concerns. Rather than spectator-oriented TV, their oppressive social problems demand grass-roots involvement away from the television to have any hope of success.

Western news receives condemnation as well. Third World politicians complain that struggling African, Asian, and Central American countries do not have the resources to compete with American, French, and British news agencies. The major agencies have fifty to one hundred correspondents abroad and expensive, high-speed transmission technology. They dominate the news holes of papers in both the developing and developed worlds. Because Western journalists define foreign news in terms of conflict and tension, people in Third World nations, and especially people outside them, get views of the developing world as bizarre, corrupt, and war-torn. This picture hinders leaders of poor nations in their attempts to develop tourism and entice investments by companies from richer nations.

The McBride Commission

Responding to concerns such as these, the United Nations Educational, Scientific, and Cultural Organization (UNESCO) appointed a commission in 1976 to propose solutions. Known as the **McBride Commission** after its chair, Sean McBride, it released a report four years later that instigated a storm of controversy.

At the core of the report was the commission's insistence that developing countries had the right to place "nation building" as an objective of their media activities, in news as well as in entertainment. Comprehensive government communications policies should guide the portrayal of nation building in different media. Economic priorities and development needs of the society should take precedence over freedom of the media. The commission added that journalists as well as other media personnel working in those countries should be expected to cooperate with these goals.

The McBride Report became the takeoff point for even more radical recommendations. Third World advocates proposed nothing less than a true **new world information order** (NWIO), meaning fundamental changes in the access of rich and poor countries to the channels of world communication.

U.N. Ambassador Mustapha Masmoudi of Tunisia, for example, argued that inequalities of legal and technological resources in global communication had to be corrected if the poorest countries were ever to move ahead economically. The best positions for satellite orbits, for example, should not continue to go only to the countries that can afford them, because that would exclude developing countries from getting good "slots" in the future.[19]

Masmoudi and others from developing nations also helped pass a resolution that UNESCO should sponsor regional news agencies for nations that had none. Accompanying the resolution were suggestions that these agencies regulate the news coming out of their regions. Some Third World politicians also proposed licensing Western journalists. The aim was to make sure that only those journalists who cooperated with a government's development aims could report from that country.

A number of the NWIO premises, such as licensing and news monopolies, flew in the face of long-held Western ideals of "free speech" and the "free flow of information." Even so, some observers from the West were sympathetic to the notion of a new world information order. They argued that the global situation already prevented true free speech and free information flow from developed to developing nations. Media resources of the former were so much greater than those of the latter that the poor nations could gain control over their destinies only through drastic steps that would forcefully release the chains of inequality.

U.S. Response

Journalists, politicians, and mass media executives in the United States did not buy this argument, however. They countered that the invocation of a new world information order by Third World politicians was, in many cases, just another excuse to solidify dictatorial power over their people through control over the news. They rejected licensing and news monopolies as contrary to the best interests of informed citizens everywhere, and accused UNESCO of being a bastion of antidemocratic policies. To underscore these points, and to remove from the organization the necessary resources for carrying out its new world information order goals, the United States, along with Great Britain, withdrew from UNESCO in 1984.

The loss of subsidies from these two major powers crippled the organization and derailed implementation of broad changes that would characterize a new world information order. In the late 1980s, the United States and England rejoined a quieter, less insistent UNESCO. The tensions between developed and developing nations over global communication issues have remained, however. They bubble to the surface now and then as the activities of Americanized global media operations clash with the objectives of leaders having very different traditions.

In rapidly industrializing Singapore, for example, issues of The Asian *Wall Street Journal* were removed from circulation after the government passed a new law that required foreign publications to be licensed yearly and to post a deposit against legal rulings. An official decree had already reduced the newspaper's circulation in that country from 5,000 to 400 after government officials became angry with material in the publication.[20] Clashes such as these reflect ways of looking at the world that are fundamentally at odds with each other. Although not as noisy as the UNESCO debate, they are likely to continue far into the future.

AMERICAN MASS MEDIA
AND THE FORMER SOVIET BLOC

Of course, there have been governments around the world that try to isolate themselves as much as possible from any First World versions of mass communication. Such governments have upheld ideologies that often directly oppose the capitalist-driven engines of news and entertainment that characterize the West. Nations that hold fundamentalist Islamic beliefs ban public displays of Western entertainment, though the use of American VCR tapes in the home is common. Also in the exclusionary category are communist nations such as North Korea, Albania, and Vietnam. In other communist countries, such as the People's Republic of China, Western media, including advertising, have made some inroads.

From the standpoint of Western media, the nations of Eastern and Central Europe are probably in the greatest state of uncertainty and change. No one seems to be quite sure what the limits to Westernization will be or who will define them. This is because transformations taking place in what many have called the former Soviet empire have been nothing short of astonishing, even to longtime observers of the region. The declaration that the Cold War with the West was over; the dissolution of the Soviet Union's hold on the region and the creation of autonomous states; the public rejection of communist philosophy among many key leaders in the area — these activities are merely the tip of a huge iceberg of changes that have been moving nations through uncharted waters. Horrendous conflicts in Bosnia, Georgia, and elsewhere have shown how dangerous these waters can be.

Media Transformations

Mirroring Eastern Europe's political changes have been transformations in mass communication. Until just a few years ago, the Eastern Bloc's communication policy reflected beliefs about media, society, and the state that were expressed by the founding fathers of modern communism: Marx, Engels, and Lenin. The approach was called **Soviet media theory** by most observers because it developed its earliest and most detailed exposition in the USSR. It provided the model for media practice and training within the broad Soviet sphere of influence.

Four fundamental premises guided traditional Soviet media theory:

- Mass media should not be owned by private individuals. Rather, the media should be subject to control by the agencies of the working class — that is, by the various arms of the Communist party.
- The press should play a positive role in educating the society toward socialism and should avoid activities that could cause divisiveness.
- When reporting events, journalists should present them according to an objectively true — that is, Marxist — interpretation of historical reality.
- Flowing from the above ideas, mass media and the personnel who run them are part of the general political and educational structure of the state and so are subject to controls by the state — for example, censorship or punishment — to make them operate properly.[21]

Soviet journalism theorists noted that the creators of news and entertainment were expected to be responsive to the interests of their audience as determined by research and letters. They were also expected to investigate situations in the society that were not conforming to the aims of the government — for example, lazy workers — with the aim of urging things to be set right.

In practice, though, the creators of mass media materials felt hindered from casting critical eyes on their surroundings. In both the USSR and its satellites, mass media creators often chafed under the pressure of governments that expected to be able to manipulate images directly — even lie — in the service of their power. The situation seemed to cultivate widespread cynicism of Soviet media theory even among Soviet mass media practitioners. When the Soviet Union fell apart, they knew their media system was going to change. But how would it change? How fast would it happen? And who would be involved?

The answers varied for different countries in the region. To a large extent, though, what was emerging is mostly in the Western mode of private enterprise regulated by the government. Moreover, because of fairly open regulations on foreign entry in both broadcast and print media, Eastern and Central European countries became yet more sites of competition between global mass media firms eager to spread their influence. The Czech Republic and

Hungary seemed more hospitable than Russia to Western media ambitions in the mid-1990s. Prague, in the Czech Republic, has been a particularly fertile area for U.S. expatriates trying to find gold in new media opportunities.[22] Yet throughout the old Soviet Bloc, Western media conglomerates and entrepreneurs are setting up shop in a broad range of media and advertising activities, from magazines to radio to television. As was the case elsewhere during the decade, the players in this region were not only Americans. In addition to Time Warner, Viacom, and the McCann Erickson ad agency, giants from Germany, France, and other parts of the First World were deeply involved. In Hungary, for example, Germany's Springer Verlag publishing firm took advantage of a free-for-all privatization in the early 1990s by buying seven of its daily newspapers.[23]

Were these activities attempts at cultural colonialism by Western capitalist countries? Or were they just examples of the competitive advantage of nations? Perhaps they were both.

GLOBAL MEDIA COMPETITION AND THE U.S. MARKET

Many — probably most — American viewers and readers in the mid-1990s have little awareness of such international competition among media firms. It is likely, in fact, that most Americans have little awareness of foreign media products. Traditionally in the United States, foreign-language periodicals and broadcast stations have been considered only temporary outlets for immigrants.

Historically, Germans, Poles, Italians, Scandinavians, Jews, and others immigrating to the United States continued to use their language of origin for one, perhaps two, generations. Newspapers and other mass media in foreign tongues typically blossomed to accommodate the needs of the first generation of arrivals and then disappeared or continued in a much weakened state to serve ever-older audiences.

This is less true in the case of many Hispanic groups living in the United States, most notably the Puerto Rican and Mexican communities. Spanish-language materials comprise a large part of the daily media diet for generations of Hispanic-Americans. Although Hispanics are the largest and fastest-growing minority in America, advertisers have not been lavish in their support of Hispanic media, probably because most Hispanics do not have the disposable income advertisers crave. This reluctance on the part of advertisers especially influences television programming, since it severely limits the amount of money available for indigenous production.

In regard to Hispanic TV, then, the United States is a large importer of programming. Univision and Telemundo, the two major Hispanic TV networks in the United States, program two-thirds of their materials with Mexican, South American, and Spanish product.[24] A third network, Galavision, directs itself specifically at Mexican-Americans and uses exclusively Mexican material.

U.S. Made

For the great majority of Americans, however, the sound and look of mass media have always been U.S. made. A middle-aged listener to mainstream American music stations has grown up hearing almost exclusively English lyrics. For decades, the major American television networks have aired almost no foreign programming.

Foreign movies are alien to the great majority of U.S. citizens. Only 16 non-American movies were among the 164 titles circulated by the major U.S. film distributors in 1990. Moreover, of these 16, almost half (7) were made in English in the British Commonwealth. Independent distributors, however, circulated 67 foreign movies.[25] The likelihood that a large percentage of movie-goers would see these products was minimal, though, because the major distributors collectively have a tight grip on the overwhelming number of theaters around the country. Few American cities have theaters that exhibit movies made outside the United States.

To be sure, many Americans knew of Sony's purchase of Columbia Pictures and Matsushita's buyout of MCA in the early 1990s. Yet news stories about these sales were couched not in considerations of international media but more narrowly in concerns about Japan's increasing ownership of American business. Moreover, these stories emphasized claims by both Sony and Matsushita management that they would be leaving their new American subsidiaries the independence to continue producing output as in the past. Stock analysts went out of their way to predict that the purchases would have little impact on the movies Hollywood made.

As a result, most Americans probably hold the notion that the U.S.-created, America-centered, English-speaking media world that they and their parents have known will remain intact. Production executives from countries such as France and Italy blame the major U.S. distributors and theater owners, who, they say, have purposely not marketed foreign films properly to the American public so that American movies will get top box-office draw. One U.S. independent distributor of French films agreed; he finds it difficult to gain theatrical, TV, or even homevideo acceptance. He recommended that the French film industry fight back with its political resources by considering harsher quota restrictions on U.S. film and video productions if U.S. theaters and TV networks are not more open to French product. "If that would happen," he contended, "I'll promise you, you'd see French films as two-part miniseries in prime time on NBC."[26]

Of course, as suggested earlier, the American audiovisual industry has been conducting its own lobbying efforts with the French and U.S. governments to ensure that such quotas do not get instituted. It is highly improbable that Americans, so long accustomed to U.S.-made entertainment, will consistently welcome foreign products with open arms. Nevertheless, it seems that the content of American mass media will be affected at least to some extent by the struggle over global media resources. Rather than extending influence through product made primarily for the French or Italian or German market, though, it is likely that in the next quarter century, foreign influences will make themselves felt primarily because of the increasingly international nature of the production business.

International Products in the American Mainstream

In the future, it is likely that a substantial segment of American mass media will be made with an aim toward the world market. Although print media will undoubtedly reflect these changes, they will probably be most apparent in the audiovisual realm: theatrical movies, TV shows, records, home video, and the technologies that follow them.

International Films

These changes are happening already. The theatrical movie industry is particularly in the vanguard. It used to be that Hollywood producers saw foreign distribution as a lucrative afterthought, a way to make money after the major dollars were made in the U.S.A. In the 1970s and 1980s, however, Hollywood producers, distributors, and investors began to target the international market in the planning stages of movies. Foreign theatrical rentals are increasing more than domestic ones, and the projection of foreign ratings has become an integral part of financial considerations about whether a movie should be made, and on what budget.

Hollywood producers have long known that certain movies that do well at U.S. box offices perform stunningly on foreign shores. The *James Bond* film series, for example, continued to be strong in the international market even as rentals for new episodes decreased in American theaters.[27] The foreign popularity of the series primarily kept it going in the 1980s and inspired still more in the 1990s. Although major movie studio executives have increasingly considered the foreign market as a factor that can influence a movie that may have only moderate U.S. possibilities, a number of independent producers have actually been tailoring product specifically for the global market.

To do so, they choose a cast of actors from a variety of key countries, then select story and production values to minimize the need for talk and emphasize action. In practice, this means a male-centered movie based on war, vigilante activity, or some sort of police action. Think of films with Steven Segal, Sylvester Stallone, and Arnold Schwarzenegger. These types of action films are shot in English, because it has become the international language; dubbing or subtitles are added to match the needs of particular countries. The violence (or "action") makes reading the subtitles almost unnecessary. The films are marketed around the United States, but the producers consider the world market even more lucrative.

Another kind of international film making an increasing presence in American theaters fits what the trade magazine *Variety* calls the Continental English-track category. This type used to be dominated by European products created for their countries of origin. Imported to the United States, with sound tracks dubbed into English, the movies at first hardly made ripples in the American market.

During the past few years, however, the category has begun to be filled with French, Italian, Spanish, German, and Dutch productions shot in English for the international market. Until the late 1980s, the major Hollywood distributors tended to steer clear of distributing these hybrid films. As a result, independents circulated such ventures as *The Cook, the Thief, His Wife, and Her Lover* (with Miramax as distributor), *Last Exit to Brooklyn* (Cinecom), and *Santa Sangre* (Expanded Entertainment).

In the early 1990s, however, the majors began to show interest in joining European companies in producing English-language films made on the continent. In the early 1990s, for example, the French pay-television cable service Canal Plus announced that it had entered into a coproduction deal with Warner Brothers to produce movies in French.[28] One possible reason for Warner's involvement was that by supporting European filmmaking, the European Economic Community would not threaten to impose tariffs on its im-

TABLE 9.4 TOP U.S. CITIES IN HISPANIC POPULATION, 1990

City	Hispanic Population
New York, NY	1,783,511
Los Angeles, CA	1,391,411
Chicago, IL	545,852
San Antonio	520,282
Houston, TX	450,483
El Paso, TX	355,669
San Diego, CA	229,519
Miami, FL	223,964
Dallas, TX	210,240
San Jose, CA	208,388

SOURCE: *U.S. Census, 1990.*

Hispanics make up the fastest growing ethnic group in the United States. These figures are taken from the 1990 U.S. census, and are undoubtedly lower than today's numbers. The table does, however, give an accurate current picture of the cities and parts of the country where advertisers and programmers to Hispanics concentrate their activities. Unlike TV programs and movies for most Americans, audiovisual programming aimed at them tends to come mostly from other countries.

ported American-made product. Another reason could be the feeling that Continental English-track films may recover their investment through combining revenues from French pay-TV and the global market. These and other considerations led Disney to buy Miramax, the preeminent distributor of foreign films in the U.S. and other markets. Many of its successes (*The Piano, Pulp Fiction, Kids*) have been made in English-speaking countries, even the United States. Yet Miramax has been on the lookout for films from around the world, especially Europe. Disney and the other majors clearly feel that there is long-term money to be made in films created by non-American firms.

International Films in the U.S. Market

The global market includes the U.S. market. International films will show up on broadcast, cable, and home video, if not in theaters. The homevideo market will be an outlet, because many of the American coproduction partners have home distribution operations. Local broadcast and cable channels will carry them because those firms' executives, burdened by small audiences (compared to those of the broadcast networks) and tight budgets, have made it their business to hunt for relatively inexpensive programming sources with sophisticated production values. Increasingly, they could decide that, if marketed properly, films such as those funded by Canal Plus and Time Warner will attract viewers and cost far less than movies produced by the cable channels themselves.

Even American commercial television networks have experimented with international coproductions. In 1990, for example, CBS signed an agreement with British independent broadcaster Granada Television to develop and produce as many as six TV movies over the following three years. CBS also agreed to pay a U.S. firm and a French company to coproduce an action series called *Paris Metal* for its late-night (11:30 P.M. – 12:30 A.M.) slot. (This was before David Letterman's takeover of that time period.) The series was shot in English and French, and the license fee paid to the network was 40% of the regular license fee for a U.S. prime time network show of similar technical quality.

Cheaper location costs are not always the reason that foreign-made shows can be had for less. Sometimes, the foreign coproduction firm is so interested in getting on an American network and sees so much value in international sales that it will accept lower payment and put up the extra money itself. An example from the early 1990s was the CBS late-night adventure series *Dark Justice,* produced by Lorimar in association with Spain's TV3, and shot in Barcelona. According to one source, CBS and Lorimar got off relatively cheaply. However, TV3 put up "an enormous amount of money" that brought the program very close to the budget of a prime time show.[29]

A Break in the Walls?

It is difficult to argue that these deals have signaled a revolutionary break in the cultural walls separating mainstream American mass media from voices and images of the rest of the world. For one thing, the networks seem to have decided that these coproductions did not work very well, because they have not repeated them in the mid-1990s. For another, the voices and images these shows projected were hardly those of the rest of the world. Made in English, with characters and plotlines that fit formulas common to U.S. television (*Paris Metal,* for example, dealt with a CIA agent), the output actually underscores how powerful American cultural materials have become. They have even become programs of choice outside the United States. The forms are so popular in such wide areas that even non-American companies want to get in on their international production and distribution.

One interpretation of this phenomenon is that television is becoming globally homogenized along American lines. It seems likely, however, that not all signs of a program's origins will always be erased. Even if created in the American style, programming and musical scores generated in foreign countries by foreign personnel will bring something of the other cultures with them.

Some of the Canal Plus TV movies, for example, will surely be truly French. Over time — and it may be a long time — programs with themes, locales, and sensibilities now absent from American screens will appear with more frequency. An optimist might hope that in a world where Americans are beginning to realize the economic importance of understanding foreign countries, audiences will even begin to welcome TV shows that provide insight into other cultures. Slowly, the face of American programming will accept some views from foreign lands.

CONSIDER THIS

1. Talk to friends from other countries and see how much they learned there about U.S. television and movies. Compare this with your knowledge of television and movies from their countries.
2. In the area of telecommunications, what are the comparative advantages that Japan and Singapore seem to possess? How do these compare to the perceived comparative advantage of the United States?
3. Why might it be argued that an awareness of the popular culture of other societies can be helpful to Americans?

NOTES

1. Carl Bernstein, "The Leisure Empire," *Time,* December 24, 1990, p. 57.
2. Herbert Schiller, *Mass Communication and the American Empire* (New York: Kelley, 1969).
3. Richard Collins, Nicholas Garnham, and Gareth Locksley, *The Economics of Television* (London: Sage, 1988).
4. Don Groves, "MTV Enters USSR," *Variety,* November 12, 1990, p. 58.

5. See Curtis Prendergast with Geoffrey Colvin, *The World of Time Inc.,* vol. 3 (New York: Atheneum, 1986), pp. 369–375.
6. See Sid Adilman, "New Canadian Pic Fund," *Variety,* April 15, 1991, p. 56.
7. Karen Murray, "A Hearing Lands CBC in the Middle of a Flap," *Variety,* April 15, 1991, p. M-98; and Sid Adilman, "Indie Producers Seek Independence," *Variety,* April 15, 1991, p. M-98.
8. "TV Newcomer Grabs a Quarter of the Field," *Variety,* October 29, 1990, p. 40.
9. Carl Bernstein, "The Leisure Empire," *Time,* December 24, 1990, p. 57.
10. Deborah Young, "MEDIA Gets 5-Year Lease on Life in 11th Hour Vote," *Variety,* December 24, 1990, p. 23.
11. Young, p. 23.
12. Young, p. 23; and Morrie Gelman, "Valenti Spurs Pols to Keep U.S. Showbox in GATT Gab," *Variety,* November 12, 1990, p. 12.
13. Gelman, p. 12.
14. Michael Williams and Rex Weiner, "Deep Thaw in Beaune," *Variety,* November 6, 1995, p. 31.
15. "Top Ten US Series," *Rap Ratings Roundup,* March 20, 1995, p. 5.
16. Elizabeth Guider, "US Seller See Green as 'A' Product Pulls Top Coin," *Variety,* October 2, 1995, p. M3.
17. Elizabeth Guider, p. M3.
18. "MTV International," *Broadcasting & Cable,* April 1995, p. 34.
19. See Denis McQuail, *Mass Communication Theory: An Introduction,* 2nd ed. (London: Sage, 1987), pp. 119–121; and S. McBride et al., *Many Voices, One World; Report by the International Commission for the Study of Communication Problems* (Paris: UNESCO, 1980).
20. "Dow Jones Halts Singapore Circulation of the Asian Journal," *Wall Street Journal,* October 15, 1990, p. B7.
21. See McQuail, p. 118.
22. Sheryl Lee, "Tales from the East," *Advertising Age,* October 2, 1995, p. 1.
23. Sheryl Lee, "Hungary's National Daily Makes Gains on Springer," *Advertising Age,* July 17, 1995, p. I-20.
24. Peter Besas, "Mexicans Ride Again in Hispano TV Sweeps," *Variety,* April 11, 1990, p. 41.
25. Will Tusher, "Nation's Screen Tally Reached a New High in '90," *Variety,* January 28, 1991, p. 3.
26. Gelman, p. 12.
27. Charles Fleming, "Bond Bombshell: 007 Goes on the Block," *Variety,* August 8, 1990, p. 1; and Charles Fleming and Richard Natale, "Sequel Opportunity as Film Franchises Falter," *Variety,* June 29, 1991, p. 52.
28. Bruce Alderman, "Cash-Rich French Firms Invest Francs in Film," *Variety,* December 17, 1990, p. 35.
29. "CBS to Co-produce for Prime Time, Late Night," *Broadcasting International* 3:1 (January 1991), pp. 7–8.

CHAPTER 10

The Challenge of Synergy

This chapter

- considers the future of the media system.
- approaches the future by exploring the way media conglomerates are attempting to marshal the resources of their many divisions to work together.
- reflects on the challenges these activities hold for the public.

Turn on broadcast children's television on Saturday morning, and you are likely to see *The Little Mermaid,* the hit cartoon series starring the characters from the hit Disney movie. Go to a toy store, and you will find *Little Mermaid* toys, dolls, coloring books, records, party favors, games. Want more? Your local mall's Disney Store may have videos or other *Little Mermaid* products to sell. But that is not all. For parents, and many children, too, the *Little Mermaid* characters recall the Disney movie version. The movie, in turn, sparks interest in the panoply of Disney animated films. In their original form, they live on on the Disney Channel, Disney's cable TV division, as well as in videos for sale and rent virtually everywhere.

Replicas of the characters and playthings based on them also populate Disney Stores as well as toy stores, comic-book stores, and trade bookstores not owned by the Disney Company. They, in turn, promote California's Disneyland, Florida's Disneyland, and the new Disney theme parks in Japan and France, which, in turn, boost the Disney Stores, the Disney Channel, and all the other Disney products. Disney characters on boxes of food and other products around the world make more money for the company while keeping up with children even when they eat. And with Mickey Mouse as the character introducing every Disney Company video, all of Disney's children's products are bound into continual reference to one another.

Through activities such as these, the Disney Company has achieved a special kind of success. It has been able to make various parts of its business — parts that represent different media — operate so that they help one another. During the 1980s, executives came increasingly to applaud this "synergistic" approach to business. **Synergy** means the coordination of parts of a company so that the whole actually turns out to be worth more than the sum of its parts acting alone. When the TV production division of Disney promotes the company's theme parks and they drum up business for the music and video division, which, in turn, promotes the book division, which, in a circular action, abets the TV division's programming, that is synergy.

The term was so overused that in the 1990s, media leaders have tried to avoid it. Sometimes, they have even played down its importance as a strategy for growth. They have pointed out that many companies have not been as successful as Disney at cross-divisional activities. Still, the process continues briskly among the biggest mass media firms. In fact, synergy has become the hub of a series of related strategies that companies have been using to maximize their presence across as many media channels as possible. These strategies have become major building blocks of the mass media system as it moves into the twenty-first century.

This chapter examines that architecture. Bringing together concepts developed through the course of this book, it explores how companies approach synergy and its related strategies. This chapter also uses present trends to speculate about concerns that executives and consumers might have concerning the future. First, we can assess the effects of synergy and related strategies on the structure of the U.S. mass media system. Then we can consider their implications for the menus of media materials available to different segments of American society.

A basic theme is that media executives' interest in cross-media undertakings built around synergy is a response to a number of key changes that have affected the U.S. and other media systems over the past couple of decades. These executives are using synergy and other cross-media activities to face, and shape, their future amid these developments. In so doing, they are raising important challenges for members of the public as well as for the mass media system.

SYNERGY AND MEDIA FRAGMENTATION

You might remember that in Chapter 1, examples of cross-media ventures similar to Disney's were described as **linking pin activities.** There it was noted that linking pin activities involve the movement of completed material, or of people representing that material, from production firms in one mass media industry to production firms in another mass media industry. From this standpoint, attempts at achieving synergy represent a particular form of linking pin work, one in which the media channels that are used belong mostly to one company. Such a company with many mass media holdings is called a mass media **conglomerate.**

As Chapter 1 suggests, organizations that take on the linking pin power role have always been standard features of mass media systems. Synergy deserves special attention, though. During the past few decades, it has become the strategy of choice for many major media corporations in the United States and elsewhere. But synergy's attractiveness to mass media conglomerates has not been limited to the mass media systems of their home countries. To the contrary, firms have used the approach to organize their cross-media activities across national borders. In other words, synergy has become a central strategy shaping the international mass media system.

The Rise of a Fragmented Media World

This increased concern with synergy is the result of a number of developments in the media world that have threatened long-standing ways in which mass media firms have obtained their resources. The most important of these developments is what people who work in the business commonly call the **fragmentation of audiovisual mass media.** This phrase refers to the splintering of channels during the past two decades so as to theoretically make each channel's percentage of the audience pie smaller. The change has been dramatic. To get a picture of it, consider the media menu that faced most Americans in the early 1970s:

> Watching television meant watching ABC, CBS, or NBC. Public television was available to many communities, but independent commercial broadcast stations were few. Even by 1979, there were only about 100 independent broadcast stations in the United States.
>
> Apart from the relatively new notion of "made-for-TV" movies, seeing a new film meant going to a theater. The home video cassette recorder was not an option. If a person could not see a particular movie in the theater, there was a fair possibility it would show up on one of the TV networks in a few years.
>
> Radio mostly meant listening to AM. The number and popularity of FM stations were still low in most areas.
>
> Besides radio, listening to music via mass media usually meant playing 33⅓ and 45 rpm records. Audio cassettes were just beginning to become popular, with bulky eight-track players competing in the home and car with more streamlined dual-track cassette players. CD laser players were not to be found in either place.
>
> Home computers did not exist. Neither did direct broadcast satellite programming.
>
> Cable television was around, but in a form quite different from that of today. Fewer than 8% of the nation's homes had cable in 1970, and they tended to be in rural areas, where people had difficulty receiving over-

the-air channels.[1] Despite great pronouncements that the medium would create a "wired nation" with a cornucopia of programming choices, cable TV in the early 1970s was essentially a retransmitter of broadcast signals. The cable TV industry generated very little of its revenues through advertising, and pay-TV channels such as HBO were only glimmers on the horizon.

The central elements of the U.S. mass media system in the early 1970s, then, were primarily the traditional publishing enterprises — newspapers, magazines, books, billboards — together with a few audiovisual industries: theatrical movies, vinyl discs, tapes, broadcast TV, and radio. At the time, mass media executives undoubtedly considered the number of basic mass media channels to be quite high. Most of them probably had little inkling of the startlingly greater fragmentation that would exist just twenty years later. By 1994, there were 339 independent TV stations alongside the network affiliates, a 450% increase over the past twenty-five years.[2] Cable TV had spread to about 65% of the nation's homes, along with channels carried only by cable.[3] VCRs could be found in about 85% of U.S. homes, and personal computers, as well as Nintendo-style game computers, were increasingly common among the middle and upper-middle classes.[4]

Threatening Long-Standing Approaches

How has this increased fragmentation of media channels threatened long-standing ways in which media firms have obtained resources and used them efficiently? One part of the answer begins with the effect that fragmentation has had on the size and type of audiences for certain key mass media. The increase in audiovisual channels has tended to decrease the audiences for most individual channels. This is because people have taken advantage of their expanded menus.

According to market research, the shift in habits has been substantial. Particularly surprising has been the weakening of the most widespread distributors of audiovisual entertainment: the commercial television networks. From the earliest commercial TV days of the late 1940s to the mid-1970s, the combined prime time Nielsen shares of ABC, CBS, and NBC totaled at least 90%. This means that 90% of all those watching television were tuned in to one of the broadcast networks. By the early 1990s, however, the three networks' share had slid to approximately 65%. The other 35% belonged to a combination of independent broadcasters and advertiser-supported cable stations, with VCRs also making a showing.

Executives at the major networks angrily contested the Nielsen data in the early 1990s.[5] Major advertisers and their agencies by and large accepted the findings, however. They approached the media system with the aim of finding vehicles with which to reach people they felt were not using broadcast TV as much as before. For many marketers, the reported fractionalization of audiences was convenient because it meshed with an increased interest in reaching ever-narrower slices of the population with messages tailored specifically for them.

Some advertisers looked down on traditional broadcast television as aiming at too many types of people at the same time. Rather than "all women, 18–49 years old," for example, they might be interested in reaching upper-middle-class married women 18 to 25 years old who were working full time and were actively interested in the intellectual growth of their children as well as in purchasing home furnishings. These marketers were looking for distribution channels that deliver desirable **demographic** and **psychographic** categories, as described in Chapter 5. In the evolving U.S. media system, they often concluded that some of the new mass media vehicles, from cable TV channels to home computers, would be better places to find people who fit the profile than at the TV networks, or even at newspapers or radio stations. These marketers began to shift substantial advertising funds away from the networks and toward other forms of media.[6]

This new approach by advertisers caused a ripple effect across the power roles that organizations took on with respect to producers in key industries of the U.S. media system. The situation virtually forced production organizations to design their output with an eye toward moving it across mass media boundaries. The broadcast TV networks were deeply involved in these changes. In their roles of clients for, and distributors of, prime time programs, ABC, CBS, and even leader NBC found that they could not make their money go as far as in decades past.

Firms producing comedies and dramas found network executives more reluctant than ever to pay the full cost of creating series or movies for the privilege of airing each episode or film only a few times. The network people had to insist that since the production firms owned the rights to material, they should cover a fair part of the expenses with the aim of making them up through linking pin activities — in U.S. syndication, on the world market, or in other ways.

New Windows

The new media system was such, however, that even the winners forced producers to move their programs across media boundaries. Ad-supported cable networks, for example, were among the types of firms that were doing better than previously as clients for, and distributors of, programming. In contrast to cable networks in the early 1970s, they were flush with cash from advertising revenues as well as from cable systems on the basis of the number of subscribers. This allowed them to make deals with major production firms for series and made-for-TV movies.

Still, these revenues did not always represent the full cost of creating the materials, and producers often had to approach cable deals with the notion that the expenditures would have to be made up elsewhere. The same was true for cable networks supported not by ads but by subscription — for example, HBO and Showtime. Producers within and outside these organizations realized that to justify the cost of creating "network-quality" fare for these channels, they would have to find opportunities to recover costs elsewhere.

An executive for the Gannett Corporation put the issue this way in 1982: "As audiences become fragmented, the dollars available for programming [on any one channel] will decrease, because everyone's share of the audience will be smaller."[7] The best solution, he said, was not necessarily to make less expensive programming. Rather, it was to evaluate the ability of news and entertainment materials to pay for themselves when moved through different channels, or **windows,** of distribution.

This approach was already becoming standard in the movie industry. When deciding whether or not a film would recoup its costs, planners at the major Hollywood studios were considering more than its ability to pull people into U.S. theaters. They were factoring into their budget estimates of the money the movie would draw across a variety of other windows: foreign theatrical rentals, video cassettes, pay–cable TV, foreign TV, U.S. network TV, local U.S. TV, and basic U.S. cable. The timing of a release from one window to another was planned carefully to maximize the audience at each stage and, by extension, the money the distributor could demand. For example, the time gap between the movement of a film from its first theatrical window to video cassette would have to be long enough so that audiences would not stay away from theaters with the notion of waiting to rent it, but short enough for the target audience to still remember the excitement generated about the film in its initial theatrical release.

This increased emphasis on adding distribution windows because of the increased fractionalization of media led many executives to perceive a strong risk. They reasoned that if competitors could control access to major channels, they could refuse to carry the firm's materials or exact an enormous price for doing so. This could harm the profit-making potential of the firm. On the other side of the coin, taking control over these channels themselves could be richly beneficial. For one thing, cable executives could be sure that the material their firm produced would have at least the opportunity to make its costs back in places they considered appropriate. For another, they could accumulate a great deal of power within the mass media system and still not be subject to restrictions on monopolies that authorities might enforce if they tried to control individual mass media industries.

Executives saw the globalization of mass media activities discussed in Chapter 9 as providing yet another incentive for managing many distribution channels. The international reach of marketers and their advertising agencies, along with the growth of sponsorship-driven broadcasting in many parts of the world, indicated to companies with advertisers as clients that opportunities existed for non-U.S. expansion of their product lines. More generally, growth in an era of giant international mass media corporations seemed based on the idea that companies had to have the ability to play off their production materials in a variety of media in a variety of countries. Not having these channels at a firm's disposal meant not being able to accumulate the resources required to grow strongly. This, in turn, seemed to mean not remaining among the top tier of mass media firms in the United States or elsewhere.

Multimedia Acquisitions

Stock brokerage firms, banks, and other firms taking on the investor power role tended to agree. The general merger-and-acquisition fever throughout U.S. business in the late 1980s and mid-1990s helped fuel public and private enthusiasm for multimedia acquisitions. Some of the biggest deals were Time Inc.'s merger with Warner Communications to form Time Warner; the purchase of MGM's library by Ted Turner; the buyouts of Columbia Pictures, MCA, and 20th Century Fox by Sony, Matsushita, and News Corp, respectively; the purchase of CBS by Westinghouse, of ABC by Disney, and of Turner Broadcasting System by Time Warner.

Even these huge deals, though, do not give the flavor of this ongoing change. The reason is that the number of holdings alone was not the point. Many large media conglomerates, such as General Electric and Times-Mirror, had existed long before the 1980s.

The key change in the 1980s was that conglomeration was now seen as a way to link media holdings actively in the interest of greater profits. Power would accrue not just to those that owned vast media holdings but also to those who could use them synergistically to play out materials across a gamut of holdings for the most value possible. Consider, for example, the following words from a top executive at Time Inc. Magazines, the magazine division of Time Warner. He describes how planners in his firm saw the requirements for a successful company in the fractionalized, globalized mass media environment in the months leading up to Time Inc.'s decision to merge with Warner Communications.

> A media company that intended to compete successfully in this environment would have to be big enough to be heard and big enough to hold consumer attention. It would have to propose products and synergies that only a large, versatile organization could offer.
>
> It'd have to be able to move its products throughout the emerging global marketplace and amortize its costs over as many distribution networks as possible. Advertisers would be demanding more speed, responsiveness, flexibility, and teamwork.
>
> Time, Inc. was big and strong and successful, but not big enough or strong enough for the challenges we saw on the fast-approaching horizon.
>
> Long-term, we saw the world accommodating perhaps a half-dozen global media companies. And we intended to be one of them. Bigness for bigness sake didn't interest us very much. We certainly didn't want to get caught up in an old Gulf and Western or ITT type of diversified conglomerate where the core business can get lost along the way.

What we wanted was solid vertical integration so we could offer synergies that would bring together magazines, publishing ventures, studios, cable channels, and other activities into a coherent operation. We wanted to be able to offer more than the Murdochs and Maxwells of the world.[8]

MAKING SYNERGY WORK

This view of the requirements for being a world-class competitor explains why synergy has been the guiding activity among mass media executives. To talk about synergy and praise its possibilities is not, however, to make it work as its strategists want it to work. In the 1990s, executives in both huge and smaller conglomerates have realized that synergy brings with it problems as well as possibilities.

Perhaps the most obvious difficulty is debt. Most of the giant conglomerates had to borrow tremendous amounts of money in order to carry out their multimedia acquisitions. The Time Warner merger, for example, led to an interest bill of $5 million per day. That kind of burden could make getting cash to respond to future opportunities very difficult. And it poses the danger that top managers could become so preoccupied with paying back debt that they would lose track of the actual media business of their corporation.

Another problem that synergy brings relates to implementing it. After their broadly optimistic statements about the advantages this approach would bring, even after the careful strategic planning that leads to multiple acquisitions and mergers, executives have found that deriving advantages from their new multimedia enterprise is not as easy as it sounds.

One reason is that the people who come from different companies, with different approaches, have no experience working together and thinking about projects that can help other parts of the firm as well. Even more of a problem, perhaps, is the difficulty of knowing how far to go with the strategy. It is not clear that synergy can or should be the core strategy for most firms just because a firm like Disney uses it to great advantage. In tackling their conglomerates' future, executives need to ask basic questions both before and after the acquisition:

Should most of the actions of the firm's divisions be geared to cross-linkages that support the firm as a whole?

Should planners try to think up ways in which the firm can create cross-media activities?

Or should cross-media work be carried out only reactively — that is, only when situations in the environment present clear opportunities for synergy?

These questions have been faced by many mass media corporations in the 1990s. The answers have come slowly, as executives have learned to relate their different divisions to the service of activities that mass media firms have been engaged in for a long time. It is through challenges posed by advertising, creative rights, and public relations that approaches to synergy have evolved.

Advertising, Strategic Partnerships, and Synergy

One obvious way for a mass media firm to use its holdings synergistically is to encourage advertisers to buy ads across them. A corporation that owns several newspapers might induce national sponsors to buy space across most of its dailies. A company with radio networks and billboards might sell time across both media. A firm with several magazine titles and a number of TV stations might offer that cross-title *and* cross-media buy.

Of course, offering these deals is different from getting advertisers to accept them. To be persuaded, sponsors would need a good reason to believe that they will get a better deal when working with a multititle or multimedia company than if they approach firms with only one individual outlet. One way they might be convinced would be to offer a lower price for purchasing the package than that of an à la carte approach. A multichannel offer would also be attractive if the package put together by the media firm fit the audience profiles that marketers were targeting. If a company's radio networks and billboards tended mainly to reach an audience of African-American consumers, for example, it might make the joint offer attractive to certain advertisers.

It was not until the 1980s that many media firms began to try to find or create synergies among their divisions that could be used to pursue increased advertising revenues. Often, competitive pressures in the environment led executives to look in that direction.

The Case of Magazines

Consumer magazines in the 1990s provide a good example. Executives in this industry faced a relatively "soft" advertising market, partly because of a sluggish economy; marketers making less money were placing fewer ads. The magazine ad decline was also partially due to a decision by many advertisers to shift substantial portions of their ad funds to other kinds of marketing activities.

This grim situation led magazine executives to offer clients more for their money in order to attract a greater share of a shrinking magazine advertising pie. They set up ad packages across different magazines (**cross-title packages**) and across different media (**cross-media packages**) that offered substantial discounts on costs per thousand compared to their own individual title buys as well as those of their competitors.

The action that especially set the course toward package discount was an announcement by the Time Inc. Magazines division of Time Warner that it would be offering to advertisers large discounts if they advertised in a package of the firm's very popular consumer magazines: *Time, Fortune, Life, Sports Illustrated, Money,* and *People.* This move shook up the industry. Hearst Corporation, Murdoch Magazines, and the New York Times Company's magazine group were among the largest conglomerates with substantial magazine holdings that announced internal discount programs.[9]

Another result was that executives in firms with only one or two consumer magazines felt threatened, especially if their titles competed directly with one or more periodicals in the lineups of the larger competitors. The solution some found was to search out marketing alliances with other, often bigger, firms that could fold the one or two periodicals into a strong package that would offer an attractive discount. *Newsweek,* the only periodical owned by the Washington Post Company and a direct competitor with *Time* for ad dollars, is one magazine that felt a great deal of pressure to look for alliances. The Time Inc. Magazines discount announcement was followed by several weeks of gloom-and-doom talk by ad industry pundits about *Newsweek*'s inability to survive in the wake of its arch rival's discount coup.

Eventually, *Newsweek*'s executives formed a strategic sales partnership with the huge Times-Mirror conglomerate's substantial magazine group to offer discounts to advertisers. The idea seemed to be catching on, both within and across mass media. As the trade magazine *Advertising Age* noted, the relationships helped both sides: "While the larger companies have been able to increase the number of ad vehicles for advertisers, smaller companies get a boost in credibility and a surge in audience by linking with bigger players."[10]

Strategic Partnerships

The last two examples highlight an important feature of the cross-media activities that conglomerates have been carrying out. While they have tried to maximize the in-house synergies that can be achieved, they have gone outside the conglomerate to use the channels of other firms if linkups could be profitable. The phenomenon is by no means limited only to magazines. In 1991, for example, Turner Broadcasting System's Cable News Network (CNN) and Gannett's daily *USA Today* newspaper began offering advertisers sponsorship of a joint Cable News Network–*USA Today* weekly college sports poll. Sponsors would be credited in both the print and TV versions. At around the same time, *U.S. News & World Report* magazine and NBC's Consumer News and Business Channel (CNBC) on cable TV announced a deal that allowed advertisers to buy space in annual guides published by *U.S. News* along with CNBC specials based on the guides.[11]

Executives call such joint ventures **strategic partnerships.** In carrying them out, executives of large conglomerates have often made deals with mid-size and small mass media firms as well as other huge conglomerates. From the standpoint of the giant companies, deals with mid-size and small firms often expand the conglomerate's coverage in particular media industries. As for the smaller firms, they have been pushed toward such linkups in order to stay alive. Strategic partnerships with the largest firms are often viewed by executives as the best way to stay afloat in a tumultuous environment in which a few large companies are dictating the rules of the game within and across mass media industries. Going it alone seems to be near-suicidal.

"Linking with bigger players," in fact, appears to be even more popular across mass media industries than within them. In the case of advertiser-sponsored mass media, a good deal of the encouragement to connect big and small mass media firms across industry boundaries has come from large marketers such as General Motors and Kraft General Foods. They want their advertising agencies and the mass media they use to help them maximize the efficiency with which they reach their target consumers. By *efficiency,* they mean hitting only those people the marketer has determined are potential buyers of the particular product. Marketers have refined their understanding of such target consumer groups through batteries of market research techniques, including the focus groups and data bases discussed in Chapter 5. The result is that reaching likely consumers has become a process of understanding their life activities and following them through the course of their day as they turn to different sources for news and entertainment. The chief executive of DDB Needham Worldwide, New York, a major advertising agency, noted that this change has been making his firm's media buyers think of mass media in new ways:

> We have 12 major clients on our personal media network, tracking prospects by using syndicated and proprietary research. We are no longer thinking media form or media vehicles until we have tracked the target consumer. We no longer think of print vs. TV vs. radio but rather in terms of how can we combine vehicles to which the consumer is extremely loyal in some sensible consumer pattern and also come out that smaller might be better and more protective.[12]

Clearly, this approach rewards companies that can help marketers send ads to targeted consumers efficiently across several of their own media channels as well as across channels with which they have established strategic advertising partnerships. Picking up on this trend, the Time Magazines division of Time Warner pioneered a technique of joining computer data bases on its magazines' subscribers to high-speed printing and binding technologies.

Using the data bases, the company can single out for an advertiser likely targets among the subscribers of *Time, Sports Illustrated, People, Money, Fortune,* and *Life.* It can then individualize the message of an ad to match the subscriber's interests or lifestyle. Finally, it can bind different individualized ads into the regular issue of the various magazines during the regular process of printing and mailing. To both Time Warner and interested advertisers, this activity takes advantage of the synergies of different subscriber data bases in the service of advertising efficiency.

SYNERGY BEYOND ADVERTISING

As the 1990s have unfolded, marketers and mass media executives have extended their interest in synergy beyond the realm of advertising. They have contended that setting up vehicles for efficient advertising should be only one factor guiding approaches to synergy in mass media corporations. Just as important, they have claimed, is the need for mass media firms to guide their divisions toward serving many broad marketing needs of their clients.

The reason behind this broadened approach is mass media executives' realization that marketers have begun to reevaluate their strategies to encourage sales. Advertising has long been king of the hill when it comes to marketing consumer products. Of secondary note have been various kinds of promotion and direct marketing.

Direct marketing involves contacting individual prospects by phone, computer, or mailed catalogs. A **promotion** is a specific act that calls attention to a firm or its products in ways other than advertising. Examples are such tactics as skywriting or underwriting sporting events (activities called **event marketing**), creating contests, giving free gifts **(premiums),** offering discounts, and even giving salespeople cash incentives to persuade stores to push the products on consumers.

Traditionally, companies marketing to the general public have treated advertising funds as separate from, and more important than, promotion and direct marketing monies. In recent years, though, marketing executives in many firms have concluded that advertising should not automatically be given higher standing than other methods of reaching potential customers.[13] One explanation for this change in attitude is the belief that modern data bases on customers allow implementation of promotion and direct-marketing efforts in ways that are more precise than advertising in traditional mass media.

In addition, some executives support promotion over advertising because they feel promotion holds greater credibility with the consumer. Marketers know that advertising calls attention to the fact that the marketer is trying to manipulate the consumer, which the latter may resent. Activities such as the support and underwriting of sporting events, however, may be evaluated favorably by target customers as indicating the firm's sincere interest in their lifestyles. The marketers believe that although promotions are more subtle than advertising, they can sometimes be more effective in creating good feelings about the marketer, which may translate into long-term product purchases.

In the 1990s, commercial on-line services such as American Online and the public Internet service have become popular promotion vehicles for advertisers and media firms trying to attract advertisers. Almost every major advertiser has created a home page on the World Wide Web. The "Web," as it is called, is a section of the Internet that accommodates graphics easily. A **home page** is an area of the Web created and maintained by a person or organization. Zima Clear Malt's home page is chock-full of information about Zima, a made-for-the-Web soap opera, and an interactive refrigerator.

Media companies have also created home pages that reflect the personality they have cultivated in print, broadcast, film, and video. Disney has a Web page, as does virtually every major magazine and motion picture firm. NBC and Microsoft, the huge computer firm, jointly run a Web page as well as a cable network, MSNBC. The aim of many of these sites is promotional — to highlight the activities of the company to the millions of young adults, mostly male and affluent, who use the service. Increasingly, though, media firms see their on-line activities as potentially profitable businesses that go beyond highlighting the firm's activities in other media to deliver entertainment, news, and information. The MSNBC Web site, for example, draws on the software capabilities of Microsoft and the news archives of NBC to allow users to access photos of famous events and request the routine transmission of information (stock quotes, the weather) customized for the person making the request.

Although some companies charge individuals fees for certain Web services, most hope to pay for their on-line sites by enlisting advertisers' interest in promoting their own on-line sites to their target audiences. For example Zima in the mid-1990s was paying *Wired* magazine's *Hotwired* site thousands of dollars for a **hot link** (a direct click on the computer mouse) to its home page. Marketers and media firms were also trying furiously to make on-line services secure enough for use in efficient direct marketing.

This increased emphasis on promotion and direct marketing, along with a decrease in advertising expenditures in some areas, has been leading executives in mass media conglomerates to work on ways in which they can profit from the trend. They have been asking two questions: How can we find synergies between our media holdings that can meet our firm's needs for promotion and direct marketing? And how can we find synergies between our media holdings that can encourage marketers outside our firm to approach us with their promotion and direct-marketing funds, in addition to their advertising funds? They have begun to find answers by exploring synergies that can result from two broad types of marketing activities they carry out: the sale of creative rights and the use of value-added incentives.

Creative Rights and Synergy

Creative rights are the legal control that organizations exercise over characters, titles, and other original materials their personnel have generated in the course of creating mass media materials. The Nine Inch Nails recording group owns the rights to its name and image, for example; anyone using it without permission (a license) may be sued. Children's Television Workshop controls the use of Big Bird, the name *Sesame Street,* and its **logo** (the design that expresses the organization's name). Similarly, the Dow Jones Company owns the rights to news stories that appear in its *Wall Street Journal,* whether printed or carried electronically in computer data bases.

The licensing of creative rights allows a production firm to make money from its creations in forms that go beyond their initial purpose.[14] Firms paying for the right to use the characters, titles, or logos expect a large benefit in return. They hope that the increased costs they incur for adding the images to their products will be more than made up by the instant recognition and interest the mass media images bring with them. For example, some parents would pay more for a pacifier with Big Bird's picture on it than for one with designs that are unconnected to any personalities they know.

Although the sale of creative rights often occurs with mass media materials that are used by children, adults have by no means been excluded. In the early 1990s, when Cher and Sheena Easton appeared in commercials for Bally's Health and Tennis Clubs, their images from films and records were the assets the advertiser was actually buying. Such assets can become big business in the adult realm. Consider publishers that have sold film rights to books they published for millions of dollars. Or the several celebrities who have clothing and perfumes, even spaghetti sauces, named after them.

Despite such occasional bonanzas, for decades creative rights held little interest for the profit-making potential of mass media firms. Their relatively minor importance is reflected in the term by which they were called in media industries: **subsidiary rights.** The word *subsidiary* referred as much to the marginal place of these activities in the production firm as to the monetary value of such rights. Creative rights activities were typically divorced from the larger strategic concerns of the firm. They involved merely arranging agreements with companies that wanted to use certain characters or logos for their own benefit and were often handled by a division of low status in the firm.

Times have changed. In an era of mass media conglomerates, companies have increasingly found that their rights to characters, plots, images, logos, and even news can be used synergistically to fuel lucrative activities throughout the firm. Product development teams can concentrate on images that are exploitable in different mass media by various divisions in the firm, or through strategic alliances with other companies. Here are some examples:

- Sony Corporation, which owns Sony Music (formerly called CBS Records), Columbia Pictures, and the Columbia House mail-order business, has been finding ways to make the three work together. Creative rights have been an important consideration in this area. In 1991, for example, Sony signed recording artist Michael Jackson to a feature film to be produced and released through Sony's Columbia Pictures. At the time, Jackson was a major moneymaker for Sony's CBS Records division. It undoubtedly made sense to Sony's management to maximize the cross-media nature of their relationship with Jackson in the interest of both the record division and the corporation as a whole. Columbia noted that other such crossover projects were in the works.[15]
- Mass media mogul Ted Turner has made linking creative rights from his various holdings a mandatory part of the work of his executives. In 1991, Turner Publishing and Citadel Press coproduced a book called *Kisses* as a Valentine's Day gift. The book included 150 pages of black-

TABLE 10.1 THE RETAIL VALUE OF LICENSED MERCHANDISE

Product Category	1989	1988	1987	1986	1985	1984	1983	1982	1981
Apparel and accessories	35.5%	35.0%	34.5%	34.6%	36.0%	38.0%	38.0%	38.0%	32.0%
Toys and games	12.0	13.0	14.0	15.5	17.0	19.0	20.0	19.0	23.5
Publishing stationery	10.5	11.0	11.5	11.5	12.0	12.0	15.0	14.0	16.5
Gifts and novelties	10.0	10.0	9.0	9.0	9.0	11.0	13.0	10.0	10.0
Home furnishings housewares	10.5	9.5	9.0	8.0	8.0	7.0	8.0	9.0	8.0
Sporting goods	3.0	3.0	3.0	3.0	2.0	2.0	3.0	5.0	5.0
Other	0.5	0.5	1.5	2.0	2.0	2.0	3.0	5.0	5.0
Foods and beverages	8.0	8.0	8.0	7.0	7.0	5.0	—	—	—
Health and beauty aids	5.0	5.0	5.0	5.0	4.5	3.0	—	—	—
Electronics	5.0	5.0	4.5	4.5	2.5	1.0	—	—	—
Total dollar value retail (in billions)	$64.6	$59.8	$55.9	$54.3	$50.1	$40.1	$26.7	$20.6	$13.7

SOURCE: Advertising Age, Advertising supplement on Licensing, May 28, 1990, p. L4.

Tying into an image that has high mass media visibility is a key aim of licensing, which accounts for more than $60 billion in retail U.S. sales.

and-white photos from Turner Entertainment's MGM archive. At the time of its release, Turner's TNT cable channel aired a TV special tied to the book and its subject. The strategy was clear: The firm's film library inspired the book, and the firm's cable channel would help promote it. "Whereas a lot of big corporations talk about synergy," boasted the head of Turner Publishing, "at Turner synergy exists routinely."[16]

- Knight-Ridder, Inc. is best known to many Americans for its twenty-eight daily newspaper holdings, including the *Philadelphia Inquirer,* the *Detroit Free Press,* and the *Miami Herald.* During the 1980s, however, the firm drew on the information-gathering expertise developed by its news divisions to fuel its growth as a vendor of news-related data bases for businesses. Knight-Ridder's Business Information Services Group includes a variety of divisions that can easily draw on one another and on the firm's news operations. Especially notable are Dialog Information Services, the world's largest on-line and full-text information source; Vu/text, a data base containing the full text of more than fifty newspapers and more than twenty other publications; and Knight-Ridder Financial News, a worldwide, real-time news service delivered via computer to major participants in the financial marketplace.[17]

- The Dow Jones Company, owner of the *Wall Street Journal,* the leading national business newspaper, and of *Barron's,* a business weekly, has also used its expertise in creating business news to enter the information marketplace. In 1980, the firm started its Information Services Group to coordinate the computerization and marketing of information that Dow thought it could sell. In 1990, the group merged its electronic libraries with those of Datatimes, a firm owned by Dow Jones and the Oklahoma Publishing Company. As a result, Dow Jones has been selling researchers the right to search electronically through the computerized files of 640 newspapers, magazines, news services, and financial data sources — its own and others.[18]

In all these examples, creative rights from particular divisions typically benefit other divisions within the conglomerate in addition to making profits on their own. A twist in this pattern that is common among entertainment conglomerates is to promote division activities even further through deals with outside marketers. The Disney Company's movement of its characters across a maze of both Disney-owned and non-Disney-owned products is a case in point. As described earlier, Disney's children's book division, video division, store division, and theme park division reinforce one another through extensive crossovers. Yet the company also promotes its own creations by leasing the creative rights for Mickey Mouse, Donald Duck, and other characters to clothing companies, food firms, and other manufacturers. Those companies, in turn, benefit from the cross-media exposures within the Disney conglomerate.

TALKING POINT 10.1   Licensing Hype

Licensing companies are constantly trying to sell their creative rights to toy manufacturers, clothing companies, sporting equipment companies — anyone who will pay to put the licenser's name in a place that will help the image sell even more. The result is that hyperbole comes with the territory.

Imagine a license seller trying to peddle a client's image to a toy maker. Here, according to *Variety,* are licensing's "top ten hypes":

10. The days of just slapping a license on everything that moves are over.
 9. They offered it to us first, but we decided to take a pass.
 8. It's going to be bigger than Batman.
 7. We don't want to overplay the merchandise at the expense of the programming.
 6. We've turned down over 100 licensees already.
 5. We're not just selling a product, we're selling an attitude.
 4. It's similar to the Turtles, only better.
 3. You don't have to hit a home run every time up. There's nothing wrong with singles and doubles.
 2. We're only aligning ourselves with quality vendors.
 1. You can fool parents and you can fool Wall Street, but you can't fool a child.

SOURCE: *Variety,* May 30, 1990, p. 41.

Another tactic used by conglomerates to attract marketers to their cross-media promotion synergies is called **product placement.** This involves charging manufacturers for the use of their products as part of the action in movies. In 1991, for instance, Disney was demanding $20,000 for a visual, $40,000 for a brand-name mention with a visual, and $60,000 for an actor to use the product in one of its movies, *Mr. Destiny.*[19]

As this example suggests, most product placements are made in movies initially bound for the theaters. Still, manufacturers benefit from a movie conglomerate's synergies with its other divisions, because those movies later move through a number of the conglomerate's divisions, including home video, network television sales, and syndication. Manufacturers that link up with films in this way often build their own ad campaigns and promotions around their product as it moves through the various media windows. They might even lease creative rights from the media firm to hype their product. Consider the presence of Teenage Mutant Ninja Turtles on Domino's Pizza boxes as a result of using this food in the Turtles' first live-action film.

Value-Added Incentives and Synergy

Apart from the exploitation of creative rights, executives in some mass media conglomerates have been moving toward a second way to find synergies in their holdings: a **value-added incentive.** This means that a mass media outlet (such as a magazine or radio station) promises a marketer extra inducements if it uses the outlet for advertising.

The kinds of incentives offered have been evolving over the past several years. Although long popular on radio (where DJs would plug products on and off the air), value-added inducements were once considered shady and relegated to the margins of many mass media industries. For instance, segments of the business periodical press were known for a value-added practice that was not considered legitimate among most media practitioners. A publisher of a trade newspaper might promise an advertiser that if the firm bought ad space in a forthcoming issue, the newspaper would write a favorable article about the firm in the following issue. Such activities, though not infrequent, were (and generally still are) considered unethical.

Since the late 1980s, however, the notion of a value-added incentive has taken on strong legitimacy and new meaning as executives in mass media conglomerates attract advertisers to individual outlets by offering benefits of synergies with other parts of the corporation. Much of this activity has taken place in magazine divisions. A major reason is economic; in the early 1990s, many magazines were hard hit by declining advertising revenues.

One cause of this decline was the nation's economic recession, which affected the earnings of companies and lowered the amount they could spend on advertising. Another cause was the decreasing attractiveness to advertisers of several types of periodicals (notably, the major women's magazines) because of declining newsstand sales. A third factor was the advertisers' shifting movement of some funds away from magazines. The cash was used to support other mass media, such as cable TV, as well as promotion and direct-marketing work.

As these problems grew, both marketing and magazine executives suggested that the companies responding most creatively to the situation were those going beyond their roles of selling space to advertisers in the issues of individual titles. They were working with the marketer to create inserts, publicity materials, point-of-purchase tie-ins to the ads — even videos — that would help tell the marketer's story in ways that would extend the advertising.

These activities sometimes encouraged magazine owners to develop mass media expertise beyond their periodicals. Meredith Publications, publisher of *Metropolitan Home* until the mid-1990s, provides a good example. In an attempt to work out a lucrative advertising deal with Kraft Foods, Meredith suggested to Kraft that they work together to create cookbooks and contests that would extend the message of the ads beyond individual issues. Similarly, in structuring a magazine advertising sale with the Sherwin-Williams paint company, Meredith became closely involved in an extensive promotion campaign

TABLE 10.2 STRATEGIC PARTNERS IN TOYLAND

Toy Maker	Product	Partner
Bandai America	Mighty Morphin Power Rangers	Syndicated TV Series
	Teenage Mutant Ninja Turtles	Syndicated TV Series
Hasbro (Kenner division)	Batman Forever	Syndicated TV Series
	VR Troopers	Syndicated TV Series
Tyco	Little Mermaid dolls and toys	Saturday Morning TV Series
Hasbro (Playschool division)	Barney	TV Series on PBS

SOURCE: Advertising Age, *February 20, 1995, p. 38.*

A small sample of popular toys shows the importance of close alliances between toy manufacturers and other media. Increasingly among toy manufacturers, TV has become the medium of choice. The TV series in particular, along with traditional ads, movies, and cross-promotional tie-ins, provide toy manufacturers with several opportunities to form partnerships.

for the firm's products. The marketing plan included in-store displays, books, and videos in addition to the magazine ads.[20]

Another example is a deal *Sports Illustrated* magazine announced with Diet Pepsi. Pepsi agreed to commit to two years of advertising in the magazine. In exchange, the magazine created an elaborate consumer promotion for Pepsi that would be highlighted in two midwinter issues. Called "Right Ones Fantasy Sports Vacation," it gave winners one of seven "fantasy vacations." Diet Pepsi paid for the trips while *Sports Illustrated's* event marketing staff handled the logistics. As an additional link to the *Sports Illustrated* image, Pepsi agreed to sponsor a "Super Shape-Up" trilogy of fitness home videos that *Sports Illustrated* was creating for release by its Time Warner parent.[21]

Putting It All Together

Just how synergistic such linkups could become in the service of advertising, promotion, and direct marketing can be seen in a Time Warner deal with Chrysler Corporation that was much larger than the *Sports Illustrated* – Pepsi linkup. When it was announced in 1990, everyone in the marketing business was certain that the $40 – $50 million contract was the largest of its kind. The agreement, which was to extend for over two years, opened the door for the automaker to use all the media firm's divisions.

Creative rights and value-added incentives would be interconnected. The theme for Chrysler's 1992 campaign, "Rediscover America," would be subtly tied to the five-hundredth anniversary of Christopher Columbus's first voyage to the New World. This connection would be drawn through an elaborate cross-media marketing campaign using eleven **advertorials** (long ads with social points of view) inserted in five Time Warner magazines. In addition, the Time Magazines division of Time Warner would create special issues of *Fortune, People,* and *Life* in which the automaker would be the only advertiser. Beyond using Time Warner's extensive magazine resources to get its ad messages out in these traditional and nontraditional ways, Chrysler also expected to target customers using the magazine division's selective binding and ink-jet printing technologies.

As incentives and premiums in this marketing effort, Chrysler would use products from Time Warner's Warner Bros. Records, Time-Life Books, and Time-Life Videos divisions.[22] Going beyond the Columbus theme, Chrysler also said it would be using other Time Warner divisions to help it reach likely customers. Warner Bros. Television and another Time Warner division, Lorimar Productions, would develop TV programming for Chrysler to sponsor. Chrysler would place its cars for publicity purposes in Warner Bros. movies. And, to bring Time Warner's expertise directly to the showroom floor, Chrysler would use Time Warner Direct Marketing to aid in local dealers' sales efforts.

People in the advertising industry heralded the deal as signifying the future. A vice-president for the Ogilvy & Mather Worldwide ad agency claimed that "joint marketing efforts with publications are just another type of nontraditional media activity we must get involved in because of the changing media environment, the changing society."[23] His counterpart at the Bozell agency agreed and suggested that mass media firms that took advantage of the synergies possible through cross-media ownerships and strategic partnerships would have distinct advantages. The challenge for mass media executives and marketing executives, he noted, lay in finding the most effective synergies. "Integrated communications programs," he concluded, "are going to become much more of a factor in the 1990s and beyond."[24]

CHALLENGES FOR THE PUBLIC

"Integrated communication programs" and other new features of the mass media environment raise an important question for society as a whole: How will these developments affect the news, information, and entertainment flowing through mainstream media channels as the world moves toward the next century? The answers are not yet clear. Nevertheless, examining the evolving media system with a critical eye on this question is necessary if members of the public are to understand the forces shaping the way they think about and act in the world.

The final pages of this book are aimed at igniting speculation on this subject. No attempt is made here to be inclusive, to cover every challenge to the public that mass media synergies may bring. Instead, the following issues are raised briefly as examples of the kinds of concerns that ought to be discussed and investigated. Among them are conglomerates' control over the mainstream menus of choice; the changing relationship between marketing, news, and entertainment; and the gap between "knowledge-rich" and "knowledge-poor."

Conglomerates and Menus of Choice

When fragmentation of mass media due to the spread of cable TV and VCRs began in the 1970s, some observers hoped that the multitude of channels would offer a large number of options for unusual choices that challenge the boundaries of typical news and information offerings. Some optimists still hold out this hope, pointing to the new streams of information, news, and entertainment that fiber-optic, computer, and video disc technologies can bring into the home. They insist that these technologies will force a diversity of voices to be presented to the great proportion of the population.

This does not seem to be the case, however. To the contrary, the way mass media systems have been developing in the United States, Europe, and Japan, it is likely that menus of choice will not be nearly as diverse as they might at first appear. The reasons are industrial, political, and economic. A counterforce to fragmentation has developed: conglomeration.

Earlier in this chapter, an executive at Time Warner was quoted that his company "saw the world accommodating perhaps a half-dozen global media companies." He also noted that "bigness for bigness sake" did not interest Time Warner. Rather, what the firm wanted was "solid vertical integration so [it] could offer synergies that would bring together magazines, publishing ventures, studios, cable channels, and other activities into a coherent operation."

Time Warner is not alone in voicing the expectation that six to ten mass media giants will develop by the turn of the century. By many accounts, the mainstream mass media channels in the United States and much of the world will be managed in one way or another by a small number of global firms acting to make the most of the synergies among their holdings.

The consequences of this remain to be seen. However, by their actions, Time Warner and other conglomerates have already indicated a number of probable consequences. One has to do with the range of choices that will be available across the most important TV stations, radio stations, newspapers, cable stations, video stores, and bookstores. Increasingly, these channels are becoming extensions of one another. VCR stores extend the reach of theatrical films; theatrical films extend the reach of books; music videos, on TV or video cassette, extend the reach of CD and tape recordings — all in the interest of a conglomerate's synergy. The result is to offer not content diversity but **time-shifting capability** — that is, the capability to listen, read, or watch something at one time rather than another.

This does not mean that a few companies will "lock up" and determine all the choices that face individuals when they watch TV, read books, go to movies, or watch VCRs. In democratic capitalist societies, there will always be room to start up independent firms that aim to be heard. In an age of conglomerates, though, these firms, even while increasing in number, may be pushed to the margins of their industries even more than before.

The reasons have to do with production costs and distribution clout. The large and mid-size conglomerates will be able to attract investments to create the materials they need to shape the synergies they want across media. Small companies that go with the typical flow of content and make deals to link up with the conglomerates will make it into the mainstream as well. On the other side, firms that steadfastly try to challenge the formulas of mainstream mass media will probably find it increasingly difficult to approach the busiest public outlets. People may well have to look hard to find their products, if they can find them at all.

Links between Marketing, News, and Entertainment

Countering the potential diversity possible with channel fragmentation might be only one consequence of conglomerates' push toward synergies. The process seems, in addition, to be encouraging new, potentially problematic links between marketing, news, and entertainment. Tendencies are at work that may encourage practices that were unacceptable to mass media workers just a few years ago.

As Chapter 4 notes, marketing needs have always shaped the kinds and amounts of news and entertainment available to different publics. If advertisers wanted to sponsor a TV news series, for example, it would be broadcast. If not, the company might not find the resources to air it. Stories have also long circulated about direct influences that marketers have had over the selection and display of particular news items. For example, powerful advertisers have occasionally used their power over newspaper publishers to get favorable mention or to exclude items that might harm them. Generally, though, such leverage has been considered disreputable. Over the decades, major mass media companies have made a public point of not allowing direct pressures from clients to influence the presentation of specific stories.

Similarly, journalistic organizations have long touted the creation of newswork as separate and distinct from the creation of entertainment. As noted in Chapter 1, both kinds of mass media work involve telling stories that cast up images of society for society. News executives, however, have always insisted that their creative personnel follow different rules than the creators of entertainment. Newspaper reports, broadcast documentaries, newsmaker interviews, and evening news spots are expected to stick to the facts in ways that fictional presentations do not. One reason news organizations have kept a distance from entertainment is to assure the public that news holds a credibility regarding "the facts" that neither marketing nor entertainment has.

The rise of synergy-oriented conglomerates that have both news and entertainment divisions under their umbrellas has raised the strong possibility that the long-standing tradition separating news from marketing and entertainment is in danger of breaking down. The mandate of synergy may be altering the norm that newsworkers separate their stories from the stories their advertisers tell. The cross-media deals that firms such as Time Warner and Meredith have formed with marketers such as Chrysler and Kraft seem to ignore many questions about the relationship between sponsorship and editorial matter that in previous years would have raised powerful doubts in the minds of news professionals over the wisdom of making such connections.

How, for example, would *Time* editors and writers cover a story embarrassing to Chrysler or other automakers during the two years in which Chrysler was becoming identified with the news magazine and other Time Warner products? More to the point, what kind of credibility would any type of coverage of this sort have for the magazine when it would be clearly identified with Chrysler? And what is a media observer to think when an entire special issue of *Time* or *Fortune* or *Sports Illustrated,* sponsored by one marketer, is devoted to subjects that are involved intimately with that marketers' products?

Even if no executives from the advertiser or its agency were involved directly with the articles, would the creators of such custom-made issues not tilt their stories to create an environment and perspectives that mesh with the marketer's desired image?

It may be that questions were asked, and satisfactorily answered, by Time Warner and its advertisers. Perhaps they were answered less satisfactorily at Meredith, Hearst, or other magazine firms following the same strategy. At any rate, during this period of profound change in the mass media system, readers should demand public answers to these questions.

They should also ask questions when conglomerates appear to be dropping distinctions between news and entertainment in the interest of synergy. Here, again, Time Warner provides a good example, because it has been so blatant in proclaiming its interest in using its various divisions for the good of the larger corporation. Careful observers of the media business noted that the Time merger with Warner had immediate impact on the flagship magazine's coverage: *Time* was highly favorable in its coverage of the controversial merger as it unfolded and as Paramount Communications tried to derail it. When the merger was finally completed, at a huge debt to the merged corporation and lower profits to shareholders than otherwise might have been the case, the magazine's editors purposely avoided reporting on it. The magazine's editors knew that word of the merger had leaked to the *Los Angeles Times.* Yet the editor-in-chief, after consulting with the business side of the firm, decided not to cover it. The excuse of *Time*'s editors was that because the word came close to deadline, they would not have been able to put a balanced story together for that week's edition. Others, however, felt that hesitation to report on their own company had much to do with this omission.[25]

This consequence of the merger hardly made a ripple in other media. A conflict of interest that did reach the public stage related to the handling of author Scott Turow and his hit books *Presumed Innocent* and *The Burden of Proof.* At the precise moment when Warner Books was releasing *Presumed*

Innocent in paperback and a few months before Warner Bros. would release the film version, *Time* magazine drew up a cover story on the author that trumpeted both the book and the film.

Both on and off the record, *Time* magazine executives have denied an interest in using their journalistic media to hype their entertainment products, in this or any other situation.[26] They point to a long tradition of separating the editorial process ("the church") from business and marketing ("the state"), a tradition stronger than that in any other magazine firm. Moreover, they argue that such activities could weaken their journalistic credibility over time.

This claim might hold up if readers, viewers, and listeners really knew of the bewildering maze of ownerships and relations that exist within the mass media system. It is unreasonable to expect that people will keep up on such links. As for the church-state separation blocking attempts on the part of other Time Warner divisions to use the magazines to hype their activities, that tradition may well make such conflicts less likely than in other firms. Nevertheless, conversations with writers and executives at *Time* suggest that the division is getting fuzzier as the Warner Communications entertainment culture begins to take hold.

One *Time* writer, for example, said that although he was sure from personal experience that the Scott Turow case was not orchestrated to help Warner Books and Warner Bros., he was convinced that conniving of this sort was going on. He pointed to a *Time* article about *Scarlett,* a big Warner Books sequel to *Gone with the Wind,* which had appeared far in advance of the book's release to the public. The purpose of the *Time* piece, he suggested, was to generate public interest in the manuscript so that the book company could make a lot of money selling the paperback and movie rights to other firms.

Whether this inference was correct or not, it indicates that even people in the magazine company believe these sorts of "church-state" violations are going on. It also suggests the confusion and concern felt by people in the know, and even at one of the most highly respected journalistic firms. Most of the time, such concerns are not voiced outside the firm. In the Scott Turow incident, public discussion of *Time*'s conflict of interest was sparked by an article in *Time*'s rival, *Newsweek* magazine, which sniped at the act.

Newsweek's vigilance, however, may well have been a one-shot deal, peculiar to that point in time. It seems to have been written, half-jokingly, by a *Newsweek* staffer who had left *Time*. Moreover, it appeared as the advertising trade press was predicting *Newsweek*'s declining appeal to Madison Avenue; its owner, the Washington Post Company, had nowhere near the cross-media property of *Time*'s parent. Observers speculated that *Newsweek* would not be able to compete with *Time*'s decision to offer deep discounts to clients who purchased advertising in several Time Warner properties at the same time. *Newsweek*'s instigation of the public controversy about *Time* may have been motivated in part by personal jealousy and corporate fear.

A few weeks after the incident, though, *Newsweek* signed a cross-media advertising agreement with the huge Times-Mirror conglomerate. Now it was in the orbit of a firm with major interests in synergies. As a result, *Newsweek* was in a position that might inhibit its executives from making a big deal about such things in print. In fact, as news-entertainment synergies within conglomerates become common, *Newsweek*'s chastisement of *Time* over Scott Turow could be viewed as one of the last gasps of old values in an old system. Executives in mainstream mass media organizations may hold little interest in exposing the complex conflicts of interest over news and entertainment, because they might be involved in such activities themselves.

SOME FINAL QUESTIONS

The increasing ability of wealthy corporations to tinker with the mainstream menus of news and entertainment that people confront in their daily lives brings up a clutch of additional questions. For example:

> How will the growth of data bases on target audiences affect the way mass media conglomerates create materials? Will the targeting of audiences and the fragmentation of mass media result in separation between the kinds of material to which relatively poor and unattractive groups in society have access and the kinds aimed at relatively well-off and attractive groups? If so, what will this increasing "information gap" imply about the different pictures people from the "preferred" and "unpreferred" parts of society have about each other and the rest of the world?

> Will the mandate toward synergies within mass media conglomerates encourage or discourage unconventional thinking by creative personnel? To what extent will creators move freely across divisions, and if they do, what will this mean for the materials they create?

> How will new relationships between divisions within mass media conglomerates affect the way people are hired and trained by the conglomerates? As noted in Chapter 7, members of minority groups have often tended to be pigeonholed in certain segments of certain industries. In large recording companies, for example, African-American executives have usually been assigned to black music divisions. To what extent will the evolving conglomerates, searching for synergies across divisions, allow greater mobility of all types of employees across divisions? And how will this affect the kinds of mass media materials the firms produce?

> What consequences will the search for synergy have for conglomerates that have holdings in a variety of countries? Will the conglomerates try to link only those divisions that speak the same language? Or will they try to translate the materials from one division into the language of another? And if they do push their far-flung holdings toward translation, will it affect the kinds of materials those divisions generate and release to the public?

How will the domination of mainstream media channels by six, ten, or fifteen huge corporations affect the influence of public advocacy groups over mainstream media activities? What influence will government agencies have on corporations that often plan their cross-media activities from foreign countries? In general, what should U.S. policy be regarding the ownership of U.S. mass media companies? Federal regulations currently prohibit foreign firms from purchasing only broadcast properties. Should federal regulations also be sensitive to a conglomerate's country of origin when the firm is purchasing "culture-producing" operations in nonbroadcast industries?

Still more questions can be asked about the way the American mass media system is developing, or ought to develop. Other questions can be asked about mass media systems that are developing around the world. The challenges that face mass media firms searching for the most lucrative synergies for their businesses are more than matched by challenges that members of the public face when they confront the results of these synergies. This book has provided a framework to see mass media systems in society with informed, wide-open eyes. Asking the right questions, providing the right challenges for yourself and others, is the first step toward making a real difference in the symbolic environment that surrounds us all.

CONSIDER THIS

1. Often, a merger between two media conglomerates is carried out because it benefits the *distribution* capabilities of the firms, not just their production capabilities. What global and national distribution capabilities did the Disney-ABC merger of 1995 bring to each company?

2. Strategic partnerships sometimes produce unusual alliances. NBC's early relationship with Microsoft to give the latter a news source on the Microsoft Network is one example. What examples can you find? Trade magazines such as *Advertising Age, Variety,* and *Multichannel News* are good sources.

3. Can you think of "challenges for the public" that this chapter has left out?

NOTES

1. Christopher H. Sterling and John M. Kittross, *Stay Tuned* (Belmont, CA: Wadsworth, 1990), p. 661.
2. *Business Horizons,* August 21, 1995, p. 13.
3. *Broadcasting and Cable,* July 10, 1995, p. 17.
4. *Consumer Electronics,* April 21, 1995, p. 13.
5. See Wayne Walley, "Nets Force Nielsen Showdown," *Advertising Age,* September 24, 1990, p. 3.
6. For advertisers' views on TV during this period, see "The Upfront TV Season," a special insert in *Advertising Age,* May 28, 1990.

7. Quoted in "Corporate Planning," *Atari* 2:1 (1982), pp. 2–3.

8. Donald Elliman Jr., "Trends, Synergy, and the Time Warner Merger," talk presented at the Annenberg School for Communication, April 3, 1990, p. 17.

9. Scott Donaton, "Magazines Turn to Buddy System: Books Build Synergy, Ad Pages with Creative Hook-Ups," *Advertising Age,* November 26, 1990, p. S-6.

10. Donaton, p. S-6.

11. John McManus and Janet Meyers, "TBS-Gannett Build Ad Package," *Advertising Age,* October 22, 1990, p. 1.

12. Quoted in Ira Teinowitz, "Bigger Not Always Better: Media Execs," *Advertising Age,* November 19, 1990, p. 25.

13. Teinowitz, p. 25.

14. See Larry Carlat, "New Kids Are a Chip off the Old Block," *Variety,* May 30, 1990, p. 42; and Larry Carlat, "How It Really Works," *Variety,* May 30, 1990, p. 41.

15. Richard Gold, "Singers Add Reelin' to Their Rockin'," *Variety,* November 26, 1990, p. 3.

16. William Stevenson, "Turner and Citadel Press Cut a Cuddly Deal with *Kisses,*" *Variety,* January 21, 1991, p. 96.

17. Knight-Ridder 1990 Annual Report.

18. "Dow-Datatimes Deal," *New York Times,* July 4, 1990.

19. Marcy Magiera, "Madison Avenue Hits Hollywood," *Advertising Age,* December 10, 1990, p. 24.

20. "Value-added — the New Medium," *Advertising Age,* April 9, 1990, pp. S-36–S-37.

21. Scott Donaton and Patricia Winters, "Diet Pepsi Teams Up with SI," *Advertising Age,* April 9, 1990, p. 35.

22. Raymond Sarafin, "Chrysler Ups Ad Budget for Time Warner," *Advertising Age,* November 19, 1990, p. 16.

23. Quoted in "Value-added — the New Medium," p. S-36.

24. Quoted in "Value-added — the New Medium," p. S-36.

25. Connie Bruck, "Deal of the Year," *The New Yorker,* January 8, 1990, pp. 82–83.

26. *Time,* July 2, 1990, p. 8, and personal interviews. See also Bruck, p. 81.

Index

About the Author

Joseph Turow is Professor of Communication at the University of Pennsylvania's Annenberg School for Communication. He earned his B.A. degree from Penn in English and went on to earn an M.A. and Ph.D. in Communication, also from Penn. After receiving his doctorate in 1976, he taught at Purdue University, returning to The Annenberg School in 1986.

Professor Turow is the author of more than thirty-five articles and five books, including *Getting Books to Children: An Exploration of Publisher-Market Relations* (American Library Association, 1979); *Entertainment, Education and the Hard Sell: Three Decades of Network Children's Television* (Praeger, 1981); *Playing Doctor: Television, Storytelling and Medical Power* (Oxford, 1989); and *Breaking Up America: Advertisers and the New Media World* (University of Chicago Press, 1997).

Professor Turow has also written media criticism for the popular press, most recently a number of articles about television for *The Los Angeles Times*. His research has received financial support from the FCC and the National Endowment for the Humanities, among other groups. He serves on the editorial boards of *The Journal of Broadcasting and Electronic Media,* the *Journal of Communication,* and the *Sage Annual Review of Communication Research*. For 1995–1997 he was elected chair of the Mass Communication Division of the International Communication Association.